changing the way the world learns

To get extra value from this book for no additional cost, go to:

http://www.thomson.com/wadsworth.html

thomson.com is the World Wide Web site for Wadsworth/ITP and is your direct source to dozens of on-line resources. *thomson.com* helps you find out about supplements, experiment with demonstration software, search for a job, and send e-mail to many of our authors. You can even preview new publications and exciting new technologies.

thomson.com: *It's where you'll find us in the future.*

CONTEMPORARY ISSUES IN CRIME AND JUSTICE SERIES
Todd Clear, Series Editor

Media, Crime, and Criminal Justice

Images and Realities

Second Edition

RAY SURETTE
University of Central Florida

West/Wadsworth
I(T)P® An International Thomson Publishing Company

Belmont, CA • Albany, NY • Bonn • Boston • Cincinnati • Detroit • Johannesburg • London
Madrid • Melbourne • Mexico City • New York • Paris • Singapore • Tokyo • Toronto • Washington

To my family
my wife, Susan
and my children,
Jennifer, Paul, and Timothy

Criminal Justice Editor: Sabra Horne
Assistant Editor: Claire Masson
Editorial Assistant: Kate Barrett
Marketing Manager: Mike Dew
Project Editor: Jennie Redwitz
Print Buyer: Karen Hunt
Permissions Editor: Bob Kauser

Copy Editor: Hilary Powers
Illustrator: Natalie Hill
Cover Design: Craig Hanson
Cover Image: © 1997 PhotoDisc, Inc.
Compositor: Thompson Type
Printer: Maple-Vail

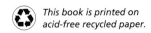
For more information, contact Wadsworth Publishing Company, 10 Davis Drive, Belmont, CA 94002, or electronically at http://www.thomson.com/wadsworth.html

International Thomson Publishing Europe
Berkshire House 168-173
High Holborn
London, WC1V 7AA, England

International Thomson Editores
Campos Eliseos 385, Piso 7
Col. Polanco
11560 México D.F. México

Thomas Nelson Australia
102 Dodds Street
South Melbourne 3205
Victoria, Australia

International Thomson Publishing Asia
221 Henderson Road
#05-10 Henderson Building
Singapore 0315

Nelson Canada
1120 Birchmount Road
Scarborough, Ontario
Canada M1K 5G4

International Thomson Publishing Japan
Hirakawacho Kyowa Building, 3F
2-2-1 Hirakawacho
Chiyoda-ku, Tokyo 102, Japan

International Thomson Publishing GmbH
Königswinterer Strasse 418
53227 Bonn, Germany

International Thomson Publishing Southern Africa
Building 18, Constantia Park
240 Old Pretoria Road
Halfway House, 1685 South Africa

Library of Congress Cataloging-in-Publication Data

Surette, Ray.
    Media, crime, and criminal justice : images and realities / Ray Surette.—2nd ed.
        p.   cm.—(Contemporary issues in crime and justice series)
    Includes bibliographical references (p.   ) and index.
    ISBN 0-534-50863-4 (pbk.)
    1. Mass media and criminal justice.   2. Crime in mass media.
I. Title.   II. Series.
P96.C74S87   1997
364.2'54—dc21

97-18989

Contents

Foreword

Not long ago, a Santa Monica, California jury awarded a total of $33.5 million in punitive and compensatory damages to the families of Ron Goldman and Nicole Brown Simpson. The civil award follows a "not guilty" verdict from a Los Angeles jury in the sensational murder trial of Orenthal James Simpson that riveted the nation for over a year. The daily television coverage of the trial introduced Americans to criminal jurisprudence and criminal procedure in a way unmatched by the thousands of college courses on criminal justice offered every year. Whatever the viewer's bias about the case, strong opinion was evoked in virtually everyone's mind, and the public's opinion of the fairness and reasonableness of the justice system was indelibly shaped by those events. In a news release shortly after the second verdict, Simpson promised that the case was not yet over. And so we can anticipate even more opinion-forming results as the appeal and its coverage by the media go forward.

We are a media nation. Almost every small town has its newspaper, and larger towns have local television coverage to go with it. The "nightly news" is, in many homes, a moment when family members sit down together to consume the events of the world around them. The lead story—and the front page headline "grabber"—is more often than not a story about crime and justice. But this is only part of the overall picture. Chances are, when an American contemplates an evening's social activity at least some thought is given to a movie, and the choices under consideration will include a number of tales depicting crime and justice. Not only are we a media nation, but a major portion of the media's attention is devoted to crime and to concepts of justice.

It is not too extreme to say that most of what Americans know about crime and justice comes from the popular media's portrayal of these topics. For this reason, I am pleased to present the second edition of Ray Surette's *Media, Crime, and Criminal Justice* to The Wadsworth Contemporary Issues in Crime and Justice Series. The Series seeks to provide thorough and current treatment of important topics in crime and justice that are neglected or covered inadequately in available texts. Authors in this series deal with theoretical and practical problems of crime and justice, and expose the reader to the most recent research and analyses of these problems. Our hope is not only to inform the reader, but to stimulate thought and discussion on topics of undeniable importance to our field.

Professor Surette's book fits especially well with the objectives of this series. Surette makes the point that reality is elusive, but *perceptions* of reality are concrete products of the way the world is informed about contemporary life. In American culture the way people learn about the world is through media. But this is not a neutral media, this is a media with an interest in presenting issues in ways that captivate the audience and stimulate passions. Thus, we learn about crime from sources designed to make us feel passionately about it. No wonder crime remains high on the list of public concerns even when the levels of serious crime are falling.

Professor Surette's thesis is that the media are simultaneously seen as a cause of crime and as a way to combat crime. This paradox stems from the way in which the media are simultaneously responsible for telling us about our crime problem and telling us how crime might be combated. We not only learn about crime from public, mass media, we learn how to live with crime from the same source. The idea of a "socially constructed reality" about crime, in which processes of information flow create our understanding of this complex world in which we live, is a central and profoundly important aspect of knowing about the crucial point where the truth about crime ends and the truth about media begins.

Todd R. Clear
Florida State University
Series Editor

Preface

Media, Crime, and Criminal Justice: Images and Competing Realities

Although it has been only six years since the first edition of *Media, Crime, and Criminal Justice*, public and academic interest in the area have grown enormously. Massively covered criminal trials, advances in media technology, new types of media content—and new ways of delivering the content—have brought the subject to the forefront of attention. Increased concern with the idea that media violence may cause social violence, parallel efforts to employ the media to reduce crime and violence, and development of popular culture that is media-driven, intrusive, and intensive have all worked to feed the growth in interest. While new questions have emerged, research has also shed new light on old questions. More is known about what the media can and cannot do and what it can and cannot be used to do. This second edition expands on the issues raised in the first edition, and, like the first, structures and organizes a large amount of research, public concerns, and policy efforts from far-flung areas. Appropriate for a book about the impact of a multifaceted media industry, findings and knowledge are drawn from criminal justice, criminology, sociology, political science, law, public administration, journalism, medicine, psychology, communication, and Internet journals as well as popular magazines, newspapers, films, and the World Wide Web. As before, the central tenet of this edition is that the media is a major force in society and is a primary engine in the social construction of reality.

Most people interact with the mass media as passive consumers rather than as thoughtful and critical consumers. They have been conditioned to receive the entertainment and knowledge the media provide without considering where this material comes from, what effect it has on their attitudes and perceptions, and how it affects society. Not only are the mass media frequently pointed to as a cause of crime and violence but we receive most of our facts and impressions of crime and justice through the mass media as well. In the last few years the relationship between the media and the criminal justice system has continued to develop rapidly; the second edition's primary purpose is to keep pace with this development.

This book has five goals:

- To provide an orientation and introduction to the ideas of the social construction of crime-and-justice reality and the media's role in the construction process.

- To introduce criminal justice students and personnel to the relevant mass media research and encourage interest and research into the varied aspects of the relationship between the media, crime, and justice.

- To summarize and interpret what is known about the mass media's effects on crime and justice.

- To teach readers to be critical media consumers and insightful observers of the relationship between the media and crime and justice.

- To provide researchers with a broader context for their specific studies and access to a wider range of literature.

To create a foundation to be a critical media consumer and provide a theoretical conceptualization to interpret the body of media, crime, and justice information, Chapter 1 introduces the concepts associated with the theoretical perspective of the social construction of reality. It is this perspective that underlies the discussions and interpretations found throughout this book. The book assumes no background in either communications or journalism on the part of the reader. In that this book addresses significant issues in media, crime, and justice, it will be of interest not only within the field of criminal justice but within the mass media and communication fields. The book is also directed at the practicing professional in both journalism and criminal justice. It provides insights and understanding for each in their dealings with the professionals from the other discipline. As in the first edition, jargon and specialized terminology have been avoided. The book is designed to be a primary text in courses that examine crime, justice, and the media, and a supplemental text in special-topic courses in such disciplines as mass communication, public administration, and journalism.

PHILOSOPHY

The theoretical perspective that guides this work is that the media are a major force in cultural change. The mass media are considered as a part of a "social construction of reality" process. People use knowledge gained from the media to construct an image of the world and behave based on the perceived reality of that image. The media are felt to be especially important for the construction of a crime-and-justice reality in society. The media are also considered as more than television, differentiating between print and electronic visual media and drawing examples from various media. The book conceptualizes the mass media as a vast web of interconnected communications channels, events, technology, and knowledge that works to mold what we believe the world to be like. The contemporary mass media are influential because of this overlapping and pervasive web. Its many forms and interconnections must be acknowledged in any discussion of its effects. The development of the electronic media has also involved the development of sophisticated new communications technology and this book will also discuss media technology and its application in law enforcement and judicial settings.

The phrase *media technology* refers to the audio and visual communications equipment that has become available because of mass media telecommunications advances. The ultimate goal in using the technology in the criminal justice field is to simulate a live person-to-person encounter and conversations. In practice, however, its use diminishes live face-to-face encounters in criminal justice, undercutting a principle on which the legitimacy of the criminal justice system was founded.

A book about the media, crime, and justice should encourage further reading and research. At a minimum this book will hopefully encourage readers to ask questions about the media such as why certain images of crime are linked together in newscasts, why one crime story is placed on the front page and another on page 11, and why some explanations of crime and some policies are emphasized over others. This edition will be a success if a reader can never again sit through a crime show or crime newscast without a thoughtful reaction and a realization of the underlying social construction process.

ORGANIZATION, SCOPE, AND CONTENT

This book is organized into seven chapters. The first introduces the media, crime, and justice area and provides the theoretical grounding in social construction of reality for the balance of the text. The second through seventh chapters delve into specific aspects of the media, crime, and justice relationship beginning with crime and justice in the entertainment media and continuing through the news media, media and the courts, the media as a cause of crime, media-based anticrime projects, and media effects on crime-and-justice attitudes and policies. It is possible to read the chapters independently or in a different order if desired. To obtain a feel for the full range and complexity of the media, crime, and justice relationship, all are recommended.

TEXT REVISIONS

To increase readability and flow the text has been significantly changed from the first edition. The use of sidebars and boxed material has been greatly reduced. While hundreds of new citations have been added, a different style of citation has been employed that removes the citation information from the body of the text. Research and case summaries that are primarily of interest to researchers and graduate students have been placed in appendixes to further reduce chapter clutter. The breadth and quality of reference material, praised in the first edition, is preserved and enhanced. The result is a text that is easier to follow and less disrupted by tangential material. The chapters themselves have been reorganized and reduced in number. As the book concerns the media, examples from the media are liberally included and more photos and contemporary examples have been added. It is strongly suggested that additional media material be incorporated into a course plan. Any commercial video rental store, newsstand, or typical evening of TV news and shows will supply a rich source. Inviting criminal justice public information officers and newspaper or television reporters as speakers is also highly recommended.

ACKNOWLEDGMENTS

I would first like to thank the individuals at Wadsworth who contributed to the development and production of this book. Sabra Horne provided encouragement and support in the early development of the text and Claire Masson was helpful in keeping the developmental process going. Jennie Redwitz husbanded the project through to completion. Hilary Powers did a superior job as copyeditor. Bobbie Broyer diligently acquired the photographs. Bob Kauser assisted in obtaining permissions. Natalie Hill created the artwork and graphics. All of them exhibited an attention to detail that I lack, and I thank all of them for their patience and professionalism.

Others deserving thanks include the many reviewers. To Randolph William Boucott, Northeastern Illinois University; Michael A. Hallett, Middle Tennessee State University; Marianne O. Nielsen, Northern Arizona University; Lucien X. Lombardo, Old Dominion University; and Ric S. Sheffield, Kenyon College, I extend my sincere appreciation, for the final work is much improved due to their insights and suggestions. Finally I would also like to thank colleagues Frankie Bailey, Joel Best, Gray Cavender, Steve Chermak, Donna Hale, John Lynxwiler, and Garrett O'Keefe for directions, materials, and knowledge that strengthened the final result.

1

⭕

Media and the Construction of Crime and Criminal Justice

This chapter begins by discussing why it is important to explore and understand the relationships between the mass media, crime, and our criminal justice system. The balance of the chapter examines basic concepts used throughout the book, drawn from the disciplines of criminal justice and mass communications. These concepts will orient the reader to the two disciplines. From the area of criminal justice come the opposing ideas of due process and crime control. From the area of mass communications comes the distinction between print media and electronic media. These ideas will help bridge the separate realms of criminal justice and the mass media. The concepts of front-stage and backstage behavior also appear. Later chapters use these concepts to explain some of the activities the media have emphasized in portraying crime and justice. Also introduced in this chapter is the basic theoretical premise of the book: that people use knowledge they obtain from the media to construct a picture of the world, an image of reality on which they base their actions. This process, sometimes called "the social construction of reality," is particularly important in the realm of crime, justice, and the media. The ideas and processes of this perspective are defined and described, and examples of its application to crime and justice are provided.

THE STUDY OF MEDIA, CRIME, AND JUSTICE

This book concerns the collision between two massive social institutions, both central to modern society. One set took its present shape only recently but has its roots in the sixteenth century. The other acquired its modern elements five centuries ago and can be traced to antiquity. They are, respectively, the mass media's news and entertainment systems and the criminal justice system. Interest in both as independent entities is long-standing. Although we normally study these institutions as separate and autonomous, the level of interaction between them has soared in recent years, ranging in form from subtle media influences on citizens' attitudes toward crime and justice to the direct use of mass media technology to combat crime. And while the media have emphasized crime and justice in their content, there have been regular attempts to criminalize popular media and to define the social effects of art, music, and visual media as criminogenic.[1] The dynamics of the media are felt to define the process of criminalization as much as the inner workings of the criminal law and criminal justice system.[2] The concerns and issues raised by the increasingly complex interactions have accompanied a heightened interest in the role of the media in society and, in particular, their role in crime and justice in the late twentieth century.[3]

Research interest in the relationship of the mass media to crime and justice has been elevated for most of this century, and the media have regularly moved in and out of public concern in steady ten- to twenty-year cycles. If a consensus has emerged from the research and public interest, it is that the sources of crime are complex and tied to our most basic nature as well as the social world we have created, and that the media's relationship to crime and justice is extremely complicated. Crime is embedded in larger historical and social forces and phenomena, and the media are only one component of a larger symbolic information system that creates and distributes social knowledge about the world. The media and crime and justice must all be approached as parts of larger phenomena that have numerous interconnections and paths of influence among them. Too narrow a perspective oversimplifies the problem and nowhere is this more apparent than in the current concern about media, crime, and justice.

The media are also related to crime and justice in ways not usually considered in the public debate, such as their effects on public policies and general social attitudes toward violence. Adding to the complexity of the media relationship, there are many other sources that either interact with the media or work alone to produce crime. These sources range from individual biology to facets of our history and culture. The importance of nonmedia factors such as neighborhood and family conditions, individual psychological and genetic traits, social structure, race relations, and economic conditions for the generation of crime are commonly acknowledged. The role of the mass media is confounded with these other sources and their significance is often either lost or exaggerated. One task of this book is to dispel the two popular but polarizing positions that have dominated the public debate. The first position is that the media are a primary cause of crime in society. The second is that the media have no or very limited effects. The relative validity of these two dichotomous positions, the media as central and the media as insignificant in fostering crime and violence, has dominated the public discussion, resulting in much confusion and public posturing by various groups and individuals. The actual relationship of the media to crime and justice lies somewhere between these two extremes.

The view of the media as a source of primary effects is often advanced along with Draconian policy demands such as extensive government intervention or direct censorship of the media. However, a number of points support the counterargument to this position. The most basic is that we were a violent nation before we were a mass media nation and there is no evidence that the removal of violent media would make us nonviolent.[4] Research into copycat crime additionally forwards scant evidence of a criminalizing effect from the media. The media by themselves cannot turn a law-abiding individual into a criminal. In sum, the sources of crime cannot be blamed primarily on the media, and policies directed only at the media have little effect.

The other argument—that the media have limited to no effect on levels of crime—resembles both in posture and approach the tobacco industry response to research on smoking and lung cancer, and rings just as hollow. The argument simply expounds inherent weaknesses in the various methodologies of the media research, triumphantly pointing to the lack of evidence of strong direct effects while ignoring a persistent pattern of positive findings.

Despite the persistent ongoing debate, however, there remain few works that discuss the impact of the modern media's effects on the judicial, law enforcement, and correctional systems. This work is offered as a broad introductory survey of the evolving meshing of the mass media and the criminal justice system. It focuses on the media's effects on our system of justice, rather than on a review of the judicial decisions, legislation, and law enforcement efforts that have influenced the mass media. The basic question addressed in this book is How have the mass media changed the reality of crime and criminal justice?

From a practical standpoint, a better understanding of the underlying dynamics of society can be gained by examining the points of contact between society's primary information system—the mass media—and its primary system for legitimizing values and enforcing norms—the criminal justice system. The criminal justice system acquires its legitimizing function by serving as a social arena in which the significance and value of various social behaviors are determined. It serves not only as an institution through which legal disputes are resolved but also as a mechanism through which a society's laws and system of government are legitimized. Hence anything that influences the public image of the criminal justice system also influences its legitimizing function and in turn affects the functioning of the total society and all its institutions.[5] The advantages of simultaneously studying justice and the media have begun to be exploited more fully, but the research conducted thus far has produced more questions than answers. The following chapters address some of the questions remaining to be answered, including:

- Is the crime and justice content of the media changing in response to new media technology or social changes?

- What is the impact of new media offerings that are combinations of news and entertainment?

- Has the introduction of news cameras to courtroom proceedings changed the process or perception of justice?

- Does violent media coverage increase tolerance for violence and how prevalent are copycat crimes?

- Can the media or related technology be used to reduce crime and what are the social effects of trying to do so?

- How does the media affect our criminal justice policies and our crime and justice reality?

Beyond academic interest, the study of the media-justice relationship is important for a number of reasons. First, the media are not neutral, unobtrusive social agents providing simple entertainment or news. The media's pervasiveness makes their influence extensive. One medium alone, television, is on more than seven hours a day in a typical American home, and individual Americans watch, on average, more than four hours of television daily.[6] Add time spent on films, video and audio recordings, radio programs, video games, the Internet, and newspapers and magazines to these figures and exposure to the mass media is virtually unavoidable. The components of the mass media form a popular culture web that to some degree ensnares everyone. Indeed, the media's influence reaches even those who are not exposed to broadcast and published messages.[7] Even if one does not watch, listen, or read, one buys products, wears fashions, talks with other persons, and lives under government policies influenced by the media.[8]

It is a basic assumption of this book that the media's impact on crime and justice can be better understood by recognizing the media's role in the social construction of reality and the inherent nature of media institutions as business organizations. Although the media collectively constitute a major social force, they are more often driven by organizational needs than by political ideologies. In practice, however, in the competition among individuals and groups representing various ideologies to gain media attention, particular perspectives do fare better than others—a fact that is reflected in the way the media cover crime and justice and that has significant implications with regard to policies affecting crime and justice.[9]

The crime and justice policy impact of the mass media leads to a second reason to study media, crime, and justice. Over the last fifty years, massive amounts of money have been spent in the United States to control crime. Despite these huge sums, however, notable successes against crime have been few and crime waxes and wanes seemingly independent of our efforts. The public's subsequent frustration has paradoxically resulted in the mass media's simultaneously being attacked as contributing to the crime problem and increasingly being looked to as a possible solution to crime. The resultant policy efforts have worked to both limit and expand the domain of the media with regard to crime and justice in America. The causes of these conflicting and ambiguous effects are explored and clarified.

Third, amid all the confusion surrounding the effects of the media, the study of media, crime, and justice also offers a unique potential for increasing our understanding of society. A society's ideas of criminality and social justice reflect its values concerning humanity, social relationships, and political ideologies. These ideas are put into operation and legitimized within the criminal justice system, spread and given final legitimization through the mass media. And though the mass media are only one source of citizens' knowledge about crime and justice, they are the most common and pervasive source of crime and justice information.[10] The media's social influence is focused therefore through their role in the social construction of our crime and justice reality.

MEDIA AND THE SOCIAL CONSTRUCTION OF REALITY

"Reality is a collective hunch."

The theoretical perspective known as the social construction of reality or *social constructionism* can help us better understand the impact of a pervasive mass media.[11] Under this theoretical view, people create reality—the world they believe exists—based on their individual knowledge and from knowledge gained from social interactions with other people. People then act in accordance with their constructed view of reality. Social constructionism has its philosophical roots in the sociology of knowledge. It contrasts with the dominant Western tradition of *logical empiricism*, in which social knowledge is felt to be independent of social processes and grounded in events in the world. Valid knowledge, which everyone should share regardless of experiences or background, maps or mirrors the real world.[12] The sociology of knowledge view differs in that it looks at knowledge of the world as a socially created product. In the social constructionism perspective, knowledge is not something possessed, but rather something done.[13] Opposite to the view that knowledge reflects objective reality, constructionism says knowledge reflects subjective society. Culture and history are crucial for determining what we see as reality and understanding the realities of others.

> Conceptions about the nature of society are shared conceptions: They permit meaningful social behavior precisely to the degree that they are held in common with, or at least understood by others. It is for this reason that our conceptions of the social world are constructed. . . . On the

other hand, [in] that conceptions about the nature of society are specific with respect to the time, place, and situation of the social group which shares them . . . [t]he same circumstances which make them general and "objective" with respect to the individuals who hold them, make them particular and "subjective" with respect to others who do not share the same social world.[14]

Social constructionism takes as its point of departure the social basis of all human knowledge. What one person sees as an objective fact about the world, another may see as a subjective interpretation. Knowledge is by necessity conditioned by the structure of society and the social conditions that at least partly determine what constitutes knowledge for a particular group.[15]

This perspective does not question the reality of the world but rather focuses on human relationships within the world and the way personal relationships affect how people perceive reality. Understanding of the world is sought by studying its shared meanings.[16] Shared meanings are in turn the result of an active, cooperative social enterprise and the degree to which a given constructed reality prevails is not directly dependent on its empirical validity, but is strongly influenced by the shifting effects of social trends and interactions.[17] The perspective recognizes the fact that a social condition can become a major social problem and then subside, without the situation it concerns having undergone any significant change.[18]

Underlying this framework is an understandable interest in American popular culture and the role of the mass media.[19] This is due to the fact that individuals gain the knowledge on which they construct their social realities from four sources: personal experiences, significant others (peers, family, friends—whose input is sometimes referred to as *conversational* knowledge), other social groups and institutions (schools, unions, churches, government agencies), and the mass media.[20] The first source, also termed *experienced reality*, is one's directly experienced world—all the events that happen to you.[21] Knowledge gained from experienced reality is relatively limited but has a powerful influence on one's constructed reality.

The next three sources of knowledge are shared symbolically and collectively form one's *symbolic reality*. The media are centrally involved in these sources of world knowledge. This symbolically shared knowledge is dominated by language, which allows the vicarious sharing of someone else's experienced reality. All the events you didn't witness but believe occurred, all the facts about the world you didn't personally collect but believe to be true, all the things you believe to exist but haven't seen make up your symbolic reality. The difference between experienced and symbolic reality can be shown by a few questions: How many believe the moon exists? Why? Because you can see it directly—you have experienced-reality knowledge of its existence. How many believe the moon has an atmosphere? Why not? Because you've been told it has no air, you've read it has no air, and you've seen pictures of men in space suits on the moon. Except for a few astronauts, everyone else has only symbolic-reality knowledge of conditions on the moon. And it is because so much of our social knowledge is gained symbolically that there is concern over its content and correctness, particularly its use in deception. Can you think of an example where such a deception is accomplished? How many readers once believed in Santa Claus?[22] Symbolic knowledge also allows the creation of abstract ideas to be part of our reality such as alienation, love, anomie, and fear of crime. Symbolic knowledge is also central to the idea of culture in that much of the socialization process involves the symbolic transferring of cultural knowledge. What a people hold to be real, true, valued, and just is largely acquired symbolically rather than directly.

Regarding the three sources of socially acquired symbolic reality (significant others, social groups and institutions, and the mass media), knowledge from all these sources mixes together with the knowledge from personal experiences, and from this mix, each individual constructs his or her personal world. This socially constructed world is composed of events individuals experience or believe to be happening; facts they observe or believe to be true; causal processes they accept and believe to be operating; and values, attitudes, and opinions they hold or believe are valid and should be upheld. Not surprisingly, individuals with access to similar knowledge and who frequently interact with one another tend to construct similar social realities.

Since the sources of knowledge people use to socially construct reality vary in importance, the degree of media contribution to the individual's construction of reality is a function of one's direct experience with various phenomena and consequent dependence on the media for information.[23] The symbolic reality knowledge you obtain from significant others is usually more influential than what you receive from social institutions or the mass media. In modern, advanced, industrialized societies with strong popular cultures, the mass media have emerged as a main engine in the social construction of reality process. In practical impact, the mass media increase in importance as other sources are less available.[24] In addition, the mass media tend to be more important in societies like the United States, because other organizations and institutions must depend on the media to disseminate information from and about them.[25] Because we get no more than a glimpse of the events of the world firsthand, we depend heavily on the social reality created by the media.[26] In their operational routines, the media impose constraints on the images that are socially available while presenting social problems within familiar frames and cultural terms. Mass media knowledge is not accepted directly and uncritically, however, but rather is part of the social-reality production process and a means for various constructions of crime, law, and justice to compete for public acceptance.[27] In the end, the media dominate the distribution of shared social knowledge and their effect is fourfold:[28]

- We record and analyze history in terms of what the media define as significant.

- People with potential historical importance must rely on media exposure to ensure their place in history.

- Media reports become an essential determination of what is held to be significant as media influence becomes ever more widely known and accepted.

- Institutions find they must present their own message and images within the accepted respectability and familiarity of media-determined formats.

Finally, because the organizations that constitute the media are also businesses, both organizational and economic factors come into play in determining the content of what they broadcast, print, or sell—and therefore the social knowledge that people receive. Media organizations help construct reality but are bound by organizational constraints in the information they contribute to the construction. Given this fact, it follows that the media's organizational nature and for-profit business values strongly influence content.

The Media's Role in the Process

Research into how the process of social constructionism works has been grouped into either *strict constructionism*, neutral studies of the construction process that do not examine the validity of the reality constructed, or *contextual constructionism*, which argues for counter versions of reality, in the process identifying and debunking what are deemed incorrect versions.[29] The strict constructionists can be said to be more concerned with the mechanisms of reality construction, the contextual constructionists more concerned with the effects of the constructed realities. This book leans toward the second approach, pointing out the many inconsistencies between available measures of crime and justice and the media-constructed images of crime and justice. A contextual social construction process model, composed of four phases, is shown in Figure 1.1.

In Phase I, the physical world represents the actual conditions in society. This is a factual base of events, the real reality that exists before social interpretations and construction. Phase II is dominated by competition. There is a social competition among different constructions of reality over being accepted as the general, dominant construction of reality—as the view that is accepted as best reflecting and explaining the conditions observed in the physical world. In Phase III, the media distribute and are involved in interpreting knowledge of the world and serve as the main playing field for the competition among the competing constructions of the world from Phase II. In Phase IV, a dominant construction emerges from the competition and becomes society's generally accepted view of reality.

The second phase, competing constructions of the world, involves a number of theoretical concepts significant for social constructionism. These include *claims* and *claims-makers*, *ownership*, and *linkage*. *Claims* are the descriptions, typifications, and assertions regarding the extent and nature of phenomena in the physical world. These statements are promoted as facts about something in the world. For example, "crime is out of control" is a claim about the factual condition of crime in society.

Claims-makers are the promoters, activists, professional experts, and spokespersons involved in forwarding specific claims about a phenomenon. Social problems emerge—become a focus for concern—through a process of

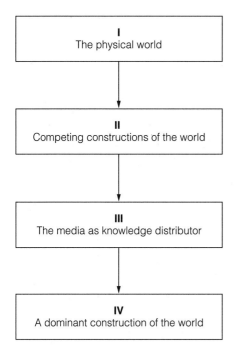

FIGURE 1.1 Phases of Social Construction

claims making. The process determines not only which phenomena come to be designated social problems, but what characteristics are ascribed to those problems. Claims-makers do more than draw attention to particular social conditions, they shape our sense of what the problem is. Each social condition can be constructed as many different social problems. For example, crime can be constructed as a social, individual, racial, sexual, economic, criminal justice, or technological problem—and each construction implies different policy courses and solutions.[30] The social roles and ideologies of claims-makers affect their characterization of problems; where moralists see sin, medical authorities detect disease, and criminal justice personnel see crime. The news story in Box 1.1 is an example of a media construction of serial killers presenting competing claims and claims-makers. The headline itself makes a claim. In the text, you can see other claims, printed in italic type, and assorted claims-makers in boldface.

Ownership is the identification of a particular phenomenon with a particular set of claims-makers who come to own the issue in that they are sought out by the media for pronouncements regarding its nature and the reasonableness of social policies directed toward it. Some groups—by virtue of their superior power, finances, status, organization, technology, or access to the media—have greater resources to make their constructions appear legitimate, to make their version of reality stick, and to take effective ownership of an issue.[31] Because of their media access and control of crime data, law

---

BOX 1.1 Claims and Claims-Makers in the News

**Random Killings Inspire
Increase in People's Fear**
*However, multiple slayings account
for less than 1 percent of the nation's
homicides.*

*NEW YORK — They are the killers every-
one fears. They are those who, perhaps
through pure happenstance or a logic
known only to themselves, repeatedly
attack strangers. They have no numerical
objective that will cause them to stop,
and they may pick you as their next
victim.*

In one astonishing week, three men
whom authorities describe as belonging
to this macabre fraternity were caught in
the New York area, in something of an
arrest spree that mocks such killers' own
repetitive behavior.

The fear inspired by random slayings
can magnify beyond reason, *especially
since multiple killers account for less than
1 percent of the nation's homicide rate.*

Still, because of whatever complex
blend of sociological currents, **criminologists** say *the slayings of strangers has in-*
creased enormously in recent decades.
Since 1960, they say, it has soared from
an insignificant number to probably at
least a quarter of the nation's homicides.

*"There's not a serial killer behind
every tree, but you fear them because
anyone, including you, could be their
next choice,"* said **John Douglas,** who
recently retired as head of the FBI unit
concerned with serial killers.

In the space of a week, **the police** say,
*John Royster, 22, a drifter from the
Bronx, has confessed to four brutal assaults on women, one of whom died,
while another loner, Heriberto Seda, 28,
of Brooklyn, admitted killing three people and wounding five others in the so-
called Zodiac shootings.*

Last Thursday, Staten Island resident,
Larry Stevens, 31, was linked by **the
police** *to at least two slayings and a wave
of vicious robberies of suburban elderly
people.*

SOURCE: *New York Times.* Reprinted by permission.

Orlando Sentinel, June 23, 1996, p. A-7. Note the
contradiction between the second and third claims.

---

enforcement agencies thus often obtain proprietorial ownership of the crime
problem.

Lastly, *linkage* involves the tying or association of an issue with other issues.
For example, drugs are often linked to other social problems such as crime.
The linkage of one social phenomenon to another generally seen as more
harmful raises the concern and importance of the linked issue.[32] Thus the social importance of drug abuse is heightened when drugs are linked to other
social problems, and the same linkage makes other causes of crime appear less
significant.[33] Examples of claims, claims-makers, ownership, and linkage occur
frequently in the mass media and recognizing them and their functions helps
to understand much of the mass media crime and justice content.

In Phase III, the role of the media in constructing reality in large industrialized societies is brought into play. The media serve the role of world knowledge conduit and playing field for the competition between claims-makers.
Claims-makers compete for media attention and the media favor claims that

are dramatic, sponsored by powerful groups, and related to established cultural themes. The media also play the role of claims filter, making it difficult for those outside the cultural mainstream to gain media attention and hence to publicly establish their claims.

As the distributors of social knowledge, the media also legitimize people, social issues, and social policies for the general public. And though the media do not control the process of cultural change, the fact is that in large industrialized nations with hundreds of millions of people, cultural change without media involvement does not occur. The media simultaneously change, react to, and reflect culture and society[34]—in the process making available explanatory frameworks to perceive and understand issues like crime.[35] In the United States, four frames regarding the cause of crime compete: (1) a faulty criminal justice system hindered by due process procedures, (2) a population reacting against blocked social and economic opportunities, (3) a social breakdown of family and community life, and (4) an oppressive and racist criminal justice system. The frames that are held and defended most strongly by individuals are those in which individuals have access to both media and personal knowledge sources. Thus *faulty criminal justice system* and *social breakdown* do well, especially among whites, because many individuals have personal and media knowledge of social disorder to draw upon. In addition, a large store of cultural knowledge forwarding the tenets of self-reliance and individualism and social myths of rampant predatory strangers also support these explanatory frames. In a similar fashion, *racist criminal justice system* does well among blacks because of personal, cultural, and media information sources that tend to bolster this frame.[36]

The media's knowledge distribution role eventually ends up with a dominant construction of reality emerging from the competition. The process is clearest in politics but the goal of molding reality in the media is carried on by many groups and organizations through so-called spin doctors and image control. The dominant construction is inevitably a social product. The most important effect of a dominant constructed social reality emerging from the competition is that the dominant construction steers public policy.[37] Policies and the solutions sought are tied to the claims of the successful winning construction. The linking of claims to policies involves claims-makers who often describe a social problem in a simplified, dramatic, worst-case scenario launching media-based moral crusades and panics.[38] Their claims influence the formation of social policy and the solutions that are seen as workable. Whatever the problem, it is seen as having one particular nature and thus needing one specific solution.[39]

At the individual level, the dominant constructed reality is hence an expanded personal reality constructed from knowledge from both experienced and symbolic realities. It is perceived as the "real" world by each individual— what we individually believe the world to be like. It is subjective in that it will differ from individual to individual because the experienced realities will differ. People of the same background, however, will usually see the world more alike than different because they will share the same symbolic reality and much of the same experienced reality. In large heterogeneous societies like the United States, however, the constructed realities are not always shared. Some Americans, for example, believe in magic, ghosts, voodoo, luck, ESP, astrology, or flying saucers. What is important for society is that this constructed subjective reality leads to social behavior. The objective world and its symbolic representations provide the basis for the individuals' social actions.[40]

Pragmatically, Phase I, the physical world, and Phase IV, the dominant construction of the world, can't be diametrically opposed to one another—but they can differ on significant points, even points of fact. For once a dominant constructed reality is established, it is resistant to change and dislodgment. Thus, people may feel and act as if the crime rate is increasing even when it is generally declining, as was the case in the early 1990s.

The media's depiction of crime-related topics in particular has been cited as playing a prominent role in the social construction of our crime and justice reality.[41] For example, the success of Crime Stoppers programs (in which citizens are encouraged to provide crime tips for reward money) required a change in the social construction of anonymous informing from a disparaged, unacceptable social behavior to a legitimate, socially supported civic act. The media presentation of informing as moral and of crime as a growing concern played a key role in reversing the prior negative connotation associated with anonymous informants.[42] The eventual normalization and legitimation of anonymous informing made Crime Stoppers programs a viable, socially acceptable public policy.

Because crime and justice permeate all forms of media and an ever-increasing number of such examples are coming to light, the usefulness of studying the media's role in the social construction of crime and justice has become more commonplace, and more writings exemplifying the social construction process via the media in crime and justice have been produced.[43]

Examples of the Media in Action

This section provides three examples of the media's role in the social construction process of crime and justice.

Rodney King. Probably the best-known example of a specific event that epitomizes the interaction of media, social constructionism, and criminal justice is the Rodney King beating caught on video on the night of March 3, 1991. This episode provides an example of the social construction competitive process in which different constructed realities strove to become the dominant view of the Rodney King beating. Even though the event was videotaped and many facts about the event were unquestioned, such as how many times Mr. King was struck, a competition regarding cause and interpretation of the beating—the constructed meaning of the event—developed.

Three different constructions of the cause and meaning of the event competed, with each construction suggesting widely different policies. In construction A, King resisted arrest and the beating was justified by King's prior actions. The law enforcement policy implications from this construction are

A frame from the citizen video showing a Los Angeles police officer striking Rodney King. The disagreement over what the footage meant resulted in three different constructions of the Rodney King beating vying for public acceptance.

John Mantel

minimal. The police were justified, therefore the police officers were not acting inappropriately and no changes are required.

In construction B, the beating was unjustified but was an isolated incident of unwarranted police violence carried out by a few renegade police officers. The officers were not acting appropriately but were also not typical or representative of L.A. police officers. This version implies the policy response of firing the bad apples and reprimanding the officers involved in misrepresenting the incident. Targeted internal individual discipline is all that is needed.

In construction C, the beating is unjustified and an example of an endemic problem of unwarranted and consistent police violence toward minorities. The officers involved acted as many L.A. officers would have and the beating reflects an organizational tolerance of excessive violence toward minorities. The policy changes required from this construction involve drastic change in L.A. police culture. It indicates the need to revamp the top administration and training of the department and to make extensive organizational changes.

In the end construction C and its explanation of the beating became the dominant one. The L.A. police chief was fired and a new black chief was hired. The Rodney King beating displays how even for events in which factual information is not disputed, vigorous competition among constructed interpretations of those facts can occur.

Highway Violence. Joel Best describes the media's role in the construction of a new crime problem, highway violence.[44] In describing highway shootings, the media used a set of descriptors such as trend, wave, spate, spree, upsurge, fad, rash, and plague, all of which suggested a new, rapidly growing crime problem. Once defined by the media as a new and growing concern, crime events were searched for and redefined to fit the newly constructed crime category of violent highway encounters.

Having created a new category of violent events, the media proceeded to offer explanations of the events. Initially, Best found that various interpretations competed regarding what sort of problem highway violence is, each with their own policy suggestions. He found highway violence referred to as:

- *Traffic problems*, implying a policy of new freeways, mass transportation, and reducing congestion.
- *Gun availability problems*, implying a policy of gun control.
- *Courtesy problems*, implying a policy of counseling to reduce aggressive and self-centered driving habits.
- *Medical problems*, implying a policy of mental health counseling and stress-reduction techniques.
- *Crime problems*, implying a policy of enhanced law enforcement—increased patrols, better investigation and prosecution, and freeway-violence laws.

Regarding the explanatory competition in the media for the new crime, Best relates that individual-level, violent predatory personality explanations dominated. The popular culture (dominated by the entertainment media) was the primary source of the media images used to describe the newly constructed phenomenon—Road Warriors, Mad Max, Freeway Rambos—and the most common element of news coverage was the emphasis on the random, senseless quality of the events. Ordinary drivers, about their everyday business, were potential victims. Highway violence was eventually constructed and interpreted predominantly as a crime problem and criminal justice policies became the preferred response.

Serial Murder. Phillip Jenkins describes the social construction of serial murder in the 1980s.[45] He attributes the shaping of the serial murder image to three forces: law enforcement agencies, news media, and popular culture. These three groups coalesced to construct the dominant image of the serial killer as a roaming lone white male predator; as an emerging, rapidly increasing new type of crime; and as an interjurisdictional crime needing federal law enforcement expertise and resources. The construction process also saw the linkage of serial killing with other phenomena to raise those phenomena in importance and threat. During the course of the construction, for example, serial murder was tied to missing children, pedophilia, sexism, racism, and homosexuality by various groups of claims-makers. Serial murder thus was constructed as an exploding, pervasive social problem and used to increase the social significance of a number of other social issues. As in other construction competitions, there were winners and losers. The FBI emerged as the main winner, gaining ownership of the serial killer crime problem and funding for a behavioral science unit to address the problem. Losers were the social groups that failed to successfully link serial killing to their pet social concerns and thus saw their social problem degraded in terms of social importance.

A common element in these examples is that the social construction of crime and criminal justice follows a large amount of attention being focused on a few criminal events—a single videotaped beating, a handful of highway incidents, a half-dozen serial killers.[46] The attention is promoted by intense, often brief, but influential mass media coverage. The end result of the social construction process is that relatively rare criminal events create new criminal justice policies. Los Angeles gets a new police chief, Congress passes highway violence legislation, the FBI launches a new initiative. A well-known recent example of this policy effect is shown by the kidnapping and murder of Polly Klass in California, which eventually resulted in the passage of Three-Strikes legislation.[47] As these examples reflect, as the mass media have become more pervasive, technically capable, and intrusive, their role in the construction of crime and justice reality has become more significant. It is on that role and its ongoing evolution that the balance of this book will focus.

THE MASS MEDIA AND CRIMINAL JUSTICE: SOME INTRODUCTORY CONCEPTS

Because our focus is the interaction of two institutions normally considered separately, we will additionally use two sets of concepts, drawn respectively from the criminal justice and mass communications disciplines, to bridge the gap between them. An understanding of these concepts will aid in understanding the dynamics and policy ramifications of the ongoing interaction between the mass media (see Figure 1.2) and the social construction of crime and criminal justice reality.

Criminal Justice: Due Process and Crime Control

The concepts of due process and crime control can be used to represent two opposing models of the operation of the criminal justice system. These models serve as conceptual frames for understanding the criminal justice system, its goals, and the mass media's effects on the system.[48] The models are abstract, of course, and do not represent existing criminal justice systems; rather, both models describe organizational case flows and can be understood as competing constructed realities for the criminal justice system. Under the *due process* reality model, the criminal justice system is seen as an obstacle course in which the government must prove an accused person's guilt while conforming to strict procedural rules. The system's most important goal under this model is the protection of citizen rights and the prevention of arbitrary and capricious government action. The key determination in this model is legal guilt, which

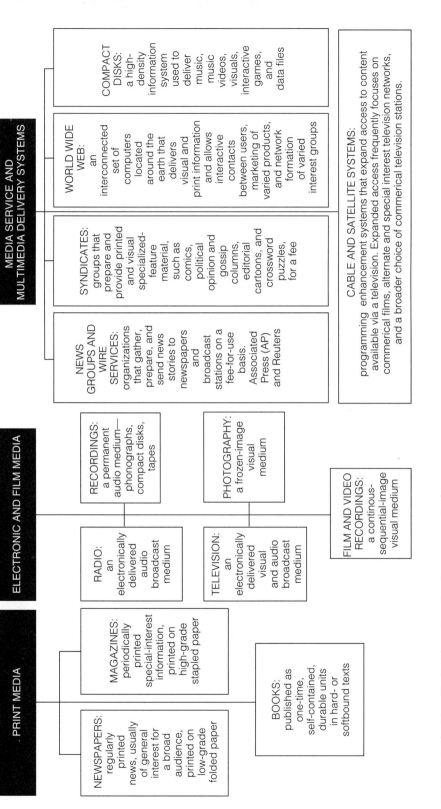

FIGURE 1.2 The Mass Media. The categories shown are not, of course, mutually exclusive, and there is much overlap among the media. For example, magazines and newspapers often use photographs, films may be shown on television, and recordings are a mainstay of radio.

is decided at the end of a long and exacting process. In contrast, in the *crime control* model of criminal justice reality, the criminal justice system is perceived as an assembly line along which defendants should be processed as quickly and efficiently as possible. The primary goal of the system here is to punish criminals and to deter crime. The key determination in this model is factual guilt, which is decided early in the process in accordance with the perceived strength of each case and professional judgment.

These models of reality make clear the basic source of conflict between the police and the courts, as police agencies are dominated by crime control advocates and the courts are normally more sensitive to due process considerations. Sometimes one or the other of these two competing realities dominates social policy; at such times, judicial decisions, too, tend to reflect the dominant model. During the 1960s, for example, the civil rights movement brought due process values to the fore, and the Supreme Court rendered a number of decisions limiting police practices. During the 1980s, when crime control values became dominant, the Court relaxed its position on several earlier strict rulings.

Beyond aiding in understanding the criminal justice system, these models are also useful for understanding the conflicting perceptions that exist within the criminal justice system regarding the mass media and their impact on crime and justice.[49] Conflicts arise because some view the media as mainly promoting a due process reality by ensuring that the courts do not exercise power capriciously, while others view them as retarding due process protections by increasing the difficulty of finding impartial juries and conducting fair trials. Paradoxically, some also see the media as promoting crime control by educating the public about the functions of the justice system and by enhancing deterrence as a result of publicizing punishment of criminals. On the other hand, others see them as hindering crime control efforts by interfering with the efforts of law enforcement to investigate and prosecute crimes, by negatively reporting unethical but effective law enforcement practices, and by withholding information and evidence from the courts. Hence even if people agree on the effects of the mass media on the criminal justice system, they may disagree as to whether these effects are good or bad. The same media effect—such as making it more difficult for the police to conduct evidence searches—can be seen by some observers as promoting due process and therefore good, while other observers see it as hindering crime control and therefore bad. Given these competing interpretations and the lack of empirical data and understanding regarding the media's true effects, the media can be constructed as either enhancing or hindering the criminal justice system. The media do what they do, and their effects are seen as promoting (or interfering with) due process or crime control depending on the observer's point of view.

The Mass Media

Front-Stage and Backstage Behavior. Within a socially constructed reality, specific types of behavior are expected of people in specific social roles and places. Front-stage behavior is formal, planned behavior performed in professional and public settings. Such behavior is designed for public observation by a specific audience and is usually associated with a formal societal role, such as student, professor, attorney, or police officer. Given that a person can have different social roles, his or her front-stage behavior can also differ with the situation and the audience. Thus a police chief may behave one way in front of patrol officers, another way in front of higher-ranking subordinates, another way in front of other police chiefs, and yet another way in front of civilians. In contrast, backstage behavior usually consists of informal, unplanned, private actions that are not normally expected to be observed by anyone but the individual's intimates. Even with backstage behavior, however, individuals may act differently with different audiences. Hence police chiefs might act differently depending on whether they are with their family members or with personal friends. In their simplest conceptions in this work, *backstage behaviors* can be thought of as behaviors that a generation ago would have been considered private and in bad taste for the media to portray or report. *Front-stage behaviors*, on the other hand, are those public behaviors that, if not especially created for the media, are at least not hidden from the media's attention.[50] As we shall see, the ideas of front- and backstage behavior can be used to understand the content of the media. When applied to media content, the concepts of front-stage and backstage behavior highlight a seminal difference among the basic types of mass media: print, audio, and visual.

Print, Audio, and Visual Media. As used in this work, the term *mass media* refers to media that are easily, inexpensively, and simultaneously accessible to large segments of a population. Systems for mass production and mass distribution of information must be in place before a society can have a mass medium. Historically, mass media did not begin to develop until the technology for printing was generally available. In addition, a significant or mass proportion of the population must be able to use the medium—requiring widespread literacy in the case of print, and access to the technology for other media. These preconditions were not achieved in the United States until the 1830s.

The first of the mass media to develop in the United States was a print medium: newspapers. Today, many people think of the media as a monolithic, singular entity comprising interchangeable parts—or, alternatively, think only of television. But neither view is accurate or adequate. Print media—newspapers, books, magazines, and much of what is communicated via computers and the Internet—are a vital part of the mass media. Audio media—radio, records, tapes, and compact discs—are neither print nor visual, but bridge the two by delivering their information in a linear fashion akin to print and evoking mental images and emotions analogous to visuals. Visual media—photography, film, television, video games, and also much of the content of computers and the Internet—are far from interchangeable with print or audio media. Historically, the different media have had very different social impacts.

Although film and radio were not without influence, print media dominated the mass media realm until the 1950s. With the advent of commercial television, however, came a shift from a print-dominated culture to a visual, electronic-dominated one.[51] Although not as dominant as once believed, the electronic visual media have challenged and caused changes in all other media—as well as causing changes in society. Consequently, to be able to follow developments in the relationship between the media and crime and justice, we must understand the basic differences between electronic visual media and print media.

The Shift from Print Media to Electronic Visual Media. The electronic visual media, exemplified by television, are accessible and easy to comprehend. In contrast, print media, exemplified by newspapers, are difficult to use and distribute and require the learning of a difficult skill—reading. Because print makes controlling the dissemination of information to selected groups easy, it encourages elitism—the division of society into experts and nonexperts, segregated socialization, and social hierarchies. The visual electronic media, however, remove information access barriers that divide people of different ages and reading abilities. The impact is equivalent to allowing everyone to be present at wars, funerals, courtships, seductions, crimes, and cocktail parties.[52] The electronic media make it difficult to limit access to specific content to specific groups.

Among other effects, the print media's fostering of elitism led to the development of distinct branches of literature for women, adults, children, academics, practitioners, professionals, and laypersons. The trend toward separate realms of information that were accessible only to select groups was also evident in the proliferation of professional jargons. Each professional group felt compelled to create special code words and language so that members could communicate in front of clients without revealing what they saw as privileged information. Medicine and law best exemplify this process, and these fields have been the most affected by the electronic media's promotion of common, open communication systems.

Another significant change that followed the shift from print to electronic media resulted from the kind of news each medium encourages. The electronic media lend themselves to instantaneous or same-day reporting of events that emphasize holistic impressions and emotions. In contrast to print media, their nature makes presenting complicated, analytical, fact-heavy reports difficult. Over the long term, this characteristic led to a shift in emphasis from reporting front-stage behavior to exposing backstage behavior.

When the print media dominated, large aspects of a public person's life were simply not reported. It wasn't that reporters didn't know private facts about public personages, but that reporting them would have been seen as in bad taste and beyond the acceptable purview of the media. In addition, though the print media can offer more analytical reporting and can cover an event in more detail (and thus might seem better able to cover backstage behavior), they are less suited to emotional, visceral reporting than, say, television. As the electronic media became dominant in the late 1950s, the scope of acceptable reporting expanded to include more backstage areas. Under the influence of the electronic media, the social norms regarding what is private and what is fair game for media coverage also changed.[53]

Spurred in the 1960s and 1970s both by competition within the industry to expose new behavior and by the advent of aggressive, investigative, exposé-style reporting, the electronic media, followed by the print media, have pursued and reported more and more backstage, previously private behavior on the part of individuals.[54] This development is most apparent in regard to politicians, who used to be able to control much of what was known about them through selective front-stage events such as speeches and political rallies, and who now try to manage and limit media coverage to these orchestrated events.[55]

The pervasiveness and invasiveness of the present-day electronic media, however, coupled with investigative reporting and a journalistic norm under which no behavior is regarded as off limits, have weakened the ability of individuals and institutions to keep backstage events and behavior private. At the same time, this development has paradoxically caused the creation of staged media events (termed *pseudo events*)[56] to try to direct the media's coverage of front-stage behavior. But despite the large market for staged media events—events full of visual appeal that appear spontaneous but are actually scheduled and planned to meet the electronic media's needs—the long-term trend in both the print and the electronic media has been toward more and more intensive coverage of backstage behavior. The media now make little distinction between front-stage and backstage behaviors. As many public figures have ruefully learned, today there is frequently only onstage or offstage behavior. A person or an event is either open to full exposure or ignored by the media.

Compounding the effect of exposing backstage behavior, the electronic media—unlike the print media—are easily available to everyone. The content of modern electronic mass media therefore has the potential to create rapid social change, not because its content is necessarily new but because its information was previously available to fewer people. Even conservative content may be revolutionary when disseminated in new ways to new groups.[57] The social knowledge available to people to construct their realities is simultaneously expanded and homogenized. People now have access to information they previously did not have, and everyone tends to be exposed to the same information. The social effects are multiple.

For one thing, arcane social realms have been demystified as more information about them has become available. The recent opening of previously closed social institutions (such as prisons, schools, private clubs, courtrooms) reverses a trend several hundred years old, one at least partly supported by the print media's inherent fostering of separate realms of information.[58] Such a trend has also been noted in the judicial system, with some arguing that the use of electronic media has caused legal interactions to become less abstract and more accessible.[59] As the amount of available information has increased, many social roles have become extinct, inappropriate, or severely altered—the All-American sports idol, for example. In addition, the idea that special events need a special place is rapidly fading. Like religious services and churches, and teaching and classrooms, the concepts of trials and courtrooms are no longer invariably linked. One need no longer be in the latter place to take part in the former activity. Finally, in a looping effect, information the public receives from the media ultimately affects the information the media distributes.[60] Thus, previously hidden backstage behaviors become acceptable media entertainment content—homosexuality, for example, is portrayed by characters of many current, highly rated television shows such as *Roseanne* and pre- and extramarital sex is a mainstay of many adult dramas.

These developments have of course not been restricted to crime and justice. They have however, resulted in a number of paradoxical relationships among media, crime, and justice. Chief among them is the way the media are simultaneously perceived as both a major cause of crime and violence and an untapped but powerful potential solution to crime. We look to the media to help reduce violence and drug use, deter crime, and bolster the image of the criminal justice system, especially the courts. In law enforcement we look to the media to aid in criminal investigations, manhunts, and street and vehicle patrols. In the courts we look to the media for assistance in processing criminal cases, reducing case backlogs, conducting trials, and presenting testimony and evidence.

In another paradox, the media more often than not portray the criminal justice system and its people negatively and as ineffective—yet the cumulative effect of these portraits is increased support for more police, more prisons, and more money for the criminal justice system. And although the criminal justice system is not shown positively, crimes are nearly always solved in the media—estimates put the solution rate on television at greater than 90 percent. Despite their long history of portraying stories of crime and justice, the media persist in presenting a wholly and often absurdly unrealistic picture of crime and justice.

A third paradox follows from the way the news media and the criminal justice system normally react to criminal events in much the same manner, concentrating their resources on investigating the facts for later presentation to a specific audience. In the end, however, the two systems are often placed in adversarial positions—with the judicial system called on to resolve the disputes. Within these resolutions, trial courts and judges generally also use the least effective means available to counteract possible prejudicial effects of media publicity—and are encouraged by the Supreme Court to do so.

And last, while crime news is portrayed as being objective and chosen for its newsworthiness, it is routinely created and prepackaged by and for news agencies, which then present the news within the framework of preestablished stereotypical themes. And as the technical capability to cover crime news has expanded, media organizations have instead increasingly blurred news and entertainment. In the process, crime news has become the mainstay of new hybrid news-entertainment, or *info-tainment*, shows.

The criminal justice system and its institutions have been significantly affected by the pervasiveness and invasiveness of the media.[61] These paradoxes and other common misconceptions about the effects of the media on crime and justice demonstrate the complex nature of the media, crime, and justice nexus and will be fully explored in later chapters. The prognosis is that the legitimacy of the criminal justice system will come to be questioned more and more as more of its daily backstage operations are exposed through the efforts of the media.[62] It is no coincidence that concern over the demystification of the criminal justice system and its attendant loss of legitimacy, along with outcries against the prevalence of plea bargains, case delays, and arbitrary discretionary decisions, arose as the electronic mass media grew and the constructed reality of crime and justice changed.

CONCLUSION

The mass media, crime, and criminal justice are seen to be intricately intertwined. An understanding of crime and justice cannot be gained without acknowledging and examining the mass media and their effects. Guided by the perspective of social constructionism and through the criminal justice models of due process and crime control, and the mass communications concepts of front-stage and backstage behavior and print versus electronic visual media, many aspects of the contemporary crime and justice scene can be related and better comprehended.

The balance of this book examines the social construction effects of media on justice. Each chapter deals with a unique facet of the media–justice collision. The next two chapters review the historical development and content of the entertainment and news media—the raw material, so to speak, for the social construction of crime and justice. The media have a long history of employing crime themes, and crime's popularity is tied to its being the ultimate backstage behavior, with the associated enticement of voyeurism. Taken together, Chapters 2 (entertainment) and 3 (news) provide the historical foundation necessary to comprehend the contemporary content used by most to construct their crime and justice reality.

CHAPTER CONCEPTS

Social Construction of Reality	Print and Visual Media	Sources of Social Knowledge
Mass Media	Symbolic Reality	Claims-makers
Due Process and Crime Control	Front-stage and Back-stage Behavior	Ownership and Linkage

DISCUSSION QUESTIONS

1. Thinking back to your childhood, what changes can you note in the way crime and justice are portrayed in the media? Are they positive or negative changes in your view?

2. What were your expectations of college when you were in high school? What were your sources of information about college life? Why or why not was media-supplied information important? Was the expected constructed reality you had of college in high school similar to the reality you found?

3. Take a local newspaper story about crime in your area and identify the claims-makers and their claims. What influence do you feel their social role played in the formation of their claims?

4. Do you feel that the mass media promote crime control or due process goals?

2

⌀

The Entertainment Media and the Social Construction of Crime and Justice

This chapter covers the historical development and present-day content of the popular entertainment media in regard to crime and justice. First discussed is how crime and justice were portrayed in entertainment prior to the development of the twentieth-century mass media. This review of the *pre–mass media* shows that the broad stereotypes of criminals and the view of crime as an individual problem found in today's media were established by the late nineteenth century. Also forwarded within this discussion are insights about the long historical popularity of crime and justice themes in entertainment.

Following this developmental period, cinema emerges at the turn of the century as the first true mass entertainment medium. The chapter traces major trends in the depiction of crime and justice in film, up to its replacement in the 1950s by television as the primary mass entertainment medium. Television's emergence is discussed with a review of its organizational and business roots in commercial radio, its phenomenal growth, and its reliance on crime themes for prime time shows. Crime is seen to be the single most popular story element in the fifty-year history of U.S. commercial television, with crime-related shows regularly accounting for one-fourth to one-third of all prime time shows.

A review and summary of the recent content analysis studies on crime and justice follows. This research has consistently reported a sharp divergence between crime and justice as depicted by the entertainment media and any real-world measures of crime and justice. Detailed in this discussion are the media images of law enforcement, the courts, and corrections—none of which are especially positive.

The chapter concludes with a discussion of the major implications of entertainment media content with regard to the kind of society it describes, the explanation it offers of crime, the public policies it suggests, and the social reality it constructs. Mass entertainment media today form much of the reality of crime and justice for much of the public. The end result is that in contemporary society, the entertainment media are the anchoring strands of a web of popular culture that enmeshes everyone. For crime and justice, this web involves more than just the elements of the media but also ensnares sets of associated crime-related products, attitudes, and policies.

CRIME AND JUSTICE IN
THE EARLY POPULAR MEDIA

Crime has been attractive to the entertainment media precisely because it is the preeminent backstage behavior. By nature and necessity, most crime is private, secretive, and hidden, surreptitiously committed and studiously concealed. To the degree that entertainment involves escapism and novelty, the backstage nature of crime inherently increases its entertainment value and popularity. The more serious the crime, the more backstage it is—and the more novel an audience is likely to find its portrayal. Portrayals of crime also allow audiences voyeuristic glimpses of rare and bizarre acts—often coupled with lofty discussions of justice, morality, and society.[1] As a means of showing people new places, new activities, and new perspectives, as escapism and as exposé, the portrayal of crime has been a rich source for the entertainment media.

Crime and justice has been a theme in popular entertainment at least since Apollo successfully defended Orestes on a charge of matricide in Aeschylus's *Oresteia,* and some of the earliest tales of crime can be found in the Bible.[2] English literature continued the trend, with criminals appearing as common figures in ballads, songs, and tales of medieval England, frequently portrayed as romantic and heroic.[3] Likewise, crime and criminals have been ubiquitous elements in American entertainment since the beginning of the republic.[4]

However, with large-scale industrialization, urbanization, and ethnic immigration in the nineteenth century, crime for the first time became one of the nation's principal concerns.[5] Spurred by growing public worry about crime, by the second half of the nineteenth century the dominant image of the criminal in the popular media had shifted from earlier romantic, heroic portraits to more conservative and negative images. The media of this period were already presenting the stereotypical portraits and themes of crime and justice that would later dominate movies and television—portraits and themes still to be found in modern entertainment media.[6]

CRIME AND JUSTICE IN
NINETEENTH-CENTURY PRINT MEDIA

Detective and Crime Thrillers

The two most popular genres to emerge in nineteenth-century print media were detective and crime thriller magazine serials and books (dime novels). Both were escapist literature, and by the latter half of the nineteenth century they described crime as originating in individual personality or moral weakness.[7] By downplaying wider social and structural explanations of crime, these works helped reinforce the existing social order—the status quo. In addition, the "heroic" detectives in these works closely resembled the criminals they apprehended—calculating and often odd loners, operating in the world of justice but not bound to it.[8] In contrast to earlier crime fighters, who were harsh social critics and whose concerns about legal fairness were more in line with the due process model, these heroes had become darker agents espousing social order and crime control.[9] Detective and crime thrillers of the late nineteenth century thus mark the beginning of a trend toward more violent popular media, less critical of social conditions and contributing to the construction of a social reality in which crime is predatory and rooted more in individual failure than in social ills.[10]

It was also in the late 1800s that the popular media industry divided itself into distinct marketing genres (Westerns, romantic novels, detective mysteries, crime thrillers, and so forth). It followed up this diversification with extensive advertising and standardization of its products.[11] By the 1890s, writers for the entertainment mass market were highly specialized professionals working within well-organized branches of an immense "culture industry" in which production, marketing, and consumption were all meshed.

For example, the theme of the Western, popularized after the West was actually won, reflects a desire for an uncomplicated system of law and order, easily understood and administered, coupled with a distrust of legal nuances of right and wrong that are difficult to decipher and interpret. In Westerns, the common man and frontier justice always win.[12] In a way, frontier justice reflects a desire for due process fairness combined with crime-control efficiency. Ideally, a man was given a fair opportunity to make things right, but once guilt was established, punishment was quickly and usually violently administered.[13] This ideal is best reflected in the popular Western books of Louis L'Amour and the classic Western films such as *Shane* and *High Noon*.

The cover from one of the popular
nineteenth-century dime detective novels

Culver Pictures

The constructions of crime and justice produced during this time are surprisingly similar to those found today, because the crime-and-justice themes established by the late nineteenth century are in many ways the same as those found in today's entertainment media. Both present images that reinforce the status quo, promote the impression that competent, often heroic individuals are pursuing and capturing criminals, and encourage the belief that criminals can be readily recognized and crime ultimately curtailed through direct law enforcement efforts.[14]

Thus the primary difference between early popular print media and today's electronically based visual entertainment media is the development of new delivery systems—the portrayal of crime and justice is the same. From the nineteenth-century media dominated by print (novels and magazines) through the modern media now dominated by electronically delivered visual images (television, cable television, and home video), the broad constructed message of crime and justice has remained relatively constant, with only a few evolutionary changes.

Movies and television are commonly acknowledged as the most influential, accessible, and pervasive of today's communications media. And because of these characteristics, they have been the subject of the most research, speculation, and public concern. The print media, however, also construct images of crime and justice as entertainment. Crime and violence have been longstanding components of American literature,[15] and historically the content of novels and magazines abounds with depictions of crime,[16] as well as concerns that these media portraits of crime would be imitated by youth.[17] Originally created by Edgar Allen Poe in *The Murders in the Rue Morgue*,[18] the detective novel is today more than 150 years old. Magazines were first published in 1741 but until the late 1800s were targeted chiefly at an elite, affluent social group. Mass-marketed crime magazines proved themselves popular in the nineteenth century, however, and a number of specialty magazines devoted entirely to stories of crime (such as *True Detective*) still appear on the newsstands.

Comic Books

Comic books have long been presenting crime-and-justice images, often constructing some of the more sophisticated images and analysis of crime and justice found in the entertainment media.[19] Like popular music, comic books regularly undergo periods of public concern and attack, the strongest coming in the late 1940s and early 1950s and (as with films) resulting in a self-adopted industry code banning torture, sadism, and detailed descriptions of crimes.[20] In the late 1940s, increased concern about delinquency coupled with increased press coverage resulted in the public implicating popular culture and specifically radio, the movies, and comic books as a cause of delinquency. Comics were the most vulnerable target and the attack upon them in the 1950s provides an excellent example of the social construction of a social problem, in this case delinquency, and the dual social role of the media as both villains and lofty moderators of the social construction contest. Nyberg describes the claims and claims-makers that abounded in the 1950s as a battle to assign the cause of delinquency to the comic book industry and enact anti–comic book legislation.[21] The 1950s story of comics is one installment in a recurring moral crusade in America that regularly aims at some component of the popular media.

The prime difference between print media and contemporary electronic visual media is not found therefore in the constructed image of crime and justice or the nature of the social construction contests but in media access and social penetration. With print, the consumer needs to be literate, have access to the materials, and make a clear decision to use or not use them. Exposure to their content has always been less "mass" and more selective, unlike exposure to the modern, electronically dominated mass media, whose images and messages can hardly be avoided.

CRIME AND JUSTICE IN
FILM AND ON TELEVISION

The Development of the Film
Industry and Its Social Impact

Movies at the beginning of this century first provided the popular entertainment media with the ability to blanket all of society with constructions of justice and criminality. The movie industry was able to accomplish what the print media, limited to books, newspapers, and magazines, previously could not. It nationalized the content of entertainment by making its portrayals available to every social, economic, and intellectual stratum. Initially silent and inexpensive to go see, the movies did not even require a common audience language. The images were universally available and widely consumed, and the film industry rapidly came to reflect and shape American culture.

In 1895, in Paris the first paying audience saw the first film. By 1905, movies were established—a separate, profitable entertainment businesses installed at 5-cent Nickelodeons that showed short features. In 1915, the first major motion picture, *Birth of a Nation*, was released, launching the motion picture industry as we conceive it today. The studio system, feature films, and stars soon became a staple of U.S. culture.[22] By 1917, the motion picture was established as the premier commercial entertainment form in the world. The American film industry began its domination of the worldwide film industry during the 1920s, and movies maintained their dominance of the entertainment media until the advent of commercial television in the 1950s.

Within three decades of film's introduction in 1895, the film industry was the most influential popular entertainment medium in America. By 1923, there were approximately fifteen thousand movie theaters in the United States.[23] By the 1930s, some 80 million people per week in a U.S. population of 122 million (or two of every three Americans) attended a movie.[24] With their immense popularity, the movies were the first modern mass medium, and their emergence heralded the creation of a twentieth-century mass culture, a culture that is homogeneous across geographic, economic, and ethnic lines.[25]

The social impact of the cinema was pervasive and extensive, affecting the American public's values, political views, social behavior, consumption patterns, and perceptions of the world.[26] Concerns about the movies' widespread influence developed nearly as quickly as the industry.[27] By 1915, the Supreme Court had already considered and ruled that movies were not protected under the First Amendment of the U.S. Constitution as a form of free speech.[28] In a number of jurisdictions people began trying to regulate this new medium as soon as it emerged.[29] Later concern with the popularity and possible criminogenic effect of gangster films in the 1920s and 1930s led to a review by the U.S. Motion Picture Association and the decline of the gangster genre.[30]

The movies were important for the construction of crime and justice for several reasons. By the twentieth century, urbanization, industrialization, and a national communications system made up of the telegraph, postal, and telephone systems had increased our economic and cultural interdependence and social homogeneity. As a result, the similarity of our socializing experiences and social knowledge increased. Movies became a major contributor to this ongoing homogenizing process. As both a social event and a source of social information, movies were the first medium able to bypass the traditional socializing agents of church, school, family, and community and directly reach individuals with information and images useful in constructing personal reality.[31]

Film was therefore the first mass medium with the ability to construct a mass public—a large homogeneous consumer group composed of individuals from many ethnic, social, and economic strata who, regardless of their differences, now shared much in the way of social information. The movies helped create a national social perspective and contributed to a collective vision of people and life.[32] Messages about the nature of society and the kinds of individuals it contains were projected again and again to the public. From repeated messages and images related to crime and justice, recurring themes and a widely accepted crime-and-justice reality emerged.

Historical Trends in the
Portrayal of Crime and Justice in Film

Portraits of crime-and-justice appeared early in film's development, and they have continued to be a popular staple of film. Besides being the central theme of police, detective, robbery, and gangster movies, crime and justice are often secondary plot elements in love stories, Westerns, comedies, and dramas. Though, of course, not every movie produced during a particular time frame portrayed the same crime-and-justice theme, dominant themes have been identified with certain periods, and the evolution of the image of crime in film can be conceived of as a dramatized documentary of twentieth-century American history.[33] Thus the first film criminals were descendants of Western outlaws, but unlike the "bandit heroes" of Western dime novels, early film criminals were usually portrayed as urban capitalists.[34] Most of these early portraits depicted ruthless crooks engaged in corrupt business practices in the pursuit of wealth, a motif that has remained popular to this day.[35] Also common in film plots between 1910 and 1920 were nostalgic portrayals of a pure and simple youthful criminality, reflecting street gang experiences among working-class immigrants. Such films reflected the social impact of large immigrations into the United States during the early part of the century.[36] Their sentimentality mirrored an earlier pattern in the presentation of criminals in crime novels, which began with sentimental portraits of criminals and later moved toward more negative depictions.[37] From the 1920s to the 1950s, the film criminal slowly evolved from an early-twentieth-century immigrant into a returning World War I veteran, again transformed into a high-rolling bootlegger and ruthless Depression-era gunman, and finally into a modern corporate or syndicate executive-gangster.[38]

Thus in the 1920s the media image of criminals was of a socially tolerated "pseudo small businessman."[39] Reflecting the extravagant, materialistic lifestyle

One of the movies' first criminals in *The Great Train Robbery*

The Bettmann Archive

of the Roaring Twenties, an aura of romantic idolatry surrounded the criminal during this period. This shifted somewhat during the early Depression years, however, when positive portrayals of Robin Hoods competed with negative portrayals of robber barons, and criminals were shown both as heroes and as villains. It is important to note that in both the heroic and the villainous portrayals, criminals enjoyed full lives and were often decisive, intelligent, attractive individuals. Whether basically good or bad, criminals were shown as active decision makers who went after what they wanted, be it money, sex, or power. They controlled their lives, lived well, and decided their own fates, in contrast to the helplessness much of the public felt during the Depression. Besides casting criminals in a positive light, this construction projected the strong message that worldly success often indicated criminality on the part of the successful individual. To be successful in America, some larceny was acceptable and probably necessary. By extension, this portrait reflected negatively on all real

The Keystone Cops portraying the traditional
law enforcers of the criminal justice system

Culver Pictures

individuals who were successful and powerful, painting them as probable
crooks.[40]

Concern that such a message could influence people to turn to crime and
delegitimize authority sparked investigations and censorship drives against the
media in the beginning of the 1920s. In 1929, the Payne Foundation under-
wrote the first large-scale study of the impact of mass media—in this case, the
consequences of movies.[41] The research examined the effects of movies on

deviant, asocial, and violent behavior on the part of juveniles. These research efforts, combined with public concerns about the influence of the cinema, helped prompt the film industry to create its own internal review panel, the Hays Commission, to oversee the content of films and thereby quell increasing calls for government intervention.[42] In response to these developments, in the 1930s the movie industry shifted to G-man films in which federal law enforcement agents rather than criminals were the heroes, a shift mirrored in the radio crime dramas of the time as well.[43] Stars such as James Cagney who had previously played only criminals now found themselves cast as crime fighters. However, this was a limited change in that local police continued to be portrayed negatively: as incompetents in the Keystone Cops and Charlie Chaplin films of the 1920s, and as heavies in the film noir productions of the 1930s and 1940s. Early portrayals of the police so upset the International Association of the Chiefs of Police that its members passed a resolution at their 1913 meeting, pledging to do as much as possible to change those depictions.[44]

In the 1940s, depictions of violence, terrorism, and murder also became more graphic, as gangsters, policemen, and detectives (many now with weapon fetishes) became more violent.[45] In response to the introduction of television in the 1950s, Hollywood began marketing crime syndicate films using a pseudo-documentary style and biographies to enhance movies' realism and suggest that deeper, truer backstage criminality was being revealed. As with the earlier gangster movies of the 1920s, the tendency in these organized-crime films was to romanticize the criminal lifestyle as the way of life within violent criminal brotherhoods.[46]

Radio drama, particularly at its height during the 1930s and 1940s, also included a substantial—though never a dominant—proportion of crime-related programming, carrying such programs as *The Shadow*, *Sherlock Holmes*, and *True Detective*. Television programmers also borrowed from this tested set of plots and themes in developing their shows. Radio portrayals of criminality were not significantly different from those on film, the primary difference being, of course, that violence could not be shown but had to be imagined.

The decline of film as the primary mass medium portraying images of crime and justice began in the late 1940s with the introduction of commercial television, a medium even more pervasive, direct, and influential than film. Criminality in the cinema (and in radio), however, had provided a fifty-year pool of plots, themes, and portraits for television to develop. Not surprisingly, television entertainment largely constructed images of crime and justice similar to the ones that had been created in film and radio.

Television's Emergence

Introduced between 1948 and 1951, television soon replaced radio as the primary home entertainment medium, and as noted, forced the movie industry to restructure and drove radio dramas into history.[47] Television's growth and public acceptance was phenomenal; it quickly dominated the media industry. The existence of established business and organizational models in commercial

James Cagney (*right*) portraying the dynamic,
shrewd criminal in *Public Enemy*

Culver Pictures

radio facilitated television's rapid emergence. CBS and NBC already existed as
radio networks, and broadcasting was unquestioningly accepted as a legitimate
for-profit business venture. Because the nature and needs of the market dominated programming decisions from television's beginnings, television programming has always been aimed at attracting and holding the largest possible
audience.[48] The medium quickly came to be criticized for the role that ratings
and competition for advertising dollars had in determining its programming
content. Borrowing its basic themes and programming ideas from film, radio,
and stage, and reformatting them in broadly palatable, noncontroversial products, television came to be commonly described as a vast wasteland of recy-
cled, mediocre programs.

Despite the critics among them, Americans by and large embraced television. In 1977, the ratio of television sets to Americans reached 1 to 1 and has
never declined.[49] Television viewing constantly ranks as the third most time-
consuming activity (after sleep and work or school) for Americans.[50] Americans spend nearly half their free time watching television and television today
is a more consuming socializing agent than school and church combined.[51]
More Americans now have televisions than have refrigerators or indoor
plumbing.[52] As an indication of how much time Americans spend watching
television, for every ten years an average American will watch one solid year
of television—with a household average greater than six hours per day.

A key to understanding television and its content is to remember that it is made up of competing business organizations that have to make a profit. The broadcast shows (news shows included) must as a first priority attract and hold viewers to retain sponsors. The larger the audience, the more the sponsors are willing to spend for advertising and the greater the profits. Television shows themselves are therefore best thought of as packaging or vehicles for commercials and only secondarily as entertainment. From a business perspective, a mediocre show with a large audience is a better product than a high-quality show with a small audience. A successful television show is one that is not turned off; it does not need to be well done, accurate, or enlightening. This does not mean that the television industry or its executives are ideologically opposed to high-quality programming. Networks will sometimes carry excellent shows at a loss, but overall they must make money in a highly competitive business. In television, where networks must draw in the same viewers week after week, this means attracting—but not alienating, irritating, or angering—those viewers. Content must also not be ideologically offensive, and so an ideological bias that supports the status quo emerges. The end result is a broadcast spectrum full of largely noncontroversial, bland, poor-to-average shows that attract and hold without engaging or stimulating. It is only recently, in response to home video and cable television, that network programming has begun to venture into controversial areas.

As for content, television executives apparently found a gold mine in crime programming. Remember that although television was modeled after radio, crime was never a dominant part of radio programming (ranging from 4 percent in 1932 to a peak of 14 percent in 1948). Television programming, however, developed differently. As noted by Joseph Dominick,[53] "crime shows became a staple of prime time [television] entertainment [in] the late 1950s, when, prompted by the introduction of 'adult Westerns' on ABC, and later by the success of a program called *The Untouchables*, crime shows began to account for around one-third of all prime time [shows] from 1959–1961." This trend leveled off during the 1960s but began to increase again during the early 1970s until it reached its peak in 1975, when almost 40 percent of the three most successful networks' (ABC, CBS, NBC) prime time schedules contained shows dealing with crime and law enforcement.[54]

Table 2.1 details this historical trend, showing that after the decline of Westerns in the sixties, crime programming came to average about one-fourth to one-third of all prime time television entertainment through the 1970s.[55] The proportion of crime shows declined somewhat in the early 1980s. By 1985, however, their level had again surged, with the largest number of crime and justice shows aired in 1987. Crime-related programming again declined in the 1990s, fluctuating between 20 percent and 25 percent through 1996.[56]

On average, then, about one-fourth of all prime time shows from the 1960s into the 1990s have directly focused on crime or law enforcement. While there is some recent evidence that the major television networks are deemphasizing crime and portraying it less positively, the total amount of crime-and-justice programming available via television is greater than ever.[57]

Table 2.1 Prime Time Programming Related to Crime and Law Enforcement on the Three Major Networks, 1953–1996

Year	Number of Shows	Number of Hours	Percentage of Prime Time Programming*
1953	5	2.5	4.0
1954	6	3.0	4.8
1955	3	1.5	2.4
1956	2	1.0	1.6
1957	7	3.5	5.6
1958	8	4.5	7.1
1959	13	8.5	13.5
1960	13	10.0	15.9
1961	13	12.5	19.8
1962	7	6.5	10.3
1963	5	5.0	7.9
1964	3	3.0	4.8
1965	5	4.5	7.1
1966	4	3.0	4.8
1967	7	5.5	8.7
1968	10	8.0	12.7
1969	7	5.5	8.7
1970	12	9.0	14.3
1971	12	10.5	16.7
1972	13	13.5	21.4
1973	18	18.0	28.6
1974	17	17.0	27.0
1975	20	21.0	33.3
1976	16	17.0	27.0
1977	12	12.0	19.0
1978	9	9.0	14.3
1979	12	12.0	19.0

Overall, the proportion of television time devoted to crime and violence makes crime the largest single subject matter on television, with crime themes found across all types of programming.[58] Special programming, such as movies shown on television, miniseries, program promotions, syndicated programs, and local network programming, has similar if not greater proportions of crime-related content.[59] There is little question that a significant amount of crime-related programming has been offered on television for a long time. The potential impact of such programming has been heightened not only by increases over the years in the amount of daily viewing of television, especially by children,[60] but by the increased access to this programming through cable stations, satellite systems, VCRs, and new networks.[61]

Table 2.1 *Continued*

Year	Number of Shows	Number of Hours	Percentage of Prime Time Programming*
1980	10	10.0	15.9
1981	10	10.0	15.9
1982	12	12.0	19.0
1983	10	10.0	17.5
1984	19	18.5	29.4
1985	22	21.5	34.1
1986	19	17.5	27.8
1987	25	23.5	37.3
1988	15	15.0	23.8
1989	14	14.5	23.0
1990	16	15.5	24.6
1991	16	14.0	22.2
1992	17	16.5	26.2
1993	13	13.0	20.6
1994	15	15.0	23.8
1995	15	14.5	23.0
1996	13	12.5	19.8

*Based on a total of 63 hours of prime time programming per week for the three networks (ABC, CBS, and NBC) combined.

SOURCE: Compiled by author from *Complete Directory to Prime Time Network TV Shows, 1946–Present,* eds. Tim Brooks and Earle Marsh, 1953 through 1984, *TV Guide* fall preview issues for 1985–1996. The hours 8 to 11 were chosen to standardize "Prime Time" to the same three hours each evening across all years. If a crime show began at 7:30 and ran to 8:30, it was counted as a half hour. Classification of a show as crime or criminal justice was taken from the classification scheme and description provided in the *Complete Directory to Prime Time Network TV Shows.* This table does not include westerns, war, horror, adventure, or spy programs. It also does not include programming on the DuMont network in the early 1950s or the Fox network from the late 1980s. This table therefore under-measures the total amount of crime- and criminal–justice related programming on television, estimated to be as high as 80 percent in the mid 1980s by one reviewer (Newman 1990, citing Berman 1987). By standardizing the prime time hours and the crime and criminal justice classification, the table does show the relative emphasis on crime and criminal justice from one year to the next and over the history of U.S. television.

The popular mass entertainment media, first in the form of film and today led by television, have thus become a significant social factor, conveying thematic messages and lessons about whom to emulate and fear in society, what the basic causes of crime are, and how crime should be fought. An overview of entertainment media constructions of crime and justice follows.

PORTRAITS OF CRIME AND JUSTICE IN THE MODERN ENTERTAINMENT MEDIA

Of the many themes to be found in the media—love, death, married life, coming of age—that of crime and justice is said to be the most revealing about society, because it encompasses notions of good and evil, morality, social achievement, and social structure.[62] In addition, criminality is an area about which the viewing public has limited alternative sources of information (everyone knows married people; few personally know convicted criminals), in part because of its backstage nature. The backstage nature of crime increases its entertainment value and popularity—hence the enormous number of media portraits of crime and justice. There has been a persistent interest in the content of these portraits since the 1930s, and a number of studies analyzing the crime and justice content of the entertainment media have been carried out. The majority of these studies—including the most recent, thorough, and enlightening—focus on television, since its pervasiveness and ready availability, especially to children, raises the most concern. The more ambitious have tried to find a link between viewing content and subsequent viewer behavior, particularly aggression (see Chapter 5).

As noted earlier, the major difference in the modern entertainment media from past portrayals is not a matter of content—it is the sheer variety of media delivering images and constructions of crime and justice. The most notable recent additions to the mass media web are rap music, music videos, video films, and video games. Rap music is not a new medium but a combination and extension of popular music and counterculture street poetry. The concerns and criticisms directed against rap and its derivatives are the same type of attacks leveled in the 1920s and 1930s against jazz and in the 1950s and 1960s against rock and roll. All three types of music have had claims forwarded by various groups linking them to promiscuity, drug use, and the undermining of the American family and values.[63] The latest emphasis on gangsta rap has also included the linking of popular music to violence, particularly violence against women and law enforcement officers.[64] The social construction of jazz, rock, heavy metal, and rap music as dangerous relies on obscenity arguments to portray the music as criminal and anecdotal copycat effects to argue that it is criminogenic. What is ironic is that popular music and its stars, which are developed and delivered through the mass media, find themselves criminalized through the same mass media. They both depend on the mass media for their cultural life and are demonized by it.[65]

Video films and video games are an additional source of contemporary concern. Combining the explicitness of film and the easy access of television, video films rouse concern by the way they give youth access to graphic violent and sexual media.[66] Here again, the content is not new but the social distribution and access—and thus the social impact—is.[67] Video games are a unique addition to the entertainment realm, however. Here the concern is with the interactive, direct involvement in game violence by the game player, with interactive "sinister combat violence" emerging as the greatest concern.[68] Some computer-based CD-ROM games revolve around the concept of terrorizing women.[69] No longer just a vicarious observer, the video game player extends the media experience to more than symbolic reality while stopping short of experienced reality. The experience is commonly termed *virtual reality*, and the player—most frequently a young male—actively enters this new reality and creates the observed, often deadly violence within the video game, in the process escaping to a place where forbidden acts are frequent and rewarded. Video players enjoy an encapsulated, immanent justice of the sort pursued in the Middle Ages via trial by ordeal and suggested throughout the media-constructed crime-and-justice reality.[70] Not surprisingly, the nonpassive role of the video game consumer coupled with the graphic violence and popularity of video games has raised public concern. While remaining an ongoing area of debate, however, video game crime and violence has sparked little definitive research into actual effects on users.[71] Like film, comic book, and music producers before it, the video game industry has responded with a self-imposed ratings system to distinguish the games' content. Research to date indicates that boys do behave significantly more aggressively after playing violent video games when compared with nonviolent game players.[72] Similar findings along attitudinal dimensions have been reported for college males.[73]

Though the other media do not precisely mirror television's content with regard to crime and justice, the content of television programming does seem to reflect the emphasis of the broader spectrum of entertainment media. There is certainly no evidence that the dominant crime-and-justice portraits in other media differ significantly from television's, and as discussed earlier there are theoretical and historical reasons why they would not.[74] Accordingly, the balance of this discussion will focus on television, cautiously extrapolating the findings to the broader general popular entertainment media.

What are viewers likely to see in the media? Are they exposed to situations and behaviors they might not experience in reality? In terms of crimes, the offenses that are most likely to be emphasized on television are those that are least likely to occur in real life, with property crime underrepresented and violent crime overrepresented.[75] And while there are recent reports of declines in television violence and fewer portrayals of violence as graphic or heroic,[76] media portraits of crime greatly overemphasize individual acts of violence.[77] If one looks at combined criminal and noncriminal violence on television, the levels are even higher.[78] Murder and robbery dominate, with murder accounting for nearly one-fourth of all television crimes.[79] In a representative content study by Lichter and Lichter, murder, robbery, kidnapping, and aggravated assault made up 87 percent of all television crimes. In contrast, murders account for only one-sixth of 1 percent of the FBI Crime Index. At the other extreme, thefts account for nearly two-thirds of the FBI Crime Index, but only 6 percent of television crime.

Thus a large difference exists between what viewers are likely to experience in reality and what they are likely to see in the media.[80] This perhaps would not be a concern if the portrayals of crime and justice in the media were balanced in other aspects and presented various competing constructions of the world. That, however, is not the case.

For example, there is also almost no correspondence between media portraits of criminals and official statistics of persons arrested for crimes.[81] The typical criminal as portrayed in the entertainment media is mature, white, and of high social status, whereas statistically the typical arrestee is young, black, and poor—all they have in common is that both are male.[82] The single most common television portrait of a criminal features an upper-middle-class person gone berserk with greed.[83] Indeed, greed, revenge, and mental illness are the basic motivations for criminality in the vast majority of the crimes on television.[84] The repeated message in the visual entertainment media (film and television) is that crime is largely perpetrated by individuals who are basically different from the majority, that criminality stems from individual problems, and that criminal conduct is freely chosen behavior (see Box 2.1). In effect, the media constructs criminals in narrowly specific archetypes: for example, the professional deviant who lives a life of crime or the apparent community pillar who uses crime to maintain or better his standard of living.[85] The archetypes are social predators not bound or restrained in any way by normal social rules and values. In contrast, the media portray victims of crime as passive and helpless. Television crime victims are also predominantly white and male—but even so, television overrepresents young women in excess of their real victimization rates.[86] The victimization rates of persons shown on television, in fact, correlate more with viewers' fear of crime than viewers' actual victimization risk.[87]

Equally distorted are media portraits of the criminal justice system and its procedures. Entertainment programming emphasizes the early steps of the justice process—law enforcement, investigation, and arrest—to the near exclusion of subsequent steps.[88] The construction loads on the front end of the criminal justice system, providing increasingly less information on the process as it moves beyond law enforcement activities. And when the rest of the criminal justice system does appear, the depiction is rarely positive. Law enforcement not only dominates, but dominates as a glamorous, action-filled process of detection, one that often legitimizes the use of violence.[89] The media's portrayal of the criminal justice system usually ends with the arrest or killing of the offender.[90] This emphasis on law enforcement allows the entertainment media to forward the illusion that they are revealing backstage crime-fighting techniques and criminal behavior and simultaneously implies that the criminal justice process after arrest is relatively unimportant. A consideration of the content of the media's direct and indirect depictions of the individual components of the criminal justice system—law enforcement, the courts, and corrections—is revealing.

Law Enforcement: The Police and Crime Fighters

Regarding those who fight crime in the entertainment media, the basic distinction is whether the crime fighter is a member of the established criminal justice system or an outsider. Outsiders are far more common than criminal justice system personnel. And while there has been an upsurge of policewomen in films in the last decade, female crime fighters tend to be stereotyped as either hypermasculine women or hyperfeminine sexual creatures.[91] For female police officers in film, myths of femininity remain evident. Whether an outsider or not, the successful crime fighter is most frequently a heroic white man of

---

BOX 2.1 Portraits of Criminals in Film

In the cinema, as in television, most criminals are portrayed as predatory, greed-driven individuals. However, other images of criminals appear in film as well, portrayed within themes ranging from that of hero, supermale (most criminals are still portrayed as male), victim, businessman, or working professional to that of psychopath. Cinematic criminals, who frequently dominate their films, and their antagonists—crime fighters—often share many characteristics (see Parish and Pitts 1976; Pate 1978, p. 5).

Psychopaths and Supermales

The psychopathic criminal has been a theme in many films and television programs. In addition, filmmakers sometimes combine a psychopathic antagonist with a supermale theme to create seemingly indestructible murderous supercriminals such as have become popular in recent slasher films. Psychotic supermales generally possess an evil, cunning intelligence, and superior strength, endurance, and stealth. Crime in these films is generally an act of twisted, lustful revenge or a random act of meaningless violence. A historical trend in such films has been to present psychotic criminals as more and more violent and bloodthirsty and to show their crimes more and more graphically. Hence, murderous violence that once took place completely off screen (for example, in *M* in 1931) came first to be represented in scenes that were violent but not graphic (the shower murder in *Psycho* in 1960) and then to be shown in graphic close-up (*The Texas Chainsaw Massacre* in 1978—a theme currently represented by numerous series of slasher films such as the *Jason* and *Freddy Kruger* series).*

Victims and Heroes

Although the criminal as hero and the criminal as victim appeared early on in the cinema and have been presented regularly, such portrayals have always been less frequent in number than those of the criminal as a psychopath or supermale. These themes usually have the common element of portraying the criminal in either a sympathetic or an envious light. Films that portray criminals in such light often also portray crime in a similar light. Thus films in which the criminal is a hero (*Robin Hood*, 1922, 1938, 1991; *The Mark of Zorro*, 1922; *The Shadow*, 1994) usually present crime as either a moral crusade or a thrilling adventure. Films such as *High Sierra* (1941), *I Am a Fugitive from a Chain Gang* (1932), *Billy Budd* (1962), and *A Bullet for Pretty Boy* (1970), which portray the criminal as a helpless but essentially good victim of external factors, present criminality as an unavoidable, unchosen career. Other examples include *Falling Down* (1993) and *Thelma and Louise* (1991).

Businessmen and Professionals

The theme of the criminal as professional is also sometimes combined with that of the supermale, with the criminal businessman characterized as a shrewd, ruthless, violent ladies' man. The professional-criminal theme extends from portrayals of the corporate syndicate executive *(The Godfather*, 1978; *Goodfellas*, 1990; *Bugsy*, 1991) through those of the skilled technician (*The Mechanic*, 1972; *The Professional*, 1994; *The Specialist*, 1994) to those of the working-class day laborer (*The Thief*, 1978; *Taxi Driver*, 1976). The central message of such films is that crime is simply work, similar to other common careers but often more exciting and more rewarding. The surfer crime movie *Point Break* (1991) is another example.

---

*Full descriptions of the movies cited can be obtained from the following anthologies: R. Armour, *Film* (Westport, Conn.: Greenwood Press, 1980); W. Everson, *The Bad Guys* (New York: Citadel Press, 1964); W. Everson, *The Detective in Film* (New York: Citadel Press, 1972); C. McArthur, *Underworld U.S.A.* (New York: Viking Press, 1972); J. Parrish and M. Pitts, *The Great Gangster Pictures* (Metuchen, N.J.: Scarecrow Press, 1976); E. Rosow, *Born to Lose* (Oxford: Oxford University Press, 1978); J. Shadoian, *Dreams and Dead Ends* (Cambridge, Mass.: MIT Press, 1977); and J. Tuska, *The Detective in Hollywood* (New York: Doubleday, 1987).

action. Media crime fighters are the dramatic embodiment of American individualism and romanticism.[92] Indeed, crime fighters are usually portrayed as antisocial, unattached loners even when they are members of an established law enforcement agency—the *Dirty Harry* and *Die Hard* films being prime examples. The media supercop is accordingly usually not a regular cop at all but someone from outside the system or a maverick officer within it.[93] Crime fighters are portrayed as being very effective in solving crimes and apprehending criminals, but not at all effective in preventing crime. In general, media police are reactive and incident driven, rather than proactive and community problem oriented. The basic crime drama plot is that the early crimes are successful and often represent a criminal enterprise that has been going on for years. Only later and final crimes are unsuccessful.

The main message these crime fighters convey about crime is that the traditional criminal justice system is unable to cope with it. The system needs the assistance of either a rebellious law enforcement insider who is willing to bend the law or, more often, a civilian outsider—private eyes being the most popular and successful. Justice, which in the entertainment media means law enforcement, is achieved by individual stars, not by the justice system as a whole.[94] Effective conformist law enforcement officers are rare, and when they are portrayed, they often have to resort to innovative special tactics, weapons, technology, and enforcement units to successfully fight crime.

Furthermore, in the investigation and apprehension stages of fighting crime, civil liberties are often violated and due process procedures ignored.[95] The message is that standard police practices are not effective and that extraordinary and extralegal means are necessary to successfully fight crime.[96] These extraordinary means often include such absurd practices as sticking a finger in a substance, tasting it, and pronouncing it "pure heroin" or the like. Not only is this impossible to do, but real law enforcement officers simply do not taste unknown substances, not wanting to sample powdered LSD, PCP, cyanide, arsenic, or other drugs.

Though the entertainment media continue to portray the police as largely ineffective—a tradition that can be traced to Poe's seminal detective stories, in which the French police fumble and fail while hero-detective Dupin, outsider to the system, solves crimes—Lichter and Lichter found that on television the police are portrayed more positively—and more often—than other criminal justice personnel such as attorneys, judges, and correctional officers.[97] Even so, the Lichters found that for every heroic police officer, two others performed incompetently and another two actually broke the law. And nearly half the time, the police shown on television are not engaged in solving crimes—they just perform other minor tasks.[98]

Who does solve crimes in the media? The Lichters found that private investigators did well, surpassed only by interested private citizens. Crime fighters of every other type failed to capture the criminal more often than they succeeded. By contrast, private eyes proved almost incapable of failure, and involved private citizens were 100 percent successful in the Lichters' study. The high failure rate of most law enforcement officers, combined with the fantastic success of private eyes and private citizens, is striking. In the media, clearly, it is the outsider who saves the day when ordinary law enforcers prove unequal to the task.[99]

Significant in media portrayals of law enforcement is the use of violence. Violence has been an element in the depiction of crime and justice throughout media history, but in the twentieth century the entertainment media have come to portray both crime fighters and criminals as more violent and aggressive and to show this violence more graphically. Indeed, so brutal have media crime fighters become over the course of this century that they are now more gangsterlike and violence-prone than law-abiding.[100] In film portraits such as *Die Hard* and *Lethal Weapon* and television shows such as *Walker Texas Ranger, Nash Bridges,* and *The X-Files*, the distinction between the crime fighter and criminal disappears in regard to who initiates violence and how much force is used.

The increasing emphasis on graphic violence has also resulted in a kind of weapons cult within the entertainment media, with weapons made increasingly more technical and sophisticated but less realistic over the years. Guns are shown as useful problem solvers and necessary tools for life in modern America. In entertainment, the people who get their way, both heroes and villains, are the ones who have guns. Furthermore, weapons—especially handguns—tend to be portrayed as either ridiculously benign, so that misses are common and wounds minor and painless (usually when the crime fighter is shot at), or ridiculously deadly (usually when the crime fighter is shooting), so that shots from handguns accurately hit moving, distant people, killing them quickly and without extensive suffering.[101] Persons (usually middle-aged white males) who use guns seldom suffer repercussions—and when the camera turns to a gunshot victim, it rarely picks up the victim's pain or that of the victim's family or friends.[102] In sum, the media up-plays the violence and downplays the pain and suffering associated with criminal violence and gunplay.

The Courts: Lawyers and Judges

According to the most prominent media image of lawyers and judges, law school graduates secretly want to be crime fighters. Although shown less frequently than police officers in the entertainment media, attorneys and judges, when they star, often spend as much effort solving crimes and pursuing criminals as they do interpreting and practicing law.[103] Similar to the portrayals of policewomen, female attorneys—while enjoying a longer history in the media—are frequently defeminized as career women or projected as creatures dominated by sexual conflicts or repression.[104] Female attorneys appear to fare somewhat better than policewomen in films in that some aspects of their real world are accurately portrayed. The films do reflect the scarcity of female lawyers, the gender-based attitudes prevalent toward women lawyers, and the existence of the femininity-achievement conflict that pits their traditional female social role against their functioning as effective attorneys. However, they, like policewomen, are likely to have their sexuality and sexual relationships dominate their portrayals and to be more often shown as young, white, single, and childless. They also share with male portrayals the unrealistic overemphasis on dangerous and sensational criminal law cases.[105]

And although criminal law is only one aspect of the field of law and most attorneys practice other specialties, most media lawyers are criminal lawyers. Thus, in the media, officers of the court usually specialize in criminal law and are often crime fighters and crime solvers. And solving crimes is clearly more demanding and significant than their legal work. When the primary advocates of due process in real life are thus portrayed, it is small wonder that the entertainment media's overall construction of crime and justice supports the crime control model. Overall, Lichter and Lichter found that lawyers are shown negatively nearly as often as positively (31 percent versus 44 percent of the time).[106] Compared with police officers, they are more likely to be shown as greedy but slightly less likely to be directly involved in crimes.

In accordance with the media's myopic concentration on the rare crime of murder, court procedures, when shown at all, emphasize the rare-in-reality adversarial criminal trial.[107] In contrast to real court systems, in the entertainment media, one can expect to go to trial. Seldom are preliminary procedures or informal plea bargaining shown, and posttrial steps are even rarer. The media image of the courts and the law as directly constructed is that of a high-stakes, complicated, arcane contest practiced by expert professionals and beyond the understanding of everyday citizens. The confrontations, the oratory, and the deliberations in the media courtroom are in stark opposition to the criminal justice system's daily reality of plea bargains, compromises, and assembly-line justice.[108] Furthermore, in that people are often wrongly accused in the entertainment media's judicial system, the fairness of the real-world judicial system is brought into question. As one researcher noted in referring to the 271 cases tried by Perry Mason in his ten-year law practice on television, "What would you think of a police force that always accuses the wrong subjects, or a district attorney who unquestioningly prosecutes them?"[109]

Though trials still dominate media portrayals of the courts, recent courtroom portraits have evolved from focusing on the highly unrealistic courtroom of *Perry Mason* to showing more nontrial backstage aspects of practicing law in the increasingly popular soap opera format.[110] The soap opera format became popular in police shows as well, beginning with *Hill Street Blues* and continuing with *NYPD Blue, New York Undercover,* and *Homicide: Life on the Streets.* This general trend can be traced to the television industry's need to revitalize the crime show genre following a decline in the early 1980s. To appeal to an audience that had been raised on television, program developers looked to add more realism to their shows by revealing more of the backstage behavior and private lives of their crime fighters and criminal lawyers.[111] The next step has been to develop courtroom docu-dramas in which real cases are reenacted, tried, and entertainmentized in seemingly realistic courtroom scenes in such daytime television shows as *The People's Court* and *Trial by*

Jury.[112] And spurred by the immense popularity of the O.J. Simpson trial, the soap opera format has been incorporated into a number of contemporary prime time television dramas like *Murder One* and *Law and Order*.

Directly and indirectly, the media paint distorted images of the courts. In shows focused on law enforcement, the courts are often alluded to as soft-on-crime, easy-on-criminals, due process–laden institutions that release the obviously guilty and dangerous.[113] The fact that most media criminals are recidivists implies that they have been through the court system at least once and have been returned to the streets undeterred. When shown, court officers are often engaged in fighting crime or in highly dramatic criminal trials. None of these images comes close to representing the reality of the courts.[114] Indeed, Harvard Law School professor Alan Dershowitz once quipped, "Perhaps the most realistic TV show on justice is a situation comedy—*Night Court*."[115]

Corrections: Prisons, Guards, and Prisoners

In entertainment programming, corrections is the least shown component of the criminal justice system—and therefore presumably the least important. The few television programs that have featured jails or prisons have either been slapstick comedy or featured the inmates rather than staff.[116] More often, corrections is portrayed through indirect negative allusions to its alumni of ex-con offenders in law enforcement shows. With habitual criminals outnumbering first offenders by more than 4 to 1, the entertainment media construct the corrections system as at best only marginally equipped to rehabilitate offenders.[117] Instead, the media imply that the corrections system is simply a way station for criminals, from which they frequently return to society at the end of their sentences worse criminals than when they were sentenced.

In contrast to television, the film industry has not ignored corrections—motion pictures are the primary medium of popular knowledge about corrections.[118] Unfortunately, the image portrayed there is as negative as that indirectly conveyed on television. Prison films make up just 1 percent of all films, however, and with most people having no direct information sources regarding corrections, the public is restricted in both media and personal information sources about corrections. Compounding the lack of information access, the historical animosity between corrections personnel and the media has left the public dependent upon the rare and unrealistic images found in the entertainment media to construct its perception of corrections. This vacuum encourages public acceptance of the correctional stereotypes found in the entertainment media, which commonly show either harsh, brutal places of legalized torture or uncontrolled human zoos that barely contain their animalistic criminals.[119] Films of women's prisons focus chiefly on lesbianism and sexual relations. And unlike crime films, which at least focus as often on crime fighters as on criminals, correctional movies usually focus on the inmates, ignoring the staff and administration or showing them negatively as smug hacks—caricatures of brutality, incompetence, low intelligence, and indifference to human suffering.[120] Reflecting on these media images, Zaner commented:[121]

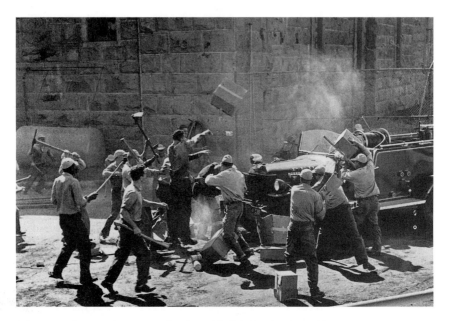

Prisons are frequently portrayed as brutal hell-holes dominated by
animalistic prisoners and sadistic guards.

Penguin/Corbis-Bettmann

The bad rap corrections takes in the movies may translate into a lack of
public support for real-life correctional institutions. . . . The perpetuation
of the stereotype that correctional officers and administrators are "dis-
gruntled, alienated hacks prone to violence under pressure" misleads the
public, giving it an unrealistic view of the corrections professions. . . .
Many of the films made about prisons in the early '30s and '40s highlighted the harshness of inmates' lives. Yet, movies made in the [1970s
and 1980s] show little progress. What's really bad, is that the inmates often
end up as more sympathetic characters than the [correctional] officers.
The pervasive attitude is that the crowd should be rooting for the kept,
not the keepers.

In sum, neither the criminal justice system nor its professional employees
are well presented in the entertainment media, and the further one moves into
the system, the worse the image becomes. If not shown as corrupt and brutal,
the system is shown as bureaucratic, cumbersome, and ineffective, so burden-
ing its few good employees that only those who are willing to bend the rules
and the law can be effective. While some aspects of the portrayals ring true,
the bulk of the constructed picture remains false.[122] People completely outside
the system, who do not have to consider department rules or government
policies and are unconstrained by due process considerations, appear more effective than those within it. Ironically, to enhance the system's appearance of

reality to viewers, the entertainment media present more backstage behavior within the criminal justice system, and this paradoxically shows a construction of crime and justice that has little basis in reality. From these images of crime and justice emerges a recurrent picture of social reality.

THE BIG PICTURE: CONCERNS REGARDING THE ENTERTAINMENT MEDIA'S CONSTRUCTION OF SOCIETY

The Law of Opposites

The entertainment media's pattern with regard to portraying crime and justice can be summarized as follows: Whatever the media show is the opposite of what is true. In every subject category—crimes, criminals, crime fighters, the investigation of crimes, arrests, the processing and disposition of cases—the entertainment media present a world of crime and justice that is not found in reality. Whatever the truth about crime and violence and the criminal justice system in America, the entertainment media seem determined to project the opposite.[123] Their wildly inaccurate and inevitably fragmentary images provide a distorted reflection of crime within society and an equally distorted reflection of the criminal justice system's response to crime.[124] The lack of realistic information further mystifies the criminal justice system, exacerbating the public's lack of understanding of it while constructing a perverse topsy-turvy reality of it.

Underlying this construction is a persistent, if often unstated, explanation of crime that has ideological and policy implications. The media consistently point to individual personality traits as the cause of crime, and to violent interdiction as its solution.[125] If one accepts the media's explanation of crime as being caused by predatory personality traits, then the only valid approach to stopping crime is to hold individual offenders responsible for their past crimes and forcibly deter them from committing future ones. In the entertainment media's simplistic notion of crime, the most effective solution is dramatic, individual action.[126] Media solutions emphasize individual violence and aggression, with a preference shown for weapons and sophisticated technology.[127]

The entertainment media ultimately project the idea of immanent justice and divine intervention.[128] This divine intervention becomes most clear in the displays of gunplay, where weapon accuracy and killing power are unequally held by criminal and crime fighter. Sinful, evil criminals miss or inflict benign flesh wounds while blessed, good crime fighters hit and kill. Similar to the constructed worldview supporting medieval trial by combat, the modern entertainment crime drama relies on the moral superiority of the crime fighter to defeat crime, which is reduced to a simplistic moral battle of good versus evil. Evil is personified in the proverbial dangerous criminal classes run amok,[129] which in turn justifies the wide use of violence.[130] This perspective on crime and justice is also reflected in the common crime fighter motivation of personal revenge spurring involvement. This portrait of an individual personal stake in fighting crime is found even for media law enforcement officers and ties into an overall emphasis on individualism and personal justice as the appropriate solution to crime and victimization.[131] These constructed images gain support from our basic cultural tenets, with the end result that an individualized, revenge-oriented justice dominates. The pursuit of individualized justice in the media tends to crowd out other competing constructions of crime and justice.[132]

Additionally, in the entertainment media, crime is separated and isolated from other social problems that in reality tend to come bundled together—crime, poverty, unemployment, poor health, poor schools, high divorce rates, high pregnancy rates, community decay and deterioration, illiteracy, drop-out rates, and so on. Communities and societies that experience one of these problems tend to experience all of them, but the entertainment media present crime as largely autonomous from other social problems and not as linked to them in any way. As noted in Chapter 1, linkage between crime and other social problems tends to be pursued by various claims-makers striving to raise the social importance of their particular issues. The entertainment media, however, link crime to only a few selected individual-based factors such as greed, mental illness, and drug abuse. With its individually rooted causes, crime in the entertainment media is constructed as an independent plague on society, its genesis not found or associated with other historical, social, or structural conditions. It follows that criminological theories that are individually focused gain more support from the entertainment media construction of crime and justice than do group or culturally focused theories. Lombrosian-like theories of born criminals and psychological theories of defective criminal personalities triumph. Retribution and deterrence are forwarded; rehabilitation and social reform are belittled.

In contrast to their focus on individual causes, the entertainment media portray responses as collective but focused on technology. Crime control is portrayed not as a social problem, but as a technological engineering problem equivalent to traffic control in media entertainment. As a technological problem, it needs a technological solution. Within this construction it makes sense to ignore social and structural sources like racism, sexism, and economic inequality and focus on solutions requiring more equipment, manpower, and resources. It suggests that we can engineer our way out of crime with enough technology, money, and manpower. Such an approach works well for true technological problems like reaching the moon, and the money and resources poured into NASA accomplished that goal. For social problems like crime and poverty, unfortunately, technological moonshot solutions do not work.[133] In so depicting crime and its solution, the entertainment media also depict a particular social structure.

The Social Reality of Crime in the Media

The repeated viewing of these portrayals imposes on the audience a "media reality" of the world.[134] Such a portrait of the world has been associated with the development of a "mean worldview"—the feeling that the world is a violent, dangerous place—and attitudes of fear, isolation, and suspicion.[135] The social dynamic underlying the image of crime forwarded by the media—an image that has not changed much over the hundred-year history of the mass entertainment media—is one of a trisected society composed of wolves, sheep, and sheepdogs. In the mass entertainment media vision of society, evil and cunning predator criminal wolves create general mayhem and prey on weak, defenseless—and often stupid—victim sheep (women, the elderly, the general public), while good crime-fighting hero sheepdogs (middle-class, white, and male) intervene and protect the sheep in the name of retributive justice. Over the course of this century the character of this portrait has darkened. Media criminals have become more animalistic, irrational, and predatory—as have media crime fighters—and media crimes more violent, random, senseless, and sensational. In parallel, media victims have become more innocent. The differences portrayed between the general public and criminals have thus swollen. In a subtle shift, the earlier predatory but rational criminal wolves have become unpredictable, irrational mad dogs, while over the years the noble sheepdogs have become wolflike vigilantes for whom the law is an impediment to stopping crime.

By depicting a predatory social dynamic the entertainment media project messages to the audience, both criminal and law-abiding, concerning whom to trust, whom to victimize, and how victims and criminals should act. The consistent message is that crime is caused by predatory individuals who are inherently different from the rest of us—more ruthless, greedy, violent, or psychotic. Combating these predators requires a special person, an equally tough, predatory, and (most important) unfettered crime fighter. Criminality is an individual choice and other social, economic, or structural explanations are irrelevant and ignored. Furthermore, by focusing attention on contests between individual criminals and crime fighters, the media's ecology of crime ignores the broader social connections underlying crime—for example, the origins and destinations of illegal moneys.[136] Though films are generally more explicit than other entertainment media, even filmmakers have consistently remained vague as to the uses of illegal income and the business tactics and organizational activities of criminals. The media may allude to illegal sources of money (bootlegging, drugs, extortion, prostitution, and so forth), but few media portraits spell out details about how the money is made or depict the connection between such sources and businesses and government. Instead, a highly individualistic picture of the genesis and conduct of crime continues to appear. Few writers or works have presented criminals as not personally responsible for their own fates.[137] The result is backstage glimpses of some types of criminal behavior without accurate backstage knowledge of crime.

Limited to this simplistic, incomplete picture of crime as mostly individual, socially isolated acts, members of each group involved (criminals, crime fighters, and the public) have for generations been receiving a misleading constructed reality in how to engage in and respond to crime. All three groups derive role models from the media.[138] Criminals can learn how to actually commit crimes, whom to victimize, and when to use violence and weapons and disdain sympathy. Crime fighters and the public are shown that counterviolence is the most effective means of combating crime, that due process considerations hamper the police, and that in most cases the law works in the criminal's favor. The public is further instructed to fear others, for criminals are not always easily recognizable and often are rich, powerful, and in positions of trust.

These images of society and criminality, combined with the emphasis on the front end of the justice system, investigations and arrests, ultimately promote pro–law enforcement and crime control policies.[139] Crime shows may be about law and order, but they are light on law and heavy on order.[140] This emphasis has led to a number of concerns regarding the entertainment media's faulty portrayal of crime and justice. These concerns include the reduction of people's sense of personal safety,[141] an undermining of the Bill of Rights,[142] unrealistic expectations about the ability of the police and the operation of the criminal justice system,[143] and negative police behaviors such as overuse of guns and emulation of supercop role models.[144] Concern with negative consequences has also been extended to offenders. Letkemann[145] reported that experienced bank robbers feel their work is made more difficult, and the victim's situation more dangerous, by the tendency of the mass media to depict bank robberies as phony, "toy-gun stuff." Robbers feel they must now first convince their victims the event is "not a joke." This may require more brutal action on their part than they would otherwise need to use. They must also convince any potential heroes among their victims that they cannot be subdued—television dramas to the contrary.

Paradoxically, although the media portray the criminal justice system unfavorably, the solutions they depict as being the most effective—harsher punishments and more law enforcement—both entail expansion of the existing criminal justice system. The entertainment media's representation of reality teaches that the best defense is an aggressive offense, the best protection is a gun, and—as an FBI agent in the television program *The X-Files* preaches—the safest course is to trust no one.[146]

CONCLUSION

The entertainment media, composed of various, ever-multiplying components, weave a pervasive popular culture web that presents a distorted, erroneous source of crime-and-justice information. Historically and consistently the entertainment media have reversed the real world of crime and justice in their media world. In this entertainment reality, traditional criminal justice systems and practices suffer. The images are not a monopoly; some alternate constructions compete, but the dominant construction shows persons outside the criminal justice system as most effective in fighting crime and supports crime control–based approaches for dealing with crime in society. In the end, the media paint for us a stark society composed of predator criminals, violent crime fighters, and helpless victims.

Of course, the media do not claim that entertainment programming is accurate or realistic in the first place, and although this does not absolve the entertainment media from responsibility for their effects on society, finding significant disparities between media portrayals and actual crime and justice is not surprising. On the other hand, the news media do claim to depict the world objectively and realistically. It is therefore more disconcerting to find considerable correspondence between the images of crime and justice put forth by the entertainment media and those put forth by the news media. The most stunning portrait of crime in the news media is found in the "media trial," a news media event that employs elements of entertainment and drama within a purportedly objective report of crime and justice. It is this concept and the history of news coverage of crime and justice that Chapter 3 explores.

CHAPTER CONCEPTS

Popular Media	Content Analysis	Predatory Crime
Pre–Mass Media	Law of Opposites	Individual Media and Media Evolution
Media Genres	Media Portraits of Crime and Justice	

DISCUSSION QUESTIONS

1. If the government guaranteed a profit for the networks and placed no constraints on content, how would you expect television programs about crime and justice to change?

2. Do you think the law of opposites is becoming more true or less true?

3. Have you ever been really frightened by crimes shown in an entertainment medium? Did you behave differently or feel differently about the world and strangers for a while afterward?

4. Where do you find the portraits of horrific crimes the most frightening—on film, in print, or on radio? Why do you feel different media have different impacts?

5. How do you feel computers and computer-based games will change the portrayal of crime and justice in the entertainment media? Do you think the portrayal will be more or less realistic and graphic?

3

The Construction of Crime and Justice in the News Media

C hapter 3 covers the historical development and present-day content of the news media in regard to crime and justice. The first section discusses news coverage of crime and justice prior to the creation of the modern mass media, noting the historical interest in crime and the items about crimes and trials in some of the earliest Western news media. The chapter then traces the development of crime news through the first mass distribution newspapers in the United States, the *penny press*, to the standardization of news-reporting styles and the creation of modern corporate newspapers at the end of the nineteenth century.

The unique task that news organizations face in producing daily news is discussed first relative to news in general and then relative to crime news in particular. Concerning news in general, three competing models of the news creation process are compared—the manipulative model, the market model, and the organizational model, of which the organizational model arguably best describes how news is actually created. This discussion develops the concepts of newsworthiness, routinization, and gatekeeping, and relates them to the selection of crime news. Lastly, summaries of two case studies illustrate how the general process of news creation applies to crime.

Having examined how the news comes to exist, the chapter presents a review of the content of present-day crime news. While the content and effects of newspapers should differ from television because newspapers contain only news and not crime dramas and because newspaper readers select which articles to read in detail and which to skip,[1] the content of newspapers and television regarding crime and justice turns out to be similar.[2] First considered is the amount of total news that is devoted to crime, then how criminals are portrayed in the news. And third, the chapter looks more closely at how the criminal justice system and its component parts—law enforcement, the courts, and corrections—are presented. Crime is a significant portion of the total news, and the news media normally portray criminals as either predatory street criminals or dishonest businessmen and professionals. The criminal justice system is frequently shown as an ineffective, often counterproductive means of dealing with crime. Of particular note is the merging of the news and entertainment formats as exemplified by the recent phenomenon of *info-tainment*. Info-tainment media are exemplified by tabloid-style docu-dramas like crime-and-justice reality television programs and by the multimedia co-optation of the justice system in heavily covered, miniseries-like "media trials." With the increased merging of news and entertainment, it is no surprise that the research shows the portraits of crime and justice in the news and entertainment media to be more alike than different.

EARLY CRIME-AND-JUSTICE NEWS

News has existed for as long as there has been communication. Formal news originated in governmental and religious decrees announcing laws or special events.[3] Printed news about crime and justice is nearly as old as printing, and a detailed account of a witchcraft trial can be found in an English newsletter as early as 1587. Pamphlets devoted exclusively to crime existed by 1600.[4] Indeed, it's been said that after 1575, "it hardly seems possible that a really first-rate murder, especially if it was complicated by an illicit love affair, or the hanging of any notable criminal, went unreported, while the very best of them inspired numerous effusions of the popular press."[5] Popular music in the form of folk ballads made the stories even more widespread and the ballad composer is the forerunner of the modern crime reporter.[6] Treason, murder, and witchcraft were the most popular song and story lines. By the mid-1600s, some newspaper weeklies (termed *broadsheets* or *broadsides*) were regularly printing accounts of court activities, many apparently written by court clerks and recorders to supplement their incomes.[7] This early crime coverage was both instructive and commercial, its constructions of crime laden with details of criminal acts intertwined with moral exhortations to the readers about the

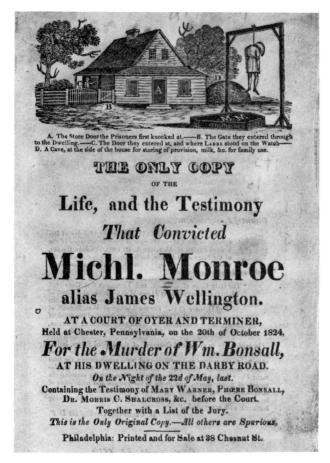

The front page of a nineteenth-century news pamphlet; note the traditional symbolic hanging at upper right and the key features of a crime site below the picture

Harvard Law Library, Special Collections

dangers of sin, crime, and downfall. The writers instructed their readers to avoid sin, crime, and punishment within prepackaged products that are surprisingly similar to the entertainment-focused content of much of today's crime news. Judging by the high public demand and the large number of writers and publishers active, this early crime coverage was also clearly profitable.[8]

Through the eighteenth and into the early nineteenth century, crime-related street literature (broadsides, pamphlets, sermons, speeches) were the main vehicles for news of crime and justice. These print media continued to fulfill an entertainment function using an informational format,[9] and at least in the British press they provided a wide range of crime-related information, including crime prevention information, suspect descriptions, accounts of foreign and domestic crimes, criminal biographies, high-profile cases, and reports of executions.[10] Driven by public demand, the broadsheets of the 1700s and 1800s maintained the already well-established tradition of crime news for profit and entertainment.[11]

However, even though examples of detailed coverage of crime and criminal trials existed and broadsheets were available in the United States well into the 1800s, the majority of U.S. crime-and-justice news consisted of brief reports about trials involving commercial or political matters and coverage of a few select murders.[12] The mainstream U.S. newspapers at this time, termed the *party press*, served as organs of political parties; they devoted their main attention to long, usually front-page editorials rather than reports of factual events.[13] No American newspaper published regular crime-and-justice news until the 1830s, when such stories became leading features in the first daily city papers in the eastern United States.[14] Prior to the emergence of these dailies, early crime-and-justice newspaper coverage is best characterized as docketlike calendar listings with rare forays into detailed coverage. Despite the relative dryness of its content, this court reporting came under early criticism for fear it would cause copycat crimes. The *New York Evening Post* of June 6, 1828, complained that it was "of little benefit to the cause of morals thus to familiarize the community, and especially the younger parts of it, to the details of misdemeanor and crime. . . . Besides, it suggests to the novice in vice all the means of becoming expert in its devices."[15] In addition, by modern standards, distribution and readership were small for this pre-1830 crime-and-justice news, so its reach and social impact did not approach that of the modern mass media until the penny press emerged.[16]

The Penny Press

Before a modern printed news medium can develop, a society must first have a generally literate population and mass distribution systems in place. In the United States, these conditions were first met in the 1830s. In the eastern cities of New York, Boston, Baltimore, and Philadelphia, the nation's first mass distribution newspapers appeared as municipal *penny press* papers distributed on street corners.[17] One of the first such newspapers, the *New York Sun*, began to include a daily police-court news column in 1833 and experienced a notable circulation boost.[18] Other penny dailies followed suit, and human-interest crime stories quickly became a staple of these inexpensive and popular newspapers. The penny press dailies were aimed at the new urban social groups (mechanics, artisans, small merchants) of the emerging literate middle class. Class oriented, these early papers portrayed crime as the result of class inequities and often discussed justice as a process manipulated by the rich and prominent.[19] They contained due process arguments and advocated due process reforms, presenting individual crimes as examples of larger social and political failings needing correction.

The penny papers were soon lamented as promoting licentiousness and the general corruption of young people[20] and setting off a wave of criticism

The front page from an 1833 issue of
The Sun, a New York penny press daily

and concern during the latter half of the nineteenth century. In 1859, some of the first published criticism complaining that court reporting interfered with the administration of justice appeared.[21] During the last quarter of the nineteenth century, law journals began to address fair-trial free press issues and to criticize the press for inaccuracies and poor taste. Before the end of the nineteenth century, criticism of the press by the bar focused more and more on the danger of prejudicial publicity.[22] By 1892, an attorney was stating flatly in *Criminal Law Magazine* that it had become a question of trial by newspaper or trial by the law.[23]

Accompanying the courts' growing criticisms,[24] during this same period concern also emerged about the mass media's ability to supersede the home and parents as a social influence.[25] Helped by the success of the penny press, which spurred an increased literacy rate, a revitalized market for weekly crime magazines like the *National Police Gazette* also emerged. By the twentieth century, magazines focusing on crime, sex scandals, corruption, sports, glamour, and show business flourished.[26] Providing an early model for contemporary proactive news creation and modern trash-TV programs, mass consumption crime news was born.

In response to the market for a steady supply of specific types of news, newspaper reporters began to specialize. Crime reporting became a prominent—though not highly regarded—specialty.[27] The emergence of specialized reporters marks the beginning of the journalistic construction of news and the aggressive marketing of social information to the general public in the United States. The evolution of newspapers and news in general has since been toward perfecting news and newspapers as salable commodities.[28] Newspapers irrevocably changed from being argumentative, politically oriented literature emphasizing editorials and openly advocating political programs to politically neutral, more sensational, but less confrontational sources of information that tended to support the status quo.[29] The marketing cycle for U.S. papers became to periodically offer sensational news to attract a new (previously non-reading) segment of the public. After circulation was established, content generally became less sensational until the next cycle.[30] After the penny press in the 1830s, the next wave of sensationalism was the "yellow journalism" of the 1890s, followed by another wave of sensationalism in the 1920s. Historically, it appears that the amount of crime news was very high from 1830 to 1850 and relatively low until the late 1890s, after which it increased quickly and remained high throughout this century.[31] Today tabloid newspapers and a set of tabloid-style television shows have made sensationalistic, exploitative crime-and-justice news a permanent segment of the media.

The Emergence of a Standard Reporting Style

Despite the early historical appearance of crime reporters, from the 1830s to the Civil War reporting on crime and justice in the United States remained a mixture of stenography and journalism. Often coverage was taken verbatim from court records and testimony. However, with the Civil War, the restraints of reporting from the battlefield and the postwar completion of the cross-continental telegraph system led to the development of the modern journalistic news style of brevity and neutrality. It also saw the adoption of the standard lead paragraph, which quickly summarizes all the main points of the story. Subsequent paragraphs contain additional and less newsworthy details. This standard allowed for rapid news editing as stories could be shortened to a needed length by simply cutting off the bottom paragraphs. The news simultaneously became less analytical and evaluative and more factual and descriptive. Once set, the practices of American crime reporters have remained largely unchanged.[32]

As noted earlier, for a brief period during the late 1800s, emphasis on crime coverage in newspapers declined. Following this transitional period, newspapers came to be produced in multiple editions by modern corporations with large advertising revenues, staffs, and circulations. Crime coverage increased again in the late 1890s with the introduction of a new type of mass entertainment journalism, known as *yellow journalism*.[33] This new style of journalism, exemplified by the Hearst and Pulitzer newspapers in New York, gave space and importance to disasters, scandals, gossip, and crime—particularly violent personal crime. This shift was aided by a number of court decisions and legislative actions that protected the privilege of reporting judicial proceedings without fear of contempt or libel actions. Large headlines and melodramatic depictions of heroes, villains, and innocent victims became the norm. Front-page crime reports became so common that crime reporters in New York had their own room in the courthouse.[34] The developing news industry emphasized standardized and increasingly generic crime reporting. Newspapers were still marketed as informational, but in reality they were offering entertaining and lively content to a much greater extent than their predecessors.[35]

By the end of the nineteenth century, and persisting to this day, two types of newspapers dominated and competed: informational newspapers aimed at upwardly mobile members of the middle class and at the elite (modern examples are the *New York Times* and the *Wall Street Journal*) and entertainment newspapers aimed at the middle and working classes (modern examples are the *New York Daily News* and *USA Today*). Unlike the earlier and cheaper penny press newspapers, however, both of these varieties were conservative and supported the status quo. They depicted crimes as individual acts, in portraits constructed to promote crime control.[36] In contrast to earlier crime news, in which the description of individual crimes played a small role and crime was frequently reported as a result of political and social factors, the new journalism emphasized the details of individual crimes and less frequently discussed crime as a social issue. Descriptive news reports of crime became more important than the editorials offering explanations of crime that had dominated the earlier press.

With this shift, police departments and police officers replaced court personnel and testimony as the primary source of information about crime.[37] Throughout the 1700s newspapers gave considerable attention to local court proceedings, seldom looking to other news sources. In the 1800s, however, reporters became more active, pursuing official sources such as the police and government officials outside court.[38] Trial reporting in the eighteenth century was frank, to the point, and reasonably detached, and reporters frequently interviewed sources on both sides of disputes.[39] The increased reliance on non-judicial official sources marks the beginning of the skewing of news toward the more easily accessible law enforcement sources. Robert Drechsel offers the following explanation for this shift: Early in this country's history, crime was synonymous with sin and trials were ceremonies of status degradation. And since the goal of justice was to reteach and heal the erring soul, confession, public humiliation, and infamy—all of which publicity could enhance—were valuable social goals. Hence publicity was seen as part of the sin-cleansing process, and newspapers were willing and encouraged to publicize even such distasteful activities as incest or infanticide. But though crime seen as sin and its punishment were to be noted, lurid details were not to be sensationalized. The emphasis on editorial moralizing over factual details that was found in these early crime stories follows as a logical extension of this view. In sum, in this early period the discovery and punishment of a deviant act might reasonably be regarded as a favorable sign from Providence and its publicity a useful example of the wages of sin to others. It follows that crime was constructed and presented along these lines by the press.

During the nineteenth century, however, crime began to be perceived as a secular problem. Though neither crime nor sin was a laughing matter, as crime came to be perceived as distinct from sin, being entertained by crime came to be seen as less harmful than being entertained by sin. Marked increases in crime and concern over immigration and industrialization during the 1800s, plus a faith in the rehabilitative power of institutions,[40] also help to explain the increased humor and melodrama to be found in crime coverage and the relative lack of concern expressed over press interference with trial fairness throughout much of the nineteenth century. Americans, fearful of crime in a violent era in which due process rights were not strongly and specifically established, saw little wrong with publicity that, at worst, might help get social undesirables off the streets and into correctional institutions.[41] By the late nineteenth century, the shift to reporting crimes as individually based, often entertaining acts rather than as manifestations of societal failures was complete. Modern corporate newspapers supplying descriptive, factual crime news were the result.[42] Once set, the format and style of reporting on crime and justice did not change much until the development of investigative journalism in the 1960s. As with the entertainment media, the primary developments affecting news media in the first half of this century had to do not with content but with the development of new visual and electronic means of delivering the news.

In the 1920s, radio came into dominance as the home entertainment and information medium, with the number of stations growing from 32 to 254 between 1921 and 1922 alone.[43] Exemplified by coverage of the *Hindenburg* disaster and the Lindbergh kidnapping and Scopes trials, radio news established itself as the first live, on-the-scene reporting medium. The current television news format of thirty- to sixty-second news spots presented within established categories (the world, the nation, sports, weather, economics, crime, and so forth) originated with radio programming. Within these news categories, temporary themes periodically prevail. The electronic news would give a topic saturation coverage for a short time, then would slack off and turn to something new.[44] Together with the producers of the film industry's newsreels, which brought weekly visual coverage of news to the public, radio producers created the style that television would embellish: short-term, visceral, emotional news coverage. Ultimately, the presentation styles developed by both the early print and electronic radio and film media combined with the competitive, profit-driven nature of media organizations to set the parameters for how current crime-and-justice news would be created and what it would contain.

PRESENT-DAY NEWS:
PROACTIVE NEWS CONSTRUCTION

On examination, entertainment and news media are remarkably similar in the distorted construction of criminality they project.[45] This is somewhat surprising in that news agencies market their material as realistic, objective, and true reports of the world and strive to maintain reputations for accuracy. An examination of the process and criteria by which most news is created reveals the origins of this paradox.

Two models for the process of news creation—the market model and the manipulative model—have been described.[46] The key for both models is *newsworthiness*—that is, the criteria by which news producers choose which of all known events are to be presented to the public as news events. In the *market model*, newsworthiness is determined largely by public interest, and journalists simply and objectively report and reproduce the world in the news. Accordingly, under this model, reporters are regarded as news collection agents who meet the needs of the public interest, and the media as mechanisms that provide the public with objective and realistic information about the world. In the *manipulative model*, news is selected not according to general public interest but according to the interests of the news agencies' owners. Under this model, the media are purposefully distorting reality and using the news as a means of shaping public opinion in support of large conservative social institutions.[47]

Both news models are simplistic and inadequate, because they ignore the organizational realities of news production.[48] Theorists now consider the assumption that there is an objective world that the news media can (under the market model) or could (under the manipulative model) report accurately to be inherently flawed.[49] It is flawed because the organizational process of transforming social events into news, by its very nature, makes rendering an objective, unbiased, mirror image of reality impossible. Rather, what the public receives as news is capsulized, stylized information that limits the news agencies' liability and is newsworthy by whatever standard the agency uses.[50] Factors having more to do with the organizational needs of news agencies than with the criteria of the manipulative or market model steer the construction process.[51] Hence, because of the organizational nature of its birth, crime news, like other news, is inherently subjective, though not necessarily ideologically biased.[52] It displays characteristics that can be interpreted as indicative of both the manipulative and market models but that can best be understood within an *organizational model* of news production—a model that better fits the historical development of news about crime and justice as just outlined.[53]

The bulk of news, then, is less discovered than formed by journalists. But journalists do not make up facts, they select facts created for them by individuals or organizations. They offer a reality constructed in part by their selection of some sources and not others. There is nothing necessarily pernicious about this, but the fact is that news claims-makers produce their own idealized versions of reality—versions that when presented as news may be perceived as representing an unquestioned broader reality.[54] In other words, news sources forward an interpretation of issues that presents the view of the world they believe to be true and wish to have generally accepted. The reporter *beat system*—under which reporters cover specific subject areas within specific locales (for example, state politics or downtown crime)—further restricts a journalist's sources and perspectives so that, in general, news journalists report on those at or near the top of the social hierarchy and those who threaten them—particularly those at the bottom—to an audience mostly located in the middle.[55] The construction of crime news can be described as the coupling of two information-processing systems—one being news agencies, the other being the government.[56] This means that in news of crime and justice we normally hear criminal justice system and government officials talking about individual criminals and street crimes.[57] Which crimes get reported is determined by each crime's newsworthiness in comparison with other crimes and other potential news.

Newsworthiness, Routinization, and Gatekeeping

Newsworthiness—that is, the value of any particular item to a news organization—is operationally defined by two components: periodicity and consonance.[58] *Periodicity* refers to the time cycle of events. If an event's cycle is similar to the publication cycle of a medium and thereby matches its organizational scheduling needs, that event is more likely to be reported as news than another event with a different cycle. Therefore, in daily news, preference is given to day-length events or to longer events that can be easily segmented into a set of day-length cycles. *Consonance* refers to how an event ties in with prior news themes and accepted public images and explanations. Unexpected or unusual events will be selected, but they will be presented in terms of previously established stories and explanations.[59] The better an event fits the established themes, the more likely it is to be selected. Other, more specific criteria for news selection include the seriousness of the event, whimsical circumstances, sentimental or dramatic elements, and the involvement of high-status persons.[60] In the case of crime news, seriousness is the primary factor. In that crimes occur in the opposite proportion to their seriousness and that the criterion for seriousness is harm to individuals rather than overall social harm, the media report those crimes that are least common and thus construct a crime reality at odds with the sociological reality of crime.[61] The result is that to the extent that reporters are encouraged to find the unique crime, it is more difficult for the public to perceive and estimate the typical crime.[62]

Another organizational pressure on news agencies is that as organizations they need to routinize their work to plan and schedule the use of their resources. But news organizations are in the unique organizational position of dealing with a commodity, news, that by definition is supposed to be unique and unpredictable. Their central organizational task, then, is to routinize the processing of nonroutine events. To do so, news media personnel must become active co-creators of the news. They cannot be totally reactive, as the market model implies, nor can they be totally proactive, as the manipulative model declares. In practice, they are somewhere in between—reactive to truly unexpected events, proactive and part of the creation process for much of the rest of the news. For example, television news agencies have the practice of stocking and maintaining "story banks"—fully taped news stories that can be pulled and aired as needed. In contrast to the manipulative model, however, even in proactive mode news agencies are generally driven by organizational pressure rather than by political ideology.[63] The more aspects of a social event that a news organization recognizes as newsworthy, the more likely that organization is to treat the event as news. Some news organizations value gossip and personal detail; some focus on financial or political themes; many prefer crime and violence.

In their efforts to routinize the creation of news, news agencies come to rely on standing social institutions from government and business as sources of news.[64] The news media favor these institutions because they represent an easy means of getting news and their personnel can be cited as credible official sources. From this reliance, a cyclic pattern develops. The media and the institutions develop a working relationship, each fulfilling organizational needs of the other—the business and governmental institutions providing the news agencies regular, ready-made news in exchange for publicity and enhanced credibility. The result is news dominated by information and interpretations that tend to support these institutions.[65] Because both the market and the manipulative models ignore these organizational constraints on the creation of news, they are inadequate. News is neither a pure picture of society nor a fully controlled propaganda message, but is instead an organizational product.

In regard to crime news, the organizational construction process has the following results. Crime news makes up a large part of the total news, because, being prepackaged (suggesting the manipulative model) and popular (suggesting the market model), it helps news organizations in their routinization task.[66] And because crime news tends to come largely from information supplied by the police, it can be gathered at little cost to the organization.[67] Additionally, criminal events are readily comprehensible and require little background information.[68] The newsworthiness of any particular crime is determined by the type of crime competitively interacting with other potential news, a reporter's time and interest, the willingness of sources to provide information, and the quality of the information being provided.[69]

A hierarchy of crime news emerges.[70] At the lowest level are crime stories that serve as space or time fillers. Next are secondary crime stories, which are potentially important depending on their characteristics and other organizational factors. Primary crime news stories are those that are given prominent space or time (front page or lead story). At the top are super-primary crime stories (exemplified by entertainment and sports celebrity offenders such as O.J. Simpson, Robert Downey Jr., Hugh Grant, Pete Rose, Mike Tyson, and Michael Irwin) that receive an enormous amount of organizational resources and develop along many dimensions. Public-interest and entertainment-style presentations increase with the level, and the stories are usually made to fit a standard crime news frame. The recurring elements of the crime news frame are the attribution of responsibility at the individual level, the reaffirmation of moral boundaries through the condemning of their violation, and the final resolution of the crime through capture, punishment, or condemnation of the criminal.[71] Within the organizational model of news production there are checkpoints where individuals select, mold, and pass on crime news candidates. Those that are processed through to the final checkpoints become crime news. First coined in 1950, the term for a person controlling the processing checkpoints is *gatekeeper.*[72]

A key gatekeeper in the crime news process is the crime reporter. A subject of much review, crime reporters are said to undergo a process of professional socialization in which, because of their low status in news media organizations and lack of alternative sources of information, they come to reflect official police positions and hold values similar to the police concerning crime.[73] To provide a steady regular pool of crime stories, a crime reporter must develop reliable police sources and maintain their access and trust.[74] Although sometimes critical of law enforcement, most successful crime reporters develop a relationship with the police that benefits both.[75] Encouraged by the fact that for both police and reporters discretion is concentrated in line personnel, over time, the two sides tend to develop similar work experiences and outlooks. Crime reporters don't gather news in the manner commonly assumed, by looking for it among victims and criminals one crime at a time; rather, they receive information from regular law enforcement sources with whom they share values and on whom they are professionally dependent. From these official sources they construct accounts of crime.[76]

A second key gatekeeper group has evolved on the law enforcement side of the news creation process—the public information officers (PIOs). Until recently there was no fixed organizational role within criminal justice agencies equivalent to the news media's crime reporter. Prior to the development of PIOs, interaction with the media was often an ad hoc, idiosyncratic process, and crime news information flow was more likely to be based on personal relationships than on formal organizational linkages.[77] The public information officers are new formal links between a criminal justice organization and the mass media. They coordinate the flow of information to the news media while promoting a positive image of their organizations. Not limited to law enforcement agencies, the courts and corrections departments have also begun to pursue and manage the media and to develop their own public information offices.[78]

Development of public information officers and public relations efforts has also led to the increased adoption of commercial models of promotion, seeing citizens as customers to whom law enforcement activities are to be sold.[79] As the marketing of crime news has developed, the competition among sources of crime news has heightened. While law enforcement agencies still hold the central position in the construction and defining of the crime problem, alternative sources such as other public agencies and private lobby and pressure groups have successfully joined the competition.[80] The public information officer has emerged as the criminal justice system's response to this competition.

Lastly, crime news sources have varying, sometimes conflicting goals when providing crime information, and their past relationship with journalists also strongly influences the access and selection process.[81]

Criminal justice agencies and the media are willing to invest substantial resources in maintaining their relationship because there are benefits for both. The police benefit by having crime news reflect their perspectives, presenting themselves as experts on crime and reaffirming police ownership of the crime problem.[82] For example, they benefit from a gatekeeping process that filters police violence events into news of police violence. As with general crime news, it is equally unlikely that news of police violence will be representative of general police violence.[83] What is newsworthy police violence is what the news media agencies decide is newsworthy after a long and arbitrary, highly idiosyncratic gatekeeping process that is disjointed from the significance of these events to either the police or the public. The end result is information about police violence that is not typical of police violence.

Crime reporters benefit by having a steady, reliable, credible, and flexible source of news that is unlikely to later need retraction or to raise charges of bias.[84] The end result is a reliance on the police for information about crime and crime news that largely reflects official police viewpoints, and—like the view of crime in the entertainment media—is front-end loaded.[85] The main exception is news of police crimes and corruption, although even in police malfeasance stories the media actively seek official police input. Typical coverage leans toward successful criminal justice steps—arrests, arraignments, and trials. Cases that drop out of the system tend to become less newsworthy. The gatekeeping process filters out the vast majority of crime from ever becoming crime news. In one study, of 7,901 crimes investigated by a city police department in one month, only 43 showed up as crime stories in the press.[86] In another study of another city, the media covered only 15 of 1,741 felonies over a three-month period.[87]

Figure 3.1 shows the seven prime processing points between the commission of a crime and the public's receipt of news about crime. At each step in the sequence is a gatekeeper, an individual who receives information on crimes from the previous step, discards some, and passes some on to the next step. These filtering steps make any correspondence between crime news and actual crime difficult. They also make ever achieving such a correspondence unlikely. The socialization of the police to pass along newsworthy crimes of interest to the media and pressure on the media to present the interpretations of the police and to report on atypical rather than representative crimes results in a biased selection of the crimes that become the news of crime.[88]

Crime News Case Studies

Two case studies of the creation of crime news describe the construction process. In the first, Stuart Hall and his associates studied the reporting of muggings in the British press:

> Mugging breaks as a news story because of its extra-ordinariness, its novelty. This fits with [the] notion of the extra-ordinary as the cardinal news

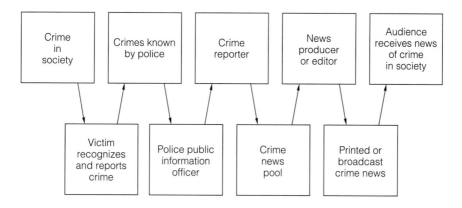

FIGURE 3.1 Gatekeeping Points in the Creation of Crime News

Adapted from "Social Creation of Crime News: All the News Fitted to Print," by S. Sherizen, p. 205. In C. Winick (ed.), *Deviance and Mass Media*. Copyright © 1978 by Sage Publications, Inc. Reprinted by permission.

value: most stories seem to require some novel element in order to lift them into news visibility in the first instance; mugging was no exception. The Waterloo Bridge killing, defined by the police as a "mugging gone wrong," was located and signified to its audience as a "frightening new strain of crime." What lifts this particular murder out of the category of the "run of the mill" is the attribution of a "new" label. Importantly, this event is mediated by the police investigating it; they provide the mugging label, and hence the legitimization for its use by the press. The journalist then builds on this skeletal definition. He frames and contextualizes the details of the story in line with the operating logic. . . . He emphasizes its novelty.

However, the news value of "novelty" is eventually expended; through repetition the extra-ordinary eventually becomes ordinary. Indeed, in relation to any one particular news story, "novelty" clearly has the most limited life span. At this point in the "cycle" of a news story, other, more enduring news values are needed in order to supplement [its] declining newsworthiness, and so sustain its "news-life." Two in particular seemed to play such an augmenting role in relation to mugging; those of the "bizarre" and "violence." In respect to both of these news values, we find a growth in the number of mugging reports, throughout our sample period, which seemed to gain news visibility primarily because of the presence of such supplementary news values.

From "The Social Production of News," by S. Hall et al., pp. 335–367. In S. Cohen and J. Young, The Manufacture of News. Copyright © 1981 by Sage Publications, Inc. Reprinted by permission.

A cycle of newsworthiness is thus created in which once a type of crime is defined as news, it will tend to continue to be news for a time because of the actions of both criminal justice and media organizations: "The relationship between [the police] and the media serves to define 'mugging' as a public issue, as a matter of public concern, and to effect an ideological closure of the topic."[89]

In a second case study, Mark Fishman (1978) reported on a similar process in the United States in which crimes against the elderly, after becoming the focus of media coverage, became the impetus for a media-generated perception of a crime wave in New York City. Here, as in Britain, the initial adoption of a crime theme by one news organization led to that theme's domination of crime news selection within the news industry over a significant time period, which in turn came to influence the activities of criminal justice agencies. News assignment editors use themes to organize and assign reporters and give structure to the presentation of the news:

> This procedure requires that an incident be stripped of the actual context of its occurrence so that it may be relocated in a new, symbolic context: the news theme. Because newsworthiness is based on [current] themes, the attention devoted to an event may exceed its importance, relevance, or timeliness were these qualities determined with reference to some theory of society. In place of any such theoretical understanding of the phenomena they report, news workers make incidents meaningful only as instances of themes—themes which are generated within the news production process. Thus, something becomes a "serious type of crime" on the basis of what is going on inside news rooms, not outside them.[90]

Because of the high level of internal monitoring and copying in the news industry, once one news organization adopts a crime theme, others will likely pick it up as well.[91] If the focus becomes industrywide, a media crime wave results.[92] Such media-generated crime waves occur regularly, the most recent and common regarding drug abuse.[93] The crimes chosen as news during these waves in effect become the typical "atypical" event (the most common news reported about a selected set of newsworthy-christened crimes) for that period.

In the views of both Hall and his colleagues and Fishman, the news media focus public attention on particular crimes without any evidence of an actual increase in victimization rates. The media thus create reality by selectively highlighting certain types of crimes from among the large, constantly available pool of known crimes. In doing this, the media create the perception of a crime wave. Media crime waves normally arise around safe crime themes. The media launch anticrime crusades that have broad public and political acceptance, for example, against crimes against the elderly, street crime, drug abuse, or child abuse.

The social importance of these media crusades is twofold. First, they enable the media to influence criminal justice policies by raising public concern about a particular offense or set of offenders, often affecting sentencing and enforcement practices, and encouraging the use of public resources to address the newly created crime problem.[94] Second, because the media tend to operate around themes, a number of socially significant events will not become news because they do not fit the current themes. For practical public purposes, such events therefore do not exist and are less likely to receive public attention or resources.[95]

In conclusion, driven by their unique organizational relationships, tasks, and deadlines, news agencies generate crime news from a relatively narrow and distinct information channel—a channel that gives preference to information from law enforcement organizations and value to certain types of crimes. The media sustain and depend upon this information channel because it is reliable and easy to use. Because of this dependence, crime and justice news is found to have a predictable content.

CRIME AND JUSTICE
IN CONTEMPORARY NEWS

The Content and Relative Prominence of Crime News

As with crime-and-justice entertainment media, the content of crime news reveals a similarly distorted, inverted image. Numerous studies using various methods and measures have established that crime news is a popular, significant, and constant component of the total news.[96] Within newspapers, crime news accounts for from 4 percent to 28 percent of all the news reported, averaging about 7 percent overall.[97] Proportions range from 22 percent to 28 percent being reported for all justice-related topics.[98] Crime-and-justice news consistently is found to constitute one of the top five subject categories for newspapers.[99] The range for national television is from 10 percent to 13 percent of total news as crime news.[100] For local television, it was found to be 20 percent.[101] Although there are differences between different media outlets (for example, between tabloid and mainstream newspapers), this range of about 5 percent to 25 percent appears to hold true for different time periods, different localities, and different media (television, newspapers, and radio).[102] Besides making up a significant portion of the news, crime news is well attended.[103] For example, in newspapers, crime news is read and remembered consistently by a greater percentage of subscribers (about one of every four) than any other type of news.[104] So popular is crime news that the reading and watching of it has been described as a daily ritual in America that sets and examines our moral boundaries concerning shock and outrage.[105]

There are a number of explanations as to why crime news is such a significant portion of news.[106] Crime news is often described as serving a positive social function by setting the boundary of acceptable social behaviors, deterring offenders, making potential victims more cautious, and providing crime surveillance and avoidance information to citizens. Crime is also an important social issue and crime news is held up as a mirror on the world. Lastly, and pragmatically, crime news boosts circulation and has entertainment value for news organizations.[107] Each of these reasons explains a portion of the amount of crime news. As the types of crime vary, so do the reasons for their coverage.

More important than the proportion is the focus of crime news. The traditional definition of news is that which is new or uncommon. Following this maxim, violent crime is seen as more newsworthy precisely because it occurs less frequently. It also follows that the rarest type of violent crime, murder, is reported the most often. Crime news has been found to focus largely on violent personal street crimes such as murder, rape, and assault, with more common offenses such as burglary and theft often ignored.[108] According to one study, murder and robbery alone account for approximately 45 percent of newspaper crime news and 80 percent of television crime news.[109] In another study it was reported that murder constituted 0.2 percent of the crime known to the police but was the subject of 26.2 percent of crime news, whereas nonviolent crime accounted for 47 percent of known crime but only 4 percent of crime news stories.[110] Crime news also focuses heavily on the details of specific individual crimes. The majority of crime news deals with crime details, whereas only a minuscule percentage deals with the personality of the criminal or victim.[111] The focus is on dramatic entertainment with a recitation of details about individual offenders and crime scenes.[112] Coverage of individual crimes has in fact been found to rank as the single most common crime-and-justice news item for both newspapers and television.[113] As an example, while rape is dramatically underreported in contrast to murder, rapes that are covered are skewed in favor of sensationalized rapes by strangers as opposed to the more common rapes committed by persons known to the rape victim.[114]

A number of criminologists and journalists have stated that the media's ignoring of certain types of crimes and criminal cases is as damaging as what they actually report.[115] Corporate crime, for example, less fits the standard crime news frame and is subsequently less frequently reported as crime news.[116] The paradox is that violent crime's relative infrequency in the real world heightens its newsworthiness and leads to its frequent appearance in crime news. Crime news thus takes the rare crime event and turns it into the common crime image. Criminologists have cited this media emphasis on publicizing the atypical crime as a serious source of misinformation and false perceptions of the true nature of crime for the public.[117] Additionally, just as crime in entertainment media minimally reflects reported crime, the variations that do occur over time in the amount of crime news reported have little relationship to variations in measures of reported crime.[118] Neither the content nor the total amount of crime news reflects social changes in the crime rate.

The Criminal in the News

The image of the criminal that the news media propagate is similar to that found in the entertainment media. Criminals tend to be of two types in the news media: violent predators or professional businessmen and bureaucrats. Furthermore, as in entertainment programming, they tend to be slightly older (twenty to thirty years old) than reflected in official arrest statistics. In general, the news media underplay criminals' youth and to some degree their poverty, while overplaying their violence.[119]

Additionally, many crime reports give no description of the perpetrator, leaving the public to fill in the image.[120] It follows that since most crime news is about violent interpersonal crime, the image that is constructed is that of a faceless predator. Thus it was found that the public's image of criminals reflected the typical street criminal—a young, unemployed, black male. The significance of this is that the public's image of crime reflects but does not exactly match the news media's image. Even though the news reports a number of white-collar, terrorist, drug-related, and business crimes[121] and describes the offenders it does identify as somewhat older and of higher status, the public appears to focus on the violent interpersonal street crimes that are reported, ignoring those characterizations that do not fit a typical street criminal portrait.[122] Although other crimes and criminals are shown, the violent and predatory street criminal dominates the public's constructed image of criminality.[123]

Although sometimes important for determining newsworthiness, crime victims are frequently ignored in crime news and in the research on crime news.[124] Victim cooperation and quality (photogenic and quotable) can occasionally provide the extra element to make an otherwise non-newsworthy crime newsworthy. Victim accessibility and involvement become more important in markets that have large crime pools to choose their crime news from, and victims are more often contacted as information sources as a crime story increases in importance.[125] The police, as with other news of crime, are the primary source of victim information. When described at all, victims tend to be portrayed as female, very young or old, or of high status,[126] and news coverage routinely depicts criminal violence against females differently from that against males,[127] while underplaying the victimization of minorities.[128] In general, to be a typical victim is not to be a newsworthy one.

The Criminal Justice System in the News

The criminal justice system and its component parts are seldom in themselves the subject of news reports. The criminal justice system serves as a background setting for a news story much more often than it appears as the subject of a story.[129] When the justice system is explicitly referred to, it is usually the courts that are portrayed. The courts are not shown as institutions, however, but as settings for individual cases. Seldom are broader judicial issues covered.[130]

Sentences reported in the media have been found to be equally atypical of actual practice. Thus Roberts and Doob[131] found that 70 percent of Canadian newspaper stories containing sentencing information report on a prison term. Fines appeared in less than 10 percent of the stories. In reality, imprisonment is rarely imposed in Canada, whereas fines make up about half of all sentences. Alternate sentences, such as restitution or community service, almost never appeared in newspaper stories. Similarly, the researchers found that crime prevention stories are rare, relative to stories of individual violent crimes—and when crime prevention does get covered, the coverage is usually negative.

An explanation of these findings is found in distinguishing between two news formats, the episodic and the thematic.[132] The more common *episodic format* treats stories as discrete events. The rarer *thematic format* highlights trends, persistent problems, or other larger social phenomena. Episodic format stories encourage viewers to place responsibility for social problems on individuals rather than on societal forces. Stories told in the thematic format have the opposite effect. With respect to crime, the news therefore reinforces the popular wisdom that says crime is an individual choice and that punishment-based deterrence is an effective response.[133]

In essence, the news supplies a large amount of information about specific crimes and conveys the impression that criminals threaten the social system and its institutions, but it provides little explicit systemwide information to help the public evaluate or comprehend the factual descriptive information provided about individual crimes and cases.[134] Rare is interpretive analysis that places criminal justice information in historical, sociological, or political perspective.[135] In the absence of news media evaluations of the police, the courts, and the correctional system, the public is left to build its own general picture of the effectiveness of criminal justice.[136]

Most media evaluations of the criminal justice system are thus implicit, conveyed through references to the ability or inability of the system to apprehend criminals, to convict and punish them when they are apprehended, and to return them to society reformed and deterred. In Doris Graber's assessment, the news media implicitly portrayed the police as doing a fair job, but the courts and the correctional system as doing poor jobs. When she queried a sample of the public, the system's components did only slightly better in the same order—police being rated as good to fair, the courts as fair to poor, and corrections as poor. The public's largely negative evaluation of the criminal justice system thus reflects overall the information and impressions conveyed by the news.[137]

Regarding corrections, the news media, like the entertainment media, mostly ignore it.[138] Indeed, corrections is mentioned directly so infrequently in the news that content analysis studies discussing corrections are rare. Marsh,[139] in a review of twenty years of newspaper content analysis literature, cites just one study (by Dossuyz in 1979) that specifically mentioned corrections—and then only to state that it is largely ignored.[140] When a news story does deal with corrections, it nearly always reports its subject in a negative light or deals not directly with corrections but with an execution or a riot.[141] The typical long-running national story about corrections features unusual and exciting events, such as the 1993 prison riot in Lucasville, or the simultaneous taking of hostages at the U.S. Penitentiary in Atlanta, Georgia, and the Federal Detention Center in Oakdale, Louisiana, in 1987.[142] As a secondary theme, the national media sometimes take up some aspect of corrections—usually negatively, as in the attack on prison furlough programs during the 1988 presidential campaign. In sum, the news image of corrections is scanty and when reported on is marketed in an unbalanced manner that emphasizes predatory inmates and criminogenic institutions.[143]

Info-Tainment: Reality Programming and Media Trials

The long-term merger of news and entertainment, or info-tainment, has resulted in two distinct developments. One is the present-day exploitation coverage of crime in tabloid-style reality television programs that mix news and entertainment formats. The second is the co-optation of criminal trials in miniseries-like crime-and-justice productions.

Reality Programming. Reality programming entertains by sensationalizing real stories about crime and justice. It presents actual crime and criminal cases in a realistic light, sometimes in reenactments, sometimes as dramatized stories, and sometimes in documentary-style stories.[144] At the high end are the network-produced news magazine programs, which began with *60 Minutes* and have proliferated into more than a dozen weekly versions. Even these shows, however, have an obsession with violent crime and exploitative stories.[145] This emphasis is also found in reality-based law enforcement programs, which have been found to contain the most violent content in this genre.[146] Table 3.1 summarizes the range of reality television offerings.

What makes these programs worrisome is that they present expanded, in-depth stories that convey the impression that an issue is being discussed from multiple sides. They feel as though they are providing a full context in their coverage, without providing the reality of context.[147] They also amplify the exposure to criminal cases and issues beyond the reporting or viewing of the cases or issues in the media. Viewer preference for reality police programs over fictional crime programming has also been linked with more punitive attitudes about crime and more racial prejudice and authoritarianism.[148] Like most popular news, high-profile, sensationalist crimes and criminals are emphasized with a focus on individual random, stranger-on-stranger acts of violence. Television news magazines also continue the process of *commodification* (the packaging and marketing of crime information for popular consumption), which has a long history. They continue the general popular culture's portrayal of crimes and criminals within constructions that are nearly always simplistic and individualistic. At the lower end are programs that are electronic versions of the supermarket tabloid newspapers. These include trash talk shows emphasizing confrontation and sexual deviance and tabloid news shows emphasizing bizarre violent crimes.[149] These programs are significant in denoting the final phase of a long trend toward merging the once distinct news and entertainment functions of the mass media.[150] As we approach the year 2000, more and more crime-focused entertainment-news shows are being broadcast. The print media have also developed a large, successful info-tainment true-crime market traceable to Truman Capote's 1965 best-seller *In Cold Blood*. True-crime books today are an established genre and include the subcategories of serial murder, mutilation, torture, mass murder, familial murder, cult and satanic worship, rape, incest, and bizarre sexual crimes.

The info-tainment crime shows are linked to the general development in the 1980s of so-called trash TV. Since its inception the genre has enjoyed continued popularity and includes a broad spectrum of junk shows such as celebrity sports, lifestyles, interview, game, and pseudoscience shows.[151] These shows present stereotypical portraits of predatory evil criminals and helpless victims; the gruesome and bizarre is shown as a commonplace fact of modern

Table 3.1 Reality Television Programming Types

Program Type	Example Program
Ride Alongs	*Cops, American Detective*
News/Documentaries	
High end	*60 Minutes, 20/20, PrimeTime*
Low end	*Hard Copy, A Current Affair*
Reenactments	*America's Most Wanted, Unsolved Mysteries*
Docu-Dramas	*The Judge, Divorce Court, The People's Court*
Talk Shows	*Jenny Jones, Geraldo, Jerry Springer, Montel Williams*

life.[152] Within their crime-and-justice construction, the crime control model triumphs. Employing real crimes, narrative styles, reenactments, and documentary-like formats, the realism these shows cloak themselves in adds to their impact. Despite their image of reality, these programs are produced using entertainment techniques, employing entertainment-style plot features of "crime, chase and capture."[153] Their acceptance and impact as true renditions of reality is underscored by viewers' frequent attempts to get the police to arrest actors who portrayed suspects in the reenactments.[154] The convoluted mix of images, and sometimes images of other media images, found in reality programming compounds the public difficulty in assessing, classifying, deciphering, and applying the crime-and-justice knowledge available in the media.[155] The development of these info-tainment shows parallels the second development in exploitation coverage: media trials that co-opt and usurp the criminal courts entirely.[156]

Court News as Miniseries—Media Trials. As noted earlier, the police appear most often on the news as spokespersons regarding specific crimes, and corrections personnel are mostly ignored and shown negatively when covered. The courts, by contrast, appear in the media as the social mechanism charged with processing offenders and dispensing justice—as the primary institutions of the criminal justice system. Their constructed portrait within the phenomenon of "media trials" illustrates both the past development and possible future of crime and justice news.[157]

A media trial is defined as a regional or national news event in which the media co-opt the criminal justice system as a source of high drama and entertainment.[158] It is, in effect, a dramatic miniseries built around a real criminal case. The trial of O.J. Simpson represents the most recent addition to a long series of high-interest, massively publicized, media-judicial events. The history of these media trials reveals that they occur with regularity. There have been at least two dozen trials called the "trial of the century" this century. Over the course of the century the interest in these trials by both the media and the marketplace has grown steadily. Following their period of intense public and media scrutiny, the trials pass into folklore and relative obscurity.

Recognition of names such as Fatty Arbuckle, Sacco and Vanzetti, Bruno Hauptmann, the Rosenbergs, Patty Hearst, and others fades from popular culture after onetime mesmerizing public interest and media attention. One of the historical factors behind the development of media trials is that news organizations competing over ratings have increasingly structured the news along entertainment lines, presenting it within themes, formats, and explanations originally found solely in entertainment programming.[159] Eventually fast-paced, dramatic, superficial presentations and simplistic explanations became the norm. As this trend developed, some criminal trials came to be covered more intensely, and organizations expanded their coverage from hard factual to soft human-interest news to emphasize extralegal and human-interest elements. This process has culminated in the total mergence of news and entertainment in the media trial.

Media trials are a small but influential subset of media-covered cases found within the larger set of *celebrity cases*.[160] Media trials, however, make up only a small portion of celebrity cases, which include all cases that make the news, whether initially or later because of subsequent appeals or court rulings. The latter are referred to as *landmark cases* and include such cases as *Miranda* and *Escobedo*.[161] Media trials involve those crimes that attract intense coverage either immediately at the time of discovery or at the time of arrest. While the phenomenon is not limited to celebrities and sports stars, their association with a case increases its likelihood of being developed by the media into a media trial. Celebrity and offbeat cases provide a pool of criminal trials that are tapped to develop media trials.

Despite their small numbers, media trials have been cited as central for the social construction of crime-and-justice reality.[162] They serve as massive public stages to disseminate crime-and-justice knowledge because they explicitly compare and evaluate competing constructions of reality before an audience of ordinary citizens.[163] As the dominant delivery medium of these trials, television directs the way they are presented to the public and their resultant serialization, personification, and commodification.[164]

Serialization, or the presentation of a trial over an extended time, is the result of television needing progressive dramatic episodes to build and maintain an audience. *Personification*, or the focus on individual human personalities and characteristics, is the result of television's tendency to focus on personal emotions at the expense of facts and issue analysis. People, personalities, and archetypes dominate the construction and this personified justice is trivialized into portraits of individual personalities and their idiosyncrasies.[165] *Commodification*, in which the trials are packaged, promoted, and sold much like any other media program, results from the commercial structure of television, which encourages viewers to see justice as part of a marketplace rather than as a public institutional space and to see themselves as consumers rather than citizens.[166] It transforms social issues such as crime into private problems with commodity product solutions like alarms. Epitomized by media trials, the entire spectrum of crime and justice in the media can be described as a marketing effort that begins with news and entertainment literature and programming and ends with anticrime productions and services.[167] Moreover the television presentation forwards the illusion that media trials are a typical judicial process and one that the viewer might someday experience. On the contrary, with the heavy-handed manipulation of information and the focus of media trials on the rich and famous, the public viewpoint is moved further from any reality of justice that members of the public are ever likely to encounter. In the end, media trials are best understood as marketed commodity vehicles produced by the mass media, paid for and usually starred in by the wealthy, and packaged and sold to the public. That understanding leads to a comprehension of the trials selected to become media trials and the manner in which they are presented.

Trials packaged as media trials involve cases that contain the same elements popular in entertainment programming—human interest laced with mystery, sex, bizarre circumstances, and famous or powerful people.[168] Media trials are distinguished by massive and intensive coverage that begins either with the discovery of the crime or the arrest of the accused.[169] The media cover all aspects of the case, often highlighting extralegal facts. Judges, lawyers, police, witnesses, jurors, and particularly defendants are interviewed, photographed, and frequently raised to celebrity status. Personalities, personal relationships, physical appearances, and idiosyncrasies are commented on regardless of legal relevance. Coverage is live whenever possible, pictures are preferred over text, and text is characterized by conjecture and sensationalism.[170] These media justice events have occurred at regular intervals throughout this century. Proto media trials can even be found in the late nineteenth century, the best known today being the 1896 Lizzy Borden ax murder trial.

In their coverage of these trials, the media offer direct and simple explanations of crime: lust, greed, immorality, jealousy, revenge, and insanity. As in the entertainment realm, recurrent themes have dominated media trial portraits of crime. The three most common types of media trials convey themes of *abuse of power, sinful rich,* and *evil strangers.*[171]

Media trials that fit the abuse of power theme include those cases in which the defendant occupies a position of trust, prestige, or authority. The general rule is the higher the rank, the more media interest in the case. Cases involving police corruption and justice system personnel in general are especially attractive to the media. Sinful rich media trials include cases in which socially prominent defendants are involved in a bizarre or sexually related crime. These trials have a voyeuristic appeal and the media coverage aims to persuade the public that they are being given a rare glimpse into the backstage world of the upper class. Love triangles and inheritance-motivated killings among the jet set are primary examples. The category of evil strangers can be considered as composed of two subgroups: non-Americans and psychotic killers. Non-American evil stranger media trials may involve—depending on the time and political climate—immigrants, blacks, Jews, socialists, union and labor leaders, anarchists, the poor, members of a counterculture, members of fringe religions, political activists, crusaders, or advocates of various unpopular causes. Psychotic killer media trials usually focus on bizarre murder cases in which the defendants are portrayed as maddened, dangerous killers. Recent examples in this category include the cases of John Wayne Gacy, Ted Bundy, and Jeffery Dahmer.[172]

All three media trial themes also appear in popular story lines in the entertainment media and help determine the content of the coverage. Thus the themes reinforce the similarity between news and entertainment, inspiring news personnel to structure content along familiar entertainment lines and entertainment personnel to create the distorted images that are frequently portrayed in the news. From both, the general audience receives the constant and congenial message that the rich are immoral in their use of sex, drugs, or violence; that people in power are evil and greedy; that the authorities should not be trusted, and that strangers and those with different lifestyles or values are inherently dangerous.

Media trials represent the final step in a long process of merging news and entertainment—a process that has often resulted in multimedia and commercial news exploitation of these cases. That the source of media trials is the judicial system eases the merger, for media trials allow the news industry to attract and entertain a large general audience while maintaining its preferred image as an objective and neutral reporter of news.[173] Furthermore, the courts have been described as already being engaged less in the business of producing decisions than in a performance for public consumption.[174] Ball described courtroom action as a distinct type of theater, judicial theater, comparing the courtroom to a stage, legal arguments to script, and a trial to a performance, with the trial itself embodying the theatrical format of protagonist and antagonist.[175]

The judicial system and its judges and attorneys thus sometimes assist the media in its own co-optation, the O.J. Simpson trial being a prime example. The end result is that in media trials, news as entertainment is fully achieved.[176] Media trials provide the news media with ready-made entertainment-style themes that give shape and direction to their coverage, and at the same time simplify the task of reporting, interpreting, and explaining a trial. Media trial themes provide the news media with a framework by which to measure, choose, and sometimes mold the various aspects of a trial that will be reported or highlighted in the production process.

The social impact and importance of media trials is thus seldom connected to the extent of harm directly resulting from the crimes. Their significance comes from the massive attention they receive and the public debate they engender. Their social importance lies not so much in what happened during the commission of the crime but in the perception and interpretation of what happened during the proceedings.[177] Because television reformats the events it covers, it affects what viewers understand the legal process to be.[178] In the coverage and marketing of these trials, they become palettes in the social construction of the criminal justice system. These trials are significant because they influence the public's attitudes and views regarding crime, justice, and society for years. Media trials, as indicated by their popularity and the resources that the media are willing to expend to cover them, are a prominent component of crime-related news. They provide concise and simplistic explanations of crime within the authoritative and dramatic vehicle of a trial.

BOX 3.1   O.J. Simpson

The Simpson trial is of the sinful rich genre. The trial's story line could be found in numerous novels and Hollywood films: handsome, rich, successful ex-athlete is accused of murdering his ex-wife and her friend in a jealous rage amid a sea of rumored drug abuse, sexual deviance, and fascinating subcharacters—racist cops, beautiful women, offbeat friends and acquaintances. Indeed, a large part of the enduring interest and ultimate social impact of this trial stems from the way it became a long-running mass media entertainment vehicle—a drama-in-real-life, covered more along the lines of a sports spectacle than a criminal trial.[179]

The actual social importance of the trial will be determined over the coming years. In terms of legal and social significance it is clearly not the trial of the century as it was christened by the media[180]—it is better described as the signal television event of the century, demanding hundreds, if not thousands, of hours of coverage.[181] Regarding the

trial's social impact, most commentators have focused on race relations, with few reporting any positive effects.[182] Other concerns specific to the judicial system generated from the coverage include the prospect of more criminal defendants refusing to plea bargain, a new skepticism about police testimony, more judicial gag orders on trial participants and less camera access, restrictions on attorneys' use of political rhetoric in front of juries, and the general degrading in the public's eye of judges, juries, attorneys, and the judicial system.[183] In that the coverage of the trial represents American culture at one of its lowest ebbs,[184] it is clear that the reputation and dignity of the judicial system will require rehabilitation after the televising, marketing, and exploitation of the latest and hopefully last "trial of the 20th century."[185]

An example of the commodification and marketing of a media trial. Books, films, photos, souvenirs, songs, toys, and games are all spin-offs of a high-profile, intensely covered trial.

Fred Prouser/SIPA Press

BOX 3.1   *Continued*

The media co-optation of a criminal trial. Television trucks and temporary studios fill the parking lot across from the Criminal Courts Building in downtown Los Angeles Monday morning, January 23, 1995, as opening statements were scheduled to start in the O.J. Simpson double-murder trial.

AP Photo/Mark J. Terrill

Part of the circus-like crowd that appeared daily at the O.J. Simpson trial. The public fascination with media trials appears boundless.

Fred Prouser/SIPA Press

Crime in these productions is nearly universally attributed to individual characteristics and failings rather than to social conditions. Media trials are significant for understanding crime news in general in that they highlight the entertainment criteria that guide the selection of all crime news. The dramatization of individual criminal acts by detailed descriptions of horrific final moments, locations, and positions of victims, as well as demon offenders and innocent victims, are found throughout contemporary crime coverage.[186] The entertainmentization of crime-and-justice news in reality programming and media trials has led to a number of basic concerns.

CONCERNS ABOUT CRIME-
AND-JUSTICE NEWS

The public's high interest in and retention of crime news, the large percentage of total news that is crime related, and the skewed content of crime news have raised concerns about crime-and-justice news similar to those expressed about the entertainment media.[187] Four basic criticisms of crime news have been described:[188]

- The majority of crime coverage pertains to violent or sensational crimes disproportional to their appearance in official data.

- Implicit explanations are primarily from criminal justice system persons and are nearly always simplistic and individualistic.

- The overemphasis on violent crimes and failure to adequately address personal risk and prevention techniques often lead to exaggerated fears of victimization.

- Coverage tends to increase the commodification of crime and justice at the expense of escalating racial divisions and fear of crime.

Furthermore, when queried, a substantial portion of the public feels that television news contributes a lot to social violence.[189] More than half of Americans feel that the news emphasis on violent crimes results in more homicide and violent deaths in the United States,[190] and more than 40 percent think it actually encourages crime.[191]

The news media's coverage of the criminal justice system also appears to lead the attending public to evaluate the system poorly while paradoxically leading to increased support of crime and justice policies that are more crime control and law enforcement oriented.[192] This paradox can be attributed to the public's adherence to an image of a street criminal and media depictions that show curable deficiencies in the justice system and personality defects in individuals as the main causes of apparently rampant crime.[193] Lotz,[194] for example, found the content of crime-and-justice-related editorial columns dominated by conservative, punishment-oriented positions. Not surprisingly, most people who pay regular attention to the media support as their first policy choice criminal justice reforms that would toughen and strengthen the existing system.[195] This is true even though these same people place a large share of the blame for crime on the criminal justice system.[196] Despite the presentation and perception of the criminal justice system as ineffective, the news media implicitly suggest that improving it, at least as a law enforcement and punitive system, is the best hope against the many violent crimes and predatory criminals that are portrayed.[197] The news media are shown to normally portray offenders in stigmatizing constructions that make reintegration into society more difficult.[198]

In the same vein, commenting on the effect of the media image of corrections, tabloid-style crime reporting and the depiction of prison riots and brutal attacks by paroled assailants has been blamed for helping to heighten the public's fear of crime, for further eroding its confidence in the ability of corrections to deter or rehabilitate criminals, and for increasing its desire to make the system more punitive for all offenders regardless of their dangerousness.[199] In the end, crime-and-justice news advances system-enhancing crime control policies and individual-based explanations of crime.[200] The media do not provide the knowledge to directly evaluate the criminal justice system's performance—but media content does steer people toward particular policies and assessments.

Another concern is associated with a hypothesized echo effect. Following a media trial, the echo of its coverage influences the processing and disposition of similar but nonpublicized cases. An echo effect was first described by Loften:[201]

> But while the impact of the press is most direct on specific cases covered, there is good reason to believe that [its] sway extends considerably beyond the cases actually appearing. . . . From the cases that are covered, officials become conditioned to expect demands for stern treatment from the press, and in the unpublicized cases they probably act accordingly.

And again by Kaplan and Skolnick:[202]

> This unwillingness [to plea bargain] appears to occur relatively infrequently. It is most likely to occur when there is strong pressure upon the prosecution to obtain maximum sentences for a particular class of crime: for example, after a notorious case of child rape, the prosecutor may refuse to bargain, for a time, with those charged with sex offenses involving children; after a series of highly publicized drug arrests allegedly involving dealers or pushers, the prosecution may be unwilling, for a time, to engage in reduction of charges from sales to possession.

The implication of echo effects is that media news coverage likely influences the disposition of a large number of cases, the majority of which receive no coverage.[203]

The overriding concern involves the image of the criminal justice system that the media constructs and the public receives. Even though the public does not read crime news in a naive search for the empirical truth about crime,[204] the inherent credibility of news means that the image of justice the news media project has serious ramifications for the public's understanding of the judicial system and its perception of the legitimacy and fairness of the entire criminal justice system.[205] Learning about the criminal justice system from the news media is analogous to learning geology from volcanic eruptions. You will surely be impressed and entertained, but the information you receive will not accurately reflect the common daily reality, whether you're looking at volcanoes or the criminal justice system. The media reality of high-stakes trials, confrontations, oratory, and detailed deliberations contrasts starkly with the criminal justice system's daily reality of plea bargains, compromises, and assembly-line justice.[206] Because the media cover crime as an act rather than an issue, most news coverage appeals to voyeuristic instincts more than it serves any educational criteria.[207]

The media could cover crime and justice better. They have the experience and a model of coverage to adopt at hand. The media provide comprehensive, contextual coverage for sporting events on a daily basis. Sports coverage stands as a model for reporting on individual events, supplemented by statistics, trend analysis, forecasts, commentary, and discussion. These events are consistently placed in their larger social context and constructed in a way that provides understanding and comprehension. An example of how crime-and-justice news might look if it were covered and formatted like sports news appears on page 81. Journalists generally disagree, however, with the contention that their role is to educate the public. They more often argue that their function is to inform the public of particular events and developments. In this view, an emphasis on noteworthy cases and unique problems is more appropriate than a comprehensive review of criminal justice operations.[208] Journalists are correct in stating that educating the public is not their responsibility, but this does not free them from responsibility for miseducating the public. News coverage does educate the public, and often that coverage is distorted.

CONCLUSION: NEWS AND ENTERTAINMENT RECONSIDERED

While the future of traditional news is questionable, the growth potential for crime news is good. Since the 1970s more than half the population report that they watch no news programs and television and newspaper news consumption has continued to fall.[209] The upside for the news industry is that among young adults and baby boomers crime news still ranks first in interest. It is easy to predict that news organizations in pursuit of this audience will increase their emphasis on crime and will offer more and more info-tainment.[210]

The impact of the media on crime and justice follows from the media's construction of crime and justice. This is true for both the entertainment and news elements of the media. It is no coincidence that similar crimes and

Inside: First chemical castrations to be held in California—See B3 for event coverage

Crime & Justice

Tuesday, February 2, 1997

SECTION **B**

Florida clinches national lead in chase deaths

By Carole Boyd
The Mirror

A report published Monday places Florida in the lead for the number of persons killed during high-speed chases involving law enforcement officials.

This report comes on the heels of allegations from state citizens' groups that high-speed pursuit policies in Florida law enforcement agencies do not protect the public. A group in Ft. Myers Beach called Citizens Against Pursuits

See Chase, B5

Deaths from high-speed chases

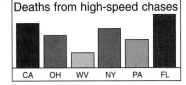

CA   OH   WV   NY   PA   FL

D.C. becomes no.1 in country in criminal justice expenditures

❏ State rankings released early today do not surprise criminal justice officials, but anger politicians.

By Maurice Jones
The Mirror

State and local direct expenditures for criminal justice activities were released this morning and the District of Columbia gained first place for the first time in 18 years.

The Top 10 States were released by the government with information broken down into state, local, municipalities, and counties. The report was published by the National Institute of Justice and is available to the public.

For the first time in the 20-year

Total Criminal Justice Expenditures 1997 State Standings
(in dollars)

Top 10 States	Per Capita	Total
District of Columbia	1,184.6	5,823,000
Alaska	572.6	6,589,710
New York	496.8	123,946,002
California	454.6	160,244,802
Florida	382.0	54,138,598
Delaware	375.8	3,272,203
New Jersey	370.7	42,335,006
Arizona	366.5	15,910,438
Hawaii	350.7	6,673,970

history of the State Expenditure Report, Florida fell to the bottom of the top 5. Florida officials say this is due to the falling crime rate in the state. Opponents argue, however, that money designated for criminal justice is being diverted to other funds that are more politically popular.

Aides to Florida governor Lawton Childs call this outrageous and say that the governor fully supports all available monies going toward state criminal justice programs.

"Governor Childs personally oversees bills that put money into correction programs, boot camps, and juvenile half-way houses," said a top aide. "He would never divert money for political gains."

See Expenditures, B7

Weekend Highlights

By Piper Chilus
The Mirror

HOME INVASIONS
❏ Two this weekend: 1 in Pine Hills, 1 in Goldenrod.
❏ Orange County ranks third in state.
❏ Florida ranks first in nation, inching above California. New Hampshire claims 5th.

DOMESTIC VIOLENCE
❏ 196 this weekend, 63 involving guns.
❏ Orange County ranks seventh in state.
❏ Florida moves up to 6th place, replacing New Jersey, which falls into 3rd.

HEROIN OVERDOSES
❏ Three this weekend; 2 minors are dead.
❏ Orange County still steady at 1st in the state.
❏ Florida moves up to 1st in nation, edging out New York.

CAR-JACKINGS
❏ Two this weekend: 1 in East Orlando that resulted in a 2-hour high-speed chase.
❏ Orange County ranks 11th in state.
❏ Florida ranks 9th in the county, falling two spaces from last week.

For complete stories, see our Crime Stats page on B6.

New teen curfew laws—Okay or No Way?

PRO

By Dianne Berrie

Juvenile crime is on the rise in Orlando and across the nation. Teenagers should not be allowed free access to busy downtown areas for the safety of tourists and the safety of the

See Pro, B7

CON

By Brett Pocock

Our government's decision to strip the rights of America's young people is as unfair as past practices not allowing women to vote. The teens, who are the future voters of

See Con, B7

Starkes receives 3 trades from 33rd Street

Name: Mike Ros
Stats: 5'10", 159 lbs.
County: Orange
MO: Strong arm robbery
Release date: 3-15-97
Habitual offender: Yes
Other: Also has battery on LEO, cocaine addict.

Name: Joe Johnson
Stats: 6'1", 205 lbs.
County: Seminole
MO: Home invasion
Release date: 12-28-97
Habitual offender: Yes
Other: Third trade; first 8 years in Alcatraz.

Name: Derek Boyd
Stats: 5'9"
County: Orange
MO: 1st degree murder
Release date: 10-6-97
Habitual offender: No
Other: Likes to wear women's clothes.

criminals appear in entertainment and news, for the goals and needs of both are to assemble the largest audience possible to maximize readership, ratings, and revenue.[211] Therefore the image of justice that most people find most palatable and popular is the image that the media have historically projected. This image is one that locates the causes of crime in the individual criminal and supports existing social arrangements and approaches to crime control.[212] The media-constructed reality of crime allows it to be more easily divorced from other social problems and highlighted as the most threatening problem. Because the image is fragmentary and presented separately from other social problems and issues, politicians can and have manipulated the crime issue, ironically through the media.

In the media, the public is paradoxically shown that the traditional criminal justice system is not effective and simultaneously that its improvement remains the best solution to crime. These messages translate into support for law-and-order policies and existing criminal justice agencies. Entertainment and news portrayals that expound social change or structural causes of crime are rare.[213] The repeated message of the news and entertainment media is that crime is largely perpetrated by predatory individuals who are basically different from the rest of us, that criminality is the result of individual problems, and that crimes are acts freely committed by individuals who have a wide range of alternate choices. That both the news and entertainment components of the media present similar portraits of crime and justice has naturally led to concern over the impact of this picture. Fear and fatalistic expectation of crime, mystification of the criminal justice system, monopolistic support for punitive criminal justice policies, and increased tolerance for illegal law enforcement practices have all been forwarded as potential effects.[214]

Escapism and voyeurism do not explain the dominance of crime and justice in popular culture's content or the emphasis within the crime-and-justice content on violent predatory crime.[215] This myopic focus on violent predatory crime is tied to a long historical interest in crime and justice as theater[216] and the palatable explanation of crime that predatory crime presents to the public. As argued, crime and justice have been sources for story lines since antiquity and predator criminality, while constructing crime as a frightening (and hence entertaining) phenomenon, also presents crime as caused by individual deficiencies, thus freeing the public from any causal role. The media's construction of crime and justice is deeply rooted in our cultural heritage, particularly our tradition of individualism and our social stereotypes. The belief in individual responsibility and individual-based explanations for crime is the primary image reflected in our crime and justice media.[217] This focus on individual responsibility for crime is distressing not because it is incorrect but because it is fragmentary. Such a perspective on criminal behavior leaves societal influences unquestioned and puts forth half the problem as if it were the whole problem. To look only at individual responsibility is to look away from any social responsibility.

The popularity of the violent predatory crime is also likely associated with a downward comparison effect. *Downward comparison* is a psychological process in which people feel better about their own situation when they see someone in a worse one. Therefore a media image of violent urban crime would have a soothing effect on middle-class suburban Americans by holding up to them a crime-and-justice construction of reality that is more violent and dangerous than what they are experiencing. And as this violent crime is shown as due to individual deficiency like greed and innate evil, the apparently better-off-by-comparison rest of America can enjoy a guilt-free boost regarding their crime situation while being encouraged to purchase security products.

The mass media have historically emphasized crime and justice in their content and have used the popularity of these topics to meet their commercial needs. Within the standard practices of crime news and entertainment, attributes of individual responsibility, the affirmation of conservative moral boundaries, and the resolution of crime via punishment and condemnation of the criminal are championed.[218] The media focus on violent interpersonal crime and explain those violent crimes as the result of individual choices and deficiencies. The public is primarily concerned with the media as a cause of crime, not with their effect on public perceptions of justice.[219] The constructed reality has gone largely unchallenged.

A final, more publicly debated concern is that mass media news coverage leads to disruption of the criminal justice process and violation of due process protections. Participants in media trials, for example, are sometimes prodded by the news media into seriously compromising cases—sometimes selling their testimony to the highest bidder.[220] In addition, extensive media attention can create social panics and result in public crusades against types or classes of individuals.[221] The mass media have been especially active in periodically creating and supporting crusades against particular types of crimes and they have been credited with significantly affecting enforcement, prosecution, and sentencing policies.[222] The media and the courts are covered extensively in Chapter 4.

CHAPTER CONCEPTS

Penny Press

Standard Reporting Style

Newsworthiness

Market, Manipulative, and Organizational Models

Gatekeeping and Routinization

Info-tainment

Media Trials

Echo Effects

Broadsheets and Ballads

Crime Reporters

Proactive and Reactive News

Public Information Officers

Episodic and Thematic News

Reality Programming

DISCUSSION QUESTIONS

1. How realistic do you feel crime-and-justice news is?

2. Discuss some types of information that could be provided about crime and justice in the news but are not. Why do you think this information is not reported?

3. If your instructor were murdered, what factors might influence whether the crime made the local news? What would be necessary for it to become national news? How many of the factors you've listed are related to the social importance of the murder?

4. How would you change the news coverage of crime and justice? Could you still turn a profit with these changes?

5. Discuss the pros and cons of the news media becoming evidence gatherers in criminal proceedings such as in the O.J. Simpson case, where they developed leads, found and interviewed witnesses, and searched for physical evidence.

6. Evaluate the relative emphasis and impact of crime control versus due process constructions of crime-and-justice reality in the media.

7. How might the discussion of criminal justice issues on radio and TV talk shows amplify the media's impact on those who do not pay attention to crime-and-justice news?

4

⌒

Media and the Construction of Criminal Proceedings

C hapter 4 examines the interplay and issues that arise when the news media interact with the judicial system. What is the effect of the media's content on the construction and proceedings of criminal cases? Conflicts arise when the First Amendment rights of the media clash with the Fifth and Sixth Amendment responsibilities of the courts to ensure due process protections. Though they are frequently at odds, the media and the courts have similar goals and reactions to criminal events. Both want to gather information, control access to this information, and present it to a specific audience. In addition, both have been pressed by the same social forces to be more open and accessible, to reveal their backstage news-gathering or case-processing procedures, and to provide information to the other. (Ironically, their disputes are often resolved in the courts, frequently by the Supreme Court.) These commonalities allow us to discuss their interaction within two broad topic areas. The first and largest encompasses news coverage and publicity issues. The second concerns the strategies the judiciary and the media use to control information and deal with each other.

The chapter begins with due process and publicity. Reviewing the difficulty the courts face in defining and identifying prejudicial coverage, the research on publicity and juries supports the surprising conclusion that the media may more frequently affect not highly publicized cases but nonpublicized ones. The chapter then discusses an additional group of publicity-related issues—privacy, media access to information, and televised trials. In all these areas, the media have striven to increase their ability to acquire and reveal information while the courts have attempted to balance the media's access against due process concerns.

The next topic concerns the efforts by the justice system and the media to maintain control of their knowledge. The courts can adopt either a proactive strategy and seek to stop prejudicial information from being published, or a reactive strategy and seek to limit the prejudicial effects of information that the media have already published. Not surprisingly, the proactive strategy, which includes closing proceedings and issuing restrictive and protective orders, and which directly constrains the media, has aroused the strongest opposition. But though the reactive, less restrictive mechanisms of the second strategy are more commonly employed, it is not clear when they should be used or how effective they are. On the media side, the media have worked to control their information by arguing that journalists have a constitutional right of privileged conversation with news sources and by lobbying for the passage of shield laws to legislatively ensure this right. These efforts have become more intense as the media have been pressed more often for information. Though the media have had successes on both fronts, their ability to avoid opening their news files or testifying varies considerably from state to state and case to case.

Concluding the chapter is a comment on the cumulative result of these separate trends on the social construction of the courts and criminal proceedings. Factors that have encouraged the opening of the judicial system to the media and the reforms that have been recommended to improve the relationship between the media and the judiciary are discussed. The trends all point toward greater access and exposure in the future, but both the criminal justice system and the mass media remain among the handful of social institutions that still aggressively resist outside access and continue to struggle to keep their backstage realms closed. The courts currently struggle to maintain socially constructed realities that are increasingly undermined by the images and portraits available in the news media.

THE NEWS MEDIA AND THE COURTS—
CONSTRUCTING SEPARATE REALITIES
FROM GRUDGINGLY SHARED KNOWLEDGE

The relationship between the news media and the courts in the United States is an area of great concern for the judiciary. As evidenced in earlier chapters, these concerns have a long history. They arise from direct conflict between the First and the Fifth and Sixth Amendments and from the continuing struggle to define and balance the rights delineated under each amendment. As early as 1807, Aaron Burr's attorney claimed that jurors could not properly decide his client's case because of prejudicial newspaper articles.[1] Only in the last seventy years, however, and coinciding with the development of the mass media, has the First Amendment been defined as a source of legal guidelines for dealing with news coverage of criminal cases.[2] More recently, the issues of reporters' privilege and shield laws, sunshine laws, media access to government files, and the live televising of criminal trials have exacerbated the conflicts between the news media and the judicial system. Ironically, despite their adversarial history and contentious interactions, the media and the judicial system normally react to criminal events in much the same manner. Both concentrate their resources on investigating facts to construct a particular version of reality to be presented to a specific audience—jurors, viewers, or readers. While the relationship between the media and the judicial system is sometimes cooperative, more often each jealously guards its information while attempting to discover what the other knows.[3]

Beyond the constitutional questions and issues regarding control of information, an additional concern arises because of the unique function that courts play in society. Besides being an institution in which legal disputes are resolved, the courtroom is also a social arena in which the significance and value of a wide spectrum of social behaviors are constructed. The courtroom functions therefore not only as a mechanism for resolving individual disputes but also as a mechanism for legitimizing society's laws and government. Accordingly, anything that influences the public image of the courts invariably influences their legitimizing function. And without question the news media are crucial in the formation of the public image of the courts.[4] Of major concern is whether or not the courts are reacting to the news media by altering their traditional practices to better match media–dictated formats. The fear is that courtroom participants will alter the way they testify, argue, and construct cases to fit the needs of the media rather than those of the courtroom. Such social construction changes have already been noted in religion, sports, and politics.[5]

The relationship between the media and the justice system is further strained because different considerations and values govern the means by which each obtains knowledge and evaluates its worth. Whereas the criminal justice system is guided by legislative and constitutional mandates and the courts have the task of separating relevant from legally irrelevant information, the media respond primarily to newsworthiness and entertainment considerations. Each side's considerations dictate what facts are presented as well as when and how they are disclosed. Traditionally, in the courtroom, information is imparted in a form and process quite different from that preferred by the news media. Courtroom knowledge is extracted point by point in long story lines by lawyers following legal procedures and rules of evidence. Moreover, the information is specially prepared for a limited audience comprising a judge or jury.[6] In contrast, news stories are outwardly directed and developed in accordance with entertainment values rather than legal relevance. They are brief time- and space-limited constructions that must make their points quickly, and they are built around whatever film or dramatic elements are available.[7] In sum, the courts have traditionally presented internally controlled, front-stage events to a small, specific audience, whereas media-produced court news tends to present dramatic backstage information to an external, general audience.

On first examination, the interactions of the mass media and the judicial system appear to give rise to a morass of complex and seemingly disparate issues. All of them, however, can be subsumed within two broad subject areas. The first and larger of the two involves news media coverage of the courts and encompasses such issues as invasion of privacy and the effects of pretrial and trial publicity on due process. A basic judicial concern is that the media undermine the fairness of a trial and that media publicity violates due process protections. This concern is at the crux of the conflicts arising from media coverage of the criminal justice system. A corollary concern is that publicity destroys privacy and that media coverage may harm or embarrass innocent persons swept up in the coverage of heavily publicized cases. Beyond the courtroom it is feared that close news media coverage can delegitimize the judicial system by revealing previously hidden information regarding case negotiations and simultaneously cripple the judicial system by forcing participants to rigidly adhere to the formal legal rules and procedures and forgo the discretion and bargaining common in case processing.

The second subject area involves judicial and media strategies for dealing with each other and controlling knowledge. The courts gear their efforts toward minimizing the negative effects of news media coverage by closing trials, imposing gag orders, granting continuances and changes of venue, and taking other judicial actions. The media gear their efforts toward both countering judicial actions that limit their activities and access, and limiting police and court access to information they hold.

ISSUES RELATED TO NEWS COVERAGE AND PUBLICITY

Due Process and Pretrial Publicity

Publicity before and during a trial may so affect a community and its courts that a fair trial becomes impossible. Due process protections such as the presumption of innocence constitutionally afforded to defendants are destroyed. The media especially create problems when they publish information that is inadmissible in the courtroom and construct a community atmosphere in which finding and impaneling impartial jurors is not possible.

Unfortunately it is not always clear when particular media content is prejudicial.[8] Prejudicial information can take two forms: factual information that bears on the guilt of a defendant and emotional information without evidentiary relevance that simply aims at arousing the emotions of an audience.[9] Factual information includes the content of confessions or allusions to confessions, performances on polygraph or other tests (usually inadmissible as evidence) and refusals to take such tests, and past criminal records and convictions. Emotional information includes stories that question the credibility of witnesses or present the personal feelings of witnesses about prosecutors, police, victims, or judges; stories about the defendant's character (he hates children and dogs), associates (she hangs around with known syndicate gunmen), or personality (he's a mean-spirited, bad-tempered degenerate); and stories that inflame the general public.[10] Judges have reported that publication of criminal records, performances on tests, and information about confessions is most damaging.[11]

Despite the concerns about prejudicial coverage, the Supreme Court has employed such ambiguous phrases as *wave of public passion*,[12] *invidious or inflammatory*,[13] *highly inflammatory material*,[14] *pervasive and prejudicial*,[15] and *a spectacle*.[16] It has not, however, operationally defined these terms for the lower courts. The resulting dilemma for trial courts is twofold. The first problem is determining when media activities infringe on a defendant's right to a fair trial. When exactly is coverage prejudicial? At what point does a news story or made-for-television movie become inflammatory rather than just colorful? The second problem is deciding how to balance media access to court proceedings with defendants' rights to fair and unbiased proceedings. How should prejudicial media content be dealt with? The problem is especially acute when the media coverage precedes any formal judicial proceedings and there are as yet no accused defendants to protect.

Faced with these ambiguous problems and forced to render largely subjective determinations, both trial and appellate courts have focused on jurors and potential influences on them as the key to determining the fairness of a trial. If a jury is considered impartial and uninfluenced by media coverage, then the proceedings are normally considered fair. The assumption is that judges, lawyers, and other judicial personnel are able to insulate themselves from media influence because of their professional ethics, legal training, and experience. Jurors, being the amateurs in the proceedings, are considered the most susceptible to media coverage. If they are unaffected and fair, the reasoning goes, the trial also should be. The difficulty has been deciding when jurors are indeed impartial and what proof is necessary to establish prejudice.[17] Some jurisdictions allow testimony or affidavits, expert testimony, public opinion polls, and various tests to establish prejudice. The most common test is a content analysis of coverage measuring fact versus opinion.

Reporting facts is perceived as nonprejudicial; reporting opinions is seen as prejudicial.[18] In practice, the operational definition of an impartial juror is derived from the Aaron Burr case: "An impartial juror is one free from the dominant influence of knowledge acquired outside the courtroom, free from strong and deep impressions which close the mind."[19] Though not a precise rule, this definition does eliminate ignorance of a case or a total lack of exposure to media coverage as a requirement for impartiality. Jurors can be exposed to extensive media content regarding a case and still be considered impartial. A reading of the case law in this area shows, however, that applying this definition has proved to be a haphazard task.

Following a set of piecemeal and not always clarifying Supreme Court decisions from the 1950s into the 1970s (detailed in Appendix I), the current judicial position is that certain extreme circumstances can be so inherently prejudicial as to require judicial remedies without requiring a showing of actual prejudice.[20] It is left to the trial courts, however, to determine on a case-by-case basis whether the circumstances before them are inherently or only potentially prejudicial.[21] If potentially prejudicial, the defendant must prove actual prejudice. If inherently prejudicial, the trial judge must intervene of his or her own accord to stem and prevent prejudicial effects. There is no set formula to look to, however; the Supreme Court has provided few guidelines to determine whether a particular case falls in the first or second category and has avoided considering this issue since the mid-1980s.[22] The response of most state courts to this ambiguity has been to demand proof of actual prejudice by the defendant, rejecting the concept of inherent prejudice. In most cases, all that is constitutionally required is that a juror be able to state under oath that he or she can render a fair and impartial verdict based on the evidence presented in court. Given that the Supreme Court has tended to reverse state court convictions only where it finds the lower court proceedings to be "outrageous" and the error of the trial judge "manifest,"[23] the safe course for the defense is to assume that the burden of proving media-generated prejudice is theirs.[24]

Social Science Research Concerning Publicity and Trials

Given the persistence of the judicial struggle over media coverage, it is appropriate to ask what social scientists studying the effects of media coverage on trial participants have discovered. How does news content actually influence jurors? The most common approach to address this question has been to create and study mock juries in pseudoexperimental situations. However, these laboratory and field jury studies (summarized in Appendix II) also have deficiencies.

Laboratory studies of mock juries, for example, normally draw mock jurors from a variety of sources, including jury pools, general community members, registered voters, high school students, undergraduate psychology students, and law school students. These subjects review the transcripts or hear tapes of cases with and without accompanying media accounts and decide guilt or recommend sentences. These laboratory-style studies generally support the conclusions that publicized confessions are especially influential on jurors, that biased news is more influential if it is the sole source of information, and that many potential jurors are able to recognize and set aside their own biases. The generalizability of these laboratory studies is weakened, however, because of the artificiality of the publicity presented and the lack of variation in the types of media used (all but the most recent used printed or audio material), the short and unrealistic time lags between exposure to the publicity and the rendering of verdicts, the questionable match between subjects and actual jurors, and the differences between deciding a verdict in the laboratory setting and doing so in an actual courtroom.[25]

In an attempt to correct the inherent artificiality of the laboratory studies, so-called "field" mock jury studies have surveyed community members and involved real cases. These studies unfortunately also report mixed results. Despite the lack of consistent findings, the results of the field research do suggest that juries can act fairly even when exposed to large amounts of information about a case prior to a trial,[26] and there are a number of examples of heavily publicized trials of notable defendants that have ended in acquittals, including those of John Delorean, Marion Barry, John Hinckley, William Kennedy Smith, Claus von Bulow, Maurice Stands, John Connally, Angela Davis, and of course, O.J. Simpson.

On the other hand, the question of the effects of pretrial publicity is far from settled, for the research also clearly shows that prejudicial effects sometimes persist despite the employment of common counteractive judicial steps such as juror instructions and expanded jury selection.[27] The research has generally found that greater exposure to publicity is associated with jurors estimating greater amounts of incriminating evidence to exist against defendants but is not associated or counterbalanced by increased juror ability to admit prejudice or to set aside information gained from news. In fact, most people state that they are impartial even when they acknowledge that they will be unable to set aside news stories.[28]

In addition, the research suggests that general publicity about events in the criminal justice system can influence jurors sitting on nonpublicized, totally unrelated cases that are similar in nature to the publicized ones.[29] There thus exists evidence of a potential generalized echo effect, in which news coverage influences the processing of cases receiving no coverage.[30] Added to the effects of publicity on the fairness of proceedings, issues involving privacy invasion, media access to government information, and the effect of television courtroom proceedings also remain unresolved.

Privacy

The media technology revolution that has magnified the intrusiveness and pervasiveness of the media has brought the question of the invasion of privacy by the media to the forefront of social concerns. Although apparently a new legal concept, the issue of privacy can be traced to a *Harvard Law Review* article by Warren and Brandeis published in 1890. Writing before the era of electronic eavesdropping and other modern technology, Warren and Brandeis were remarkably prophetic in predicting that "mechanical devices threaten to make good the prediction that 'what is whispered in the closet shall be proclaimed from the housetops.'"[31] Legal factors used to determine whether or not a person's privacy has been violated include whether or not the material published was legally obtained, whether the subject matter was newsworthy and of legitimate public interest, whether the publication would offend a reasonable person, whether the information was timely, whether consent was obtained, and whether the reported event or action was plainly in the public view. Legally speaking, violations of privacy take any of four forms: (1) an unreasonable intrusion upon the seclusion of another, (2) appropriation of another's name or likeness, (3) unreasonable publicity given to another's private life, and (4) publicity that unreasonably places another in a false light before the public.[32] In relation to criminal cases, issues of privacy normally involve the reporting of embarrassing but truthful information, usually about either victims or defendants.[33] As the British royal family and many American politicians have ruefully learned, public figures generally are deemed to have less expectation of privacy than other citizens.

The Supreme Court has argued that a balance between the gathering and dissemination of information and the preservation of privacy and chances for rehabilitation is a valid goal, and has not extended protections to shield the press from lawsuits based on truthful but embarrassing publications (see Appendix I). It has not detailed precisely where the balance between news making and the goals of the criminal justice system should be struck. Though there are few certain rules, however, there are some guidelines. In general, information of the following type is private and should not be subject to publication: sexual relations, family quarrels, humiliating illnesses, intimate personal letters, details of home life, photographs taken in private places, photographs stolen from a person's home, and contents of income tax returns. On the other hand, matters of public record are not generally considered private facts and may be published freely.[34] At present, the courts will discount privacy claims if doing so will further an important public policy interest.[35] One aspect of the continuing confusion is ambiguity about what constitutes a public record and a public interest. Legislative and court efforts to resolve the dilemma have not been greatly successful and the public perception, exemplified by the contents of the tabloid press, is that little is private and beyond the media purview.

Media Access to Government Information

In a significant number of instances, a government agency has possession of information that the media deems newsworthy. Often the government is reluctant to release control of such information and in response the press has worked diligently to increase its access to government-held data and files. The first national response to growing difficulties in obtaining information held by the government was the federal Freedom of Information Act, adopted in 1966. This act opened up numerous government files to the media and the public. A subsequent associated law was the Government in Sunshine Act, passed in 1976, which prohibits closed government meetings concerning policy. Both these efforts have been duplicated in numerous states but have had mixed results in easing the news media's access to government files and information. The federal Sunshine Act, for example, does not apply to Congress or the courts but only to agencies answerable to the office of the president—and many of those are exempted. Similarly, under the Freedom of Information Act (FOIA), agencies or persons who want information about themselves withheld from the press must list the exemption on which the denial is based, describe the materials being withheld, and relate the exemption to the withheld materials.[36] However, despite the FOIA's intention to place the burden of proof on those seeking to deny access to information, in certain instances those requesting information have been forced to show an overriding public interest in order to obtain it.[37] In practice, the FOIA has been criticized for cumbersome procedures, an excess of exceptions to the law, and often long delays in rulings and obtaining information.

Competing concerns over privacy and intrusive misuse of government-collected information regarding individuals led to Congress passing the Privacy Act in 1974 to counterbalance the effects of the FOIA and Government in Sunshine acts. The goal was to control the misuse of government information and restrict access to certain information in criminal files and judicial records. Information required to be disclosed under the FOIA cannot be withheld under the auspices of the Privacy Act, but the boundary between the two acts has always been blurred.[38] As the Privacy Act imposes greater penalties on government agencies for incorrectly disclosing private information than the FOIA does for incorrectly withholding information, the net result of both laws is less rather than more government openness.[39] As in other areas regarding the media, the lower courts, agency personnel, and the media operate without clear rules in determining when privacy supersedes public interests, and decisions are rendered on a case-by-case basis.[40] In final impact, the overall effect of this legislation seems more symbolic than significant.[41]

Because the media oftentimes are denied access to what they consider newsworthy information, limiting media access to government files has become a highly litigated issue. Since 1979, the Supreme court has held that the media cannot claim a special privilege or right of access—that news gathering is not entitled to an extended First Amendment protection but is limited to whatever information and access is given to the general public.[42]

For example, the Supreme Court has stated that the way to determine whether or not the media have a right to interview prison inmates is to examine the public's level of access.[43] This access rule has been challenged by the news media in a number of state prison systems that are implementing restrictive prisoner access policies and limiting face-to-face media-to-inmate interviews reportedly spurred by concerns that media info-tainment shows are glamorizing prisoners.[44] To date the Supreme Court has held firm to its general public access rule.

Having established the equality of the media and the public with regard to access, the courts have yet to directly address the effect of disclosing the identity of victims and witnesses, particularly in sexual offense cases. It has been strongly argued that such public identification can needlessly add to the pain of the victim and is likely to deter other victims from reporting crimes and other witnesses from testifying.[45] There is reason to believe, for example, that rape witnesses fear the publicity they will receive if they testify more than they fear testifying.[46] This issue received national attention during the Florida rape trial of William Kennedy Smith, a nephew of Senator Ted Kennedy. Florida law prohibited the publishing of the name or photograph of a victim/accuser in a sexual offense case. When the press violated this statute, the offending news media were fined and cited. On appeal, the Florida Supreme Court declared the statute unconstitutional, stating that the privacy concerns in such situations cannot override freedom of the press protections.[47]

Paralleling this issue is the concern that media publicity will result in unwarranted harm to a defendant. The appeals courts have not responded to this concern, and they have thus far not recognized media coverage as a mitigating factor in subsequent sentencing decisions. A 1980s statement by Judge Frankel of New York still summarizes the current judicial position:

> Public humiliation is the frequently heard contention that he should not be incarcerated because he "has been punished enough." Defendant's notoriety should not in the last analysis serve to lighten, any more than it may be permitted to aggravate a sentence. It is not possible to justify the notion that this mode of nonjudicial punishment should be an occasion for leniency not given to a defendant who never basked in such an admiring light at all. The quest for both the appearance and the substance of equal justice prompts the court to discount the thought that the public humiliation serves the function of imprisonment.[48]

Left unaddressed are cases in which the defendant is found innocent of criminal charges but has his or her career or reputation permanently ruined by publicity. The consequence of publicity has been described in relation to government officials who have been investigated, as follows:

> Once again the tendency to portray public officials accused of criminal or unethical activities as guilty [is displayed]. . . . We find it appalling that long after many of these individuals have been found innocent of the accusations against them, the disproved accusations continue to be repeated as almost a permanent addendum to their name in news stories.[49]

Some have suggested that live television coverage incites such negative feelings against defendants that, even if they are later acquitted, the feelings are irreversible.[50] Exemplified by the perceptions of a substantial portion of U.S. residents regarding the guilt of O.J. Simpson, the modern mass media have constructed a new category beyond the realm of the judicial system: *legally innocent but proved socially guilty*. In the process, media coverage confounds the concepts of *legal guilt* (is the defendant legally responsible for a crime?) and *factual guilt* (did the defendant actually commit the criminal behavior?). Factual guilt is not always equivalent to legal guilt, and the general public little understands and is poorly instructed by the media in the differences between the two. If defendants who have been found innocent are subsequently punished in a real sense by losing their careers or reputation because of publicity, then the system and society both lose legitimacy. And as the assassination attempt on President Reagan by John Hinckley Jr. revealed, a defendant does not have to be set free or avoid imprisonment to raise public outcry. (See Chapter 5 for further discussion of the Hinckley case.) Sensational and narrow coverage of a case that is ultimately decided on legal rather than factual guilt can result in serious loss of credibility and legitimacy for the entire judicial system and in media-driven pushes for poorly considered changes in criminal justice public policy.[51]

Televised Trials

Live televised proceedings represent the most intrusive of news media access to the judicial system. Televised proceedings raise unique and myriad questions about the impact of the modern, visually dominated electronic media in the courtroom and the widespread exposure of hidden backstage judicial processes and behaviors. The range of judicial posture toward televised proceedings is shown by its embracement in the O.J. Simpson criminal trial compared with its banishment in his civil trial.

The judiciary has long been skeptical about visual coverage of trials. Recognition of its unique potential for disruption originated in the Bruno Hauptmann trial (for the kidnapping and murder of Charles Lindbergh's baby son) in the 1930s.[52] In response to problems that arose during this trial, in 1937 the American Bar Association issued a new rule regarding the use of photographic equipment at trials:

> Proceedings in court should be conducted with fitting dignity and decorum. The taking of photographs in the courtroom, during sessions of the court or recesses between sessions, and the broadcasting of court proceedings are calculated to detract from the essential dignity of the proceedings, degrade the court and create misconceptions with respect thereto in the mind of the public and should not be permitted.[53]

This recommended ban on photography in the courtroom was widely adopted and was extended in 1952 to include television cameras as well. Despite the extension of the ABA rule, however, the first trial to receive television coverage took place in 1953 in Oklahoma City, and the first to receive live coverage took place in 1955 in Waco, Texas. These cases stand as exceptions to the more deeply held opposition to television in the courts.

The Supreme Court first reviewed the question of television access to courtrooms in *Estes* v. *Texas* in 1965.[54] The *Estes* trial received intense regional television coverage with nightly news reports broadcast from the scene. Television equipment caused a significant disruption in the courtroom, with camera operators moving about and cables and wires snaking across the floor.[55] The Court reversed Estes's conviction without clearly stating why television should be excluded but indicating that television was unavoidably disruptive

One of the nation's early media trials. Shown is the gathering
of reporters to cover the 1935 Lindbergh kidnapping trial.

Corbis-Bettmann

and should be banned from the courtroom: "Television in its present state and
by its very nature, reaches into a variety of areas in which it may cause prejudice to an accused. . . . The televising of criminal trials is inherently a denial
of due process."[56] In response most states subsequently severely limited television's access to their courts, and many simply banned all coverage. Encouraging this trend, the prohibition of television was broadly supported throughout
the legal field. As recently as 1980, a clear majority of lawyers opposed allowing television cameras to broadcast court proceedings, with 75 percent feeling
that television would tend to distract witnesses and would only be used to
show the more sensational aspects of a trial.[57]

However, encouraged by the development of less obtrusive equipment,
various states also continued to experiment with televising proceedings. In
1979, the Florida Supreme Court allowed television reporting from trial
courts, subject to coverage guidelines. The permission of the defendant was
not required. Florida's procedures were challenged and were reviewed by the
Supreme Court in 1981 in *Chandler* v. *Florida*.[58] At that time, the Court rejected many of the assumptions about television it had forwarded sixteen years
earlier in the *Estes* decision. (See Box 4.1.) The most significant assumption it
rejected was that televising a criminal trial without the defendant's consent is a
per se denial of due process. Emphasizing the modernization of the medium,
the lack of evidence of a psychological impact from televised coverage on trial

Inside an early media trial. The kidnap ladder is shown being taken
through the crowded courtroom at the 1935 Lindbergh trial.

Corbis-Bettmann

participants, and an increase in the public acceptance of television as a fact of
everyday life, the Court upheld the *Chandler* conviction, placing the burden
of establishing a prejudicial effect from television on the defendant.

The impetus for this reversal is found in the years between *Estes* and *Chandler*, during which there was growing concern among the judiciary that the
public lacked confidence in the courts' ability to control crime and criminals.
The courts were viewed as partly responsible for the increasing crime rates. In
this negative atmosphere, televising trials began to look to some judges like a
possible counter to negative charges against the judiciary. As front-stage events
purposely constructed for public consumption, trials do after all show the justice system at its best. It was increasingly felt that the camera's eye would show
impartial justice, fair procedure, conviction of the guilty, and imposition of
sentence. Though some may denigrate the trial process, it is impressive. By
contrast, the seamy side of the criminal process—the plea bargaining, the procedural inefficiency, the arbitrariness inherent in police and prosecutor discretion—will go unseen. Televising trials, in other words, was now seen as unlikely
to hurt and likely to help shore up the poor social image of the judiciary.[59]

By the 1980s, therefore, the courts saw televised trials as a means of presenting controlled, formal front-stage behavior and events to the public while
protecting their backstage assembly-line processes from further exposure. The
basic policy issue underlying the question of whether or not to allow television

---

BOX 4.1   Arguments For and Against Allowing
Television Cameras in the Courtroom

For (circa 1981 and
Chandler **v.** *Florida***):**

1. There is no research evidence that cameras in the courtroom negatively affect courtroom personnel or trial participants.
2. Modern technology has made equipment less obtrusive and smaller and eliminated the need for cables and special lighting or power.
3. The public has become so used to television as a fact of everyday life that judges no longer consider the fact that jurors are aware of the cameras or that the presence of television cameras indicates to jurors that the trial is significant sufficient to demonstrate prejudice.
4. The televising of trials could bolster the courts' image, as the impressive front-stage ceremony of the courtroom can be seen as the judicial system at its best.
5. Television promotes both crime control and due process.
6. By educating the public about the judicial process, expanding the trial audience would help promote deterrence and increase the legitimacy of the law. In the end, public confidence in the courts would increase.

Against (circa 1965 and
Estes **v.** *Texas***):**

1. Trial participants' primary audience would shift from the courtroom to the external public.
2. The judicial system would lose control, mystique, and legitimacy.
3. Courtroom distractions would increase, and witnesses already stressed because of having to appear in court would be further stressed, hampering examination.
4. Jurors, concerned with being on camera, would concentrate less on the proceedings.
5. Lawyers would be tempted to play to the cameras rather than to the jury.
6. A distorted picture of court proceedings would be portrayed, and to a wider audience.
7. Television is inherently biasing: "Television in its present state and by its very nature reaches into a variety of areas in which it may cause prejudice to an accused ... the televising of criminal trials is inherently a denial of due process" (381 U.S. at 538 and 544).

---

cameras in the courtroom was never the freedom of the media to report courtroom matters—broadcast journalists, after all, can attend and report trials on the same basis as other reporters—but the effects of expanding the trial audience to include persons not in the courtroom. In the 1960s—at the time of *Estes*—the court feared the effects of this expansion on both the trial participants and the expanded electronic audience. By the 1980s opposition to courtroom television had drastically lessened.

One reason for the original concern is the dramatic difference between the construction of knowledge in the courts and in the media. Lawyers must go slowly, following strict procedures and rules of evidence,[60] while media representatives need speed and drama.[61] Therefore, the courts are traditionally an internally controlled front-stage production, but media coverage of the courts focuses on external audiences and dramatic backstage presentations and information. The belief in *Estes* was that the presence of the electronic media would cause courtroom participants to alter the way they present testimony and arguments to suit the media instead of conforming to courtroom format, and that in the process they would delegitimize the whole judicial system by revealing previously shielded information regarding case negotiations and the influence of nonlegal factors.[62] In effect, the fear was that the social reality of the courts would be changed forever and for the worse.

Bolstered by research evidence reported between the *Estes* (1965) and *Chandler* (1981) decisions that indicated that the effects of the presence of television cameras on the traditional trial participants were benign, and acting on its own new attitude that televised trials forwarded both due process and crime control, the Supreme Court decided in *Chandler* that electronically expanding the trial audience was desirable. Whether linking courts to television will enhance or diminish the integrity of the criminal justice system in the eyes of the general public is still to be determined, but recent televised trials certainly did not seem to be improving the system's image.

The *Chandler* decision marks a remarkable shift in the attitude of the judicial system toward the presence of television. In 1976, all but two states prohibited cameras in courtrooms; in 1996, forty-seven states allowed cameras in their courts at either the appellate or trial level or both.[63] The *Chandler* decision is seen as a broad victory for the electronic media in that since *Chandler*, to prohibit broadcasting the defendant must show material prejudicial effects and interference with due process.[64] The roots of this victory can be understood by looking at how the social construction of televising courtroom proceedings changed between the *Estes* and *Chandler* cases. In sum, the Supreme Court in its 1965 *Estes* ruling was influenced by its belief that the televising of trials inherently violated the due process rights of defendants—a negative effect that was not, in the Court's view, counterbalanced by any positive crime control effect. In the 1981 *Chandler* decision, however, the Court altered its view of courtroom cameras in accordance with a change in its attitudes regarding the effects of those cameras. Television was now seen as promoting both crime control and due process, and thus was now a positive addition to a proceeding.[65]

Attitudes regarding television news coverage have changed to such an extent that an ironic reversed appeal to the *Estes* case has been argued. In *United States v. Hastings*, a defendant demanded live television coverage of his federal trial.[66] The defendant, then federal judge Alcee Hastings, asserted that he was entitled to television coverage as part of his right to a public trial and that television coverage was necessary to restore his reputation. The news media argued that recent access to criminal proceedings also gave the media the right to broadcast federal criminal trials.[67] The appeals court disagreed, however, arguing that appellate decisions stated only that television coverage is not constitutionally prohibited, not that it is constitutionally mandated.

Regarding the concerns first raised in the *Estes* decision about the inherent biasing effects of televised coverage, social science researchers since *Chandler* have not noted negative results and have been generally positive toward continued coverage. For the most part, surveys of trial participants indicate that they do not perceive serious negative effects from television coverage of court proceedings.[68]

So it is that extensive reviews of numerous court experiments with cameras have concluded that one by one the early concerns about and arguments against televising courtroom proceedings have fallen.[69] Concerns about physical disruption have declined as smaller, better equipment has become available; as judges have shown themselves able to maintain the dignity and decorum of a courtroom; and as effects on trial participants (judges, prosecutors, witnesses, and jurors) have usually been found to be slight and attitudes toward television's presence supportive.[70] For the most part, the courts have come to accept television and most feel that courtroom proceedings, participants, and outcomes are unaffected by the presence of cameras.[71]

While the effects of cameras on actual courtrooms are now seldom seen as primary concerns, the effects of those cameras on those outside the courtroom are still unresolved. Still at issue is the impact of televised trials on the external social audience and potential negative effects arising from the types of cases chosen for television coverage and the style of this coverage.[72] A number of public disturbances and full-scale riots have been triggered by court decisions.[73] Specific unresolved issues include the deterring of crime victims from reporting crimes or testifying to avoid embarrassing coverage, the heightening of viewers' fear of crime, the distorting of the workings of the judicial system, the encouraging of copycat crimes, and the pillorying by publicity of defendants eventually found innocent. As can be seen, the focus of the issues that remain regarding televised trials is no longer on internal effects, but has shifted to possible external effects, particularly attitudinal effects on the viewing public.[74] However, none of the negative effects has proved severe enough to seriously curtail televised coverage, and televised trials are now seen as having the potential to further both due process and crime control through education of the public about the judicial process, enhancement of the deterrence effect of trials, and promotion of the public's confidence in the courts. For example, it was found that viewers of a televised civil trial became more knowledgeable of the judicial process while remaining equally confident of the courts. Whether these positive results occur in massively covered media trials such as the O.J. Simpson case remains an open question. Initial feedback suggests they do not. Thus whether or not televised trials will remain in judicial favor can be predicted by examining whether or not their effects continue to be seen as forwarding due process or crime control goals, and whether or not trials continue to be the front-stage events that the courts wish to project to the public. Should trials come to be seen as expensive, ostentatious, and ineffective events, or as due process–laden mechanisms in a period emphasizing crime control, judicial opposition to their televising will rise. Not surprisingly, following the O.J. Simpson trial new calls for the banning of courtroom television have been heard.

In sum, intensive and sometimes intrusive news coverage is accepted as a fact of life in the judiciary. The courts have come to an unsteady acceptance of

Contemporary news coverage of a judicial proceeding

AP Photo/Chuck Robinson

the media in most cases but are still uneasy about the media's presence and actively resist it in certain circumstances. Future clashes between the two are to be expected as the media seek access to other backstage judicial activities and as media technology makes observing and recording them easier. These clashes will continue to revolve around the control of information and the construction of the public image of the judiciary. The courts will need to control the information juries consider in reaching verdicts, government agencies will continue to try to control access to their files, and the media will strive to gain broader access to judicial proceedings and government files while trying to maintain control over and limit access to their own news files and information. The media are aided in this process by the societywide effects of the mass media over the last forty years, which have persistently discouraged closed social institutions and information.[75] Ironically, these same forces undermine the media's arguments for secrecy regarding their own information. In response to the increasing number of requests for information, both the media and the judicial system have developed strategies and mechanisms to limit access to their information and to minimize the negative effects from the access that does occur.

CONTROLLING KNOWLEDGE

The courts have two strategies they can pursue in dealing with problems resulting from media content. One is proactive and seeks to limit the availability of potentially prejudicial material to the media. The second is reactive and seeks to limit the effects of the material after it has been disseminated by the media.[76] Under the first strategy, if a court deems information to be prejudicial, it then acts to restrict either media access to the information or, if the material is already in the media's possession, the publication of the information. This approach directly clashes with the First Amendment protection of freedom of the press and has been most vigorously resisted by the media. It has also not been a favored strategy of the courts, as shown in test cases in which the Supreme Court has been more stringent in reviewing appeals where the proactive strategy has been used. The courts have had more success using the proactive strategy when they have been able to prevent media access to information than when they have attempted to keep the media from publishing information already obtained.

On the other hand, appeals by the media have been less successful when the courts employ the reactive strategy, for this strategy allows the news media access and publication, and attempts to compensate for the resulting publicity and protect the due process rights of defendants through various judicial mechanisms. Some feel, however, that given the pervasiveness and intrusiveness of the mass media, these after-the-fact attempts to compensate are costly, disruptive, and, most important, ineffective, especially in massively covered cases. They accordingly call for greater support for the proactive restriction of media access to prejudicial information.[77] However, the proactive strategy tends to close off the judicial system and thus runs counter to the societywide, media-driven trend toward open social institutions.[78] Therefore, although still used, the mechanisms of the first strategy are likely to continue to lag in popularity, being reserved only for the rare and unusual case and challenged whenever they are used.

Court Mechanisms to Control Prejudicial Materials

Under this first strategy of limiting the availability of prejudicial information, the courts have three mechanisms they can employ. Each mechanism involves a court order restraining to varying degrees the ability of the media to report a criminal case. And all three—closure, restrictive orders, and protective orders—have been vigorously opposed and decried by the media.

Closure. Closure involves isolating judicial proceedings from outside (public and press) attendance. Given that information is kept directly from the media, closure is felt to be a very effective means of preventing prejudicial coverage once a proceeding has begun, as there can be no prejudice if there is no coverage. Though logical, closure encroaches directly on the freedom of the press to observe government proceedings and violates the long-standing tenet of open, public trials. Furthermore, a number of assumptions underlie the logic of the need for closure in a specific case:

1. Prejudicial information will be revealed during a proceeding.

2. The media will report that information.

3. The public will take notice of this information from the media.

4. Prejudice will actually result from the reports.

5. Enough people will be prejudicially influenced to make it impossible to impanel an unbiased jury.[79]

In cumulative effect, these assumptions argue that not closing a proceeding will result in a media-generated social construction that is prejudicial to a defendant. In opposing closure, the media argue that these assumptions are seldom if ever true and that it cannot be predicted when they will be valid. They further argue that the media are proxies for the general public and therefore have an inherent right of access to the courts. Proponents respond that the media have no inherent right of access and no special claim to court information, particularly information that would be inadmissible at a trial, and that the defendant's right to a fair trial supersedes any public or media interests. Proponents of closure also argue that precisely because predicting when prejudice may be generated is difficult, a conservative approach of closing a proceeding when there is any doubt is necessary. In the appeals that have arisen, the main subject of contention has been the closing of pretrial proceedings and hearings. Judges frequently close such proceedings to keep evidence and other information that might be revealed in the pretrial sessions but ruled inadmissible for the trial from reaching prospective jurors through the press.

During the 1970s, as the mass media advanced technologically and broadened their scope and influence, trial judges began to increasingly close courtroom proceedings. Encouraged by the ambiguity and tone of the 1979 *Gannett Co.* v. *DePasquale* ruling,[80] trials, pre-indictments, pretrial hearings, and post-trial proceedings were all increasingly closed.[81] Within a year of *Gannett,* however, the Supreme Court moved to reaffirm the presumption of open access to criminal trials.[82] Then—in 1986—the Court extended its negative posture toward closure and ruled that the press and public have a qualified privilege to attend a preliminary criminal hearing, stating that "criminal proceedings cannot be closed unless there is a substantial probability that the defendant's right to a fair trial will be prejudiced by publicity."[83] This ruling established a clear presumption of openness and access, and made closing even pretrial hearings extremely difficult.[84]

At present, judges can still close pretrial proceedings and criminal trials but must show cause. While voir dire, depositions, suppression hearings, and other pretrial proceedings have all been closed, and their closures upheld by the Supreme Court, a number of lower appeal courts have established various burdens of proof that must be overcome before state trial judges can issue a closure order. Most courts agree that closure orders should be preceded by a hearing to examine the necessity of closure; that counsel requesting closure should demonstrate that there is a substantial chance that unreliable, untrustworthy, or inflammatory information will reach prospective jurors; and that the media should have an opportunity to argue that alternative methods of ensuring due process are available.[85] The Supreme Court, however, has not endorsed any definitive rules. In an example of "do as I say, not as I do," with the exception of juvenile proceedings, juvenile testimony in sexual cases, grand juries, and the federal courts in general, the Supreme Court appears to wish to make closure rare and a choice of last resort for trial judges.[86] It will, however, support closure in properly documented situations, and once closed, reopening a court proceeding through appeal has not often been successful.[87]

Restrictive Orders. Second only to closure, the next most effective court mechanism available to control prejudicial materials with regard to the media is the use of restrictive orders (also sometimes termed prior restraint or gag orders). Restrictive orders prevent the media from printing or broadcasting information. Obviously, if information is not published it cannot cause bias. Not surprisingly, the media have argued vigorously for the right to publish what they have already discovered, and this right has generally been recognized.[88] A form of censorship, the granting of restrictive orders against the press is a chilling action and has been acknowledged as such by the Supreme Court.[89] However, such orders may be upheld if essential to safeguard other constitutional rights.

The current judicial support for restrictive orders originated in the Sam Sheppard case,[90] in which the Supreme Court made trial judges directly responsible for controlling the media during proceedings. In criticizing the trial judge in *Sheppard*, the Supreme Court listed possible countermeasures that could have been taken, including restricting media publications. Later, in 1968, the American Bar Association recommended that judges use contempt rulings to back restrictive orders. The combined result was an increase in the number of restrictive orders, starting in the late 1960s and climaxing in the mid-1970s.[91]

The Supreme Court did issue guidelines for issuing restrictive orders, rather than leaving the situation vague as with rules for closure. In the 1976 case *Nebraska Press Association* v. *Stuart*, the Court reversed a restrictive order and described the standards that such an order would need to meet. To justify a request for an order, the accused must show a clear and present danger that unchecked news reporting will prejudice his or her right to a fair trial. If, however, alternative methods can be used, they should be, and the inadequacies of each alternative must be explained. The judge must examine the nature and extent of the publicity and find that unrestrained publicity is certain and would prevent the court from finding unbiased jurors. The judge must also consider the practical limitations of restrictive orders. As the Court noted in this case, courts have jurisdiction only over persons in their jurisdiction. Therefore, national press coverage is largely beyond the reach of restrictive orders by local courts. Finally, if the trial judge feels that prospective jurors may receive information from other sources besides the media, such as through word of mouth, prior restraint requests should be denied.[92] Clearly, the free use of restrictive orders was not encouraged. Currently, recognizing that restrictive orders are frequently overturned and that the Supreme Court favors the media in generally opposing this method, lower courts seeking to deal with media effects have looked more to closure of proceedings and less to the contentious reactive mechanisms, which are aimed at limiting the effects of information already revealed.

Protective Orders. The third judicial mechanism that can be used to limit the availability of prejudicial materials is the protective order. Trial participants are a common source of prejudicial information, and these orders, in which a trial judge prohibits statements made outside the courtroom, are most effective in the early stages of a case.[93] Problems arise because protective orders restrict trial participants' freedom of speech. The legal rationale for allowing their speech to be restricted is that they possess privileged information regarding a criminal case and no longer have the same First Amendment right to speak as a member of the general public. Though the Supreme Court views protective orders in a better light than restrictive orders, uncertainty remains as to whether or not a trial court must first exhaust other, less contentious measures before resorting to a protective order. As it now stands, it is currently easier for a trial judge to restrict the speech of a trial's participants, excluding the defendant, than to close a proceeding or to restrain the media from publicizing information and statements they have obtained. Since the mid-1980s the Supreme Court has purposely avoided considering these issues despite a number of *certeria* cases forwarded from the lower courts. Protective orders therefore are on the increase in the trial courts.[94]

Court Mechanisms to Limit the Effects of Published Prejudicial Material

Failing to limit access to and dissemination of prejudicial material, trial court judges can invoke a number of reactive mechanisms to limit the potential negative effects of information reported by the media. These mechanisms are generally preferred over closure, restrictive orders, and protective orders, as they do not directly limit the activities of the media and thus do not directly undermine First Amendment freedom of the press. They rest on the premise that even if most of the public may be influenced and biased by media information, an unbiased jury can still be assembled and an unbiased trial conducted.[95] Within this second, reactive strategy, judges can expand the jury selection voir dire, grant trial continuances, grant changes of venue, sequester jurors, and give special instructions to the jury to counteract the effects of publicity. However, current case law and legislation provide little direction concerning the appropriate use of these mechanisms, and little empirical research is available regarding their relative effectiveness.[96] Therefore, although each mechanism has recognized strengths and weaknesses, its application is based on unproved but commonly accepted assumptions concerning its effectiveness and appropriate use.

Voir dire ("to speak the truth") is a process in which prospective jurors are queried regarding prejudice. Attorneys can prevent jurors from serving either through challenges for cause, where they must state a valid reason for eliminating a juror, or peremptory challenges (normally limited in number) that do not have to be supported by a reason. Voir dire will only identify those jurors who admit knowledge and prejudice about a case and is based on the premise that jurors will recognize themselves as biased and truthfully admit it. The proportion of potential jurors who have detailed knowledge and prejudice about a case is often used as a measure of the level of prejudice in the general community.[97] Despite its limitations, judges and lawyers generally feel that the process is an effective means of choosing an impartial jury.[98] Although Buddenbaum and her colleagues concluded in 1981 that voir dire is a more certain remedy for the effects of publicity than a change of venue, recent research questions the effectiveness of voir dire as a means of identifying biased jurors and thus of countering the effects of prejudicial publicity.[99] Voir dire conducted in groups and with yes-or-no questions is felt to be particularly weak in uncovering bias.[100]

A *continuance* is simply a delay in the start of a trial until media coverage and its effects are thought to have subsided enough to allow an unbiased trial. The practice is based on the premise that media interest in the case will wane and that jurors will forget details of past media reports.[101] Disadvantages include its inconsistence with the defendant's right to a speedy trial, and the possibility that witnesses and evidence may not be available at a later time.[102] Also, the reality is that highly newsworthy trials are not normally helped by continuances.[103] The latest research has found that continuances help to mitigate the biasing effects of factual publicity but not of emotional publicity.[104]

A *change of venue* occurs when a trial is moved from a location in which the case has received heavy media coverage to one in which it has received less coverage and is of less interest, and where residents, therefore, are assumed to be less biased. However, even a quarter century ago, a change of place was not often found to mean less bias,[105] as prejudicial news items tend to be widely disseminated and coverage outside the community where the crime occurred is often similar to that within it.[106] Thus the basic premise underlying changes of venue is questionable, and the effectiveness of the practice appears to depend on the second community's having less interest in a case and therefore paying less attention to the coverage. No studies examining this latter question are available.

Although costly and questionable in effectiveness, venue changes are deemed necessary in certain cases—for example, in rural areas where the jury pool is limited and a major crime is likely to be the dominant news story for a long time. Thus, the Illinois Supreme Court ruled that a change of venue should have been granted to a thirteen-year-old murder defendant when evidence showed that a large proportion of the general population and half of the jury knew of the release of a codefendant due to insufficient evidence and of the results of a lie detector test.[107] The court noted that the volume of publicity, although great, was not the deciding factor, but the type of prejudicial information, an inadmissible test result, was. Once information of this type reaches a jury pool, a change of venue is required. That the amount of publicity is not crucial was again emphasized after a U.S. Court of Appeals upheld a denial of a change of venue after reviewing the nature of the publicity.[108] The appeals court found that, although widespread, the publicity was mostly objective rather than inflammatory, and the trial judge had instituted other corrective measures by expanding the voir dire and increasing the number of peremptory challenges. Unless publicity is pervasive *and* prejudicial, whatever its magnitude, it is not deemed to be in and of itself grounds for a change of venue.[109] In practice, change of venue requests are routinely denied.[110]

Sequestration is the isolation of a jury to control the information that reaches it. This practice can be very effective if the jury has not been exposed to prejudicial information prior to being impaneled. However, it is extremely costly and disruptive to jurors and is felt to generate animosity toward the accused.[111] Its actual effectiveness has not been empirically established, but judges commonly consider it effective.[112] In that many of the more dramatic revelations occur long before trial and sequestration does not prevent exposure to media activities in the courtroom, its effectiveness is felt to be muted.[113]

Jury instructions are probably the simplest and least expensive judicial mechanism that can be invoked, as they comprise only the directions the trial judge gives to the jury. They fundamentally consist of telling jurors to ignore media reports of the trial and not to discuss the case with anyone. Trial judges and other judicial participants believe that such instructions are effective with most juries.[114] Therefore, standard warnings concerning the media and outside sources of knowledge are now commonly given as a matter of course in most trials that receive any media coverage. The empirical studies that have examined this mechanism suggest, however, that for the most part standard jury warnings do not eliminate publicity-generated bias.[115] How much bias remains is undetermined, but studies have indicated that juries commonly discuss prejudicial information despite instructions not to.[116]

The primary difficulty for trial judges in using these various mechanisms is determining when action should be taken and which of the mechanisms to employ. Appeals courts have used various ambiguous terms to describe cases where a trial judge must intercede. Collectively, the decisions describe "news media based spectacles where pervasive, inflammatory materials are published and result in waves of public passion against a defendant"[117]—a colorful but not very precise set of directions for trial judges to follow. Contributing to the ambiguity is the variety of rules directing judges. For example, a federal district judge can deny habeas corpus (a legal request to release an accused from imprisonment) based on alleged pretrial publicity, without having to review all the news articles and newscasts underlying the appeal claim.[118] A judge also does not have to immediately query jurors to determine whether or not they are aware of questionable publicity every time someone reports a prejudicial news release during the course of a trial.[119] This ambiguity is not by chance but reflects a long-standing appellate preference for not spelling out specific rules: "We prefer to leave [the decision] to the trial judge's judgment and discretion, subject to later review after verdict on appropriate motion, and our review on appeal . . . rather than invoke a standing inflexible rule."[120] Besides the question of when to take action, the question of what action to take has been left ambiguous. These mechanisms interact with one another in complex ways that make their use by trial judges problematic. At the most basic level, to enforce their decision, trial judges rely on contempt-of-court rulings to deter and punish the ignoring of their orders regarding media publicity. In practice, the threat of a contempt finding normally works better with local criminal justice system personnel, as they have to consider future dealings with the court, and less well with jurors, witnesses, reporters (especially those from other jurisdictions), and other temporary participants.[121] Like most deterrence mechanisms, contempt rulings also function better when reserved as a threat than when frequently employed. Trial judges, therefore, most often rely on the reactive measures of voir dire and jury warnings, although there is little empirical evidence that these measures adequately attenuate media effects.[122] Their effectiveness remains an unsubstantiated assumption, and continued reliance on them is based largely on faith. Usually, it is only when a case has attracted widespread, adverse news coverage that more costly reactive and more intrusive proactive measures are instituted to limit the prejudicial information. As a last resort, a mistrial can be declared and a retrial ordered if jurors are exposed to or admit to being influenced by prejudicial news once a trial has begun. A retrial can be thought of as the ultimate judicial remedy for media publicity—but it also represents an expensive failure of the system and does not prevent the recurrence of renewed massive coverage.

In the end, when dealing with the media, trial judges and attorneys face a maze. All must constantly monitor media coverage of a case and act expeditiously when it is apparent that prejudicial information will be released. Exactly what course is adequate or proper in any particular case is unfortunately still determined largely by the trial judge's past experience and best guess.[123]

Media Response: Reporters' Privilege and Shield Laws

On the opposite side of the knowledge control issue, the media sometimes possess information that the courts or law enforcement want but that the media do not want to divulge. Controversy generally revolves around journalists' claim of the right of a "privileged conversation" with news information sources. Journalists argue that they should be protected from having to divulge information or identify their sources to the same extent that communications between husbands and wives, attorneys and clients, priests and penitents, and psychiatrists and patients are protected. In each of the latter relationships the courts cannot compel disclosure. Journalists argue that to fulfill their function as watchdogs of government activities, protect their First Amendment rights, and guarantee credibility of and access to information, their news sources must be similarly protected.[124]

The subject of privileged communications is an old one. The right to confidentiality between a lawyer and client was recognized during the sixteenth-century reign of Elizabeth I. At the same time, common law extended the privilege to husbands and wives. In the United States, the issue is older than the country. Benjamin Franklin describes the jailing of a publisher for refusing to reveal his news source in colonial Massachusetts.[125] Today, communications between priests and penitents, physicians and patients, and informers and the government are universally recognized as privileged.[126] Journalists, however, did not begin to seriously lobby for privileged communication protection until the 1890s.

Opponents to the extension of privileged protection to media sources have argued that the media should have no more protections or privileges than the average citizen, whose duty to provide testimony in criminal matters has frequently been affirmed. Even within the media industry, opinions differ greatly as to when sources should be protected.[127] Opinions range from the view expressed in Canon 5 of the American Newspaper Guild's Code of Ethics, which states that reporters shall always refuse to reveal confidences, to that spelled out in the Associated Press Managing Editors Association Code of Ethics, which recommends that sources should be disclosed unless there is a clear and explicitly stated reason to keep them confidential.

Most in the media industry feel that journalists are not adequately protected by Supreme Court decisions, which have failed to recognize a constitutional right of the media to privileged communication. Indeed, a trend toward the shrinking of the scope of a reporter's privilege has been observed.[128] To avoid forced testimony, many reporters therefore feel that they need legislative protection in the form of shield laws. Paralleling media efforts for recognition of a right to privileged conversation, the lobbying for shield laws also began in the 1890s. The first reporters' shield law was passed in Baltimore, Maryland, in 1896. The media have continued to lobby successfully for shield laws, and currently more than half the states have enacted some form of shield law. Most qualify the privilege and provide a test for assessing whether or not the information is relevant and whether or not it can be obtained from other sources.[129]

The effectiveness of shield laws has been questioned, though, and the protection they afford the media is subject to state court interpretation and procedural rulings. Often the degree to which reporters are shielded depends not on what a state's laws say, but on a judge's attitude toward the press.[130] A second serious deficiency with state shield laws is that they operate only within each state, and contemporary news organizations are national and international in scope. Because of these deficiencies, few journalists believe their state's shield laws provide substantial help in protecting confidential files or preventing forced testimony.[131] Some journalists believe that shield laws actually work against reporters in that for the laws to be upheld, an uncomfortable distinction must be made between journalists and the rest of the American people that may eventually lead to government regulation of the news business.[132] Box 4.2 lists the arguments for and against shield laws.[133]

Currently, the media are infrequently asked to provide information but due to the absence of new Supreme Court decisions, a narrower interpretation of shield statutes at the state level has occurred.[134] When judges and law enforcement personnel request information, reporters may be forced to divulge it—especially if the information can be shown to be crucial to a case

---

BOX 4.2   Arguments For and Against Shield Laws

For

1. A reporter's relationship with a source is equivalent to that of a lawyer with a client and forced disclosure of sources chills further news information.
2. Disclosure of crimes from information provided by confidential sources aids justice.
3. Reporters can tap sources that are reluctant to talk to police or authorities.
4. Libel laws assure adequate protection against reckless publication of unattributed information.

Against

1. Courts fear that their authority will be weakened if necessary evidence is excluded.

2. The use of unattributed information makes fair trials impossible and circumvents subpoenas.
3. Public officials could be held up to anonymous ridicule and distrust by the press.
4. Reporters would be turned into detectives, pursuing investigatory exposé stories or making alliances with the underworld in quests for information and scoops.
5. In all other classes of privilege, the identity of both parties is known, but shield laws conceal one party. Therefore, shield laws make it impossible to determine if such a relationship actually exists, thus potentially increasing the use of irrefutable "blind quotes."

---

and unavailable elsewhere.[135] The media's efforts have made obtaining their information more difficult, and in that sense they have successfully increased control of their knowledge. But like the courts themselves, the media are now more open to inspection and more often pressed for access and information. Ironically, while the media's role is more protected in the social construction of reality process, the very process they have initiated has cycled back to affect their own social reality.

CONCLUSION

While many issues remain unresolved and research continues, a paradox emerges. The courts and social science research have focused nearly exclusively on looking for effects on cases that receive news coverage. But the evidence suggests that the effects of coverage in such cases can often be successfully reduced through the properly used combination of available judicial mechanisms (although the ones most frequently used do not appear to be the most effective). Meanwhile, pervasive and systematic media effects on a large number of nonpublicized cases are indicated but have not been seriously studied, nor are judges likely to consider taking mitigative measures in these nonpublicized cases. For now, the sole problems acknowledged within the judicial system are ensuring that jurors in highly publicized cases have not been influenced and, when prejudicial coverage occurs, recognizing what cases will need extra protection against the potential negative media effects. The courts and researchers have focused on effects in publicized cases, but in the future, they need to expand their focus to encompass more general, systematic effects in which a criminal justice system is sensitized to a specific type of case and processes these cases, both publicized and nonpublicized, differently from other types of case.

Facing frequent and increasing interaction between the media and the criminal justice system, the question arises as to what reforms in the media-judiciary relationship should be pursued. Most often suggested with regard to news media coverage of the criminal justice system is the development of voluntary guidelines.[136] Indeed, some have argued that voluntary cooperation with the press is the only real solution.[137] Standards for coverage are also important. Judges' biggest complaint about news reporting is not that it interferes with fair trials, but that it is inaccurate and incomplete.[138] Creating and applying effective voluntary standards acceptable to both sides has not been problem free, however.[139] Judges do not so much want to bar the media from the courtroom as want them to be more thorough and balanced in their reporting. They also wish the media would select a more representative set of cases to cover and not emphasize those selected for entertainment value.[140]

In addition to the media-court relationship, the historical pattern of the press and police and correctional agencies' interacting only when problems arise remains the norm.[141] An underlying reason that police and correctional officers and the media have had more difficulty agreeing to and following voluntary standards is that their relationship is more adversarial than that between the judiciary and the press. Police and correctional officers are more often the focus of negative exposés and tend to see the press as a hindrance to crime control and perceive little benefit in cooperating with the media.[142] Attorneys, in contrast, are generally more sensitive to due process values and thus more sensitive to both the need to accord the media their rights and the larger benefits of both a conscientious and a robust free press. Even with this orientation, however, maintaining a cooperative relationship has been found to take considerable effort, but in jurisdictions where guidelines work well and both sides cooperate, restrictive orders and closures are rare.[143] For law enforcement and corrections, the recent emergence of public information officers and media relations departments have worked to improve relationships with the press.[144]

Phrases such as "government in sunshine" and "freedom of information" reflect a larger, media-driven social trend toward greater openness of public institutions. The two dominant social institutions, the media and the criminal justice system, play critical roles in the continuing development of this trend. That the courts, as central players in these struggles, would be pressured by the media, especially the electronic media, to open their institutions to scrutiny was inevitable. Simultaneously, the media have also felt the pressure to open their institutions, processes, and files and have suffered through their own exposés of backstage activities.[145]

In regard to the judicial system, several other factors have further encouraged greater media access being perceived as a positive step. First, many perceive the public as distrustful and ignorant of the function of the courts and believe that media access will increase public understanding and support. Second, judges have come to accept the news media more and are more comfortable with the measures necessary to control media behavior during trials. Third, the constitutional importance given to defendants' rights has diminished, with the balance swinging toward general societal interests and thus toward increased media access.[146] Fourth, led by judges' experience with television, there has been a shift in judicial attitudes toward the media regarding due process versus crime control effects. The media are no longer viewed as obstacles to due process, and crime control is now seen as an attainable and desirable role for the media, particularly television.[147]

All these developments can be understood as a social reconstruction process of the public's perception of the impact of media coverage on judicial proceedings. The construction process has changed from a view of coverage as inherently prejudicial and damaging to one of a positive and helpful impact. Nonetheless, the criminal justice system and the mass media remain among the handful of social institutions that still resist outside access and continue to struggle to keep parts of their backstage realms closed.[148] Both striving to construct contemporary public images that better align with their historical, traditional social realities—for the courts as the fair, impartial social institutions that determine truth and dispense justice by the rule of law; for the news media as the objective, credible news-gathering government watchdog businesses that represent and inform the public. Neither ever really matched these constructed images and today are more strenuously pressed to sustain them. The current reconstructed images of both institutions significantly vary from the ones they promote.

Lastly, this reconstructed image of the news media and the courts has also eased the importation of media technology directly into the case processing flow. One area in which the judiciary has not strongly resisted media influence is in the adoption of media technology to ease the courts' administrative burden—a subject of Chapter 6. A remaining area of greater public concern over the crime and justice content of the media is the content's impact on the amount of crime we have in society. The media as a criminogenic factor, their ability to construct a more dangerous, crime-ridden social reality, is discussed in the following chapter.

CHAPTER CONCEPTS

Prejudicial Information

Pretrial Publicity

Due Process

Reporter's Privileged
Conversation

Media Access

Courtroom Cameras

Information Control

Privacy

Restrictive Orders

Protective Orders

Closure

Voir Dire

Change of Venue

Sequestration

Contempt

Jury Instructions

Shield Laws

DISCUSSION QUESTIONS

1. Can media trials coexist with fair trials?

2. What aspects of contemporary news coverage do you feel are the most damaging to fair trials?

3. Should live television coverage of criminal trials be allowed?

4. Should negative publicity be taken into account when sentencing a famous defendant?

5. Discuss the pros and cons of the U.S. versus the British and Canadian approaches to news media access and coverage of criminal proceedings and investigations.

6. Is it important that reporters be protected from testifying and that their files and notes be protected?

7. Juries are unreliable because of undue media influence and should no longer be used in massively covered criminal trials. Discuss why you agree or disagree.

8. How do television and radio talk shows expand the exposure to case evidence and issues independent of news coverage? Should this content be taken into consideraton when determining media-generated prejudice?

5

The Social Construction
of Crime and Violence

Media as a Cause

Chapter 5 reviews the research and ideas concerning the mass media as a cause of crime. Few people have actually directly examined the media as a cause of crime; the bulk of the research has focused on the media as a cause of social aggression and violence. Although narrowly focused and based on an as yet unproved premise, this social aggression research has dominated public discussion. The evidence that violent media cause an increase in social aggression is clear in the laboratory but somewhat mixed in society. Though the idea that media depictions of violence have a cathartic effect has been discredited, a debate continues about the extent to which they may stimulate violence. Nonetheless, there is a rough consensus among researchers that, at least in the laboratory and likely outside it, televised or visual violence can elicit aggressive behavior in some viewers. There is less concern about a potential print media effect on social aggression. Overall, the research suggests without proving conclusively that we are a more aggressive society because of our mass media.

Social aggression is not necessarily criminal, however, nor is most crime violent. Thus, irrespective of the media's effect on aggressive behavior, this research does not directly measure the media's effect on criminality. The subsequent portion of the chapter reviews evidence of criminogenic effects from the media. Media and aggregate crime rate studies suggest that the media's effect on crime might be independent of their violent content and their effect on aggressiveness. The research results implicate the visual media more than the print media and point to increases in property crime rather than in violent crime. At least one important exception to this generalization may exist in sexually violent pornography. There is increasing evidence that even nonexplicit, non–X-rated depictions of sexual violence against women may evoke negative social effects such as trivializing rape and supporting aggression against women, and the potential influence of sexually violent material on predisposed males poses a clear danger.

A substantial review of the concept of copycat crime follows, exploring its nature, magnitude, and mechanisms of effect as well as its relationship to terrorism and a theoretical model for its operation. In sum, copycat crime appears to be a persistent social phenomenon, common enough to influence the total crime picture—but more by influencing offenders' choice of techniques than by criminalizing individuals. These effects appear to be especially apparent following a successful terrorist act using a novel approach.

On the basis of the evidence available, which is admittedly less than perfect but still considerable, the chapter concludes with the argument that the media are a factor in our crime rate. But though most reviewers accept that the media have an effect, the nature and the magnitude of that effect are undetermined. A criminogenic effect by the media is rare and highly interactive with variables external to the media, such as the characteristics of the consumer, the setting, and the social context. The chapter closes with a discussion of a general interactive model regarding the interrelationships among these sets of variables.

STUDYING THE MEDIA
AS A CAUSE OF CRIME

Crime is normally secret and hidden. Applying the concepts of front- and backstage behavior, we can regard crime as one of the furthest backstage or even offstage of social behaviors. Its surreptitious nature makes isolating, studying, and assessing individual factors such as mass media impact difficult. Not surprisingly, little research bears directly on the issue of the media as a cause of crime; most conclusions about the influence of the media on crime have been extrapolated from studies of aggression and violence. And it is these studies that generate most of the concerns about the mass media's criminogenic potential. Underlying these concerns is a general belief in and focus on the following causal proposition:

Media depictions of violence ⟶ Increased social aggression ⟶
Increased amount of crime

There are inherent problems with this proposition as a foundation for evaluating the media's effect on crime. Most seriously, it ignores the fact that much crime is nonviolent. Second, the assumption that increased social aggression leads to more crime is unproved and largely uninvestigated. Third, the evidence that media depictions of violence cause a significant increase in social aggression is at best mixed. And last, almost all the research based on this proposition has focused on the effects of the visual media.

Because crime encompasses a wide range of behavior from serious, predatory, violent crime to trivial, passive, and victimless crime, it is not reasonable to expect to be able to describe the relationship between the media and crime in a single proposition or expect it to manifest in a simple way. Nonetheless, few researchers have taken a broad, complex view of the relationship—instead, they tend to stick closely to studying the proposition that depictions of violence lead to increased social aggression.

The public meanwhile has long been worried about the criminogenic effects of the mass media. As early as 1908, the worry that the mass media (then newspapers) were creating an atmosphere of tolerance for criminality and causing juvenile delinquency appeared. W. I. Thomas wrote in *American Magazine* in 1908:[1]

> The condition of morality, as well as of mental life, in a community depends on the prevailing copies of the newspaper. A people is profoundly influenced by whatever is persistently brought to its attention. In the same way, advertising crime, vice, and vulgarity on a scale unheard of before in the annals of history has the same effect—it increases crime, vice, and vulgarity enormously.

As noted previously, the films of the 1920s and 1930s only served to increase the public concern. After World War II, this concern about media behavioral effects reached new heights. In the late 1940s and early 1950s, a New York psychiatrist, Frederick Wertham, led a public campaign against comic books as causes of crime and delinquency. Mostly ignored by social scientists but publishing in popular magazines and appearing on radio and television, Dr. Wertham aroused strong anti–comic book sentiments in the general public, convincing large portions of the public that all comics, but particularly crime-oriented comics such as *Batman*, had criminogenic and other negative effects.[2] It is interesting to note that recent attacks against rock videos and rap lyrics are of the same tone as Wertham's earlier criticism of comic books. Once television was introduced in the 1950s, the print media generated less public concern as a serious cause of crime and television became the new focus.[3] In 1955, a commissioner of the Federal Communications Commission (testifying before the U.S. Senate Judiciary Committee on Juvenile Delinquency in the United States) expressed a still-common perception:

> Millions of television receivers are pouring an unending stream of crime, violence, outright murder, brutality, unnatural suspense, and horror into

the living rooms of America, where, in constantly increasing numbers, the children and youth of the country are found before the screen. The suggestions that there is no discernible relationship between these programs and the recent appalling increase in juvenile delinquency, in my opinion, flout common sense and rudimentary sound judgment.[4]

Today the media continue to be commonly cited as an exacerbating cause of crime—some have even advocated the censorship of the media as an effective means of reducing crime. The U.S. public today has little doubt about the role of the media. Forty-three percent feel local television news crime coverage encourages crime.[5] The entertainment media fare even worse with the public. Sixty percent of Americans currently feel that television and movies contribute a lot to social violence,[6] and the majority feel that television crime shows, movies, and television news are a major reason for the high U.S. murder rate.[7] In total, three out of four Americans think that there is a relationship between violence on television and the general U.S. crime rate.[8] And not surprisingly, the vast majority of Americans (80 percent) think there is too much violence portrayed on television.[9]

Spurred by a long history of similar public perceptions, during the past thirty years numerous studies have examined the behavioral effects of the media on consumers, most focusing on television violence and children. The reason that television has been the focus of research is that television fulfills the three preconditions considered necessary for media to contribute significantly to societal violence: There must be a constant high level of violence portrayed, the violence portrayed must be unique and unavailable elsewhere, and audience exposure to this media violence must be high. Television is felt to be the first mass medium to meet all three conditions and has therefore generated the greatest long-term concern and consequently the most research.

That television meets the first condition was established through the many media content studies discussed earlier. That it meets the second is indicated by surveys that show that few people ever observe the types of violent acts commonly portrayed in the media. For most Americans, life is relatively peaceful compared to life as shown on television. Thus direct personal experience is not a source of learning about severe violence for most of the American population.[10] Regarding the third condition, the evidence is that television alone consumes on the average approximately 11 percent of every American's time. It is the third most time-consuming activity among Americans, second only to work and sleep. Young viewers often watch even greater amounts, and the total average amount of viewing time has steadily increased since television's introduction in the 1950s, while the portion of the public who are nonviewers has decreased toward zero. If any medium contributes to crime and violence, television is the best candidate. Viewers of television violence and persons arrested for crimes also tend to be drawn from similar segments of the population: male high school dropouts aged eighteen to twenty-four.[11] Although a television-aggression focus contributes little toward a full understanding of the media and crime, this area of research has received the most public exposure, and a review and assessment of the findings is a necessary first step in unraveling the relationship between the media and crime.

EVIDENCE OF MEDIA
EFFECTS ON AGGRESSION

A Brief History of Television-Aggression Research

The logic of science requires that in order to establish the causal effect of a variable, one must be able to examine a situation without the variable's effect. In terms of television and violence this requirement means that a group of subjects (a control group) that has not been exposed to violent television is necessary for comparison with a group exposed to violent television (a treatment group). Television, however, is ubiquitous and an integral part of a modern web of influences on social behaviors. Therefore, when the interest is in the effects of television on mainstream citizens in Western industrialized and urbanized nations, finding nontelevision control groups is essentially impossible. In response, artificial laboratory situations have been created or statistical controls and large data sets employed to explore the television-aggression connection. And while social science abounds with research reporting variables that are correlated with one another, research firmly establishing causal relationships is rare. Unlike the content of television, there are few smoking guns in social science. Cause must often be inferred from the preponderance of evidence without conclusive proof—rather like the conclusion reached in a judicial trial. Such is the case with television and violence.

Driven by the folk logic of *monkey see, monkey do*, establishing whether *child see, child do* holds true in terms of the media and aggression has proved more difficult than first expected. Research on the link between media depictions of violence and social aggression initially revolved around two competing hypotheses, one conjecturing a cathartic effect, the other a stimulating effect. The cathartic-effect hypothesis can be stated thus:

> Exposure to properly presented violence acts as a therapeutic release for anger and self-hatred which are present in almost everybody.[12]

In contrast, the stimulating-effect hypothesis states that:

> A constant diet of violent behavior has an adverse effect on human character and attitudes. Violent [media content] encourages violent forms of behavior and fosters moral and social values about violence in daily life that are unacceptable in a civilized society.[13]

Researchers positing a stimulating effect have explored a number of causal mechanisms through which the media could cause aggression.[14] The most commonly advanced mechanism involves social learning, imitation, and modeling processes in which viewers learn values and norms supportive of aggression and violence, techniques to be aggressive and violent, or acceptable social situations and targets for aggression and violence.[15] Advocates of a stimulating effect feel that through these processes children learn aggression the same way they learn cognitive and social skills—by watching parents, siblings, peers, teachers, and others. Accordingly, the more violence children see, the more accepting they become of aggressive behavior. Under this hypothesis, looking at violent scenes even briefly will make viewers, particularly young children, more willing to accept aggressive behavior from others, and this acceptance of aggression will increase the likelihood that the viewers will themselves become more aggressive. The content of television has been forwarded as increasing the potential for learning aggression. A high percentage of violent scenes do not show the perpetrator being punished, the target of violence shows no pain in the majority of scenes, violence is present as plausible in over half the programs, and few programs depict any long-term negative consequences of violent behavior.[16]

Other violence-stimulating mechanisms mentioned include disinhibition processes, in which viewers become less inhibited about acting aggressively; desensitization processes, in which viewers become more tolerant and accepting of violence and aggression in others; and psychological arousal processes, which are thought to increase general arousal that may in turn boost aggressiveness.[17]

In a traditional laboratory experiment, two sets of matched, usually randomly assigned subjects are placed in identical situations except for a single factor of interest. Early studies in the television-violence quest were in this vein, with the seminal work conducted in the 1960s by researchers Bandura, Ross, and Ross.[18] These laboratory studies basically consisted of exposing groups of young children to either a short film containing violence (frequently an adult beating up an inflated Bobo doll) or a similar but nonviolent film. The two groups of children were then placed in playrooms and observed. Children who watched the film where a doll was attacked would significantly more often attack a similar doll if given the opportunity shortly after viewing their film than children who had observed a nonviolent film. These and other studies established the existence of an *observational imitation* effect from visual violence. In short, children will imitate violence they see in the media and it was concluded by many that television violence must therefore be a cause of youth violence.

In addition to the laboratory studies and about the same time, a number of survey studies were reporting positive correlations between youth aggression and viewing violent television.[19] Efforts to extend the laboratory findings and determine if the correlational studies reflected real-world causal relationships led to two types of research: natural field experiments[20] and longitudinal panel studies.

The better-known and most discussed research efforts in this area came from panel studies conducted in the 1970s and early 1980s. Expensive and time-consuming, panel studies involve selecting a large number of subjects and following them for a number of years. Three such studies are particularly important due to their renown, similarities in approach, and differences in conclusions.

In the first study (called the Rip Van Winkle Study), L. Rowell Huesmann, Leonard Eron, and their colleagues used a cross-lag panel design in which television habits at Grade 3 (approximately age eight) are correlated with aggression in Grade 3 and with television viewing and aggression ten years later for a sample of 211 boys.[21] The researchers collected their data in rural New York state from students in the third, eighth, and thirteenth grades (that is, one year after graduation). Favorite television programs were rated on their violent content and obtained from the subjects' mothers in Grade 3 and from the subjects themselves in Grades 8 and 13. Aggression was measured by a peer-nominated rating obtained from responses to questions such as "Who starts fights over nothing?" The most significant finding reported was a strong positive association between violent television viewing at Grade 3 and aggression at Grade 13. However, this study was criticized for a number of reasons. For example, the measure of aggression used in Grade 13 was poorly worded and phrased in the past tense ("Who started fights over nothing?") and thus the answers were ambiguous in that the Grade 13 subjects may have been referring to general reputations rather than current behavior. In addition, cross-lagged correlation analysis has a built-in bias toward finding relationships even where none exist. Despite these weaknesses, Huesmann and Eron concluded that a causal relationship between television violence and aggression existed. The dissemination of the study's conclusions had a strong impact on the public's belief in the causal role of television on aggression.

Conducted in response to the Rip Van Winkle study, a second longitudinal panel study (the NBC study), conducted by Ronald Milavsky and his colleagues in the early 1970s, argued an opposite conclusion. This study was based on surveys of about 2,400 elementary students aged seven to twelve and 403 male teenagers aged twelve to sixteen in Minneapolis, Minnesota, and Fort Worth, Texas.[22] The subjects were surveyed five to six times over nineteen months. This study also used peer-nominated aggression measures for the younger group and four self-reported measures of aggression for the teenagers.[23] Unlike the Rip Van Winkle study, which used a parental selection of favorite program, this study used a measure of exposure to violent programming based on the subjects' self-reported frequency of viewing selected violent programs. Their analysis further controlled for earlier levels of aggression and exposure to television violence, in effect searching for evidence of significant incremental increases in youth aggression that could be attributed to past exposure to television violence after taking into account past levels of aggressive behavior.

Milavsky and his colleagues reported meaningful lagged associations between later aggression and a number of prior conditions such as earlier aggression in a child's classroom, father's use of physical punishment, family conflict, and violent environments, but not for prior exposure to violent television. Although some significant positive relationships were found between exposure to television violence and later aggression, the overall pattern and number of findings regarding television were interpreted as inconsistent. These researchers concluded that chance, not cause, provided the best explanation for their findings regarding television and aggression.

Partly in response to the NBC study and criticisms of their earlier methodology, Huesmann, Eron, and their colleagues conducted a third panel study (the Chicago Circle Study) in the late 1970s, using first and third graders in Chicago public and parochial schools as subjects.[24] Six hundred seventy-two students were initially sampled and tested for three consecutive years in two groups. One group was followed from their first through third grades, the second from their third through fifth grades. Aggression was measured once more by a peer-generated scale in which each child designated other children on fifteen descriptive statements, ten of which dealt with aggression, an example being "Who pushes and shoves other children?" Exposure to violent television was measured by asking each child to go through eight different ten-program lists, select the most-watched show on each list, and indicate how often the child watched it. Each list contained a mix of violent and nonviolent programs.

The study was simultaneously conducted in the United States, Australia, Finland, Israel, the Netherlands, and Poland. The analysis of the U.S. data showed a significant general effect for television violence on girls but not for boys. However, the interaction of viewing violent television and identification with aggressive television characters was a significant predictor of male aggression. Huesmann and Eron concluded that the relationship between television violence and viewer aggression is causal and significant but bi-directional. That is, television viewing increases aggressive behavior and acting aggressively increases the watching of violent television.

In addition to such research efforts, periodic government assessments serve as mileposts in the history of research, public debate, and policy crusades in this area. Two government commissions examined television violence in the late 1960s and early 1970s—the National Commission on the Causes and Prevention of Violence (NCCPV) in 1969 and the Surgeon General's Scientific Advisory Committee on Television and Social Behavior in 1972. Following a ten-year hiatus, in 1982 the National Institute of Mental Health (NIMH) released the report *Television and Behavior: Ten Years of Scientific Progress and Implications for the Eighties*. The conclusions stated in the 1969, 1972, and 1982 government reports reflect a consensus position. In the 1972 Surgeon General's report, the advisory committee concluded that the convergence of evidence from both laboratory and field studies suggested that viewing violent television programs contributed to aggressive behavior. The 1982 NIMH commission report agreed, adding that more recent research had significantly strengthened this conclusion. "Not only has the evidence been augmented," the report said, "but the processes by which the aggressive behavior is produced have been further examined. For example, several important field studies have found that television violence results in aggressive behavior."[25]

However, a number of researchers have argued that the media cannot be posited as a cause of aggression or violence based on the research currently available.[26] They assert that to conclude that the media cause negative social behaviors is unjustified and it is premature to conclude from the available evidence that the media are causing social aggression, rather than being simply correlated with it. In their view, the true relationship between the media and aggression is the one shown in Figure 5.1.

In this figure, exposure to violent content and violent behavior are linked—but not causally. Rather, both stem from the predispositions of some persons, who seek out violent content and act violently because of their predisposition to aggression. Significantly for public policy, if the figure is valid, eliminating portrayals of violence in the media will not reduce the level of violence in society. The number of individuals predisposed to violence will remain the same. Advocates of this model have correctly pointed out that the evidence of a link between violent content and social aggression supports a noncausal model about as well as it does a causal one.

In response to critics who ask how the media balance the assertion that advertising influences viewers' behavior with the contention that violent content and images do not, media proponents argue that the behavior portrayed in media advertising is socially acceptable whereas violence is not.[27] Therefore, that people emulate behavior shown in advertising does not prove that they will emulate violent behavior because society reinforces the behavior shown in commercials but generally does not reinforce violence. Proponents further argue that in contrast to the socially sanctioned behavior shown in media advertising, media depictions of violence often show it as undesirable and socially unacceptable.[28] In sum, these critics argue that the research used to forward a causal effect is flawed and that in reality violent media content has an insignificant or nil effect on social aggressive behaviors.

In response to media critics who argue that the evidence of a link between violent content and social aggression is supplemented by laboratory research that substantiates a causal link, media proponents argue that the laboratory experiments conducted to determine the relationship between the media and violence are biased toward finding an effect. To isolate the effect of a single factor, the media, and observe a rare social behavior, violence, these laboratory experiments must exaggerate the link between the media and aggression and create a setting that will elicit violent behavior.[29] This bias arises, critics argue, because aggression is a relatively rare event, so experimental designs must (1) minimize subjects' internal inhibitions against aggression, (2) minimize external cues sanctioning or suppressing aggression (to limit possible causes to media effects only), and (3) maximize the clarity and intensity of experimental treatments.

In addition, the way the experimenters operationalize aggression in the laboratory affects the likelihood that they will find a strong positive relationship between the media and aggression, and because of this artificiality the experiments are criticized as invalid predictors of behavior in the real world. A final target of criticism has been researchers' ambiguity in defining and measuring the concept of aggression. For some, aggression is a broad concept that encompasses many types of social behaviors. Thus conceived, its relationship

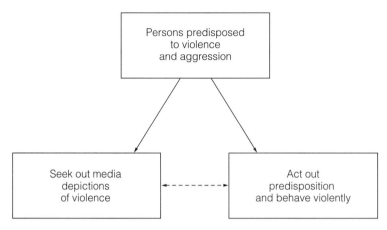

FIGURE 5.1 The Argument Against a Causal
Link Between the Media and Aggression

to the media cannot be separated from other antisocial but nonaggressive social behaviors.[30] Others narrowly operationalize aggression to a laboratory behavior, reducing it to a single, obviously artificial behavioral response such as inflicting an electric shock. The relationship of these laboratory measures of aggression to real-world aggression is unclear and questionable. The end results are unrealistic experiments and findings with limited applicability to the home and other social situations.

In summary, one cannot assume that behavior and variable relationships observed in the lab are occurring in the home or street. Thus Andison[31] reviewed sixty-seven studies, conducted between 1956 and 1976 and involving more than thirty thousand subjects, that dealt with the relationship between television violence and viewer aggression. He reported that studies employing "degree of shock administered" as their measure of aggression reported a consistent, more highly positive relationship than studies using overt physical aggression or responses to questionnaires as measures.[32] Critics argue that this laboratory operationalization of aggression is so flawed that it does not accurately reflect the watching of media violence and subsequent social aggression in situations outside the laboratory. They therefore argue that all laboratory research on the issue is irrelevant. Many also consider the effects that have been found in nonlaboratory, mostly correlational research trivial and substantively unimportant.[33] They dismiss the nonlaboratory research for lack of strict variable controls and for using designs that leave open noncausal interpretations of the results. Cook, Kendzierski, and Thomas felt that a positive bias is also likely in cross-sectional surveys and noted that field experiments produce little consistent evidence of effects, and that in the cases where an effect is claimed, the populations involved seem to be more aggressive to begin with.[34] In their view, no study yet conclusively establishes the media as a cause of violent behavior.

The research regarding pornography exemplifies the difficulty in assigning a behavioral causal effect to the media.[35] Demare and his colleagues,[36] for example, assessed their subjects' exposure to violent and nonviolent sexually explicit media content, the supportiveness of their attitudes toward violence against women, and the self-reported likelihood of using sexual force if assured of not being caught. They report no significant associations between the amount of exposure to either violent or nonviolent pornography and the degree to which the subjects supported violence against women, but a significant correlation between the amount of exposure to sexually explicit violent images and the self-reported likelihood of using sexual force. Faced with conflicting results, Demare and his colleagues[37] argue that it is the media's combination of sex and support for aggression that produces a tendency for sexual violence. However, in that it is equally likely that males with a predisposition toward sexual aggression are more likely to seek out sexually violent content, it cannot be concluded from this research that the exposure causes a tendency for sexual violence.[38] As with other research in this area, the reported correlations may be due to a third variable causing both consumption of sexually violent material and a proclivity toward sexual aggression.[39]

Other research has attempted to predict aggression against women in laboratory settings and through self-reports after exposure to violent sexual media.[40] Malamuth[41] concluded that the presence of any single factor is unlikely to result in high levels of sexual aggression. He argued that though sexual arousal in response to aggression has been used in diagnosing and treating rapists,[42] this arousal pattern has also been found in a substantial portion of the general nonviolent male population.[43]

Similar to the research on violence and aggression, the pornography research suggests but does not prove a causal connection. Therefore a noncausal explanation of the research findings remains viable. These criticisms are best summarized by Cook, Kendzierski, and Thomas,[44] who analyzed the 1982 NIMH report and concluded that the research was limited to examination of how the media's content influences viewers' perceptions and how these perceptions in turn affect viewers' attitudes and behavior. Institutions rarely come under study, and the NIMH report largely ignores the media industry, advertising, and government influences, in effect assuming that the media influence audiences directly and solely through programming content.

What should be made of the conflicting positions? After eighty years of concern and forty years of serious research, most reviewers of these studies and the subsequent research conclude that a modest but genuine causal association does exist between media violence and aggression.[45] The fact is that once mass media are introduced, the effect of media on society or an individual can never be fully extricated from all the other forces that may contribute to violence. Media influence is so intertwined with these parallel forces that searches for strong, direct causal effects are not likely to be fruitful. But as with research into smoking and lung cancer, most reviewers believe that evidence of a real causal connection of some sort has been established beyond a reasonable doubt.[46]

One undeniable finding is that the cathartic-effect hypothesis has been discredited. Contrary to what the catharsis theory predicts, when viewing is combined with frustration or arousal, viewers are more rather than less likely to behave aggressively.[47] The current debate revolves around the magnitude and significance of a stimulating effect. The research suggests that the relationship between visual media violence and audience aggression is clear, particularly for certain audiences, but the validity of extrapolating from that research evidence to a relationship between media exposure and crime remains tenuous.

The research has also revealed, however, that media depictions of violence do not affect all viewers the same way, and it has indicated that a number of specific factors play into the media's effect. In other words, whether or not a particular depiction will cause a particular viewer to act more aggressively is not a straightforward issue.[48] An aggressive effect largely depends on the interaction between each individual viewer, the content of the portrayal, and the setting in which the portrayal is viewed. The total body of research shows that the media are not monolithic in their effects but contribute more or less to aggression in combination with other social and psychological factors (see Box 5.1).

In sum, the evidence indicates that a three-prong interactive model operates with regard to violent media images and their effects on individual aggressive behavior, suggesting the model represented in Figure 5.2 for the media's effect on crime. The content of the portrayal, the setting in which it is viewed, and the characteristics of the viewer all interact to determine what effect, if any, a particular exposure to violent media images will have on the subsequent behavior of each viewer.[49] As Comstock has concluded, "Contrary results [should not be viewed] in the role of disconfirmation but in that of qualification. They simply demonstrate that in some circumstances a relationship does not occur, either because of attributes of the subjects, the particular portrayals involved, or the circumstances of exposure or subsequent behavior."[50]

At a practical social level, this gives the media significant aggregate effects but makes the effects difficult to predict at the individual level. The 1982 NIMH report conceded: "A distinction must be made, however, between groups and individuals. All the studies that support the causal relationships demonstrate group differences. None supports the case for particular individuals. . . . This distinction does not, of course, minimize the significance of the findings, even though it limits their applicability."[51] The sole individual-level impact that can be predicted is the absence of any cathartic effect leading to a reduction in aggression. This just does not occur. People do not become less violent from watching violence.

Irrespective of all the flaws noted and the doubts and criticisms expressed, however, currently most reviewers conclude that the research suggests a significant causal effect. Even Thomas Cook and his colleagues,[52] severe critics of the research, finally conclude that:

> No effects emerge that are so large as to hit one between the eyes, but early measures of viewing violence add to the predictability of later

BOX 5.1   Factors Affecting the Impact of Media Depictions of Violence on Social Aggression

Researchers* have cited the following factors as interactive and important in determining the effect that a particular portrayal of violence by the media has on a particular viewer. Note that most of the factors relate to characteristics of the media, not of the viewers, a focus that reflects a deficiency in the general research.

1. Reward, or lack of punishment, for the perpetrator of violence (Bandura 1965; Bandura et al. 1963; Rosekrans and Hartup 1967)
2. Portrayal of the violence as justified by the behavior of the victim (Berkowitz and Rawlings 1963; Meyer 1972)
3. Similarity between details in the portrayal and the viewer's real-life circumstances, such as a victim in the portrayal with the same name as someone toward whom the viewer holds animosity (Berkowitz and Geen 1966, 1967; Geen and Berkowitz 1967)
4. Similarity between the perpetrator of violence and the viewer (Rosekrans 1967)
5. Portrayal of violent behavior that is ambiguous in intent as motivated by the desire to inflict harm or injury (Berkowitz and Alioto 1973; Geen and Stonner 1972)
6. Portrayal of the consequences of violence in a way that does not stir distaste or arouse inhibitions over such behavior (Berkowitz and Rawlings 1963)
7. Portrayal of the violence as representing real events rather than events concocted for a fictional film (Feshbach 1972)

8. Portrayal of violence without critical commentary (Lefcourt et al. 1966)
9. Portrayal of violence whose commission particularly pleases the viewer (Ekman et al. 1972; Slife and Rychiak 1976)
10. Portrayals, violent or otherwise, that leave the viewer in a state of unresolved excitement (Zillman 1971; Zillman et al. 1973)
11. Viewers feeling angry or provoked before seeing a violent portrayal (Berkowitz and Geen 1966; Geen 1968)
12. Viewers experiencing frustration after viewing a violent portrayal (Geen 1968; Geen and Berkowitz 1967; Worchel et al. 1976)
13. The presence of live peer models of aggression (Murray et al. 1978)
14. The presence of sanctioning adults (Eisenberg 1980)
15. Selective attention and emotional reactions on the part of the viewer (Ekman et al. 1972)
16. Low viewer self-esteem (Edgar 1977)

Television violence has been linked to aggressive behavior whether portrayed by real or animated characters (Bandura 1971 1977; Ellis and Sekyra 1972; Hanratty et al. 1972), and only unambiguous linking of violent behavior with undesirable consequences or motives appears to inhibit the viewer's subsequent aggression (Hennigan et al. 1982; Leifer and Roberts 1972).

SOURCE: From "Media Influences on Aggression," by G. Comstock. In *Prevention and Control of Aggression*, edited by A. Goldstein and L. Krasner. Copyright © 1983 by Pergamon Press. Reprinted by permission.

*The first twelve factors were compiled by Comstock (1983, pp. 250–251) following his review of the relevant literature through 1982.

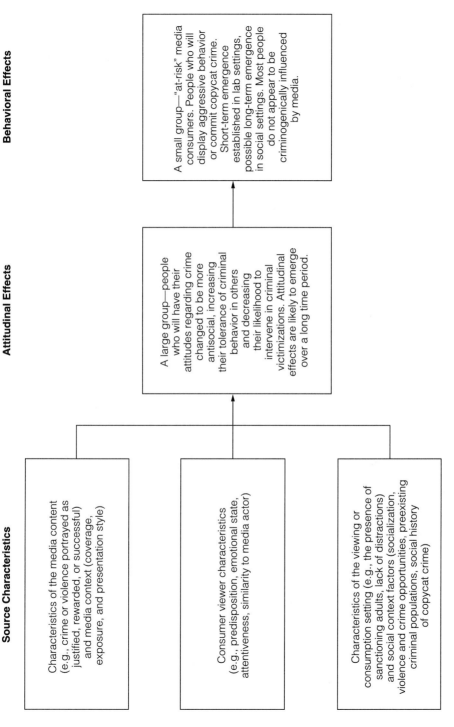

FIGURE 5.2 Factors Related to the Media's Criminogenic Effects

aggression over and above the predictability afforded by earlier measures of aggression. These lagged effects are consistently positive, but not large, and they are rarely statistically significant, although no reliable lagged negative effects have been reported. The evidence indicates that a small association can regularly be found between viewing violence and later aggression when individual differences in aggression are controlled at one time. But is the association causal? If we were forced to render a judgment, probably yes. . . . There is strong evidence of causation in the wrong setting (the laboratory) with the right population (normal children) and in the right setting (outside of the lab) with the wrong population (abnormal adults). However, trivial proportions of variance in aggression are accounted for and there exists an exaggerated sense of confidence in the research supporting an important causal connection. . . . But the effects may aggregate when large numbers of children each are affected slightly, or a small number suffer much larger consequences.

In reality, the research shows persistent behavioral effects from violent media under diverse situations for differing groups. Regarding the strong behavioral effects apparent in fashion and fad, effects that Madison Avenue touts, the argument of a media behavioral effect only on sanctioned behavior but not on unsanctioned violence is specious. The media industry claim of only having a positive behavioral effect is as valid as the tobacco industry claim that their ads do not encourage new smokers but only persuade brand switching among established smokers. First, violence is sometimes socially sanctioned, particularly within the U.S. youth and hypermasculine culture that is the target audience of the most prominently violent media. Only the unambiguous linking of violent behavior with undesirable consequences or motives in the media appears capable of inhibiting subsequent aggression in groups of viewers.

The issue for most thus comes down not to the existence of an effect but to the magnitude and substantive importance of the effect. Researchers normally measured the substantive importance of the media in generating aggression in terms of the amount of "explained variance" in levels of aggression attributable to the media—in other words, the proportion of the changes in aggression that can be statistically associated with the media. When effects are present, the explained variance is usually between 5 percent and 10 percent. Though some have interpreted these levels as important,[53] others have termed them slight or trivial.[54]

And despite clear laboratory evidence that media violence can lead to short-term imitation, researchers who have looked for an incorporation of violent behavior into the viewer's overall behavior pattern or a subsequent willingness among children to use violence as a problem-solving method have reported mixed results.[55] Exactly how and to what extent the media cause long-term changes in aggressive behavior remains unknown, and so, despite the general agreement that there is a positive relationship between violence in the visual media (particularly television) and viewer aggression, the substantive importance of this relationship is still under debate.[56]

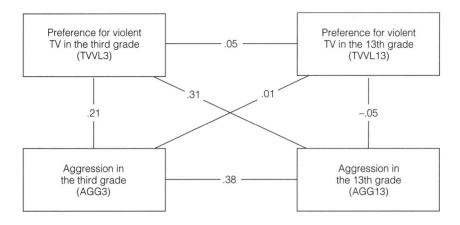

FIGURE 5.3 Correlations Between a Preference for Violent Television and Peer-Related Aggression for 211 Boys over a Ten-Year Lag

From "Adolescent Aggression and Television," by L. D. Eron and L. R. Huesmann. In *Forensic Psychology and Psychiatry*, edited by F. Wright, C. Bahn, and R. Reiber, p. 320. Copyright © 1980 by The Annals of the New York Academy of Sciences. Reprinted by permission.

Not surprisingly, various descriptions of the substantive causal impact of the media compete. Positing a significant impact, the NIMH report[57] stated regarding television that:

> Recent studies have extended the age range in which the relationship between televised violence and aggressive behavior can be demonstrated . . . to include preschoolers and older adolescents . . . [and] suggests that the viewer learns more than aggressive behavior from televised violence. The viewer learns to be a victim and to identify with victims. As a result, many heavy viewers may exhibit fear and apprehension, while other heavy viewers may be influenced toward aggressive behavior. Thus, the effects of televised violence may be even more extensive than suggested by earlier studies, and they may be exhibited in more subtle forms of behavior than aggression.

Wilson and Herrnstein[58] offer a conservative interactive model:

> Aggressive children, because they are not very popular, and low IQ children, because they have trouble with schoolwork, spend more time watching television than other children. These children identify with the television characters and may come to accept the apparently easy and sometimes violent solutions these characters have for the problems that confront them. To the extent they emulate this violence or further neglect their schoolwork, their reliance on television may increase. Television provides for such children reinforcements that are not supplied by peers or schoolwork. . . . There is no doubt that aggressive boys, including those who grow up to acquire significant criminal records, spend a lot more

time than other boys in front of the television, but we are not much closer to being able to say that these viewing habits cause much of the violence than we were twenty years ago . . . and even when all doubts are ignored, only trivial proportions of individual differences in aggression are accounted for.

Summary—Violent Media, Social Aggression

Despite some contradiction, the research reveals that in terms of magnitude, a diet of media violence correlates as strongly with and is as causally related to aggressive behavior as any other social variable that has been studied.[59] This statement describes both the media's impact and our lack of knowledge about aggression. There is a consensus among social scientists that, at least in the laboratory, television or film violence can elicit aggressive behavior in some viewers.[60] Because of the many other individual and social factors that come into play in producing any social behavior, however, one should not expect more than a modest relationship between the media and aggression to emerge outside the laboratory. Media exposure alone is not a sufficient cause of violent or criminal behavior.[61] In that since the 1950s the research has focused on visual media, there is little research and not surprisingly no evidence of an effect by the print media on social aggression. How important the relationship between the media and aggression is to society and how much it influences our quality of life is still being researched and debated. Because aggression is perceived as a persistent problem, however, even factors that contribute to it only modestly are still considered socially significant. Accordingly, in that small effects are likely to accumulate, the media cannot be ignored.[62]

Regarding specific processes, the evidence supports the stimulation hypothesis, contradicts catharsis, and suggests that the media stimulate violence through a process of observation followed by imitation.[63] There is also evidence of a normative socialization process in which exposure to mass media portrayals of violence over a long period of time socializes audiences to norms, attitudes, and values supportive of violence. Thus the more violence a person sees in the media, the more accepting of aggressive behavior he or she becomes.[64] While the media do seem influential, it is not yet clear whether their influence is through media portrayals of violence increasing the proportion of persons who assault others, encouraging already-violent persons to use violence more often, encouraging violence-prone persons to use greater violence, or some combination.[65] We do not fully understand who is most likely to respond to media violence, under what conditions the effect will take place, and in what precise way it will influence behavior.

The research available strongly suggests without conclusively proving that we are a more aggressive society because of our mass media. Violent media help create a more violent social reality. As previously stated, however, social aggression is not necessarily criminal, nor is most crime violent. Consequently, even if the media significantly foster aggressive behavior, it is a separate question whether their influence extends beyond aggressiveness to specifically increase criminal behavior—the central issue of this chapter.

EVIDENCE OF MEDIA EFFECTS ON CRIME

Aggregate Crime Rate Studies

There are inherent difficulties in researching and examining possible relationships between the media and criminal behavior. First, experiments are even more difficult to conduct in this area than in the area of social aggression; consequently most of the available evidence consists of anecdotal reports rather than empirical studies. Second, the ways in which the media may be affecting crime are numerous. The media may be increasing the number of criminals by turning previously law-abiding persons into criminals. They may be helping already active criminals succeed by teaching them better crime techniques. They may be increasing the seriousness or harmfulness of the crimes that are committed by making criminals more aggressive or violent. They may be fostering theft and other property crimes by cultivating in consumers the desire for unaffordable things and encouraging instant gratification and impulsiveness. They may be making crime seem more exciting and satisfying.[66] Any of these processes would result in more crime, more criminals, and more costly crime. Third, research is made even more difficult because an aggregate, societywide criminogenic effect is likely to be small and intermixed with many other crime-generating factors, and similarly the pool of at-risk individuals who are likely to be significantly criminally influenced by the media is also probably quite small. This makes identifying criminogenic effects and at-risk individuals for research purposes problematic.

Because of these problems, there are few empirical studies in this area. In the best-designed empirical study of media effects on recorded criminal behavior, Karen Hennigan and her colleagues examined aggregate crime rates in the United States prior to and following the introduction of television in the 1950s.[67] (See Box 5.2.) Using both statewide and citywide data, they found that the introduction of commercial television was not associated with increases in the rates of violent crime but was associated with increases in the rates of certain property crimes, particularly larceny. They attributed this correlation to the materialistic focus of television programming and advertising, which promote a high-consumption, materialistic lifestyle. Hennigan and her colleagues regarded this pervasive message of consumerism as the key through which the media affect crime, and saw it as more important than the mechanisms of imitation or stimulation hypothesized in the research on aggression. They noted that violent programming is not constant and that viewers can avoid it by being selective about what they watch, but that images of a high-consumption lifestyle are constant and cannot be avoided except by not watching. In their view, television's criminogenic effect could ultimately be attributed to the arousal of feelings of relative deprivation and frustration in viewers, caused by constant exposure to high levels of consumption, rather than to the learning of larcenous values or robbery techniques from watching theft on television.[68] Describing the process, they speculated:

BOX 5.2   A Unique Study Opportunity: U.S. Crime Rates, Before and After Television

---

Hennigan and her colleagues (1982) took advantage of one aspect of the introduction of television into the United States:

Television did not diffuse rapidly to all communities in the United States at the same time. Instead, the rapid spread of television broadcasting stations was artificially staggered between 1949 and mid-1952. Therefore, some communities gained access to television before the freeze while others had to wait until the freeze was lifted. If the introduction of television caused an increase in crime, the level of crime in the prefreeze communities should increase more than in postfreeze communities shortly after the prefreeze communities began to receive television signals. On the other hand, the level of crime in the postfreeze communities should increase relative to that in the prefreeze

communities a few years later when the freeze was lifted and the post-freeze communities began receiving signals. To be convincing, an effect found at the earlier time in prefreeze communities must be replicated at the other time in the postfreeze communities.

Graph shows larceny theft offenses known to police (logged and standardized) in prefreeze and postfreeze cities from 1936 through 1976 (the time series were standardized to aid visual inspection of the plots but they were not standardized in the analyses).

SOURCE: From "Impact of the Introduction of Television on Crime in the United States," by K. Hennigan et al., *Journal of Personality and Social Psychology* 1982, 42(3), 461–477. Copyright © 1982 by the American Psychological Association. Reprinted by permission.

Lower classes and modest life-styles were rarely portrayed in a positive light on TV, yet the heaviest viewers have been and are poorer, less educated people. It is possible that in the 1950s television caused younger and poorer persons (the major perpetrators of theft) to compare their life-styles and possessions with (a) those of the wealthy television characters and (b) those portrayed in advertisements. Many of these viewers may have felt resentment and frustration over lacking the goods they could not afford, and some may have turned to crime as a way of obtaining the coveted goods and reducing any relative deprivation.[69]

In terms of an overall aggregate effect on crime then, Hennigan's study forwards the idea that television influences property rather than personal crime, at least initially. Whether this applies today is unknown, because we can no longer separate television's influence from other contemporary social processes. Hennigan and her colleagues, however, speculate that television still does contribute to an increase in property crime rates to some unknown degree.[70]

In regard to print media, as noted earlier, there is no evidence that newspapers have any general criminal effect. After reviewing the research through 1978 concerning whether or not the reporting of crime news encourages others to commit crimes, Joseph Dominick concluded that there was little

BOX 5.2 *Continued*

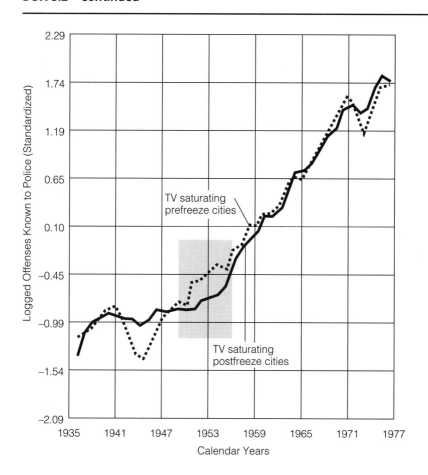

evidence supporting such an effect, and the current consensus is that there is no rigorous evidence indicating a general relationship between the print media and crime.[71] In sum, the limited aggregate research suggests that the visual media may very well affect crime independently of their effect on aggressiveness or the violence of their content. One area of research, however, does indicate that violent content in a particular context may indeed be criminogenic.

Pornography

Given that crime is normally considered aberrant behavior, an examination of aberrant media suggests itself. It is commonly believed that a link exists between pornography and criminal acts and that pornography has negative social effects.[72] The theoretical positions regarding pornography are analogous to those held concerning the general media and viewer aggression. Two basic views compete: One posits a stimulating effect, hypothesizing that pornography encourages viewers to act violently toward women; the other, a cathartic effect, holding that pornography cannot change people's fundamental sexual natures but can help them resolve inner conflicts by releasing anger toward women without overt aggression.[73] In 1972, however, the Commission on Obscenity and Pornography published findings contrary to these commonly held perceptions. In its report, the commission stated, first, that rapists reported significantly less exposure to pornography than the general public. Second, a higher percentage of male child molesters (when compared with the general public) reported never having been exposed to pornography. Third, in total, all types of sex deviants interviewed reported less than average exposure to pornographic materials than the general population.[74] In addition, in reviewing Denmark's experiment with unrestricted legalized pornography, Kutchinsky noted that Denmark experienced a large decrease in minor sex crimes and a small decrease in rape and attempted rape.[75] Finally, the commission report stated that only 2 percent of the general U.S. public considered pornography a serious problem. Because of these findings, the commission concluded in its 1972 report that pornography is generally harmless and that exposure to pornography is relatively innocuous and without lasting or detrimental effects.

Not surprisingly, given the morally laden nature of the topic, the conclusions of the 1972 report were not universally accepted.[76] In fact, perceptions of pornography apparently reversed for the majority of Americans, who over the past twenty years have reported feeling that pornography does lead people to commit rape.[77] For example, despite the lack of empirical evidence, Court[78] argued that there was a causal link between the level of access to pornography and serious sexual crime. He cited the increased availability of material featuring sadomasochism and bestiality, reports of snuff films—sexually explicit films in which a person is actually murdered—the use of rape as an entertainment theme, and a wave of sadistic pornography as all evidencing a link between pornography and sex crimes. The feminist movement also spurred new research efforts, and in the years following the 1972 report, a number of contrary findings were reported.[79]

Two subsequent federal reports—one authored by the U.S. Department of Health and Human Services and published in 1982, the other, *The Final Report of the Attorney General's Commission on Pornography*, published in 1986 by the U.S. Department of Justice—came to the opposite conclusion from the 1972 report. According to both reports, later research indicated that pornography has sexually harmful effects in certain circumstances. Studies had shown, for example, that films that are both pornographic and violent can trigger aggression toward women.[80] In comparison to nonaggressive pornographic material (sex between mutually consenting adults), "aggressive pornography" (forced, violent sex depicted as "pleasurable rape") increases male viewers' subsequent aggressiveness toward females, but not toward males.[81] It has also been reported that violent pornography increases the willingness of a man to say that he would rape a woman,[82] increases aggressive behavior against women in a laboratory setting,[83] strengthens the attitude that women want to be raped (belief in the rape myth),[84] and decreases viewers' sensitivity to rape and sympathy for a rape victim.[85]

Bolstered by these laboratory studies and the conclusions of the government reports, sexually violent material has subsequently been targeted as the most influential and socially harmful type of media content with the greater concern being generated by violent rather than sexual content.[86] As Comstock[87] notes:

> At this point the recent research on the effects of violent pornography becomes relevant. It appears that the [1972] commission on obscenity and pornography may have been precipitous in its conclusions that exposure to pornography has no influence on antisocial behavior. More recent experiments indicate that pornography featuring violence against women stimulates subsequent aggression toward women, and especially so when the victim in the portrayal appears to gain some pleasure from the violence directed against her. The factor most clearly implicated as responsible is the portrayal of violence against a female in an erotic context. It is the presence of aggressive behavior [in the media] that results in the display of heightened aggressiveness [in male subjects].

In an attempt to determine whether or not these laboratory-elicited relationships have counterparts in the larger society, several studies have examined the relationship between pornography and rape rates. These studies compared state-by-state differences in rape rates with state-by-state differences in pornography consumption and reveal a positive correlation between rape rates and sex-oriented magazine purchases.[88] However, when a measure of hypermasculinity is introduced, the relationship disappears. *Hypermasculinity* refers to support for traditional male-dominant, masculine attitudes and values; such as that women shouldn't work, that husbands should make all decisions, that men shouldn't show emotions, exhibit pain, or discuss feelings, that women should please men, and that women should be physically attractive. Segments of the population and ethnic groups that value these attitudes tend to have high rates of rape and high use of pornography.

This research therefore shows a significant relationship between sex-oriented magazine sales and rape rates but does not establish a causal one—other factors, particularly variations in the level of a hypermasculine culture, better explain the differing rape rates between localities.[89] This underlying macho ethic, when strong, is suggested as accounting for both high pornography consumption and high rape rates.[90]

General exposure to sexually explicit media does not emerge as a strong predictor of sexual crimes, but violent sexual media depictions have been clearly associated with negative attitudes toward rape victims and an increased self-reported likelihood that subjects would use sexual force.[91] As with media violence, however, it must be noted that most people are exposed to sexually explicit media (90 percent of males and 80 percent of females according to the 1972 commission report), and though most become aroused, few become sexually deviant in attitudes or behavior.[92] There is little evidence that increased availability of pornography increases sexual crimes such as rapes, and some evidence that it may decrease some sexual crimes such as child molestation.[93] Hence, few are prepared to blame the media as the primary cause of sexual violence or callous attitudes toward women, but media exposure is identified as being one among many contributors.[94] It is the linking of sex and violence in the media that emerges as especially pernicious, not the explicitness of the sexual activity. Pornography's negative effects appear to operate not through sexual arousal of viewers but through heightening the aggressiveness of a number of at-risk males and negatively influencing the attitudes toward sexual violence of an even larger number of nonaggressive males.

In sum, sexually violent pornography, because of its effects on hypermasculine males, presents the clearest and gravest danger,[95] though some still question even this link, and the methodology and generalizability of the research have been severely criticized.[96] Findings in this area continue to be mixed and the debate continues. Effects are hard to predict and when they occur tend to be haphazard, unreliable, and of low magnitude. Sexually violent images are thought to facilitate aggression by influencing cultural attitudes and beliefs regarding relationships and sex roles—specifically, by normalizing aggression toward women for men in sexual and other interpersonal encounters and increasing the tolerance for aggression toward women in the larger culture.[97] However, whether or not the connection between sexually violent content and antisocial attitudes actually causes increases in sexually coercive behavior is yet unproved.[98] Despite these caveats, there is increasing evidence that sexual violence against women need not be portrayed in explicit sexual media to have negative effects.[99] Of particular concern are the popular R-rated slasher films, which do not fit the general definition of pornography yet—due to their availability to young males—may be even more deleterious than X-rated films in their social impact.[100]

If one accepts the premise that sexually violent content has negative behavioral effects, the immediate policy problem is what to do about the pernicious effects of sexually violent material. Educational debriefings have been found to be useful in reversing the negative attitudinal effects, and some have suggested that society develop educational material to debunk the pleasurable rape myth and counter other attitudinal effects.[101] As in the recent campaign against child pornography, some also recommend a public policy goal aiming at the curtailment and eventual elimination of sexually violent material (regardless of its industry rating) that portrays violence against women as pleasurable, rewarding, and acceptable.[102]

The research findings on media violence and aggression, and pornography and sexual crimes, indicate that the media affect preexisting sets of at-risk individuals, some portion of whom will have the mix of characteristics that make them prone to display media-induced acts of aggression, sexual or otherwise. With sexually violent material there are clear links between the media and antisocial attitudes about sexual crime. Sexually violent material creates a social reality where a particular view of women and sex roles dominates. When combined with the research on media violence, the research on pornography indicates imitative modeling as the likely short-term mechanism through which the media influence individuals. Nonetheless, that these attitudes translate into an actual increase in the commission of sexual crimes, though suggested, has not been proved by the research. The implication of modeling leads to a concern with copycat crime—crime directly triggered by and emulated and constructed from media portrayals, another commonly acknowledged but poorly investigated media phenomenon. The epitome of the social construction of reality process in crime and justice is demonstrated by the phenomenon of copycat crime, for in copycat crime you have a media-constructed crime reconstructed by a copycat criminal.

COPYCAT CRIME:
ITS NATURE AND REALITY

The first issue to be addressed concerning copycat crime is whether or not it actually occurs. There is no lack of information on how to commit crimes available in the mass media. A large body of printed matter detailing how to commit specific crimes is readily available.[103] These texts come complete with diagrams and directions on how to commit robberies, murder, and numerous acts of terrorism. What seems a simple matter, however—determining when a copycat crime has occurred—is complicated by the intrinsic nature of copycat crime. For a crime to be a copycat crime it must have been inspired by an earlier, publicized crime—that is, there must be a pair of crimes linked by the media. The perpetrator of a copycat crime must have been exposed to the publicity about the original crime and must have incorporated major elements of that crime into his or her crime. The choice of victim, the motivation, or the technique in a copycat crime must have been lifted from the earlier, publicized crime. These limits make identifying copycat crimes for study problematic because two independent but similar crimes may be erroneously labeled a copycat pair, and true copycat crimes may easily go unrecognized and unidentified. Research is further complicated because the size of the at-risk pool—the number of individuals who are likely to be criminally influenced by the media—is unknown but probably small and therefore difficult to identify, isolate, and study. Moreover, not enough copycat criminals have been identified to allow for generalization or for scientifically adequate research.

Historically, references to possible copycat effects began appearing as soon as the mass media developed in the early 1800s.[104] How-to manuals for terrorist acts can be traced to the writings of Johann Most, who in his 1885 work, *Revolutionary War Science*, published instructions for making nitroglycerin and dynamite, inflammable liquids, and poisons, and advocated their use in radical bombings and attacks. The 1886 Chicago Haymarket Square bombing is thought to have been a result.[105] The film industry in the 1920s adopted a self-imposed code that forbade crimes shown on film to teach methods of crime, inspire potential criminals with a desire for imitation, or make criminals seem heroic and justified.[106] The courts have also had to address the existence of copycat crime, and there have been many attempts to hold publishers or broadcasters liable for damages when someone engages in harmful conduct shown in the media. Almost without exception the courts have refused.[107] The courts have held that "mere abstract teaching" that sanctions violence is not the same as inducing specific individuals to commit specific murders and has not held the media liable for acts performed by media consumers.[108]

The shooting of President Reagan by John Hinckley Jr., a case in which news and entertainment merged, is a prime example of a copycat crime. Hinckley's assassination attempt on President Reagan and Hinckley's bizarre life fit the psychotic-killer theme popular in crime-related entertainment (see Chapter 2). Because of this overlap, the Hinckley story provided the media with both great entertainment material and great news material, having elements of drama, celebrities, money, and filmed violence. The entertainment media provided the role model and reality structure Hinckley followed in formulating his assassination attempt, which then provided the news media the frame they used to fit the resulting news story into an entertainment-style theme:

> Hinckley's story was perfect for news media, and television news in particular, as it went beyond the usual character of a major news story. . . . The Hinckley case not only had drama, a famous person, and filmed violence, it had an unexpected and fascinating twist. . . . [Hinckley] was motivated by an apparent irrational desire to impress a movie star. As reported by network television news, the Hinckley story was also framed within the typical prime-time television perspectives of simplicity and ideal norms. To this end, Hinckley was characterized much like the psychotic killer in a fictional television drama.[109]

The Hinckley case thus displays the full range of possible effects by the media on crime and justice, from creating a tolerant atmosphere for violence, to providing criminal role models and techniques, to influencing the public reaction to the justice system's processing of the case.[110] Snow summarized the multiple media effect as follows:

> First, since Hinckley's life prior to the shooting was lived largely through the media scenario of a Hollywood film and in vicarious involvement with a media personality, media may be understood as providing a cultural context for constructing and legitimizing bizarre and even criminal behavior. Second, an examination of how network television reported the verdict supports a contention that media plays a potentially significant role in the evaluation and administration of justice. In both points, the principal idea is not that the media inevitably produce particular effects, but that the media have become an important cultural arena for defining, enacting, and legitimizing a wide range of behavior, including crime and justice.[111]

BOX 5.3   Copycat Crime in Action?

"How-to" Film May Have Inspired Subway Attack

NEW YORK — Two men armed with a bottle of flammable liquid and a match turned a token clerk's booth into an inferno inside a Brooklyn subway station early Sunday, critically injuring the clerk in an attack that officials said may have been patterned on the current movie *Money Train*.

The liquid ignited with such force that the bulletproof booth was blown apart, spraying broken glass, charred insulation and splintered wood inside the Kingston-Throop Avenue station on the A and C lines in Bedford-Stuyvesant. Trapped inside was the clerk, Harry Kaufman, 50, working an overtime shift for which he had volunteered, who suffered second- and third-degree burns over 70 to 80 percent of his body.

Judging by the power of the 1:40 a.m. blast, which was felt in apartments a block away, investigators said the arsonists, who escaped, were probably injured. A transit official said a charred glove believed to belong to one of the attackers was found on a station staircase.

Moments after the explosion, Teresa Cohen, a police sergeant responding to a 911 call, arrived at the station, where, she said, Kaufman "ran right into my arms.

"He said: 'Somebody blew up my booth. I'm hurting. I want my family. Please help me.'"

Other police officers among the first to reach the Kingston station on Fulton Street said they found an old-fashioned military assault rifle, an M-1 carbine with a clip holding 17 cartridges, lying on the floor near the demolished booth, leading investigators to guess that the attack had been a failed attempt at robbery.

Scenes from the current film depict two attacks nearly identical to the one that severely burned Kaufman, a similarity that was noted at a news conference by Mayor Rudolph Giuliani, Police Commissioner William Bratton and Alan Kiepper, president of the Transit Authority.

Kiepper and Joseph R. Hofmann, the Transit Authority's senior vice president in charge of subways, said the agency allowed some parts of the film, starring Wesley Snipes and Woody Harrelson, to be shot in the subway system. But they said the authority would not cooperate in the making of violent scenes involving arson, shootings and explosions, and that these were filmed entirely in Los Angeles sound stages.

The film deals with the robbery of the train that nightly collects each token booth's receipts.

By RICHARD PEREZ-PENA
New York Times Service. Reprinted by permission.

In the final analysis, the news media's emphasis on drama, violence, and entertainment and the entertainment media's programming emphasis on themes of violent criminality appear to work together to foster copycat crimes such as Hinckley's simply for notoriety.[112]

However, although the term *copycat crime* has appeared in the academic literature for many years,[113] few empirical studies touch on this phenomenon. Researchers have therefore relied on anecdotal evidence to argue the existence of a copycat crime phenomenon. The slowly growing file of compiled anecdotal reports does, in fact, indicate that criminal events that are rare in real life are sometimes committed soon after similar events are shown as part of a fictional show or a news story.[114] Collectively, this file provides significant and growing evidence of copycat crime.

Other research evidence that copycat crime is a real phenomenon—not just a linking of similar sequential but independent crimes—originated in the laboratory research discussed earlier, in which viewers of media violence imitated the violence. The observation that people will mimic media behavior in the laboratory lends credence to the hypothesis that people are mimicking media-portrayed crimes in society. Stronger evidence of copycat crime's significance was established through a link between the level of coverage of an event and the number of similar events occurring after this coverage. For example, a number of studies found that the suicide rate increased with the level of media coverage of a suicide of a famous person.[115] After reviewing U.S., Canadian, and European studies, Lesyna and Phillips concluded that suicides rise significantly following the front-page publicizing of a suicide. Similarly, both television news stories of suicide and fictional television suicide stories also appear to elicit imitative suicides.[116]

The Werther Effect

The media-generated copycat effect on suicides is termed the Werther effect, after a fictional hero who committed suicide in a novel by Goethe. This fictional suicide was felt to have triggered imitative suicides throughout Europe in the nineteenth century.[117] Similarly, Phillips calculated that within two months after the suicide of Marilyn Monroe in 1962 there were three hundred more suicides than would have occurred had she not died. The most disturbing finding is that media portrayals of suicide, even in the news[118] or in antisuicide programming,[119] appear to trigger imitative suicides, particularly among teenagers. The more publicity, the greater the increase in suicides, with the increase in suicides greatest in the region where the story was most heavily publicized.[120] The link is particularly strong for stories aired on multiple TV stations and for teenagers.[121] Although not without contradiction,[122] this set of research indicates that fictional and nonfictional stories widely publicized by the mass media can trigger fatal imitative behavior.

There is also some evidence of a link between the level of coverage and the number of similar subsequent events with regard to criminal acts. It has been reported that just after the appearance of newspaper and television accounts of a heavyweight prize fight, the number of reported homicides increases by about one-eighth, with the increase greatest for the most highly publicized fights, and the homicides tending to involve victims of the same race as the loser of the fight.[123]

The anecdotal cases in combination with the research on suicide and other coverage studies establish reasonable grounds for concluding that copycat crimes occur regularly at an unknown but significant rate.[124] One now-dated study did examine the ability of the media to directly criminalize law-abiding persons. In 1973 Milgram and Shotland found no evidence of an imitative effect from a single portrayal of a crime followed by an opportunity to commit a similar crime a week later. The difficulty with this study is that an effect

The aftermath of John Hinkley's assassination attempt on President Reagan. The shooting is one of the most famous copycat crimes.

AP Laserphoto

would have to be incredibly strong for a single show to affect a randomly selected group of previously noncriminal subjects to steal or not to steal.[125] The suicide studies are felt to measure the influence of the media on predisposed individuals and a media criminogenic effect is likely to affect a select number of already at-risk persons.[126]

Magnitude

The anecdotal cases broadly suggest that the copycat phenomenon may affect societal crime in two ways. First, the media coverage may both trigger the occurrence of crime and shape its form, creating crime that otherwise would

BOX 5.4   Copycat Crimes

Anecdotal examples of copycat crimes include the following:

In Texas, a group of black kids imprisoned for a string of robberies claimed that they "got hyped" on rappers Easy E and N.W.A. Four youths who shot and wounded two Las Vegas police officers are alleged to have been motivated by Ice-T's "Cop Killer." The film *Menace II Society* has been cited by a trial judge for providing a script for two youths accused of robbing and killing a motorist and four teen boys told authorities that the same movie motivated them to steal a car, wound one man, and kill another (Ferrell, forthcoming).

MTV cartoon characters Beavis and Butthead have been blamed for inciting children to start sometimes fatal fires (Ostrow 1993).

Three teenagers died when they imitated a stunt from the Disney film *The Program* (Tucker 1993).

The film *New Jack City* has been associated with theater lobby fights, the killing of a teenager during a shootout outside a theater, and the exchange of gunshots outside other theaters (*USA Today* 3/12/91).

Three drunken men in Germany were jailed for throwing manhole covers from a highway bridge after reading about a similar prank in the papers (Reuters News Service 1991).

In Seattle, a fifteen-year-old girl laced a peanut butter sandwich with poison intended for an eleven-year-old playmate. She got the idea from the movie *Heathers*. The dispute was over a videotape of the same movie (Associated Press 1991).

Two men armed with flammable liquid burned a clerk's booth inside a Brooklyn subway station, patterned on a crime in the movie *Money Train* (Perez-Pena 1995).

A Canadian boy attempted to extort $50,000 from a local mayor after watching an episode of *Starsky and Hutch* (Nettler 1982).

A nine-year-old girl was raped by several girls on a California beach a few days after a television movie was shown. In the movie a young female is raped in a similar fashion by three other teenagers in a juvenile reformatory (Pease and Love 1984b).

In Boston, a woman was doused with gasoline and set afire following a movie on television in which teenage boys roam Boston burning tramps for fun and amusement (Pease and Love 1984b).

The same evening that a television movie about a battered wife who pours gasoline on her sleeping husband was shown, a man poured gasoline on his sleeping wife and set her afire, saying he was trying to frighten her (Pease and Love 1984b).

An eleven-year-old boy murdered a postman in imitation of an adventure show (Pease and Love 1984b).

Following a television movie called *Doomsday Flight,* airlines reported a number of extortion calls making bomb threats (Schmid and de Graaf 1982, pp. 131–132).

And, of course, two of the most infamous copycat crime episodes are the Tylenol copycat poisonings, in which the initial murders occurred after the victims had purchased Extra-Strength Tylenol that had been laced with cyanide. The story received intense national coverage, and within a short time copycat poisonings and product tamperings were reported across the nation.

And John Hinckley Jr.'s assassination attempt on President Reagan. Hinckley was emulating the main character in the movie *Taxi Driver.*

not exist and turning formerly law-abiding individuals into criminals. The result would be an immediate increase in both the number of crimes and the number of criminals within a society. Second, the media coverage may shape the criminal behavior of already active criminals, molding the characteristics of crime without actually triggering it.

The scant evidence that is available concerning copycat crime does not support the first scenario as a common outcome.[127] There is no empirical research evidence of a direct media criminalizing effect.[128] The media do appear to heighten the sophistication and brutality of criminals, especially among those who rely heavily on the media for information about the world and who have a tenuous grasp on reality. For example, in the anecdotal case histories, most individuals who mimic media crimes have prior criminal records or histories of violence, indicating that the effect of the media is more likely qualitative (affecting criminal behavior) rather than quantitative (affecting the number of criminals).[129] The conclusion is that the media influence how people commit crimes to a greater extent than they influence whether or not people actually commit crimes.[130] Hence the media are important in the genesis of crime, but not as important as they would be if they were continually criminalizing individuals.

Nevertheless, most of the evidence supporting even this circumscribed view is anecdotal and the empirical research is limited. A few researchers have examined offender populations to assess the proportion of copycat criminals and the role of the media in motivating their crimes. In one study by Heller and Polsky, a hundred young male offenders were interviewed and twenty-two reported trying criminal techniques they had seen on television, with only three of them reporting failure or arrest. Another twenty-two disclosed that they had contemplated committing crimes they had seen on television. In another interesting report, compiled by an offender serving a life term, Hendrick surveyed 208 of 688 inmates at Michigan's Marquette Prison regarding their use of television as a source of crime techniques. He reported that many prisoners took notes while watching crime shows and that nine out of ten inmates said they learned new tricks and increased their criminal expertise by watching crime programs. In addition, four out of ten reported that they had attempted specific crimes they had seen on television. A random survey by Pease and Love at the federal correctional institution at Butner, North Carolina, reported similar findings.

All these results are interesting and suggestive, but because of the limited samples and methodologies and because all three efforts examined only adult male offender populations, statements about copycat crimes remain tentative. Whether or not one can generalize from the available research to a wider population of offenders or to nonoffenders is unknown. In addition, none of the researchers examined for differences between the self-reported copycat criminals and noncopycat criminals. With these limitations in mind, the anecdotal evidence and the findings of the narrow, offender-focused research together indicate that the current best supposition is that copycat crimes are largely limited to but significant among the existing offender population (influencing somewhere between 20 percent and 40 percent), and rare but not unknown among the general noncriminal population. As Heller and Polsky state:[131]

> A significant number of our subjects, already embarked on a criminal career, consciously recall and relate having imitated techniques of crimes. . . . For such men, detailed portrayals of criminal techniques must be viewed as a learning process. None of our subjects ascribed any causative role to television viewing. . . . They would, in all probability, have engaged in the same pursuits, but their style was influenced to some degree by previously having watched skillful experts perform similar tasks on television.

Hendrick[132] and Pease and Love[133] also report that offenders seldom cite the media as a motivating source. Pease and Love reported that only about 12 percent of the inmates in their study named the media as a cause in their criminality, ranking them second to last behind all other possible factors except for "too much junk food." However, 21 percent of their inmates endorsed the media as a source of information about crime techniques. Ironically, copycat criminals may be more attuned to literature than the general public as books and magazines were most often cited, followed closely by movies about crime. Overall, the media ranked fourth as a source of information about crime, behind *developed techniques by myself, friends,* and *fellow inmates*—categories similar to the general information sources used to construct one's social reality—*personal experiences, family and friends,* and *peer groups.* The development of copycat crime and the social construction of reality appear to follow similar lines. The media are active in both areas but other sources of knowledge take precedence when they are available.

If there is a consensus regarding copycat crime and the media it is that the effect is concentrated in preexisting criminals. Pease and Love conclude that except for isolated cases of mentally ill individuals, copycat offenders have the criminal intent to commit a particular crime before they copy a publicized technique. Few reports have suggested that copycat crime occurs because otherwise law-abiding people are influenced by the media to do so.[134] The same holds true for terrorist acts. The scenario of the media triggering copycat crimes is not found to be pervasive or significant. But the shaping of the activities of existing criminals, though admittedly based on very limited research at this time, appears to be substantively important and may significantly affect overall crime. Cressey,[135] studying motion pictures in the 1930s as part of the Payne Fund studies, reached the same conclusion more than sixty years ago. In his view, young men, when suitably predisposed, sometimes use techniques of crime they have seen in the movies, but movies do not entice "good" boys into crime.[136] In regard to copycat crime, the media are a rudder more than a trigger for crime.

Theory and Model

By what mechanism do the media generate copycat effects? Here again, direct research is limited. In that the concept implies the imitation of an initial crime, the most obvious starting point in discussing copycat crime is imitation. Gabriel Tarde[137] in the beginning decades of this century was the first to offer a theoretical discussion of copycat crime. Focusing on violent crime and observing that sensational violent crime appears to prompt similar incidents, he coined the term *suggesto-imitative assaults* to describe the phenomenon. In a pithy summation, he concluded, "Epidemics of crime follow the line of the telegraph." Tarde's line of research was largely ignored until the 1970s, however, when a surge of copycat crimes and media interest in them led to renewed attention to the role of imitation in the generation of crime. Picking up directly from Tarde's earlier perspective, researchers have most often attributed copycat crime to a process of simple and direct imitation generated by observation-based social learning.[138]

More recently, imitation has been criticized as too simplistic a process to fully explain copycat crime—it fails to explain why most children imitate aggression within socially acceptable limits and only a few imitate aggression with a real gun.[139] Critics have also noted that imitation theory focuses on the copycat criminal and tends to downplay other contextual social factors. Given these limitations, imitation is considered a necessary but insufficient factor in the generation of copycat crime. The primary flaw in imitation theory is that it generally implies that the copycat behavior must physically resemble the portrayed behavior and therefore falls short in explaining any generalized effects or innovative applications.[140] Note that Hennigan and her colleagues[141] earlier dismissed imitation as an explanation for the aggregate criminal effects they discovered from the introduction of TV, and that the self-report studies of copycat offenders found more links to general property crime than to violent crime.[142]

Partly in response, Berkowitz[143] has posited another mechanism, more general than imitation, by which media portrayals may activate similar behaviors. Through this mechanism, termed a *priming* effect, the portrayals of certain behaviors by the media activate a network of associated ideas and concepts within the viewer that increase the likelihood that he or she will behave similarly but not necessarily identically.[144] Priming holds that when people read or hear or witness an event via the mass media, ideas having a similar meaning are activated for a short time and these thoughts can activate related actions.[145] Thus, regarding violent media, viewers will have an increased likelihood of hostile thoughts, believe aggression is justified, and behave aggressively.[146] The mass media are perceived as *priming* consumers by giving importance to certain events and pushing the issues associated with these events to the forefront.[147] Priming can also be understood within the general perspective of this work as the forwarding of a set of ideas and beliefs that support a particular social reality—the perception that the nature of the world is such that a particular type of crime is appropriate, justified, and likely to be successful.

Berkowitz feels that priming offers a conceptual explanation of both prosocial and antisocial media effects, as well as explaining the effects reported in the studies of suicide and aggregate crime effects discussed earlier. He concludes that priming occurs within a multifactor model incorporating the media content, the viewing setting, and viewer interpretations, predispositions, characteristics, and identifications. A study by Mazur[148] offers an example of this process in the area of crime. Mazur reported that bomb threats directed at nuclear energy facilities increased significantly following increases in news coverage of nuclear power issues. Mazur's study is important in that it indicates that the media may initiate crimes even when they don't provide precise models to copy, as the bomb threats to nuclear facilities followed news stories that were not necessarily bomb-related. In Berkowitz's conceptualization, the news media coverage primed those who made the bomb threats but did not model the behavior. John Hinckley Jr.'s assassination attempt on President Reagan is a well-known anecdotal example of a crime where media priming also appears to have occurred.

The evidence concerning copycat crime supports the proposition that predisposed, at-risk individuals, primed by media characterizations of crime, are the primary perpetrators of copycat crime.[149] This proposition suggests the model of copycat crime shown in Figure 5.4. Copycat crime is seen as a result of the interaction of four factors: the initial crime and criminal, the media coverage, the social context, and the characteristics of the copycat criminal.[150] The reiterative model denotes a process in which select, usually successful, highly newsworthy crimes or crimes shown in popular entertainment media emerge as candidates for copying. The media coverage first affects individuals by inviting them to identify with the initial crime or criminal, and thereafter priming a pool of potential copycat criminals. The size of this pool is affected both by the level of media coverage and by other social context factors such as norms regarding deviance and violence; the preexistence of social conflicts; the number of opportunities available to the potential offender to copy a crime technique (there are more opportunities to copy a car theft technique, for example, than a bank robbery technique); the nature, credibility, and pervasiveness of the mass media; and the size of the preexisting criminal population. The nature of the media coverage and content and the characteristics of the social context are felt to mutually influence one another.[151] After the at-risk pool emerges, the first wave of copycat crimes results through a process of generalized imitation, limited by and adapted to the copycat criminal's opportunities (see Figure 5.4, Phase A).

Should these first-order copycat crimes receive further media attention, and particularly should they be incorporated into a news media crime theme, the likelihood of additional copycat crime increases (see Phase B of Figure 5.4). This extended reiterative process is regarded as much more likely to occur with violent crime because of the high news value of violence. Thus, the model reflects a paradox. The process is more common for property crime and property offenders through first-order copycat crimes (Phase A). But violent copycat crime and offenders are most likely to generate second- and

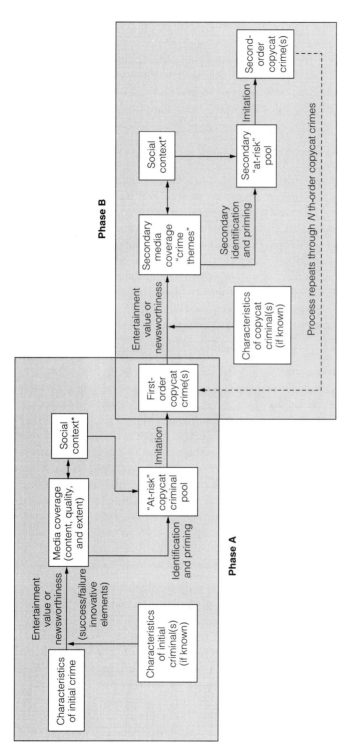

FIGURE 5.4 A Reiterative Model of Copycat Crime

*Social context includes social norms regarding crime, news reporting and entertainment; opportunities to copy; social tensions (racism, economic strife, and so forth); organization of mass media (state, private, nonprofit, accessibility, regulation, audience size, and credibility).

Adapted from Raymond Surette, *The Media and Criminal Justice Policy*, 1990. Courtesy of Charles C. Thomas, Publisher, Springfield, Illinois.

higher-order imitations (Phase B), as they are more likely to become the focus of intensive news coverage. Once more in regard to crime, the mass media take the rare real-world event and make it the more significant, better known event in the public's perception of social reality. The expanded social construction of copycat crime is more likely to be of a violent crime like a bombing—while all the evidence points toward copycat property crimes as far more common.

Copycat Crime and Terrorism

Terrorism's relationship to the media epitomizes the interplay between crime and the media and the dangers of copycat effects. Two statements capture the situation very well: "In many ways, the modern terrorist is the very creation of the media,"[152] and "If the mass media did not exist, terrorists would have to invent them."[153] The development of this symbiotic relationship can be traced to the fact that news media and terrorists share several needs. Most fundamentally, both are trying to reach the greatest number of people possible. Driven by these mutual needs, a new type of terrorist has emerged in this century— the media-oriented terrorists who script their violence to earn publicity[154] and therefore target more newsworthy symbolic victims. Media-oriented terrorism is "propaganda by deed," a symbolic rhetorical crime and a special type of coercive media event.[155] Media-oriented terrorists are guided by five principles.[156] First, their acts are aimed at the audience, not tactical in nature. Second, victims are chosen for symbolic meaning to maximize fear and public impact. Third, the media are eager to cover terrorist violence. Fourth, the media can be activated, directed, and manipulated for propagandistic effect. Fifth, target governments are at a disadvantage, their only choice is between censorship and allowing terrorists to use the media. The ample evidence of the general validity of these principles in operation has resulted in the contagion of media-oriented terrorism, which has diffused around the planet.[157]

To the degree that a failed terrorist act is one that nobody notices, terrorists have come to focus especially on and manipulate television coverage,[158] and electronic media publicity is now the sole objective in many terrorist acts.[159] Carlos Marighella,[160] a Communist insurgent terrorist in the 1960s, described the manipulation of the media by terrorists as follows:

> These actions, carried out with specific and determined objectives, inevitably become propaganda material for the mass communication system. . . . The war of nerves or psychological war is an aggressive technique, based on the direct or indirect use of mass means of communication and news in order to demoralize the government. In psychological warfare, the government is always at a disadvantage since it imposes censorship on the mass media and winds up in a defensive position by not allowing anything against it to filter through. At this point it becomes desperate, is involved in great contradictions and loss of prestige, and loses time and energy in an exhausting effort at control which is subject to being broken at any moment.

Like politicians, terrorists, too, have learned to manipulate coverage to bypass the editing and contextual formatting of journalists and go directly to the public with their messages.[161] In the process, terrorism has become a form of mass entertainment and public theater and thus highly valuable to media organizations.[162]

For the news organization, terrorism is dramatic, often violent, visual, and timely, and attracts high public interest.[163]

> Unlike wars and most revolutions which are usually protracted and highly complex events . . . acts of terrorist violence normally have a beginning and an end, can be encompassed in a few minutes of air time, possess a large degree of drama, involve participants who are perceived by the viewing public as unambiguous, and are not so complex as to be unintelligible to those who tune in only briefly.[164]

All of this transforms terrorism into high ratings and readership levels. And as the media have pursued terrorists, terrorists have become media-wise. They now understand the dynamics of newsworthiness and the benefits of news coverage: increased legitimacy and political status, heightened perception of their strength and threat, and an increased ability to attract resources, support, and recruits.

Since terrorism sells so well and coverage of these episodes has become extensive, it is hardly surprising that criticism of the coverage has been common. The negative effect from coverage that generates the greatest concern is a copycat effect.[165] Within the academic literature about terrorism, no doubts are expressed that the media motivate copycat terrorist acts.[166] In sum, the media can provide the potential terrorist with all the ingredients needed to engage in terrorism. The media can reduce inhibitions against the use of violence. They can offer models and provide technical know-how. And though extra-media factors are probably equally important, the media are felt to provide sufficient impetus in themselves to lead to imitative acts in a number of instances.[167]

Additionally, competition for news coverage tends to cause terrorist violence to escalate.[168] Many more acts of terrorism are committed than are reported in the media.[169] More violent and more dramatic acts are necessary to gain news coverage as the shock value of ordinary acts diminishes. As long as news reporting is a commercial product whose content is influenced by sensationalism, excessive coverage will afford violent terrorist acts a disproportionate significance.[170] As terrorist groups have learned to design their acts for the media and publicity, terrorist acts have become more violent. Occupation of a building, for example, no longer garners world or even national coverage in most instances and without the potential of a confrontation will not receive even extensive local coverage in many cases. The relationship between terrorism and the media is ultimately not qualitatively different from other criminogenic effects of the media on society. The relationship is clearer only because the links are more observable and because terrorists and the media so openly pursue each other.

Media-oriented terrorists will frequently use hostages or create other terrorist acts designed to gain media attention. Shown are U.S. hostages being held in Iran in 1979.

SIPA

Copycat Crime: A Summary

The available research suggests that copycat crime appears to be a persistent social phenomenon, common enough to influence the total crime picture. It works mostly by influencing criminals' choice of crime techniques rather than by motivating criminal acts. Copycat criminals are more likely career criminals involved in property offenses rather than first or violent offenders (although a violent copycat episode will receive an immense amount of media coverage when identified). The specific relationship between media coverage and the generation of copycat crime remains unknown, as do the social context factors that are most important. The most likely mechanism behind copycat crime is a process of identification and priming leading to some degree of generalized imitation. There is no empirical evidence of a significant direct criminalizing effect on previously law-abiding individuals. The media influence how people commit crimes to a greater extent than they influence whether or not people actually commit a crime.

The interplay between media coverage and copycat terrorist crime is dual. First, anecdotal evidence indicates that coverage of a terrorist crime encourages the making of false threats in pseudo copycat reactions. For example, a bombing in New York City's Kennedy Airport was followed by more than six hundred bomb threats the next week.[171] Second, real copycat events follow in significant numbers. As with general copycat crime, there is much anecdotal evidence that terrorist events such as the stealing of a corpse (of a national hero or leader) for ransom, bank robberies in which hostages are taken, kidnappings, plane hijackings, parachute hijackings (twenty-seven from 1971 to 1977), and the planting of altitude bombs on airplanes occur in clusters.[172] These effects appear to be especially strong following a successful terrorist act using a novel approach.[173] Although their number waxes and wanes, the historical pattern of these acts suggests that copycat terrorist crime has been and remains a persistent element of the total crime picture and significantly influences the nature and goals of terrorist acts, making them less tactical and more media-oriented.

In addition, the blatant competition among the media for coverage—especially exclusive coverage—tends to degrade media news reporting and journalist behavior. Families of victims have been harassed for interviews, and terrorists have been offered payment for interviews or access to hostages.[174] Regarding public policies, the basic policy problem with regard to copycat crime is deciding when to publicize information about sensational crimes.[175] In such cases as the Tylenol poisonings[176] (see Box 5.4), there is an obvious need to warn consumers, but in other types of crimes, such as bombings and hijackings, the issue may not be so clear-cut. While acknowledging that copycat effects may result, the news media argue that the decision to publish is correct in nearly every case, but law enforcement and other public officials argue for restrictions.[177] The confusion surrounding the best policy course in regard to copycat crime is exemplified by one commentator, who exclaimed, "There seems to be only one way to end the copycat tamperings. I think it will be short lived . . . before long, copycat tamperings will become so common that they will no longer provide thrill seekers with the excitement that they crave."[178]

The paradoxical reasoning is that, over time, a publicized copycat crime will become less newsworthy from having received large amounts of prior coverage, and as a result of overexposure become less likely to recur. The logic is that the coverage will eventually result in fewer crimes committed in pursuit of coverage and notoriety—a questionable and unproved position. More proactive policies focus on the initial coverage given crimes. Suggested reforms include delaying coverage, avoiding live coverage, using screen crawl lines rather than interrupting programs, downplaying staged events, avoiding the portrayal of criminals as celebrities or heroes, avoiding crime coverage that reveals the techniques used or provides coverage of ideological and political statements, reporting that most known copycat crimes are unsuccessful, and providing fuller, long-term reporting and follow-up stories that deal with prosecution and punishment.[179] For the present, the best long-term policy course may lie in defining the characteristics of those at risk of committing copycat crimes and trying to limit their number through deterrence efforts. In the final analysis, however, some level of copycat crime may be an unavoidable part of the price of a free and private mass media.

CONCLUSION

The media do affect crime rates. Though imperfect, the evidence is extensive. Still, though most agree that the media have some effect, we don't know exactly what that effect is. Because of the nearly exclusive focus on modeled individual violence generated by the media, possible media effects such as changes in people's willingness to delay gratification, in people's sense of equity and fairness, or in the deterrent effect of penalties for crimes have yet to be explored.[180]

However, the existing research and literature from all areas (media and social aggression, suicide, aggregate crime rates, copycat crime, and terrorism) suggest the following propositions. Most people exposed to pernicious media will show no negative effects. Some smaller proportion of people—the proportion is not clear—will show slight effects concentrating more in attitudes than in behaviors. Strong behavioral effects are relatively rare and are most likely in predisposed at-risk individuals. The reality of long-term effects on a large number of people remains a distinct possibility and the media's ability to generate greater numbers of predisposed at-risk individuals appears likely. Whether specific criminogenic effects such as copycat crime, criminal aggressiveness, and antisocial and crime supportive attitudes emerge in any particular instance depends upon the highly idiosyncratic interactions of the content of a particular media product (its characterizations of crime and criminals), the media's context (the amount of coverage and length of exposure, presentation styles, and supportive exposure settings), and the social context of the exposure (preexisting cultural norms, consumer dispositions, crime opportunities, number of preexisting potential offenders).

The evidence concerning the media as a criminogenic factor supports the conclusion that the media have a significant short-term effect on some individuals. And although the media cannot criminalize someone not having criminal predispositions, media-generated copycat crime is a significant criminal phenomenon with ample anecdotal and case evidence. The recurring mimicking of dangerous film stunts by youths belies the argument that the media can have only positive behavioral effects. It is apparent that while the media alone cannot make someone a criminal, they can change the criminal behavior of a predisposed offender.

The key to media effects occurring in any particular instance then are the intermediate, interactive factors. In terms of the media, numerous interactive factors have been identified as conducive to generating aggressive effects. Among the many such factors delineated in the research: reward or lack of punishment for the perpetrator, portrayal of violence as justified, portrayal of the consequences of violence in a way that does not stir distaste, portrayal of violence without critical commentary, the presence of live peer models of violence, and the presence of sanctioning adults. This effect depends on the combined influence of social context, media context, and media content interacting with characteristics of the audience. The more heavily the consumer relies on the media for information about the world and the greater his or her predisposition to criminal behavior, the greater the effect.

Therefore, violence-prone children and the mentally unbalanced are especially at risk of emulating media violence. When sex and violence are linked, hypermasculine males are most influenced. When the news media sensationalize crime and make celebrities of criminals, the danger of imitation for notoriety increases. And when successful crime is detailed either in print or in a visual medium, some criminals will emulate it. The major unsolved question is the size of the at-risk population—at present, only a small number appear to be significantly affected. But the media also slightly affect some larger portion of the general population, particularly in fostering attitudes that support crime. Both influences are therefore important potential contributors to the total crime picture.

Finally, the electronic media's pursuit of backstage social behavior they can portray as entertainment and report as news has inexorably driven crime from its backstage social position. In media-induced crimes committed for notoriety and publicity we now witness the paradoxical situation of backstage behavior being purposely performed for front-stage consumption. Real crime, particularly when committed by terrorists, is now sometimes a pseudo-event in the spirit of Daniel Boorstin's[181] usage—created and contrived solely for the media. The media reality of crime more often becomes the social reality of crime.

The media are powerful but complex social agents whose effects need not be all negative, however. For if unplanned, haphazard media content fosters crime, perhaps planned applications of the media can help reduce it. Given the strong belief in the media's social power, it is not surprising that some have tried to use the media in positive, prosocial ways. Accordingly, Chapter 6 will examine the use of the media and media technology in constructing a reality with less crime.

CHAPTER CONCEPTS

Cathartic Effects	Priming	Copycat Terrorism
Stimulation Effects	Criminogenic Effects	Contagion
Neutral Effects	Hypermasculinity	At-Risk Consumers
Cause and Correlation	Copycat Crime	
Substantive Importance	Sexually Violent Media	

DISCUSSION QUESTIONS

1. What should be done about the media's ability to generate copycat crimes?

2. What should society's policy be regarding sexual media, violent media, sexually violent media?

3. Does it make sense that the media appear to influence property crime more than violent crime?

4. Discuss whether copycat crime is increasing.

5. Discuss how to best handle an ongoing terrorist hostage-taking event. What information should be released, and what access and restrictions should be imposed on the media?

6. What factors do you feel are more important than the media as causes of crime? Do you think that the media will become more or less important as a cause in the future? Why?

6

The Construction
of Crime and Justice

The Media as a
Cure for Crime

Much has been written concerning the mass media as a cause of crime. Somewhat unusually then, this chapter deals with the increasing number of efforts to use the media to combat crime and administer justice. These modern efforts are all conceptually rooted in the success and promise of the prosocial entertainment programs and public information campaigns of the 1960s. Those successes and subsequent advances in media technology spurred the development of a number of media-based anticrime programs and the application of media technology in criminal justice beginning in the 1970s. The first half of the chapter discusses media-based anticrime efforts, and the second half turns to the use of media technology in the criminal justice system.

Media anticrime efforts have targeted two audience groups, criminals and citizens. Programs targeting criminals include mass media public information and communication campaigns geared to deterring offenders. Programs targeting citizens include mass media public information campaigns geared to reducing victimization by encouraging people to adopt crime preventive behaviors, and programs designed to solve crimes by encouraging citizen cooperation in law enforcement investigations. In that all these program types are designed to reduce crime, media anticrime programs frequently emphasize crime control values, whereas critiques of them raise due process concerns. All crime reduction programs seek to change their target audience's perception of social reality in the hope that a perception change will result in a behavior change. The limited evaluations of these campaigns show that they are effective means of disseminating information and can sometimes influence attitudes. Not established, however, is their ability to significantly affect audience behavior.

The development of the electronic media has also meant the development of sophisticated new communications technology. This chapter discusses media technology and its application in law enforcement and judicial settings, focusing on the audio and visual communications equipment that has become available because of recent advances in mass media telecommunications. In practice, the visual media have been emphasized, with videotape, television, and camera technology playing a central role. This technology can be computer enhanced, taped or live, located at a single or several sites, and linked by various methods such as closed circuitry or microwave. In general, the ultimate goal in using media technology in the criminal justice field is to simulate a live face-to-face encounter.

The area of greatest application and concern in law enforcement involves advances in media technology that have significantly improved the surveillance capabilities of law enforcement agencies. Taking advantage of a *surveillance effect*—the psychological effect of fearing that you might be under observation—surveillance programs have expanded the traditional police use of the stakeout and hidden camera to encompass more locations and conditions. Reduced costs have given more agencies these capabilities. Media technology has made constant surveillance of broad public areas possible, and cameras permanently mounted on patrol cars and in police interrogation rooms have begun to appear. Not surprisingly, the use of this potentially powerful and intrusive technology has raised concerns at the same time that it has demonstrated clear benefits.

The increasing application of media technology within the judicial system has also changed judicial reality. In these applications participants must interact through the equipment, often testifying directly into a camera or participating by watching a television screen. In contrast to the use of media equipment in news coverage, here the technology has changed from a tangential, temporary visitor to an indispensable, permanent tool of the judiciary.

Though the use of media technology has come to be widely accepted in the presentation of physical evidence and testimony, in the creation of permanent records, and in live proceedings, only limited uses are currently supported, and the prerecording of entire trials has generally been rejected.

The acceptability of an application seems to rest on whether or not a crucial element of justice is felt to be lost in the use of the technology or in effect how much the mediated judicial reality changes the traditional judicial reality. For preliminary and short procedural steps, most participants, including defendants, appear to feel that the integrity of the process is unaffected. With regard to longer, more significant, and more symbolic steps such as trials, concerns and resistance arise, especially among defense attorneys and public defenders.

The chapter concludes with a discussion of the general usefulness of the media in combating crime and delivering justice. The media are not a panacea for crime, and though useful in specific areas, these programs have not reduced the overall crime rate. Because of their other demonstrated benefits, however—the ability to impart information and influence attitudes, the short-term ability to suppress specific crimes in specific locations, and the reduction in cost and increase in speed of processing criminal cases—the consensus view is that such programs should be expanded but closely monitored and evaluated.

CONSTRUCTING LESS CRIME—
THE MEDIA AND ANTICRIME EFFORTS

Programs that use the media to reduce and solve crimes are not new. The "Wanted Dead or Alive" posters on the Western frontier and the FBI's "Most Wanted" list are two long-standing examples of fugitive searches based on available media.[1] Print-based anticrime and preventive efforts can be traced as far back as the 1772 publication of *Hue & Cry* by John Fielding in Britain.[2] The media have also been forwarded as a potential source of reintegrative effects by which offenders could be recertified as stable, law-abiding citizens.[3]

What is new is the rapid increase in the number of media-based anticrime efforts over the 1980s and 1990s. In these recent developments, the media have been increasingly employed in both traditional advertising and entertainment formats. Popular and with broad-based support, these applications use the media to construct a social reality with less crime. To better understand the expectations of the developers of these media anticrime programs, one must first look at the literature on *prosocial* uses of the media—or efforts designed to achieve positive social effects and teach values, attitudes, or skills through the media.[4]

Prosocial media applications are modern, tangential outgrowths of the public information and communication campaigns that have a history of use in the United States dating back to the 1800s. Research on media campaigns began with the Payne Fund studies in the 1930s. In a 1933 study, the film *Birth of a Nation*—a sympathetic and romantic portrayal of the creation of the Ku Klux Klan—was shown to 4,000 junior and senior high school students.

Following the screening, students reported attitudes toward blacks that were less favorable than those held prior to seeing the film. When a number of films with the same theme were shown, the change in attitudes was cumulative. Although the effects eventually wore off, they were found to persist for a significant period of time (up to eight months).

With the establishment of the media's ability to negatively affect attitudes, planners subsequently tried to employ the media to effect planned positive changes in attitudes and perceptions. Perhaps the best known of such purposeful attempts are governmental campaign efforts especially active during World War II to get people to buy war bonds, contribute tin and rubber, conserve gas, and support the war effort. During the 1950s, media campaigns aimed at changing general social practices in health and other areas also became common. Then for a time (during the 1960s) negative research findings led to pessimism about the media's ability to influence audiences[5] and it was not until the late 1960s that attempts were made to use the media to positively influence children. Based on evaluations of these efforts, in the 1970s researchers began recognizing a limited but significant media potential for influence, and some began forwarding the possibility that the media could be used to attain limited positive goals in specific controlled circumstances.[6]

The current perspective is that the media can help form, change, and strengthen attitudes and actions in certain circumstances, but that persuasion efforts that ignore communication research findings will fail. Enough campaigns have succeeded to encourage the continued emergence of planned advertising-style communication campaigns and entertainment-style programming designed to have positive social effects.[7] The expectation that these programs can succeed is bolstered by the billions of dollars spent annually by advertisers who believe correctly that brief, thirty-second exposures, repeated over and over, significantly affect the public's behavior.[8] The feeling is, if fashion designers can cause behavior changes, so can other groups and organizations.

Whereas the earlier public information and communications campaigns had been aimed at various groups, entertainment-style prosocial programming efforts initially targeted children. The basic goal was to counteract the pervasive violent content of television. Accordingly, most research on prosocial media applications has involved children's television programs. The PBS show *Mr. Rogers' Neighborhood*, for example, has been the focus of a number of studies that found that children cooperate more, display more nurturing behavior, regulate themselves more, help others more, share more, persist longer in attempting tasks, and show more empathy, imaginativeness, and creativity after watching episodes of the show.[9] Encouraged by these findings, television programmers have designed and scheduled more prosocial programs, the best-known and most successful being *Sesame Street*.[10] Evaluations of these shows have revealed that programs of various types (animated, adventure, comedy, fantasy) all have the ability to elicit socially valued behaviors from children and adolescent viewers.[11] In contrast to the bulk of negative assessments of commercial television, regarding these programs it was concluded that "television can have beneficial effects; it is a potential force for good."[12] Some evidence has even been forwarded that prosocial media efforts can cancel out negative effects from violent content.[13]

Spurred by these findings, there developed in the 1970s a newfound enthusiasm for the mass media, and an expectation that positive media effects could be elicited in a number of social arenas—including that of crime. However, the research on prosocial uses of the media focused on the short-term viewing of special programming under special viewing conditions and thus left unanswered the question of precisely how prosocial media efforts operate over the long term in a home setting.[14] The 1982 report of the National Institute of Mental Health[15] summed up this limitation:

> Potentially, children and to some degree adults can learn constructive social behavior, for example, helpfulness, cooperation, friendliness, and imaginative play, from television viewing. It is less certain whether these positive benefits are actually being achieved. Such useful material is embedded in a complicated format and is viewed at home under circumstances not conducive to effective generalizations. Additional research is required to determine the conditions under which pro-social behavior is most likely to be learned.

Thus, although the research shows that positive effects are possible, longitudinal field studies are still needed to confirm that they appear in general social settings.[16] Despite the lack of definitive knowledge about the specific manner in which the media can best influence people, acceptance of the media's ability to do so has led to an extension of prosocial media into a variety of social areas. The result is that without clear direction and through trial and error, a variety of designs for anticrime programs have developed. In practice these designs have borrowed media techniques both from entertainment and news-style television shows and from printed public communication campaigns. However, programs using the media to try to reduce crime have encountered unanticipated problems, and success has not proved as direct or as simple as first envisioned.

MEDIA-BASED ANTICRIME EFFORTS: AN OVERVIEW

With planners driven by the promise of positive effects and the continually reducing costs and increasing capabilities of media technology, media-based anticrime programs have proliferated during the last decade. Collectively, they fall into three groups. The first group—aimed at offenders—employs deterrence programs designed to directly dissuade people from committing crimes. These programs use existing mass media advertising avenues to convey anticrime messages. A second group of projects—aimed at citizens—is victimization reduction programs. Similar in form to deterrence programs, they use existing mass media outlets to distribute information, communicate appeals, and solicit help. Programs designed to reduce victimization work to reduce opportunities for crime by inducing citizens to protect themselves. The third group of projects—citizen participation programs—are designed to increase crime clearance and arrest rates by increasing citizen cooperation with law enforcement investigation efforts. Table 6.1 summarizes the three approaches and their basic designs.

These anticrime programs incorporate content and distribution elements from successful prosocial entertainment and public communication campaigns, as well as stylistic features from mainstream entertainment, news, and advertising. The projects are clearly crime control efforts, with only secondary consideration given to due process issues. And though some make use of print media, most have concentrated their resources in the electronic visual medium of television. Except for citizen participation programs, they all also share an underlying reliance on fear as a motivating agent and a belief in the criminal justice system's ability to effectively retain, process, and punish criminals.

Lastly, each of the basic programs has been forwarded as at least a partial cure for crime. To be judged a success in actually reducing crime, these programs must ultimately change their audience's social behavior. But most are actually designed to influence attitudes and perceptions of the reality of crime under the belief that changes there will lead to changes in behavior. However, research on public information and communication campaigns has established that the mass media do well in informing people about an issue, but that changing people's attitudes is more difficult, and changing behavior more difficult still. These programs thus rest on a set of questionable premises, and they have not been able to reduce crime as initially hoped.

OFFENDER DETERRENCE PROGRAMS

Both the earliest and the most recent mass media efforts to reduce crime involve public communication campaigns about drug abuse. Antidrug media campaigns have a historical tie to the *Reefer Madness* films produced by the Federal Bureau of Narcotics in the 1930s under the direction of then Commissioner of Narcotics Harry Anslinger. Although marketed as deterrence films, in their effect and purpose they had more to do with program funding and legislation and greatly facilitated the criminalization of marijuana and the expansion of the Federal Bureau of Narcotics.[17] Evaluations of media antidrug projects during the 1970s first revealed the difficulties in using the media to help reduce crime. The failure of these initial anti–drug abuse campaigns was blamed on their inability to make drug abuse a salient social issue and the irrelevance of the campaign messages to any target audience.[18] To be effective, a media campaign must tailor its content for a specific population, and that pop-

**Table 6.1 The Three Basic Types
of Media-Based Anticrime Programs**

Basic Type of Programs	Behavior Change Sought	Mechanism	Example
Targeting offenders:			
Deterrence programs	Voluntary reduction of criminal behavior by criminals	Deterrence	Antidrug public service ad campaigns
Targeting citizens:			
Victimization reduction programs	Adoption of self-protective, crime preventive behavior by citizens	Target hardening Reduction of opportunities for crime	The McGruff "Take a Bite Out of Crime" campaign
Citizen participation programs	Increased public cooperation with and involvement in law enforcement efforts	Monetary reward Anonymity	Crime Stoppers

ulation should not be simultaneously receiving conflicting or competing information. In that these early campaigns were diffuse efforts and general mass media content was rife with prodrug images, these initial projects were fatally flawed.[19]

An additional problem faced by such media-based deterrent efforts is a short-lived psychological effect related to publicity. Termed an *announcement effect*, it follows extensive publicizing of a law enforcement or judicial policy change aimed at offenders. The announcement effect means that media deterrent effects on behavior can be generated quickly by publicizing a planned policy—but this suppression effect will be short-lived. For example, significant offender behavior changes occurred in Massachusetts following heavy publicity about the introduction of a mandatory prison term for gun-related crimes.[20] Evaluation indicated that gun assaults fell significantly immediately following introduction of the law, with a displacement effect increasing the use of other weapons (knives, bats, and so forth), only to eventually return to their preannouncement levels.[21] Another example is the announced use of Breathalyzer tests to curb drunken driving in Britain during the 1960s.[22] The planned policy change was heavily publicized and an evaluation showed a marked drop in alcohol-related accidents with the introduction of the law, followed by a slow return to prior levels. The authors reasoned that as enforcement waned and this became known, the deterrent effect followed suit. A third example with similar results involved an announcement by Connecticut authorities of plans to drastically increase enforcement of speeding laws. Speeding fell initially but slowly returned to prior levels as drivers realized that enforcement had not changed.[23] In sum, using the media to deter crime has

Media-based anticrime efforts have a long history as shown by the 1930s U.S. government-produced film *Reefer Madness.*

UPI/Corbis-Bettmann

proved a difficult task. Immediate, short-term announcement effects are easy to get but difficult to maintain. A general media deterrent effect from the publicity given to executions has also been studied.[24] The media have not shown much ability to deter serious offenses such as murder, but may have some general deterrence effect on less serious crimes.[25]

Current media-based efforts targeted at offenders reflect the difficulties revealed in the evaluative research.[26] The primary reasons for the difficulty in using the media are the lack of control over the information disseminated in the media and lack of attention to fitting media messages to specific target audiences. Where these criteria are met, as in media-based antidrug campaigns, the results are promising.[27] Regarding their ability to influence offenders, the media appear best able to deter offenders involved in victimless crimes by increasing their fear of health and social consequences and encouraging self-protective behaviors rather than by increasing their fear of punishment. In that sense, successful offender-targeted media deterrence efforts are akin to victimization reduction programs. In recognition of the effects of competing information, a series of successful lobbying efforts have worked to reduce the levels of prodrug information in the media and community-based tie-in projects help counterbalance announcement effects. The more recent media antidrug campaigns—for example, the *Media-Advertising Partnership for a Drug-Free America*—are better designed and marketed and evaluations of these efforts indicate that a media campaign can significantly affect attitudes toward drugs among preteens, teenagers, and adults.[28] Whether or not behavioral changes and reduced drug use follow as a result has yet to be substantiated, although the correlational evidence suggests they might.[29]

With the long-standing concern about violent media content, it is not surprising that a recent attempt has been made to employ antiviolence public service announcements and antiviolence programming to deglamorize and reduce violence.[30] Unfortunately, analysis of seven studies of fifteen antiviolence public service announcements and an antiviolence program found no evidence that either approach significantly affected adolescent attitudes toward violence.[31] The evaluators conclude that messages to deglamorize violence may be overwhelmed by messages that glamorize violence and may never be aired frequently enough to achieve their objective. Even given the best circumstances, the media and television in particular may only modestly affect violent attitudes and behaviors.[32]

VICTIMIZATION REDUCTION PROGRAMS

Programs aimed at reducing victimization, usually by teaching and encouraging crime prevention techniques, obviously differ from deterrence programs aimed at offenders in that the target audiences differ. However, both types of programs share the goal of trying to change individual behavior, the reliance on fear as motivation, and the difficulty of empirically demonstrating behavioral effects.

What victimization reduction campaigns strive to accomplish is the increased use of personal crime prevention techniques by citizens. Crime prevention falls under the umbrella of self-protective behaviors, which include avoiding health risks and other hazards. Identified as key variables in triggering self-protective behaviors are people's beliefs about the likelihood that they will be harmed and the severity of that harm if they do not act, the efficacy of the precautionary actions being advocated, and the costs of taking action when compared with inaction. In general, persuading people to adopt more self-protective behaviors is difficult because of complex interactions among these factors. Also, programs advocating the adoption of behaviors to help prevent possible unpleasant future events such as crime tend to be less successful than those that encourage actions with an immediately recognizable return, such as an increase in health from exercising or dieting.[33] Additionally, perceptions of the importance of crime and the effectiveness of preventive behavior vary considerably among groups, so messages must be carefully matched to sub-populations to have any effect.[34] Adding to the difficulty of determining which campaigns actually work, victimization reduction programs in general have rarely been adequately evaluated. The McGruff "Take a Bite Out of Crime" campaign in the United States has received the most extensive study.[35] On the basis of the available data, media campaigns appear able to affect people's attitudes toward crime prevention more easily than their behavior.

The McGruff campaign, which began in 1979 and is still continuing, uses national public service ads (PSAs) to increase knowledge of crime prevention and to encourage the use of crime prevention techniques.[36] The desired behaviors can be divided into individual actions to reduce personal risk of victimization, such as locking cars and doors, and community actions, such as forming crime-watch groups. Despite lack of control over the placement of the PSAs, the campaign's evaluators have reported that the campaign has had some success. Overall, 80 percent of a national sample has heard of the campaign.[37] Furthermore, of those exposed, one-third report learning something about crime prevention and about one-half report changes in their attitudes.[38] In general, there is consistent evidence of positive changes in people's knowledge about and attitudes toward crime prevention. There is also some limited self-report evidence that the McGruff media campaigns influence the behavior of potential crime victims, with about 20 percent reporting changing relevant behaviors.[39]

For some citizens, a behavioral change is apparently brought about directly through simple media reminders of anticrime actions that can be taken.[40] To date, the McGruff campaign has shown a significant ability to impart information about crime prevention and influence attitudes, and it has begun to demonstrate an association with the level of crime preventive action taken in a community. Greater effects are observed among women, less educated, lower-income, and black citizens as well as among parents with children.[41]

Marketing Fear of Crime

Given that media-generated fear underlies both the offender-targeted deterrence and the citizen-targeted antivictimization campaigns, it is important to understand the difficulty of using fear in media campaigns. Research has shown that using fear as a marketing technique and as a means of influencing behavior is problem-ridden and sometimes counterproductive. In essence,

(MUSIC UNDER)

SONG: Where have all the children gone.

Long time passing.

Where have all the children gone.

Long time ago.

Where have all the children gone.

Gone to graveyards, one by one.
Oh, when will we ever learn?
Oh, when will we ever learn?

ANNCR VO: Every day, ten children are killed by gunfire. The killing won't stop, unless you help stop it.

Call 1-800-WE PREVENT, to find out what you can do.

Not one more lost life, not one more grieving family.

Not One More.

SONG: Oh, when will we ever learn?

Ad from the McGruff campaign

Reprinted with permission from the National Crime Prevention Council, 1997.

media-generated fear and concern, if not carefully managed, can result in exactly the opposite effects of those desired.

The use of fear as a means of marketing anticrime products is logical; after all, evaluations of victimization reduction programs show that unless some fear and concern over crime is generated, the public simply won't notice the campaign.[42] However, the use of fear as a motivating mechanism is not simple and has been found to be less effective and predictable than expected. Strong appeals to fear are less effective than moderate or mild appeals to fear in motivating people to alter their behavior.[43] The discovery of this negative relationship—the greater the fear, the less the effect—led for many years to a rejection of fear as a media marketing technique. However, subsequent studies reported that the use of fear could be effective in certain circumstances and successful media campaigns based on moderate fear messages such as the antismoking campaigns of the late 1960s followed.

More recent research has indicated that both very mild and very strong appeals to fear are ineffective: Too mild an appeal fails to attract attention, whereas too strong an appeal causes people to avoid the message.[44] Accordingly, a curvilinear relationship has been postulated.[45] Optimally, a message arouses sufficient fear to attract audience attention and compel acceptance of the message and its recommendations but not so much fear that the audience avoids the message and rejects its recommendations. In addition, in product marketing, portraying the intended purchaser as the victim of some type of physical harm in an appeal to fear actually works against the message. Instead, the message should portray the harm as directed toward a surrogate target such as a spouse or child or as consisting of negative social consequences.[46] Fear also appears to be an effective motivator among those who have not seen themselves as part of the market for the recommended product or brand.[47] A good example of this technique can be found in the marketing of canned mace—long a popular product among police and mail carriers—to new markets. To increase sales, smaller, key-chain-size vials were manufactured and advertised to women as a means of stopping would-be rapists.

The research on the use of fear in marketing efforts suggests that anticrime messages aimed at the occasional criminal or drug user and focusing on the negative social consequences of discovery and arrest, particularly to loved ones, will be the most effective.[48] Media campaigns aimed at offenders must raise offenders' fear of arrest and punishment or concern for their health, while simultaneously offering viable alternatives to pursuing criminal activities. Unfortunately, the research also suggests that such efforts will not influence a core of chronic, committed career criminals or drug abusers.

Underlying these campaigns is a belief in the causal relationship shown in Figure 6.1. The programs are predicated on the belief that they will cause citizens to learn more about the risks of arrest and crime and the means to prevent it. This new information, in turn, is expected to cause a change in attitude—increasing citizens' sense of the importance of crime prevention and increasing offenders' fear of arrest or, in the case of drugs, of death or illness.

These new attitudes should finally result in the adoption of self-protective actions—citizens' taking on new crime preventive behaviors, offenders' committing less crime and abusing drugs less often. Unfortunately, program evaluations and communications research in general do not strongly support this causal chain.[49] In sum, while the trends point in the desired direction,[50] behavior changes among substantial portions of the public have not been empirically established and do not appear to follow readily from media campaigns.

As one would predict from the research on public communication campaigns, using the media to change crime-related attitudes and behaviors is a complex process. Simple audience exposure to media campaigns is not enough to ensure results. Unless carefully designed, mass media appeals are more likely to reinforce people's current behavior than they are to change it.[51]

Anyone planning a media-based anticrime program must consider that a significant proportion of the population does not perceive crime as an important personal concern, that the salience of crime varies widely across categories of individuals and communities, that the relationship between exposure to mass media and perceptions of crime is indistinct and ambiguous, and that the perception of crime as overly threatening can be counterproductive. Mass media anticrime programs must balance the need to overcome audience apathy against the need to avoid scaring the audience too much.

Five guiding principles necessary for successful mass media anticrime campaigns emerge from the research.[52] First, the information must be effectively disseminated, particularly in campaigns aimed at deterring crime. Second, the relevance of campaign information must be gauged and the varying importance of crime to different segments of the public recognized. Often creating an interest in crime as a personal issue is a necessary first step. Third, optimally, no contradictory information concerning the danger of crime or the effectiveness of anticrime measures should be present. With so much information about crime being projected in entertainment, advertising, and news, however, anticrime campaigns are unlikely to be able to gain a monopoly over crime-related information. Anticrime campaigns must therefore take the nature and sources of these counterimages into account in their design. Fourth, goals must be realistically defined to allow for both evaluation of the program and efficient use of resources. Fifth, to minimize the counterproductive effects of heightening the salience of crime as an issue by making the public believe that they are likely to be victimized, the campaign must clearly communicate what anticrime behavior it is encouraging.

To date, victimization reduction campaigns are considered useful means of disseminating anticrime information to the public and sometimes influencing related attitudes, but they appear to affect behavior only marginally, and more significant effects may be beyond their reach. To be effective, programs should tailor their messages to their audience; focus their efforts on television, which seems to have the greatest impact; stay simple; and directly and clearly instruct audiences on crime preventive behavior.[53] Most important, additional local community follow-up and the creation of community support organizations

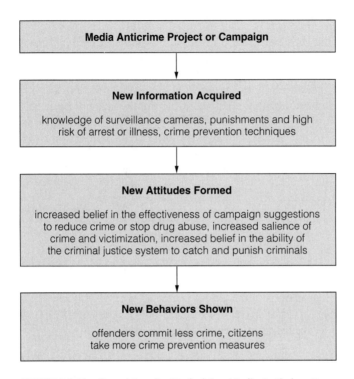

FIGURE 6.1 The Causal Premise Underlying Media Anticrime Programs

such as citizen crime watch groups are necessary to achieve lasting effects.[54] A dilemma revealed by the research is that the better the neighborhood, the less concern there is about crime but the greater the involvement in crime prevention activities and the more likely people are to report keeping watch on behalf of their neighbors.[55] Interestingly, there is also a correlation between increased knowledge of crime prevention and increased viewing of crime-related shows, indicating a general interest in crime in at least one segment of the population.[56] Recent ads in the McGruff campaign show that its developers have responded to the communications research—linking the campaign to the creation of neighborhood anticrime groups is a specific ongoing goal of the McGruff effort.[57]

Citizen Participation Programs

Programs of this last type aim to increase the level of crime-related information available to police from the public. Although having features related to the format of fact-based documentaries, these programs have many entertainment characteristics. Such programs, most commonly known as Crime Stoppers,[58] use television reenactments of crimes and radio and newspaper items to obtain information on crimes (*tips*) through anonymous phone calls. They offer reward money for useful information. The logic behind this approach is the same as that behind the "Most Wanted" reward posters of the nineteenth-century West and the FBI's "Ten Most Wanted" posters displayed in post offices. Getting the images and descriptions of wanted suspects and unsolved crimes to as many people as possible and enticing reluctant citizens with rewards increase the possibility of solving crimes and apprehending suspects. The innovation here is using the modern print and electronic mass media to distribute posters, thereby enormously increasing both the audience and the potential amount of information received.

Although such programs will normally accept information concerning any felony, specific crimes are usually selected and highlighted as "crimes of the week." Reenactments of these crimes are televised as a weekly feature and descriptions of the crimes and any suspects are carried by radio stations and newspapers.[59] Many programs also include a "most wanted" component, printing the pictures and descriptions of fugitives in newspapers and broadcasting them on television and radio. The roots for Crime Stoppers programs have been traced back to a 1960s program in Germany[60] and the first U.S. Crime Stoppers program was started in 1976 in Albuquerque, New Mexico. Currently there are more than a thousand similar programs worldwide, increasing at the rate of about a hundred programs per year.

The development of Crime Stoppers programs raises a number of issues. The first and most obvious is the effectiveness of these programs. Do they result in more arrests and solutions of crimes, and are they an efficient means of gathering information? Second, there is a question of the image of criminality that such programs project. Do they perpetuate stereotypes of criminals, victims, and crime? In publicizing crimes of the week and appealing for information, the media depict certain crimes as representative of a serious, constant, and dramatic community problem. This image of crime is felt to be the most crucial issue concerning these programs. Presented in news segments cousin to the reality programming discussed in Chapter 3, the subjects of these crime ads seem to be the real local crimes—the important, unsolved cases in the community—and the suspects look both typical and dangerous. In essence, because the crime ads are presented as representative of the actual crime in a community, the image they portray has great potential impact on the social construction of criminality. This potential leads to the third and final issue: What is the proper role of the news media in law enforcement efforts? These programs shift the media from their traditional roles as observers and reporters to being active participants in investigating crimes and hunting fugitives. In this new role, are the media rendering an acceptable public service or compromising their traditional function?

No one knows if these programs affect the crime rate. The number of cases cleared by Crime Stoppers is not great enough to expect an effect on the overall crime rate in a community unless one assumes a general deterrent effect from the mass media coverage. Neither effect has been reported. But anecdotal evidence does suggest that the programs are solving many felony cases that are unlikely to be solved otherwise,[61] and they appear especially effective in

BOX 6.1   Crime Stoppers

The structure of a typical Crime Stoppers program is as follows. The Program is under the supervision of a private nonprofit corporation. This corporation and its operating committees oversee the policy and distribution of reward money and coordinate information collection with the local law enforcement agencies. Crimes for the program are usually referred by participating law enforcement agencies; for example, detectives forward unsolved cases to Crime Stoppers for consideration. A review committee selects from those cases a number to be reenacted for television spots or described in newspapers or on the radio. The review committee reserves a veto over the acceptance of any particular crime. In addition to a description of the crime, the media coverage stresses the fact that a reward will be paid for information leading to an arrest and prosecution, the fact that the informant will remain anonymous, and the telephone number of the local Crime Stoppers program tips line. When information does lead to an arrest and felony indictment, a rewards committee reviews the case and decides on the amount of reward money (up to $1,000) to be paid.

THERE ARE THREE ESSENTIAL ELEMENTS:

 The Police

The Community   The Media

CRIME STOPPERS INTERNATIONAL, INC. (CSI)

As the world headquarters, it is the central clearinghouse for Crime Stoppers materials, and the main source of problem-solving for individual programs. There is a minimal charge for information needed to start a Crime Stoppers program.

A 30-member Board of Directors establishes CSI policy and represents the Members.

Crime Stoppers International:
- Distributes a comprehensive Crime Stoppers Manual and video tapes describing the operation of Crime Stoppers;
- Produces training, public relations and promotional tools;

concerning statistics, legal issues, fundraising, publicity, promotion, insurance, and media, board and police relations;
- Sponsors, with a host program, the Annual Crime Stoppers International Conference, where law enforcement, community and media representatives from around the world exchange information and participate in professional training and where CSI awards are presented;
- Publishes *The Caller,* a monthly magazine containing statistical information, instruction and accounts of Crime Stoppers successes;
- Provides a Crime Stoppers *Directory;*
- Develops resources for the headquarters operations;
- Makes on-site visits;
- Provides a toll-free line for incoming calls.

Crime Stoppers International, Inc.
Post Office Box 30413
Albuquerque, New Mexico 87190-0413
(800) 245-0009

solving cases involving fugitives, bank robberies, and narcotics.[62] As of March 1997, the 1,000-plus programs reporting to Crime Stoppers International claimed responsibility for solving more than 600,000 felony cases, more than 5,000 homicides, and recovering more than $1 billion in stolen property. The perception of nearly half of the program coordinators is that their programs have reduced the crime rate for specific types of crimes.[63]

The high visibility of these programs also increases their effectiveness by attracting secondary tips for unadvertised crimes. Indeed, given the large amount of unsolicited information received regarding unadvertised crimes, the advertised crimes appear to be more important as vehicles for obtaining tips regarding other crimes than as a means of solving the crimes actually publicized.[64] Crime Stoppers cases have also held up under judicial review in which the courts have allowed anonymous tips corroborated by other information and ruled that the identity of Crime Stoppers informants need not be disclosed.[65] Bolstered by these rulings—and by low program operational costs—Crime Stoppers is generally viewed as a cost-effective program and its continuance is currently assured.[66] Despite the support it enjoys and its successes, however, critics argue that the program's gains against crime are marginal and possibly outweighed by other negative social effects. The fears raised by participation programs become most clear when defense and public defenders are queried.[67]

> It seems that many of the tips are called in out of revenge. It's subject to abuse. If the police go out and investigate people based on anonymous tips, it can cause problems. The right to be secure in your home is not a technicality; it's an important right. It's what keeps the police off our backs. We're overreacting to the crime problem. *Former assistant public defender*
>
> It's frightening, chilling. It induces me to rat on my neighbor. I think it's dangerous and dumb. *University law professor*
>
> People who give tips for money are inherently suspect. People will take a suspicion and elevate it into a fact. *Defense attorney*

In addition, there is concern that the media could become a base for a mass informant system.[68] As Marx[69] has noted:

> Yet there are also potential dangers in institutionalizing such systems. They may encourage paranoia, suspiciousness, and vigilantism. They can weaken trust and offer a vehicle for malicious reporting from anonymous sources. In a different political climate, [they] would lend themselves equally well to informing on those who are merely different or unpopular rather than criminal.

Paying for information from anonymous sources is at the crux of the uneasiness felt toward these programs. The fear is that paying rewards and providing anonymity for informants will reduce voluntary cooperation and encourage retributive snitching by citizens on their neighbors, family, and friends, thereby fostering a police-state mentality. The acceptance of this practice required the social reconstruction of citizen informing on neighbors from a disparaged social act to a legitimized civic duty and an act of good citizenship. This reconstruction process was naturally carried out in the media.[70] The legitimization of anonymous informing was preceded by years of increasing fear of crime and the view that crime was increasing precipitously.[71] The resultant pessimism made acceptable previously objectionable social behaviors such as anonymous informing.

As for the effect on the public of the images of criminality projected through these programs, the image of criminality forwarded is similar to that portrayed in the general entertainment media—that of a dangerous and crime-ridden world where violent attacks are common[72] (see Chapter 2). Not only are the images similar to entertainment, but the format of the ads frequently are produced in entertainment programming styles with mood music, voice-overs, and heightened dramatic elements.[73] Crime Stoppers programs, by adding similar realistic, credible, and official images of crime, contribute to this negative worldview.

The effects on society include the polarization of society along ethnic and economic lines as people isolate themselves and grow more wary of strangers.[74] Further, by emphasizing violent crimes that appear to be due to greed or irrationality, Crime Stoppers forward individual explanations for crime and downplay broader structural, social, and economic factors.[75] The final consequence of this image is felt to be an unsubstantiated, undue support for law and order and crime control–based punitive public policies.[76] Given that media programming marketed purely as entertainment has these same effects, many believe that Crime Stoppers programs, with their presentation of selected slices of real-life crime, are likely to have even more effect on viewers' attitudes about crime and their perceptions of crime and justice reality and the criminal justice policies they support.[77]

The possibility of negative social consequences from these programs leads to the third issue, concerning the proper role of the mass media in law enforcement efforts. Should the media restrict themselves to basic reporting of events or become involved in their resolution? On the involvement side is the argument made by program advocates that the media should cooperate and become involved as a civic duty. They feel that Crime Stoppers is a natural extension of the practice of public service announcements. Nationally, most media executives appear to agree with this view[78] and program coordinators report high levels of media cooperation.[79]

The media are not always cooperative, however, apparently because some in the media perceive involvement as contrary to the philosophy of separation of press and government, particularly separation from law enforcement agencies. This reluctance is found more often within print media than within broadcast media. The print media more than the electronic media have long had an adversarial, watchdog relationship with law enforcement that conflicts with their involvement in Crime Stoppers projects. They also gain less from cooperating in terms of increased readership.[80] In essence, some within the media feel that cooperating makes them uncomfortably close to being information-gathering subsidiaries of local law enforcement rather than autonomous news agents. For media cooperation also allows the police to have their perspective reflected in the Crime Stoppers stories.[81] Some media personnel regard this as counter to their traditional adversarial relationship with the entire criminal justice system, ultimately jeopardizing their credibility as journalists.

How all these concerns are to be resolved is unclear; indeed, the nature of these programs makes a resolution unlikely. Unfortunately, we have little independent data to support or lay to rest the expressed fears. We simply do not know at this time if the hypothesized negative consequences of Crime Stoppers–style programs counteract their positive anticrime effects. First, we don't know how much positive, anticrime effect they actually have. Second, to determine whether or not the negative effects are in fact occurring and to what degree, community attitude surveys examining the relationship between viewing the Crime Stoppers ads, perceptions of criminality, and sources of support for crime-related public policies would be needed. In the interim, because the reservations are all unsubstantiated, the low cost, apparent successes, and popularity of the programs argue for and assure their continuance.

RECONSTRUCTING CRIMINAL JUSTICE: MEDIA TECHNOLOGY IN THE CRIMINAL JUSTICE SYSTEM

We now turn to the increasing application of media technology within the criminal justice system. In these applications the technology is central to the process and participants must interact through the equipment. The technology changes from a tangential, temporary new media visitor to an indispensable, permanent tool.

Law enforcement has employed media technology to increase surveillance capability and as a means of gathering evidence. In the judicial system, the uses range from the presentation of physical evidence and testimony to the creation of permanent records of proceedings and the live linking of participants for court proceedings.

Surveillance Programs

The idea of increasing surveillance to deter crime gained prominence in the early 1970s through the work of Oscar Newman, whose concept of defensible space argues that community and building designs that increase the sense of community and that eliminate conditions favorable to the commission of crimes (such as inadequate lighting) can minimize crime.[82] The surveillance capability of residents was forwarded as a key component. Surveillance applications based on media technology have been in use for a number of years in some types of sites—for example, surveillance cameras in banks, subways, and department stores—and have recently expanded to public schools[83] and highway toll booths.[84] These established uses differ from newer applications in that the areas surveyed are small and areas of public domain are not involved. In contrast, the new surveillance programs use media technology directly to prevent crime in large public areas. The programs are also often mobile.

Several issues arise in examining surveillance programs. The most obvious issue is the effectiveness of these programs: Do they reduce crime? A second issue is the trade-off of privacy for security. The criminal justice system, often in response to prodding by the public, has begun to turn increasingly to media-based technology for more innovative countermeasures against crime.[85] Because of their nature, however, such programs inevitably encroach on people's privacy, invading social realms and exposing and recording behaviors that were previously considered beyond the government's purview. Another basic question is how the social costs of these programs compare to their benefits.[86] Lastly, surreptitious camera surveillance invariably raises the specter of *1984*, with all its connotations of governmental abuse.

Interest in the use of surveillance as a crime reduction aid is not new and is based on the idea that surveillance heightens the perceived risk of committing crime.[87] Though media-based surveillance programs do not introduce new law enforcement practices, the new technology greatly enhances the reach of law enforcement agencies' surveillance capability. The practical goals of using media-enhanced surveillance include reduction of the number of officers needed for patrol; an increased ability to provide full twenty-four-hour-a-day coverage of an area; a reduction in citizens' fear of victimization; improved deterrence of street crime; an increased ability to apprehend and convict street criminals; decreased response time; and, for supervisors, an improved ability to oversee and direct line personnel and review field decisions.

On the other hand, critics have raised concerns that such programs will be difficult to control. Even when ineffective, these systems and their associated surveillance effect have been criticized as psychologically too powerful and therefore dangerous: "Agents are clearly limited in the surveillance and coercion they can carry out, but they are free to create the impression of police omnipresence and omnipotence. What they cannot do by force or by the actual power of their technology, they may attempt to do by creating a myth of surveillance."[88] Such projects have also been questioned regarding their cost and the reliability of the equipment, the community image that using such systems projects, and the likelihood that their use will merely displace rather than reduce crime.[89]

In the field, camera surveillance programs take one of two basic forms: completely hidden systems that give potential offenders no indication that they are being observed, and clearly marked, open systems.[90] Although the first form functions more as a means of gathering evidence and aiding in apprehension, both forms take advantage of a surveillance effect, using the psychological impact of the belief that one might be under surveillance to deter crime. Rapid improvement in the technology has encouraged the use of surveillance systems, but a general lack of research regarding the most useful applications has hampered it.

Research based largely on interviews with offenders does suggest that criminals do take into account the apparent level of surveillance and likelihood of intervention when deciding whether or not to commit certain crimes.[91] Nonetheless, projects to increase surveillance on the part of the general public appear to be the least effective approach to using surveillance to deter crime. On the other hand, increasing (or appearing to increase) the surveillance capability of law enforcement officers, local residents, and employees, in that order, does hold promise.[92] The limited literature available suggests that the impact of surveillance is related to the actual threat of intervention; that is, unless surveillance actually leads to intervention, like the previously discussed announcement effect, a surveillance deterrent effect will soon wane.

Despite the increasing use of camera surveillance by law enforcement agencies, there are few studies of surveillance systems' actual impact on crime. The best-known study in this area focused on the installation of closed-circuit television cameras in the London underground train system in the 1970s. Evaluation of the system showed that the cameras reduced the incidence of both theft and robbery, though there was evidence that thefts had been displaced to adjacent stations without cameras. The evaluators also cautioned that the novelty of the system contributed to its effectiveness and that in time offenders would discover that the system was less to be feared than they had imagined. They warned that the initial deterrent effect of the cameras would not last without actual law enforcement intervention to apprehend lawbreakers.[93]

And while surveillance systems covering large outside public areas are becoming common, only one system has been studied even superficially. The studied project involved the placing of television cameras linked by microwave atop traffic lights in a downtown shopping district.[94] An assessment of this project reported that crime did decline in the monitored area. It is possible, however, that the decline was part of a general decline in crime in the city or that the cameras had a displacement effect, reducing crime in the immediate area but increasing it in adjacent areas.[95] Of special interest is that the decline in street crime coincided with the installation of the camera housings, weeks before the actual cameras were available, evidence of the psychological strength of the surveillance effect.

Currently, public video surveillance projects are under way and well received in Tacoma, Washington; Newark, New Jersey; Baltimore, Maryland; and Santiago, Chile.[96] The most recent one in Baltimore is considering a $1 million expansion to blanket its downtown with up to two hundred cameras.[97] Due to their intrusive nature, such general public surveillance systems are likely to raise sensitive political issues wherever they are employed.[98]

BOX 6.2 Baltimore's Video Surveillance System

The Baltimore video surveillance system uses sixteen black-and-white fixed-position cameras to monitor a sixteen-block stretch in the downtown business district. The cameras, which are mounted on existing light poles at intersections, fif-teen feet above street level, use zoom lenses to deter muggings, drug deals, and car thefts. Baltimore police officers monitor the $58,000 project from a Japanese-style *koban*, or police kiosk.

Courtesy of Downtown Partnership of Baltimore, Inc.

The recent appearance of video cameras mounted on patrol car windshields represents an expanded, mobile use of video technology for surveillance. The mobility of the patrol car extends the practice of general law enforcement surveillance to virtually the entire society.[99] Challenges to the practice based on invasion of privacy have been rejected by the Supreme Court, which has stated that an invasion of privacy cannot result unless there is a reasonable expectation of privacy. Because there is no expectation of privacy in a traffic stop or on a public street, the use of cameras by police on patrol is allowed under almost all circumstances.[100] In this use, it can be argued that the police are as much under surveillance as the public, for police car video transforms the relationships between line police officers, their administration, and the public by providing a reviewable record of officers' street interactions. The benefits of having an audiovisual record of a patrol are obvious—administrators and the courts can later review officers' and suspects' actions, and thereby monitor liability, voluntary search consent, and misconduct claims, and obtain more credible, objective evidence of behavior and statements for DUI and drug cases. In addition, the cameras deter suspects from resisting arrest and also deter officers from mistreating suspects and engaging in other unprofessional acts.[101] The use of patrol car cameras has not been successfully legally challenged, and as its benefits—especially to officers—are obvious, its spread is predicted. Indeed, in one recent review, no disadvantages to using the technology were forwarded.[102]

A final use of media technology by law enforcement agencies involves the video recording of police interrogations. As with patrol car cameras, here again the cameras provide more objective, fuller records of interactions between police and citizens, as well as evidence regarding the voluntariness of statements, suspects' understanding of their rights, police coercion and interrogation practices, and the physical and mental condition of suspects. A two-year evaluation of a Canadian experiment in videotaping police interrogations showed that the expected advantages of protection against unwarranted allegations of misconduct, the introduction of accountability in interrogation procedures, and the reduction in challenges to the admissibility of suspect statements were all realized.[103]

The evaluators reported that suspects did not appear inhibited by the cameras and the confession rate remained the same. In fact, police, prosecutors, and defense counsel all came to support continuation and expansion of the project—police because it relieves them of the need to take written notes during interrogations and reduces their court appearances, prosecutors because it usually disposes of all legal questions surrounding the police-suspect interview, and defense counsel because it ensures that police more strictly follow legal procedures and because the defense often can use the tapes to demonstrate their client's intent and remorse for sentencing purposes. The interrogation tapes provide a record of the frame of mind and emotional reaction of a suspect much nearer in time to the actual commission of a crime than has been previously available.[104]

Summary: Media Technology, Surveillance, and Law Enforcement

More than a decade and a half ago a prophetic assessment of the difficulties of using surveillance programs to prevent crime was offered:[105]

The use of surveillance to reduce crime shares some of the usual problems of methods which attempt to reduce opportunities of crime; they do not tackle underlying factors that may motivate offenders; they can appear negatively "defensive"; and they cannot guarantee that crime is not merely displaced in time, place, or method.

The few evaluations that have been conducted indicate that a significant immediate deterrent effect follows the well-publicized start of a new surveillance capability. In fact, an announcement effect is normally the strongest effect found for surveillance programs. The primary difficulty is maintaining these immediate gains over a longer period. The initial deterrent effect dissipates over time if offenders realize that the law is not being enforced and that punishments are not being imposed. Surveillance and announcement effects are so psychologically powerful that planners can effect a quick but short-term behavioral change by convincing people that things are different—either that they are under observation or that transgressions, if discovered, will be more harshly punished. But if no actual change persists—if people discover that punishments are not harsher, that the cameras do not work, or that no one responds when offenses occur—then the deterrent effect disappears along with the falsely constructed reality of increased surveillance and enforcement. Effective use of the media and technology thus dictates that sufficient resources and effort be allocated to ensuring and maintaining actual real-world social policy changes as well as socially constructing and publicizing the planned change. Otherwise, the conditions and experiences of the real world will eventually overwhelm the perceptions of the socially constructed one.

The use of media technology is in most cases efficient, and legal questions of admissibility, privacy, and due process have been answered in favor of continued use of the technology in the United States.[106] Resistance to even greater adoption within law enforcement agencies appears to arise because law enforcement officers perceive the cameras as administrative tools, installed to watch them, more than as law enforcement tools, installed to increase convictions. In reality the cameras are both, and though their use originates in efforts to achieve crime control goals, they also generate enough due process benefits to have gained relatively broad-based support. In effect, these programs appear to protect police officers from frivolous charges of abuse and misconduct while protecting the public from actual abuse and misconduct by officers. Where they have been experimentally employed they have, to date, been permanently adopted.

Beyond technical feasibility, all the surveillance programs mentioned raise issues concerning the use of media technology in the daily policing of our society. Surprisingly, in the literature evaluating these projects, concerns over "Big Brother" and *1984* were raised only by the news media, law enforcement officers, and external observers, not by citizens under surveillance, who appear quite ready to trade off a measure of personal privacy for a potential reduction in victimization and fear. The acceptance of surveillance is associated with the acceptance of increased media exposure of private, backstage behaviors—if privacy is already rare, then surveillance becomes less offensive.[107] Another concern over the use of this technology is the prospect that it displaces crime. Thus, one eventual result could be the isolation of crime in poor neighborhoods that cannot afford such systems, permanently polarizing society into crime-free versus crime-ridden zones.[108]

Further unresolved questions concern effects on the legitimacy, symbolic impact, and the public image of justice when media technology is employed. The justice system is a mechanism for adjudicating guilt and administering punishment. It is also a means of legitimizing the whole social system. Accordingly, the police have a symbolic value. On the street, both the presence of a live police officer and the assurance of knowing when one is being observed affirm the values of voluntary consent and involvement and the public control of law enforcement. Loss of these symbols may diminish the aura of legitimacy sustaining the entire system and undermine an otherwise successful crime reduction program.[109] Misuse or overuse of this technology will construct a social reality of mistrust and cynicism, where fear of crime has been replaced by fear of authority.

The basic problem these programs present is how to balance police intervention and public safety—how much safety is gained at what cost? The equation seems clearly to be that increased fear of crime results in increased tolerance for intervention. Citizens fearful of crime are willing to open more backstage social areas to observation, even when the observers are hidden. Orwell's *1984* scenario of total surveillance is less frightening than a local mugger. The danger is that fear will drive citizens to glibly surrender personal privacy for an unknown measure of personal security. Whether or not these crime control programs actually reduce crime enough to warrant the reduction in privacy is still an open question. They do seem capable of producing short-term effects purely through psychological impact, but whether the programs themselves can maintain these effects over the long term or not remains an issue.

JUDICIAL USES OF MEDIA TECHNOLOGY

Like law enforcement agencies, the courts too have recently begun to incorporate media technology into their activities. Here, as in law enforcement, the basic incentives are the administrative benefits of increased speed and efficiency. The hope is that the technology will help the judicial system's crime control assembly-line function better without damaging the protections of its due process obstacle course. Because most of the benefits of this technology facilitate crime control, most of the concerns that have been raised involve due process. Historically, the impact of visual media technology in the courts has been resisted because of the effects of news photographic and television coverage,[110] but with the rapid development of mass media technology, especially within the areas of visual communications systems and videotape, it was inevitable that media technology would find application within the courtroom. The key difference between the new in-house applications of media technology and news media camera coverage is that in news coverage the equipment is tangential to the judicial activity and the goal is to have the participants ignore the equipment. As visitors, the media and their technology are to be unobtrusive bystanders to the proceedings. But in these new applications, the participants must interact with the equipment, often speaking to a camera or watching a screen rather than interacting face to face. No longer a temporary, passive visitor, the equipment is rather a permanent, active judicial tool.

The first recorded judicial use of television cameras was in 1962 in Michigan, where a courtroom and a law school were linked to permit law students to view trials. From this simple beginning the use of media technology has expanded, and over the past decade courtroom use of media technology has increased markedly. Currently, many potential uses are available to the courts. Already, traditional trials, first appearances, and misdemeanor arraignments have been videotaped to create a visual and audio record of courtroom proceedings. Physically separate locations have been linked through two-way networks, allowing defendants, attorneys, and judges to interact with one another across great distances. These sessions may be broadcast to a public audience; they may be electronically scrambled to prevent eavesdropping; and they may be videotaped for future use. Indeed, videotaped presentations have been used instead of the live testimony of witnesses, and videotape has been used to record confessions, physical evidence for courtroom presentation, recreations or simulations of a crime, accident, or other event, and even entire trials for presentation to a jury.

Despite the fact that many commentators have approved such efforts,[111] these applications raise a number of questions. How does the introduction of media equipment into the judicial process affect the relationships between judges, attorneys, and other court personnel? How does it affect the ability of defendants to interact with their attorneys and judges? How do defendants feel about its use? Are media-facilitated cases fair, just, and efficient when compared to traditionally processed ones? In essence, does crime control win at the expense of due process? And most important, what is the final reality of justice that results? These questions revolve around three interrelated issues: the efficiency in cost and time of using media technology versus using traditional courtroom methods, the legal admissibility of evidence and due process, and the effects on participants and courtroom atmosphere and decorum. A review of each application in turn sheds light on these issues and suggests a general explanation for the acceptance or rejection of the technology in the judicial system and its impact.

Presenting Physical Evidence

The use of media technology to present physical evidence in court has long been well received. Videotape is frequently used to record physical evidence and exhibits prior to their presentation in the courtroom. Where objects such as machinery, airplanes, and automobiles are too large to be brought into court, or where the geography of a crime scene, accident scene, or other location must be viewed, videotape can capture them for subsequent courtroom use.[112] Objects that are small or detailed may also be videotaped to highlight features and ensure that they are seen clearly. Taping can preserve for the jury objects and conditions subject to change before the trial (for example, property destroyed in a condemnation case, the alleged nuisance in a nuisance action, or unsatisfactory goods in a contract case).[113] The use of videotape in the presentation of evidence has increased markedly, and admission rules have been altered to further encourage its use.[114] In comparison with traditional methods, videotape has been found to yield more economical, more effective, and more comprehensive presentations.[115]

Judicial concerns about videotaped evidence relate to admissibility and the production of good-quality evidence without misleading or irrelevant material. To be admissible, a videotape, like a photograph, must be a fair and accurate representation, must be relevant, and cannot be unfairly prejudicial or otherwise contain inadmissible evidence. Doret identified two primary sources of prejudice as being camera angle (since the camera represents the juror's eye, the juror can watch only what is shown on the tape, and all off-camera, possibly crucial information is unavailable) and tape editing (choice of camera shots, timing and sequence, cutting of important footage or scenes).[116] However, the courts have found these concerns no greater or less than those found with any photographic evidence. The presence of a judge during taping and editing or review of a tape by the judge and litigants prior to its showing to a jury has effectively minimized problems, and using videotape as a means of presenting evidence is no longer unusual. Further aiding the use of videotaped evidence is that any print of a videotape is considered an original, not a copy. It is thus outside the scope of the best-evidence rule, which would normally bar the use of a copy as not being the best available evidence.[117] The benign history and general untroubled acceptance of videotaped evidence established a positive foundation for subsequent expanded uses of media technology in the judiciary. The natural first extension was from physical evidence to verbal evidence—the videotaped presentation of testimony in lieu of written depositions.

Presenting Testimony

The judicial acceptance of media technology as a substitute for the live testimony of witnesses is particularly important in regard to the expanded use of this technology in the courts. The resolution of the questions raised regarding videotaped testimony eased the development of the more controversial media-based communication and case-processing systems now found in many judicial systems. The videotaping of testimony directly replaces the traditional practices of having a live person in the courtroom either testifying or reading a written deposition. It therefore quickly met with close scrutiny and opposition.

In support of videotaped testimony, the National Center for State Courts has argued that the "most useful application of video recordings" is in place of an in-court reading of a typed deposition.[118] A number of authors are also enthusiastic about the use of videotaped testimony, listing among its many advantages convenience, elimination of the problem of unavailable witnesses, and enhancement of the ability to hear and follow testimony.[119] In addition, videotape alleviates scheduling problems; reduces the likelihood of last-minute trial postponements and delays; allows more clearly ordered, comprehensible testimony; and limits jurors' exposure to inadmissible material, byplay, and other potentially prejudicial, irrelevant, or unnecessary material.[120] Spurred by these advantages, procedural barriers to recording the testimony of witnesses have steadily fallen.[121] First sanctioned in the federal courts in 1970, videotaped depositions are now accepted in all but a handful of jurisdictions.

Despite assurances by advocates of the benefits of expanded use of videotape in presenting testimony, its use has raised concerns. Specific early concerns involved the admissibility of video testimony and its effects on jurors. Regarding admissibility, it is argued that videotape should be admitted into evidence only when certain safeguards have been met.[122] As with physical evidence, questions regarding editing and its control arise, as certain courts allow testimony to be taped without the presence of a judge. Admissibility remains the central concern of those seeking or opposing videotaping.[123] Other procedural concerns relate to the handling of witnesses who do not want to be videotaped and the question of whose burden it is to demonstrate that videotaping should be allowed or not allowed. Some courts rely on the requester to demonstrate solid reasons for videotaping testimony. Other courts hold that motions should be granted unless the opponent argues convincingly that video would be prejudicial.[124] Challenges arguing the inherent inadmissibility of videotape have failed, however, and its future use, although not its admissibility in specific cases, is currently assured.

A greater issue related to the social construction of justice is the effect of video on the processing of testimony by juries. Critics have cited a number of possible negative effects.[125] First, unlike videotaped physical evidence, video testimony unavoidably involves a loss in the amount of information communicated. This has both positive and negative implications in that it narrows the field of information offered the jurors at any given moment during testimony but can also filter out extraneous events and preserve a crucial moment that a juror might otherwise miss in a lapse of attention. Second, some observers fear that video cannot capture the total psychological and physical essence of a witness—that the electronic construction of communication will degrade the accuracy of the communication and limit its clarity, detail, and realism. Another source of concern is that video favors some witnesses—telegenic subjects—and not others, thereby distorting viewers' perceptions of witnesses' veracity. Lastly, one of the chief concerns associated with the use of videotaped depositions is that of boredom,[126] particularly when such presentations are compared with commercial television. The overriding fear is that the courtroom reality created through videotaped testimony will differ substantially from the reality of live testimony.[127] "To the extent that television increases the degree to which credibility is assessed on the basis of the looks of

Media-based technology has become increasingly accepted and common in court proceedings. Shown is video evidence used during the O.J. Simpson trial.

Corbis-Bettmann

the witness, it emphasizes a factor extraneous to the truth of the testimony, and renders the truth-finding process less objective."[128]

In total, the arguments against videotaped testimony are similar to those listed in the Supreme Court's *Estes* decision, which in 1966 banned television cameras from trial courts. All these concerns involve a possible effect on the interaction between witness and jury. Videotaped testimony sacrifices the elements of a two-way communication system with feedback. Video changes testimony from a live, three-dimensional face-to-face reality to a unidirectional and two-dimensional impersonal reality. Feedback from seeing witnesses' reactions to answers and questions is lost not only for juries but for attorneys, witnesses, and judges. No longer can a lawyer evaluate how well a line of questioning is being received and change tactics accordingly. This makes for a different judicial reality and may make for less effective counsel.[129]

With the courts pressured because of the administrative benefits to adopt the practice and spurred by effectiveness concerns not to do so, researchers undertook the study of the effects of videotaped testimony. These evaluations focused on jurors' attention span and boredom and their ability to retain information, reach decisions, and detect lies when viewing videotaped testimony. The most extensive evaluations were conducted in the 1970s,[130] when Miller and Fontes concluded after various experiments that "there is no evidence to suggest that the use of videotape exerts any deleterious effects on

182

the juror responses studied; in fact, as far as retention of trial related information is concerned, it appears that videotaped testimony sometimes results in higher retention levels."[131] Regarding the ability of jurors to discern lying, they reported, "our findings do not support the argument that videotape will curtail jurors' abilities to assess the demeanor of witnesses."[132] In fact, nonverbal cues may hinder rather than help jurors make accurate judgments—the highest percentage of correct judgments followed written transcripts.[133]

Despite a number of initial concerns, the use of media technology in the courts had passed its first crucial test. In fact, video is now felt to be clearly superior in certain situations. The research supports the contention that videotaped testimony is equal to written transcripts and in some ways surpasses live testimony.[134] Allaying concerns about the effect on judicial outcomes, the research indicates that the use of videotaped testimony does not significantly affect either juror verdicts or monetary awards. It should be noted, however, that this research focused on civil cases. That the effects of video testimony in criminal trials will be similar has simply been assumed.[135]

Both videotaped testimony and videotaped evidence are thus now regularly accepted in the criminal justice system, and expanded uses are continually advocated. For example, the Supreme Court now supports the videotaping and closed-circuit televising of children's testimony in child abuse cases as a solution to maintaining the right of confrontation and press access to trials while protecting child witnesses from emotional or mental strain.[136] And it has been recommended that jurors be provided trial videotape in deliberations as a matter of course.[137] Nonetheless, many still resist expanding the role of video, and even advocates of its use for depositions argue that presenting large portions of testimony by videotape is inappropriate.[138] Whereas using video for a small segment of the total testimony in a trial is acceptable, the idea of making it the dominant method of presenting testimony, and in the process drastically changing the traditional appearance, process, and reality of a trial, raises resistance. Another area where limited use of media technology has been accepted but expanded use has met resistance is as a replacement for a written stenographic record of a proceeding.

As a Permanent Court Record

Trials and other case-processing steps are sometimes videotaped as a means of creating a permanent visual and aural record of proceedings, replacing the stenographic notes of the court reporter and other paper files. Despite the potential financial merits of this use and its possible value in appellate procedures, its threat to the role and livelihood of court personnel has fueled opposition, not only from court reporters[139] but also from appellate judges.[140] Because of this opposition, enthusiasm for this application has declined in recent years. Initially, court administrators felt that videotaped records would provide advantages over the traditional written transcripts. Coleman[141] listed as the main advantages expected from videotaping court sessions that videotape captures gesture and facial expressions as well as words, the equipment is not obtrusive or disruptive to court proceedings, and the master tape can be readily copied, making a record available in much less time than is required to prepare a typed transcript.

However, contrary to the advantages initially expected from videotaped records, the practice of videotaping court proceedings for appeals has been dropped after two experimental applications. Attorneys found too much of the taped material inaudible and found reviewing the tapes time-consuming. Additionally, the appeals court found that viewing the tapes took much longer than reading transcripts, and appellants were eventually required to attach a typed transcript of the portion of the videotape supporting the appeal with indexed references to the videotape included.[142] The videotaped records neither shortened the appellate process nor reduced the expense of preparing a record for review.[143] Currently, only one appellate jurisdiction is reported to be using videotapes.[144] The videotaping of trial proceedings has not proven an acceptable substitute for a traditional transcript prepared by a court reporter.

In no application is the format and appearance of justice more changed by media technology than in the recording and presentation of full trials using media technology. Prerecorded videotaped trials (PRVTTs) involve giving the jury a videotape of the entire trial—after a judge has deleted all inadmissible questions, answers, and comments from the tape.[145] PRVTTs constitute a marked departure from traditional trials in that video becomes the exclusive means of presenting testimony, without regard to the availability of the individual witnesses. All extraneous and objectionable statements are eliminated from the jurors' knowledge, and counsel, judge, and litigating parties need not be present while the testimony is being shown to the jury.[146] The main advantages are speed and cost savings. Although not a well-known application, as early as 1973 comments regarding the use of videotaped trials and noting the difference between live and videotaped testimony appeared:

> Although similar, the videotape trial is more than a procedural extension of videotape depositions. It is not incorporated in the normal trial framework but is the sole means by which evidence is introduced to the jury. . . . The essence of the videotape system is that it allows the trial to be subdivided into three units: testimony (involving lawyers and witnesses), rulings (involving trial judges and lawyers), and presentation (involving jurors). These units proceed chronologically but relatively independently, each impinging only slightly on the schedules of the others.[147]

According to proponents, prerecorded video trials have been very successful in reducing overloaded court dockets and have cut the amount of time needed to complete the hearing of a case.[148] Setting aside the apparent advantages, however, critics have argued against the expanded use of video to present entire trials. The use of PRVTTs is not expected to increase in the near future, even in seriously backlogged jurisdictions. The reluctance to adopt PRVTTs appears to revolve around the effect of videotaping trials on the traditional atmosphere and appearance of a trial. One is inescapably drawn to

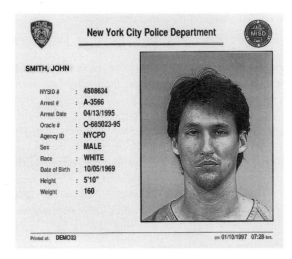

New York City Police Department

SMITH, JOHN

NYSID #	:	4508634
Arrest #	:	A-3566
Arrest Date	:	04/13/1995
Oracle #	:	O-685023-95
Agency ID	:	NYCPD
Sex	:	MALE
Race	:	WHITE
Date of Birth	:	10/05/1969
Height	:	5'10"
Weight	:	160

Printed at: DEMO03   on: 01/10/1997 07:28 hrs.

Video Mug Shot

Courtesy of XImage Corporation.

the conclusion that expanded use of video will drastically alter the trial process, its internal relationships and procedures, and, ultimately, the verdicts it reaches.[149] The presumption behind the formal court setting and proceedings is that they have an impact on witnesses' performance and perceptions, as well as on the behavior of other trial participants and observers.

> The trial process itself will be altered as will the relationships between and among lawyers, parties, witnesses, and judge. From a drama directed and to various extents controlled by a professional and "impartial" judge, the trial will be transformed to a far more "partisan" event, directed and controlled by a larger variety of participants—lawyers in all their variety of competence, personality, and partisanship; cameramen of varying degrees of neutrality and proficiency; and witnesses who will be less readily surprised or otherwise made to lose their poise.[150]

The importance of the courtroom as a mechanism of legitimization has also been noted.[151] Its symbols and processes are important in and of themselves and by severing testimony from the courtroom a crucial function of the trial in the larger social community may be sacrificed. If prerecorded trials are to be broadly accepted in the future, they must not undermine the symbolic functions of the trial process. Otherwise, the common expectation of what the reality of a trial should be must alter considerably. At present, few are convinced that either is possible.

Other, less ambitious video records have, however, shown themselves to be beneficial. Thus, videotape provides a useful record of the backstage interactions and procedural steps found early in the criminal justice process, which are simply dated and logged or otherwise not recorded. These early backstage steps include bookings, first appearances, arraignments, and bond and plea hearings.

An increasing number of police departments currently use the technology to record booking of all arrests. These video mug shots provide a pictorial record of arrestees that includes voice, accent, and a continuous front-to-profile view. The availability of these video records has also allowed changes in two other common practices—the identification of a suspect from a traditional lineup and the identification of a suspect from a set of photographs of known offenders (a mug book).[152] In a video lineup, a crime witness is shown a series of video bookings selected for their similarity. The witness chooses from this video lineup the individual he or she feels is the offender. This process is felt to be fairer than the old practices in that the individuals in video lineups more closely resemble one another than the groups usually assembled for a live lineup, and it provides a permanent record of the lineup for later review should questions of fairness arise. In video mug books, a computer searches a pictorial file for specific characteristics (for example, tattoo, bald, heavy, white male) and displays—and prints if desired—the pictures that match.

Video records of arraignments, first appearances, bond hearings, and pleas have also proven inexpensive and useful. A single videotape of hundreds of cases can be stored as a permanent record that can be consulted should the state of mind of a defendant, his or her comprehension of rights or instructions, or the voluntariness of a plea later be questioned. Unlike videotaping trials, videotaping these short, nontrial procedural steps offers both crime control and due process benefits. Crime control proponents like the savings of time and money. Due process adherents feel the knowledge that a permanent record is being created makes law enforcement and judicial personnel more conscientious in following due process procedures. Videotaping these procedural steps also provides a means not previously available of resolving any subsequent due process concerns. In addition, a bit more of the backstage world of the criminal justice system is revealed for outside review. As with the videotaping of vehicle stops and interrogations by police, once instituted these systems gain support from both crime control and due process advocates. Furthermore, the same technology used in creating a video record also allows, if desired, the separation of the participants, thus allowing a judicial proceeding to be conducted in a completely new way—in live but media-linked sessions.

Live Video-Facilitated Proceedings

This use of media technology electronically expands the traditional courtroom so that defendants, witnesses, judges, and lawyers who are physically separated can communicate. In a sense, the traditional courtroom is diffused to physically isolated but electronically linked locations. The technology allows various configurations of communication linkage; this flexibility in turn allows multiple applications. In practice, such systems primarily benefit not judges but other system personnel, who spend less time traveling and waiting for a judge to be available.[153] As with videotaped depositions, the use of video in judicial systems to conduct live proceedings has increased. Likewise, using video to conduct live proceedings has raised concerns about the constitutionality of the proceedings, the creation of a new and significantly different trial reality, the possible restriction and distortion of communications, loss of judicial legitimacy and decorum, and effects on the norms, values, and interpersonal relationships within the system. One advantage over videotape for live, media-facilitated proceedings is that communication, while restricted, remains a two-way system with feedback. Although the capability to conduct live video proceedings has existed for over twenty years, it is only in the last decade that it has been employed significantly.[154]

Live interactive video has been most extensively used in misdemeanor arraignments. Media-facilitated misdemeanor appearances were introduced to reduce the number of court and correctional personnel involved in first appearances, to reduce costs, to increase security, to alleviate courtroom crowding, and to speed up the handling of cases—all administrative benefits that further crime control goals. The expense of a system is the most often cited reason for discontinuation. Technical unreliability, even when a system appears to be down for significant amounts of time, has not been a common complaint. Also, despite criticism of video images as inadequate substitutes for live interaction, appeals based on a loss of due process protections and the inherent unfairness of a video-facilitated proceeding have all failed.

However, reviews have largely ignored questions of the effect of the technology on the attitudes of participants, concentrating instead on the efficiency and cost of the equipment. Therefore, little is understood regarding the differences between successful and unsuccessful implementations or the technology's long-term effects on judicial systems. In general, video systems usually ease courtroom logistics and reduce the cost of processing defendants, and evaluations have been more approving as the technology has improved. Acceptance is also aided because the technology affects a relatively invisible component of the judicial process, and each individual hearing is short.

Even at the trial level, however, live media-linked sessions have been gaining favor. The high-profile trial of the "Chicago Seven" in the 1960s,[155] during which disruptive defendants were bound and gagged in the courtroom, led to criticism of the use of restraints on defendants and to the practice of removing such defendants from the courtroom. The Supreme Court subsequently upheld this practice, stating that disruptive behavior on the part of a defendant constitutes a waiver of the right of confrontation.[156] Thus ordained, closed-circuit television is today commonly used in many jurisdictions to enable disruptive defendants who have been removed to at least watch their trials on television. The Supreme Court has also supported the live, one-way, televised testimony of children in child abuse cases, allowing the defendant and defense attorneys to view the child testifying but protecting the child from having to confront the defendant.[157] Though concerns remain, expanded use is likely for the future.

UNRESOLVED CONCERNS OF THE
JUDICIAL USE OF MEDIA TECHNOLOGY

Concerns about media technology rarely involve questions of technical feasibility and constitutional due process; they tend to be more deeply rooted in established social attitudes, perceptions, and expectations with respect to the judicial process. The technology's impact on trials has been a particular hotpoint. Ultimately, judicial acceptance or rejection of the technology rests on whether or not its use leads to a perceived loss of a crucial symbolic element of justice. When the traditional, familiar reality of the judicial system is changed drastically, resistance to the new reality rises. For preliminary and short procedural steps, most participants appear to feel that the integrity of the process is unaffected. The technology's use in longer, more significant, and more symbolic steps such as trials triggers greater concern and resistance.

Even for the now-common and accepted applications, the alteration of the reality of the judicial system gives rise to three concerns: the technology's effects on working relationships among courtroom personnel, its depersonalization of the criminal justice system, and its impact on the constructed image and legitimacy of the judicial system. Though uses of the technology have been initially promising, questions regarding the effects of this technology on participants, on the judicial system, and on the public's perception of the criminal justice system as a whole—and thereby ultimately on justice itself—have not been answered.

Regarding the technology's effects on the relationships among courtroom personnel, comments from attorneys (especially public defenders) and judges indicate that the relationships among courtroom personnel can be upset by the introduction of media equipment. It is significant that in a number of pilot projects public defenders remain largely skeptical of the technology's advantages even for short procedures. The question arises whether attorneys deliver equivalent representation if they feel legally and organizationally disadvantaged in media-constructed proceedings. If their morale suffers, does their subsequent effort also suffer?

An examination of case outcomes revealed no significant aggregate differences between cases conducted using media technology and those not using the technology.[158] The possibility remains, however, that such an effect could be operating in other locales or develops only after a large number of cases over a significant period of time have been processed.[159] These systems also have the potential to increase the administrative supervision of courtroom personnel and thereby decrease the substantial discretion they now have. What effect this would have on morale, effectiveness, and case outcomes, or whether it would have crime control or due process implications, remains unknown.

A second concern is that expanded use of this technology within the judiciary will almost certainly lead to further depersonalization of criminal justice proceedings. Adjudication within the criminal justice system is based on face-to-face interaction, particularly on the premise that the accused are entitled to face their accusers. Extended use of media technology, however, will reduce live, face-to-face encounters between witnesses and defendants, police and the public, attorneys and clients, judges and defendants, and jurors and all the previous groups, thereby seriously altering the interpersonal structure of the system. This process will most likely be hastened by equipment advances that make this technology more economical, less obtrusive, and more approximate (but never equal) to live meetings. The full effects of these changes will become apparent only after such practices have been in place for a long time.

Critics of this technology also frequently mention the effect on juries and jury deliberations.[160] It is feared that jurors will bring their television experience to their interactions with the technology, expecting entertaining, engaging sessions.

> Research has demonstrated that the whole juror comes to court: he brings to the courtroom his entire experience with the media. That experience includes watching soap operas, tv westerns and gangster movies, where actors may die ghastly deaths, but spring to life to play new roles again. Further research is necessary to tell us whether we can fully separate tv as reality from tv as entertainment. We don't know what unconscious forces might be at work affecting our judgment when we see a trial in the form of a television program.[161]

A third key unresolved concern is what is lost in legitimacy and the public image of justice when media technology is employed. The justice system is a means of adjudicating guilt and administering punishment. It is also a means of legitimizing the whole social system—its rules, laws, and government. Accordingly, the courtroom and its personnel have a symbolic value. The majesty and mystery of actions in the courtroom embody the sanctity and well-being of the larger society. Loss of these symbolic qualities may diminish the aura of legitimacy sustaining the entire system. If the reality of the system is altered, will the system lose or gain public support? From this social construction perspective, how the system treats individuals is crucial.[162] If people become alienated from the system or if they feel intimidated or dehumanized by it, whatever benefits that result from the use of media technologies in the courtroom may cancel out. If these systems ultimately result in the further isolation and separation of the police from the policed and the courts from the public, the social costs of such losses would outweigh any administrative benefits that might accrue from their use.

A crucial unexamined factor within this area is the technology's effect on courtroom visitors and friends and family of defendants. These external observers participate significantly in the social construction of reality with regard to the criminal justice system. It is reasonable to expect that defendants, who are immediately threatened by punitive sanctions, would be more concerned with procedure outcomes than with the process itself. However, unthreatened observers may receive an image of the system that is unacceptable if they see the use of technology as a degrading means of keeping the defendant out of the courtroom and as insulating those in authority from those under authority. Inasmuch as these observers represent a larger part of society than the actual defendants, effects on them cannot be ignored. But to date, no information regarding the affects of the use of media technology on the perceptions of the larger public is available.

As crime control values become more popular there is considerable desire, especially on the part of administrators, to make the court system more effective and efficient. Nevertheless, the system must remain moral in the public's eyes if it is to remain a legitimate and viable system of justice. The visuals created by these projects are used frequently in news reports and thereby also contribute directly to the social construction of the public's image of justice. They have therefore changed the reality of justice on many levels and have opened previous backstage judicial activities to public scrutiny. Ironically, although the courts are still wary of the news media, their pursuit of media technology will ultimately have many of the same effects that are feared from news coverage. The judicial process will become, for good or ill, a less arcane, more open and accessible system as its processes become more visible due to this technology. The overriding concern remains whether this new reality of justice is ultimately seen as an impersonal, unfair, and unacceptable substitute.

CONCLUSION

The media can be used prosocially to influence people's attitudes about crime and make more crime-related information available to the police. Such use can speed the processing of criminal cases. The technology of the media can be used to videotape police patrols, vehicle stops, and interrogations. And the technology can be useful in the investigation, surveillance, and deterrence of crime. The technology can also be useful in the judicial processing of criminal cases in various ways. The administrative, mostly crime control, benefits associated with these uses follow quickly, and the projects have consistently been assessed as efficient and cost-effective. Their increased use will be hastened by technological advances that make the equipment more economical, more flexible, more capable, and less obtrusive. However, there are concerns about potential social costs and infringements on due process that do not emerge quickly and are difficult to quantify. The difficulty is that, should evidence of negative effects be found, curtailing established practices could well be impossible.

Despite their popularity, no media-based crime reduction program has empirically demonstrated a significant reduction of the crime rate without displacement. Regarding existing programs, deterrence programs that do not include surveillance show no behavioral effects. It appears doubtful that the mass media can by themselves deter criminal behavior—much as it was shown to be unlikely that they alone can criminalize an individual (see Chapter 5). Media surveillance programs show short-term deterrence effects similar to the announcement effect observed for heavily publicized law enforcement changes, but their long-term ability to deter crime without simply displacing it remains unproved.[163] Media efforts to reduce victimization by teaching crime preventive behaviors have had mixed results. Campaigns aimed at potential victims have shown an ability to attain high recognition levels among the general public and have both increased public knowledge and changed public attitudes about crime prevention, but they have not been shown to significantly change behavior. Programs designed to increase public cooperation by advertising crimes appear effective in gathering information and in solving specific types of crimes. Their effect on the overall crime rate is not known but is likely negligible. Neither the mass media nor their technology offer crime control panaceas.

Media technology has also proven itself useful in the judicial system, especially as a substitute for personal, in-court testimony and as a means of presenting evidence and courtroom exhibits. There is less agreement, however, about its usefulness as a substitute for live proceedings and written records. In general, the use of media technology in the processing and recording of brief, nontrial procedural steps and small portions of a trial is accepted; more extensive uses are not. In all these projects the trend is for crime control benefits to emerge quickly and to overshadow the possibility that due process losses may emerge over the long term. As these systems are increasingly instituted, long-term studies are needed to address whether such effects do in fact develop. With this in mind, we may consider media technology an extremely useful tool but, again, not a panacea for the judicial system's problems. There are invariably costs that accompany its benefits.

All anticrime programs have potential costs that include increased depersonalization of the criminal justice system, isolation of the police from the policed, increased citizen fear and suspicion of surveillance, polarization of society due to the creation of affluent, technologically secured garrison communities, and decreased citizen support and legitimization of the criminal justice system. A final problem from media coverage of these uses is the conveyance of the message that these efforts are working to reduce overall crime rates and that such media-based programs are indeed panaceas for the general crime problem. To the extent that the public believes this, resources for other and ultimately more beneficial approaches will be drained away.[164]

To solve crimes and deter criminals the government must intervene in its citizens' lives. The media provide a means to do so in new ways, ways that are felt to be both more efficient and less obviously intrusive. In practice, however, such applications cannot avoid opening up for view areas of public life, of the criminal justice system, and of police-citizen interactions that are even further backstage. In certain instances, such as in the use of patrol car cameras, which record police actions as much as citizen actions, this is clearly seen as a positive course. In other instances, such as in the use of hidden police surveillance systems, the desirability of doing so is not so clear. Still, these programs provide unique opportunities to study the interaction of media and justice from a new perspective. They let us look at the media as part of a solution to crime rather than as part of its cause.

In addition, in using the media and media technology, and in being news themselves, these programs increase the dimensions of interaction between the media and the justice system. Study of this expanded interaction, in particular of the social dynamics that develop in support of and in opposition to these programs, would improve our knowledge of the influence of the media on crime and justice in our society. The impact of these programs on citizens' construction of criminality and criminal justice still needs to be assessed. Do such programs increase the fear of crime, perpetuate or exacerbate the stereotypes promoted by the entertainment media, and create support for or opposition to specific criminal justice policies? For now, the mass media and their technology are an additional, potentially positive, but limited resource to be used in reducing crime.

The preceding chapters have detailed the manner in which the expanded capabilities of the media affect how the news media report on the criminal justice system and how the system responds to crime. The ever-increasing popularity of crime-and-justice programming and the potential of the media to extensively cover live all aspects of the criminal justice system raise the final but most important question concerning media, crime, and justice: What kind of crime-and-justice social reality do the media construct?

CHAPTER CONCEPTS

Prosocial Media	Surveillance Effect	Systems
Announcement Effect	Marketing Fear	Video Records
Deterrence	Video Evidence and Testimony	Self-Protective Behaviors
Victimization Reduction Program	Live Media Proceedings	Public Communication Campaigns
Citizen Participation Program	One- and Two-Way Communications	

DISCUSSION QUESTIONS

1. Are the media more effective as a cure for crime or more damaging as a cause of crime?

2. Discuss the possible conflict in using the media in anticrime efforts and unduly increasing fear of crime in society.

3. Do you think the media are more effective at influencing offenders or victims of crime?

4. Discuss ways in which people are under surveillance in their daily life due to media technology.

5. Discuss the social factors that make it easy for the media to impart knowledge but difficult for them to change behavior.

6. What do you see as the impact of declining face-to-face interactions in the criminal justice system?

7. Do you feel comfortable about using the media to gather information about crimes or hunt down wanted persons?

7

❦

The Media and the Social Construction of Crime-and-Justice Attitudes and Policies

T his final chapter reviews the evidence concerning the effect of news and entertainment on crime- and justice-related attitudes, beliefs, and policies. It deals with the public and political social construction of crime-and-justice reality that the media portrayals and applications discussed in previous chapters provide. The media effects discussed in this chapter may be less dramatic and more abstract than behavioral effects on crime and violence, but they may well be more important to society.

What crime-and-justice reality do the media construct? Does a particular reality emerge from the portraits of crime and justice projected in the media? As a prelude to examining the research, this chapter examines first the media's planned and purposeful efforts to influence attitudes and beliefs through public information or public communication campaigns. Evaluations of these campaigns provide a sense of what to expect and not to expect regarding reality-constructing effects from the relatively unplanned but pervasive content of news and entertainment. If we then conceptualize news and entertainment media as a long-running, continuous, but poorly designed public information campaign to forward specific claims by various claims-makers, we can reasonably hypothesize that the media have unplanned but significant effects. The research suggests that such effects will interact with other social factors and will be difficult to discern and counteract once established. Following this discussion, the chapter analyzes in turn media influences on crime and justice agenda setting, beliefs and attitudes, and public policy with regard to crime and justice. Public policy discussions about crime and criminal justice issues are themselves important input into the knowledge base from which the public constructs its reality of crime and justice. A self-fulfilling cycle of a policy-supporting construction leading to specific criminal justice policies is common and exemplified in the passage of Three Strikes laws and public support for prison construction in times of declining crime. The importance of crime-and-justice images in the political arena cannot be overemphasized.

Regarding the forming of the public agenda, a process closely related to claims and claims-makers, the research indicates that the media have a haphazard relationship. When effects occur, they appear highly sensitive to local factors, and no consistent, generalizable effects have been observed. The concept of *agenda setting*, in which the order of issues on the public agenda is studied, has given way to *agenda building*, a wider conceptual view that explicitly incorporates policy makers and claims-makers and claims about social and political conditions into a media effects model.

The effects of the media on beliefs and attitudes about crime and justice have received more study. Most studies have built on or reacted to two concepts formulated by Gerbner—those of a "mean-world view" and "mainstreaming." Overall, researchers have found that media effects differ depending on the audience, the medium, and the content communicated. The effects of newspapers and television, in particular, have been found to differ. Newspaper content tends to be associated with differing factual beliefs about crime, whereas television more affects crime and justice attitudes such as fear of crime. In sum, differing media tend to advance different types of crime-and-justice claims.

The final set of research involves the most significant social effect of the media on crime and justice, the shaping of crime-and-justice public policies and by extension crime-and-justice social reality. A number of studies have reported consistent positive correlations between media consumption and support for punitive criminal justice policies among the general public. In addition, a fair amount of anecdotal evidence exists describing media effects on policy decisions within the criminal justice system. Spurred by these reports and building on the earlier research on agenda setting, researchers are currently studying the media's effects on criminal justice policy from an ecological approach, a method that combines case studies with data analysis. Presently, this research is still in a developmental stage, but some studies have reported significant media causal effects. No one has yet been able to specify the structure of the causal relationship, that is, to offer a general process by which the media influence criminal justice policy.

The chapter ends with a discussion of the implications of the research. As a group, the findings indicate that the media, to various degrees, do influence the social construction of crime and justice. Our mass media alter reality by affecting the way people perceive, interpret, and behave toward the world, and our socially constructed world of crime and justice is far from immune to their influence.

THE MEDIA AND
OUR CONSTRUCTED REALITY

People today live in two worlds: a real world and a media world. The first is limited by direct experience; the second is bounded only by the decisions of editors and producers.[1] Linking exposure to the media world with beliefs, attitude formation, and policy effects in the real world has long been a goal in mass communications research and a concern of the public.[2] To what extent the media actually influence people's socially constructed reality remains the subject of some argument, however. The origins of attitudes, beliefs, and opinions are diverse and idiosyncratic, ranging from internal psychological factors to sociological, environmental, and historical influences. It is no surprise that attempts to tie one possible source—in this case the media—to specific constructed realities have had mixed results.

Those asserting that the media significantly affect people's realities about crime commonly argue that the vast majority of our exposure to crime and violence comes from the media.[3] Public surveys have reported that as many as 95 percent of the general population cite the mass media as their primary source of information about crime,[4] and as established in Chapters 2 and 3, crime is an extensively covered, prominent topic in the media. And because most people have little direct experience with crime, it follows that the media would be a significant force in the public's formation of attitudes and perceptions about crime and justice.[5] This reasoning gives rise to both a common belief in the importance of the media and a long-standing concern regarding the media's potential ability to influence and manipulate the social construction of public opinion regarding crime and justice.

Despite concerns and many studies, however, the question of the extent to which the news and entertainment media actually affect attitudes, beliefs, and policies with regard to crime and justice has not been fully resolved. Although unresolved, the available research does allow the drawing of some basic conclusions and suggests some working suppositions regarding the media's role in the formation of crime-and-justice attitudes and policies.

Before considering the research on news and entertainment's effects, however, a useful first step is to examine the research on the purposeful use of the media to influence the general public through public information or communication campaigns. In general, these planned media information campaigns have been aimed at generating specific effects in a large number of individuals through an organized campaign of media activities.[6] The research findings regarding such efforts suggest much about the potential for effects from unplanned, unorganized general depictions of crime and justice in the news and entertainment media.

PUBLIC INFORMATION AND COMMUNICATION CAMPAIGNS

Public communication campaigns have a long history in the United States. Through the nineteenth century, such campaigns were normally conducted by private interest groups or political parties. But by the end of the 1800s, as people became more accessible to printed mass media, these campaigns expanded from local and regional efforts to encompass larger populations and regions. Following the construction of the national wire services, and with the emergence of large-circulation newspapers and magazines after the Civil War, the shift from local media campaigns to broad, national, mass campaigns was complete.[7] After the turn of the century, the federal government became directly involved in campaigns involving various social reforms and legislation. The end result of these trends is that as mass media technology improved and expanded during the 1920s and 1930s to include film and radio, the idea of using the media as an agent of social change was already well established.

Serious research into the effectiveness and impact of these campaigns did not begin until the 1930s, however. Until then, people simply assumed that the media's effects on attitudes and opinions were direct, universal, and immediate. The mass media were conceived as hypodermic needle–like mechanisms that could be used to inject information and attitudes directly into the public. Spurred by this perception, government propaganda efforts as well as academic and public concern about the mass media increased significantly during this period.[8]

The first major research efforts on media effects were the Payne Fund studies (1928–1933), a set of research projects that examined the effects of movies on U.S. society. This research appeared to substantiate the perception that the media constituted an extremely powerful means to influence the public. The concerns about movies then were similar to the concerns about television in the 1960s, and one set of these studies focused upon possible negative effects of movies on society. In the Payne Fund study on the effect of film on children, *Movies, Delinquency and Crime* (1933), Herbert Blumer and Paul Hauser concluded that movies played a direct and powerful role in criminal careers.

It wasn't until the late 1940s that a study of a presidential campaign dealt a death blow to perceptions of strong, direct, and universal media social influence. That study, published in the 1950s in *The People's Choice*, showed that the media did activate some voters to follow their predispositions and reinforced the positions of other voters, but the media's ability to convert voters from one position to another was minimal. A second set of studies, the Decatur studies, which traced informal opinion patterns in relation to marketing, fashion, public affairs, and movie attendance, further attacked the idea of strong, direct media influence. The Decatur studies showed social ties between people, and the social structure in which the media operated, to be more important than the quantity of media messages in determining the media's actual impact.[9] Lastly, the *Revere Project* study in the early 1950s, which studied message diffusion through leaflet distribution, revealed that inaccurate social communication quickly blurred media messages and that the proportion of a total population receiving a media-communicated message is subject to the law of diminishing returns. Increasing spending and the total number of media messages becomes less and less effective—quickly reaching a saturation level where additional expenditures have no additional benefits. All told, these studies suggested that the media were a rather weak, ineffective means of reaching and influencing the public.

A seminal work of the time declared that even if all the physical barriers to communication were removed, five basic barriers would still block effective use of the media to change public attitudes.[10] To begin with, 10 percent to 20 percent of the audience are "chronic know-nothings"—irredeemably apathetic people who are unreachable by any media techniques. In addition, only motivated people will acquire significant amounts of information about a subject. Third, people seek information compatible with their current attitudes, tastes, and biases. Fourth, people interpret the same information differently. And fifth, new information does not necessarily change existing attitudes.[11]

Throughout the 1950s and 1960s, additional research showed that the effects of public information campaigns were largely unpredictable and uncontrollable. A number of evaluations of these campaigns reported that they had no significant effects.[12] Apparently, the mass media could only reinforce attitudes already existing in an audience. The researchers blamed the media's lack of influence on inherent and apparently irreversible characteristics of the public. Rather than as *passive*, the research view during the 1930s and 1940s, the public was now described as *obstinate*.[13] The resultant pessimism regarding the usefulness and effectiveness of media campaigns caused their general dismissal as a social tool. The prevalent view into the 1970s was "When the media hypodermic needle failed, the public was to blame."[14]

In the 1970s, however, some researchers began to recognize in the media a limited potential for influence in specific, controlled circumstances.[15] This renewed perception of the media as influential can be partially credited to societal changes that had occurred since the 1940s. First, television had developed into a pervasive, dominant, and encompassing medium unavailable in earlier periods. Additionally, and perceived by some to be associated with the rise of television,[16] traditional social ties, structures, and values had weakened and people were more geographically and socially mobile.[17] These factors combined to encourage more reliance on the media rather than on other people for social information, thereby increasing the media's potential ability to influence the social construction of reality process. Lastly, the social sciences had developed more sensitive statistical and computerized research techniques, enabling researchers to search for and discern previously hidden, more complex relationships between the media and consumers. Influenced by these developments, academics developed and adopted the current view—that mass media campaigns, if properly designed and employed, can be effective under certain conditions[18]—and a new set of guiding principles regarding the media's influence on public attitudes emerged:[19]

- The mass media may help form attitudes toward new subjects where little prior opinion exists.
- The mass media may influence attitudes that are weakly held.
- The mass media may strengthen one attitude at the expense of a series of others when the strength of the several attitudes is evenly balanced.
- The mass media can change even strongly held attitudes when they are able to report new facts.
- The mass media may suggest new courses of action that appear to better satisfy existing wants and needs.
- The mass media's strongest and most universally recognized effect remains the reinforcement or strengthening of existing dispositions and attitudes.

Besides noting the media's potential usefulness and effects, these principles also highlight the difficulty of using the mass media effectively and the limited scope within which they can be used. Within planned applications, the mass media tend to be more effective at building citizen awareness of an issue, but for complex attitudinal or behavioral changes, they must be coupled with more direct forms of citizen contact and intervention.[20]

Associated with this current moderate perception of the media's influence is a revised theoretical model under which influence and information flow through multiple pathways between the media, interpersonal communication networks, and the individual members of the public.[21] Only in the case of socially isolated people do the media appear to have a primary influence on attitudes.[22] Paradoxically, because of the multiple paths and complex social networks lying between the public and the media, it is also generally accepted that the media's influence can reach even those who do not watch, read, listen, or directly attend to the media in any way.[23]

What are the implications for the social construction of crime and justice from this body of research? When discussing the impact of the news and entertainment mass media on the social construction of crime and justice, remember that, as a whole, media campaigns expressly designed to influence attitudes and perceptions on health, safe driving, safe sex, drug use, and smoking have had rather limited success.[24] This raises some doubt about the ability of the mass media to affect reality construction through the "unorganized, unplanned" content of news and entertainment. If deliberate influence is difficult, should the general crime and justice content of the mass media be a concern?

If the crime-and-justice content of news and entertainment were mixed, accurate, or ignored, the answer would clearly be no. Chapters 2 and 3, however, establish that this is not the case. Unfortunately, the fact that planned media effects appear hard to elicit or control does not mean that unplanned media effects are necessarily absent or innocuous. But the research does imply that if unplanned effects are occurring, they will most likely be highly interactive with other social factors, difficult to isolate and discern, and, most important, difficult to counteract once established. The repetitiveness and pervasiveness of the media's general crime-and-justice content increase the possibility that the media have significant unplanned effects, particularly in the area of crime and justice and especially for persons with limited alternative sources of information. And because of the media's content emphasis on law enforcement and predatory crime, it is expected that any media reality effects would promote crime control constructions more than due process ones.

What public communication campaigns establish is the existence of significant but ephemeral media effects. To the extent that the content of entertainment and news can be perceived as a continuous, long-running, but poorly designed public communication campaign about crime and justice, it is reasonable to hypothesize that unplanned and uncontrolled social construction effects are occurring. The search for these effects has focused in three areas: the social construction of the public agenda and crime's rank on it, the construction of public beliefs and attitudes about crime and justice, and the construction of public policies related to crime and justice.

CONSTRUCTING THE
CRIME-AND-JUSTICE AGENDA

Agenda-setting research considers whether the media, by emphasizing or ignoring topics, influence the list of issues that are important to the public—what the public thinks about rather than what the public thinks.[25] The working hypothesis is that people tend to judge a social concern as significant to the extent that the media emphasize it. In time, some argue, through the process of claims-makers forwarding their claims in the media, the media construct the public agenda. A weak to moderate correlation between the media's coverage of issues and the public's agenda of social concerns has appeared regularly in research findings.[26] Spurred by this association, most of the research has concentrated on the media's effects on the public's ranking of issues in the belief that issues that receive governmental attention are chosen from those issues.[27] In accordance with this focus, a key assumption in the initial research on agenda setting is that the media influence public policy through a linear process: stories of an issue appear, the issue increases in importance to the public, the public becomes alarmed, interest groups mobilize, and policy makers respond.[28] Evidence of a linear process has not emerged from the research, however. Linearity simply fails to capture the range of actions and influences that media attention can set in motion.[29]

Additionally, at its strongest, the media's influence on an individual's agenda of social problems appears to be secondary to other factors such as age, sex, or income.[30] The media's influence is also seldom direct. More often it is mediated through multiple steps and social networks[31] and the acceptance of media-promulgated crime-and-justice claims by the public is an unresolved process. Important questions remain about the strength, form, and extent of the relationship between the media and the public agenda.[32] The correspondence between the media agenda and the public agenda is rather rough, and far more needs to be known about the conditions that maximize and minimize this correspondence.[33] It may be, for example, that individuals whose agendas already match the media's tend to seek out the media for confirmation of the correctness of their priorities, whereas those who disagree with the media tend to avoid them. If so, the greater match between the media and those who attend to the media more would be due not to the media's constructive influence on the public's agenda but to a selective exposure and retention of information on the part of the public.

In sum, the research indicates that media effects are variable; are more common for television than for newspapers; appear to increase with exposure (those who watch more match the media more closely); are more significant the less direct experience people have with an issue; are more significant for newer, concrete issues than for abstract ones but diminish quickly; and are nonlinear, sometimes reciprocal, and highly interactive with other social and individual processes.[34]

Taking something akin to a social construction perspective, researchers have expanded their focus from media agenda-setting effects to what they term *agenda building* in an effort to better comprehend the relationship between the media and social agendas. The original framework of agenda setting studied whether specific issues depicted by the media became more salient to the public. A major deficiency, however, is that such research documents the media's effect on policy making only if one assumes that increases in an issue's salience among the public necessarily trigger policy actions, a conclusion that is usually incorrect.[35] In that policy makers may act without public attention or may ignore public concerns, in the agenda-building perspective, researchers examine the media's relationship to policy makers' agendas. For example, research into the effects of investigative reporting has revealed that the most consistent factor in determining the impact of the media on policy is the relationship that forms between the media and local policy makers.[36] In terms of actual policy effects, the largely passive public, its constructed crime-and-justice reality, and its agenda can often be circumvented even when there is widespread public outrage.[37] Indeed, the interactive and often reciprocal influences between the media and policy makers help to determine the likely composition of the public agenda, hence the term *agenda building*.[38] As the situation now stands, a media effect on the public's agenda is generally acknowledged, but unless the effect also appears among policy makers, it is usually regarded as socially insignificant.

Despite its limitations and current status, the agenda-setting approach was instrumental in changing the view held until the 1970s that the media have only minimal effects.[39] The approach invigorated the search for special cases in which the media had a significant effect and refocused attention on policy formation. And although most of the literature concerning agenda setting analyzes media effects in the political arena, the findings are thought to be equally applicable to the criminal justice system.[40] Specifically regarding crime and justice, the media emphasis on crime and associated claims about the nature of crime has been credited with raising the public's fear of being victimized to disproportionate levels and hence giving crime an inappropriately high ranking on the public agenda.[41] It is felt that crime's high ranking also encourages moral crusades against specific crime issues, heightens public anxiety about crime, and pushes or blocks other serious social problems such as hunger from the public agenda.[42]

Regarding the media-agenda relationship and crime's place on the agenda, the best hypothesis at this time is that the media, policy makers, and the public have an unspecified but mutually reinforcing causal impact on one another's views of the world. In some cases, the media do seem to heighten crime's significance as a social problem, and some individuals do appear to construct their personal social agendas largely from what the media tell them to be concerned about. Not surprisingly, those who are exposed the most to the mass media are most likely to show this association. Because crime is so prevalent in the media, those exposed the most are also most likely to rank crime higher on their agendas. However, effects on the rank of crime on the public agenda may not be as important as once believed. More important are effects on policy makers and on public attitudes and beliefs about crime and justice that support particular crime and justice policies.

CONSTRUCTING PUBLIC ATTITUDES AND BELIEFS ABOUT CRIME AND JUSTICE

Crime-and-Justice Attitudes and Beliefs

The methodology of studying media and public attitudes and beliefs about crime and justice is exemplified in Table 7.1. Researchers typically measure news content, media preferences, or media consumption levels and then determine whether or not the public's beliefs have changed as a result.[43] Using a similar strategy, others have contrasted the news media's depiction of particular crimes, criminals, and law enforcement with the facts contained in official statistical reports.[44] Where the public's beliefs have more closely approximated the media coverage than the statistics, researchers have concluded that those beliefs have derived from claims forwarded in the less accurate media portrayal.[45] Although the bulk of the research has been on television, some research tying newspapers to crime-and-justice beliefs and attitudes also exists and has led to theoretical "newspaper-crime attitude" models reflected in Figure 7.1. Despite the apparent substance of such models, however, the exact nature of the relationship between the media-based claims and public attitudes and beliefs about crime and justice is far from resolved.

In examining the evidence of a relationship between exposure to claims and claims-makers in the mass media and a person's beliefs and attitudes about crime—respectively, the statements about crime a person accepts as true, and the feelings about crime a person believes to be justified—a beginning point is the work of George Gerbner. Gerbner and his colleagues investigated the association between watching large amounts of television and general perceptions about the world, with the idea that the medium creates a particular and pernicious social reality for its audience.[46] This process, initially described as worldview cultivation, was first felt to be directly related to the number of hours of television viewed.[47] The researchers hypothesized that through exposure to television's content most everyone comes to have a similar view of the world—a mainstream, media view. Over time the repetitive themes and content of the mass media homogenize the viewpoints and perspectives of the public. People come to think like the media and, consequently, to think alike. Gerbner's group concluded that even the most sophisticated viewers may receive many facets of their personal knowledge of the real world from purely fictional media representations of that world.[48]

They tested this thesis by having viewers choose among answers to a series of questions about world conditions. One set of answers reflected the media portrayal of reality and the other a real-world measure. One question, for example, asked, "What proportion of people are employed in law enforcement, 5% or 1%?" Gerbner and his associates found that heavy television viewers were significantly more likely to choose the television answers (for this question 5 percent) and also to view the world as "mean"—an outlook characterized by suspicion, fear, alienation, distrust, cynicism, and a belief that the world is a violent, crime-ridden, dangerous place. They suggested that heavy television viewers fail to differentiate between the television world and the real world. The television world either supplants and distorts the viewer's conception of the real world or confirms and then magnifies the viewer's real-world experience.

Prodded by critiques of their initial research,[49] Gerbner and his colleagues subsequently amended their hypothesis of worldview cultivation, according to which all media viewers are affected, to one of mainstreaming, which posits that the media affect some viewers more than others regardless of exposure level. They now argue that the media are homogenizing society, influencing those heavy television consumers who are currently not in the mainstream to move toward it, while not affecting those already in the mainstream. They further argue that the media's effects would be greater among

Table 7.1 Rankings of Relative Frequency of Index Offenses by Police, Media, and Public

Offense	Police	Times-Picayune	TV Stations*	Public
Homicide	7	4	1	4
Robbery	3	1	2	1
Rape	6	6	5	3
Assault	5	3	3	5
Burglary	2	2	6	2
Larceny	1	5	4	7
Vehicle theft	4	7	7	6

*All three television stations were so similar in rankings that they are reported here as one.

Note: $W = .397$; p = n.s. W signifies the Kendall Coefficient of Concordance for use in measuring the relations among several sets of rankings.
SOURCE: From "Crime, Crime News, and Crime Views," by J. Sheley and C. Ashkins, *Public Opinion Quarterly*, 1981, 45:492–506. Copyright © 1981 by the University of Chicago Press. Reprinted by permission.

viewers whose experienced realities were resonant with the media's image of reality.[50] Media effects should be stronger when they reflect or resonate with real-life experiences.

In this perspective it is felt that by sending pervasive, uniform messages or claims concerning the structure and operation of society, television streamlines and standardizes the perceptions of its more dedicated viewers.[51] Ultimately, the media—led by television—are felt to influence even isolated, light-media consumers to adopt the claims and more closely reflect the views of middle America.[52] Other research has revealed, however, that the extent of this influence on beliefs is not absolute and may be reduced substantially when social background and individual characteristics are controlled. Some now argue that television's effects on worldviews are severely limited[53] and that mainstreaming effects are haphazard, with some groups appearing especially susceptible and other groups appearing to react opposite to the theoretical predictions of mainstreaming.[54] Other significant but mixed findings regarding the relationship of the electronic and print media to attitudes about crime have also been reported in a number of studies.[55] Overall, this research suggests that newspaper exposure tends to be associated with beliefs about the distribution and frequency of crime, whereas television exposure is associated with attitudes such as fear of crime and victimization. However, some of the findings reported in these studies directly contradict findings reported in other research.

One factor that has consistently emerged as important in determining the impact of the media is the local environment. In effect, local conditions make the acceptance of media-based claims about crime and justice more likely. For example, television viewing and mean-world attitudes tend to diminish when actual neighborhood crime levels are taken into account. In essence, if one's world truly is mean, television has less effect on one's view of the world. This finding is consistent with the general proposition that media effects are most powerful for issues that are outside a subject's personal experiences. Thus,

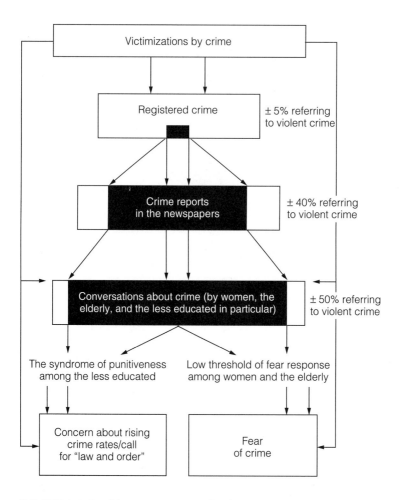

FIGURE 7.1 A Graphic Representation of a Theoretical Model. This model tries to explain the emergence of public attitudes toward crime. The different volumes of the blocks should not be interpreted to represent the exact ratio of the phenomena. Feedback loops have not been taken into account.

From "The Extent of Public Information and the Nature of Public Attitudes Toward Crime," by J. van Dijk. In *Public Opinion on Crime and Criminal Justice*. Vol. XVII. *Collected Studies in Criminological Research*, p. 36. Copyright © by Council of Europe. Reprinted by permission.

media-based claims would be expected to have less impact on beliefs about crime among those who have had direct neighborhood experience with crime and thereby a powerful alternative source of information about crime.[56] Even in high-crime neighborhoods, though, it is not that television has no relationship to beliefs about crime and justice. Consistent positive correlations between heavy television viewing and factual misperceptions about criminality and violence, and between television viewing and support for certain crime-related policies, such as higher spending on police or support for carrying a weapon, are found both in high- and low-crime neighborhoods.[57]

The most relevant crime-and-justice attitude that has been linked to the media is fear of criminal victimization. Fear of crime has long been attributed to mass media influences[58] and is closely related to perceptions of personal vulnerability and the seriousness of the consequences of being victimized.[59] Fear-of-crime levels are socially important because they influence support for punitive criminal justice policies and encourage increased social isolation.[60] As the most accessible and pervasive potential source of fear, the role of the mass media in generating fear is therefore important—but that role is not clear at this time.[61] Because so much media crime and violence goes unpunished, however, the current consensus is that the media significantly contribute to fear in some people.[62]

The literature examining the media's role presents five competing hypotheses as to the media's relationship with fear:

- *Substitution*: Persons lacking alternative sources of knowledge substitute media information, which raises fear.

- *Resonance*: Persons with victim experience or knowledge focus on media information, which compounds preexisting fear.

- *Vulnerability*: Persons less able to prevent victimization are made more fearful by media information.

- *Affinity*: Persons who demographically resemble media victims are made more fearful by media information.

- *Ceiling effects*: Persons who already have high levels of fear are therefore beyond the media's influence.[63]

As can be readily seen, the various hypotheses argue contradictory effects on different audience groups and persons in different social situations from the media. As with other areas of media study, the media's role in the generation of fear has been linked to sets of characteristics. For fear of crime, the relevant characteristics are found in the type of media, the media's content or claims, and the audience's characteristics.[64]

Concerning media type, research regarding the effects of television has found that at least some television programming is correlated with fear of crime for some viewers.[65] Viewer belief in the credibility of the television content is seen as crucial in finding an effect.[66] There is debate however, regarding the causal relationship between television viewing and fear of crime. Some research suggests that more fearful people seek out crime media as a coping mechanism.[67] For example, viewing justified violence in which good guys win appears to generate less fear than viewing unjustified violence in which bad guys get away unscathed.[68]

The relationship between newspapers and fear of crime is equally complex and has produced a similar set of mixed research results.[69] Content factors include the proportion of print space devoted to crime,[70] local versus distant crime news,[71] and random crime or sensational crime reports.[72] Regarding the characteristics of media content and fear, newspaper crime news seems to affect readers' fear of crime differently depending on how the crime news is reported.[73] In Britain, tabloid newspaper readers as well as heavy television viewers have been found to be more fearful of crime.[74] Specifically, if a high proportion of crime news focuses on local crime and portrays it as predominantly sensationalistic or random, those consumers report fearing crime more. If, however, local crimes make up little of a paper's crime news, the public report less fear, regardless of how many crimes are portrayed. The impact of crime news depends on whether the crime is local or distant. Interestingly, factors such as sensationalism, which increase fear when a crime is close at hand, reassure when the crime is distant.[75]

This unique finding is explained by people having an intrinsic need to feel in control of their immediate social environment. In response, they will engage in a process of *downward comparison* when assessing their immediate crime threat. News of distant, sensationalistic, random crime allows people to reduce their anxiety about local crime by allowing them to compare themselves with others who are seen as worse off.[76] Random crime is frightening when close because it suggests loss of control, but reassuring when distant because it suggests that conditions in other places are worse and one has less to fear in one's own immediate, apparently less dangerous environment.

Studies of audience characteristics have focused on belief in the reality of television content,[77] preexisting viewer apprehension about crime victimization, and direct victim experience.[78] In sum, the type of program, the credibility of its claims about the world, the resolution of crimes portrayed, and pre-viewing fear levels when viewing television and the level of sensationalism, randomness, and location of crime when reading newspapers have all been found to be important factors in the generation or lack of generation of fear of crime.[79] The relationship between fear of crime and the new media technologies has just begun to be explored. The directing hypothesis is that because media technologies like VCRs, remote controls, and cable increase content choice for viewers, access to the technology should allow viewers to avoid fear-generating content without having to forgo the mass media. An initial investigation reports that VCR ownership and cable access are associated with less fear of crime, but that videotape rentals and remote control devices are not.[80]

Currently, the latest research suggests that media exposure is more strongly related to fear of distant social conditions than to personal fears.[81] Not surprisingly, the public is more likely to accept fear-generating claims about locales known only via the media. Thus, media consumption is more strongly related to fear of social violence than to fear of personal victimization,[82] fear of nonlocal places more than local,[83] and fear of urban areas more than fear of nonurban areas.[84] Regarding the five competing hypotheses, if ceiling effects occur, supportive evidence appears to apply only to black females.[85] There is also little support for resonance or vulnerability as explanations. There is some support, however, for the process of substitution and affinity.[86] For example, Chiricos and his colleagues found the strongest media fear-of-crime effects concentrate in white middle-aged women and for television news. They conclude that affinity, the identification of white middle-aged women with the victims of crime shown in the media, with a secondary role played by substitution, as the current best explanations for significant correlations between media exposure and fear of crime. Such a conclusion is supported by prior research in violent media and viewer aggression where modeling increases when the violent media persons are demographically similar to the viewers and by the general precepts of the social construction of reality perspective, which argues that indirect sources of information such as the media will be more influential when identification occurs and direct experience is lacking.[87]

In general, this body of research has substantiated an association between the media and crime and justice beliefs and attitudes for specific audiences.[88] The importance of this line of research is that it provides support for the media's role in the social construction of a crime and justice reality. At the least, heavy consumers of television do share certain beliefs about high societal crime and victimization levels and live in a world socially constructed to be more violent and dangerous—to inspire more fear—than the world as constructed by others. The significance of this for society is found in the connection between these socially constructed, media-influenced worldviews and support for various crime and justice policies.

Pornography and Crime-Related Attitudes

As the foregoing indicates, the research picture concerning the media and beliefs and attitudes about crime and justice is suggestive but not consistent. One area in which somewhat clearer results are emerging, however, is that of the relationship between pornography and its explicit and implicit claims about sex, violence, and crime, and consumers' attitudes. Much research has been conducted in this area. On the basis of a series of experiments, depictions of sexual violence rather than of explicit sex per se appear to affect attitudes the most.[89] Specifically, studies that have compared subjects exposed to sexually aggressive material with subjects exposed to nonaggressive but sexually explicit material indicate that nonviolent sexual material results in fewer antisocial attitudes and beliefs than sexually violent material.[90] Most consistently affected have been perceptions, judgments, claims, and attitudes about rape and women who have been raped. Perceptions, judgments, and attitudes about males in general, and about violent male sexual offenders in particular, have been unaffected, or the research results have been contradictory.[91] For example, one study found that males who read a sexually violent passage were more punitive than a control group toward a rapist,[92] whereas another reported that males and females exposed to sexually violent media presentations were less punitive than a comparison group toward a fictional rapist.[93]

Overall, the data do not show that exposure to nonviolent pornography significantly affects attitudes toward rape as a crime or more general assessments of female rape victims. A recent review concluded:

Most consistently in both long [exposure greater than one hour] and short [exposure of less than one hour] term studies, negative effects such as lessened sensitivity toward rape victims and greater acceptance of force in sexual encounters emerge when media portrayals of violence against women or when sex is fused with aggression are used. This is especially true for "slasher" films. Every study that has included a "slasher" condition has found anti-social attitudinal effects. Anti-social effects arise either from exposure to violent pornography *or* from materials that are sexually violent but not sexually explicit.[94]

Depictions of sexual violence appear to foster antisocial attitudes about women and rape, such as the myth or claim that women unconsciously want to be raped or somehow enjoy being raped. Virtually none of the research, however, reveals direct main effects for pornography, and even violent pornography does not negatively affect all male viewers.[95] The research instead indicates an interplay between violent, sexual material and individual dispositions.[96] Many cultural and individual factors appear to mediate the effects of sexually violent material on attitudes.

Individual conditions and the broader social climate are postulated as the originating environmental influences on the individual. The mass media are considered one of many social forces that may, in interaction with a variety of many other cultural and individual factors, affect the development of intermediate attributes, such as thought patterns, sexual arousal patterns, motivations, and personality characteristics. These intermediate variables, in complex interactions with each other and with situational circumstances, such as alcohol consumption or acute arousal, may precipitate [effects] ranging from passive [attitudinal] support to actual aggressive [behavior].[97]

A population identified as hypermasculine[98] appears particularly likely to be influenced, especially by violent pornography.[99] What is not clear is what effect the removal of pornography would have in society. There is little evidence that the number of sexual offenders would be reduced,[100] for the mechanism linking the media and sexual crime is thought to operate through the process illustrated in Figure 7.2. The key unresolved issue is the placement of the hypermasculine at-risk males. If they exist prior to exposure to sexually violent media content (in position 1) rather than following it (in position 2), then exposure to sexually violent media is not as causally significant in the development of antisocial attitudes. In position 1, already-hypermasculine males would simply be seeking out sexually violent content, which would be reinforcing rather than creating their antisocial attitudes. In addition, it is not clear whether or not the third variable, "sexually coercive behavior," actually develops or can be predicted to develop as a result of any antisocial attitudes caused by exposure to sexually violent content.[101] The sole link in the process that has been empirically established (although not without dissent)[102] is that between sexually violent content and antisocial attitudes.

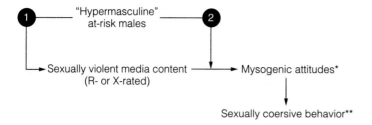

FIGURE 7.2 Hypermasculine Males and
Sexually Violent Media Content

*Increased support of aggression against women, increased belief in the rape myth (that
women secretly want to be raped), higher likelihood of blaming rape victims, increased belief
in general female promiscuity.

**Includes an increase in self-reports of the likelihood that a subject would commit rape.

This is no small result and lends credence to the argument that the media, sexual and nonsexual, are influencing wider attitudes in regard to crime and justice.[103] But as with other aspects of crime-and-justice attitudes, neither a causal link between misogynic attitudes and sexually coercive behavior nor the causal placement of hypermasculine males has been established. As in other media and behavior research areas, outside the laboratory the relationship between these variables is much weaker than the relationship generated within laboratory settings.[104] In other areas of media research such as crime prevention, little evidence of attitude change leading to behavior change has been found.[105] It appears that even after attitudes have been changed, influencing changes in behavior seems to require additional impetus such as learning new skills and instilling increased confidence.[106] This means that sexually violent media may change attitudes about sexual aggression but remain unable to significantly affect sexually aggressive behaviors. Applied to other social behaviors, these findings also imply that media-induced behavior changes that follow from media effects on attitudes and beliefs will only occur haphazardly in individuals and be limited in scope and impact at the aggregate level.[107]

Summary: Media and Crime-
and-Justice Beliefs and Attitudes

What does this research say about the media and people's beliefs and attitudes about crime? The evidence remains mixed concerning the impact of news and entertainment on people's perceptions of crime. Media exposure has been found to be related to particular beliefs about crime, but the relationship is not straightforward or universal. Credibility has been found to be a primary factor in the generation of effects.[108] Especially true for television, the more real or credible the information source is perceived to be, the more it will influence perceptions, suggesting a need to closely study the impact of the increasingly popular crime-related reality programs.[109] When effects do occur, the most common are increased belief in the prevalence and spread of crime, victimization, and violence, and increasingly cynical, distrustful social attitudes. If nothing else, the research indicates a strong, if not understood, interplay between media coverage of crime and public perceptions of it.[110] The media provide both a knowledge foundation and the bricks in the form of individual events and claims about crime and justice for the public's crime and justice construction—plus the attitudinal mortar with which the public binds together its social reality. In sum, the media's portrayal of crime creates and defines a broad public reality of crime, which—with many other factors such as social and physical environment—have much to do with the final shaping of public beliefs.[111]

A few definitive conclusions emerge. For one, an important distinction exists between the respective effects of print and visual electronic media.[112] Television is more related to fear of crime; print, to people's knowledge about crime and adoption of crime preventive actions.[113] These distinctions also likely differentiate between the bottom and top ends of the print media, with tabloids more influencing fear of crime and the elite press affecting knowledge and crime prevention.[114] These differences likely stem from the style in which crime is journalistically portrayed in each medium. Television and the tabloids, being more visceral and emotional in their content, would naturally tend to affect emotional attitudes such as fear and concern. High-end newspapers, being factual and analytical, naturally would tend to affect fact-based beliefs and preventive responses. Second, some individuals appear more susceptible to media effects than others—predisposed hypermasculine males to sexually violent content, socially isolated individuals to belief effects, and nonmainstream individuals and perhaps females who feel that news and entertainment is credible to attitudinal effects. The relationship between the media and beliefs and attitudes about crime ultimately depends on the interaction of three factors: the medium being discussed; the medium's style of presentation and its crime-and-justice content; and the experiences, predispositions, and immediate environment of the consumer. In that the media tend to construct a particular crime-and-justice reality for their consumers, the logical next question is whether or not effects on beliefs and attitudes translate into support for specific crime and justice policies.

CONSTRUCTING CRIME-
AND-JUSTICE PUBLIC POLICIES

Arguably, the relationship between the mass media and the formation of criminal justice policies is one of the more important.[115] Policy effects are important because effects translate into the expenditure and allocation of social resources and define how society will react to crime. Effects on policy are therefore the ultimate prize in the construction of crime and justice reality competition. Claims-makers forward their competing crime-and-justice claims in an effort to steer the social construction of crime-and-justice policy, gaining power, resources, and credibility in the process. Do the media influence the formation of public policies with regard to crime and justice? A way to begin answering this question is to look first at the relationship between the media and public policy unrelated to criminal justice. Recent research does suggest that the news media, at least, significantly affect policy preferences among the public for general social issues.[116] The content of television news broadcasts favoring or opposed to specific policies consequently shifts public opinion in the same direction as the news coverage. In one study, nearly half of the variation in public opinion concerning the examined public policies could be explained on the basis of newscast factors.[117] A journalist's comment in favor of a policy, for example, was associated with an average opinion shift of more than 4 percent in the same direction. Although the public opinion shifts could simply reflect the impact of a preexisting consensus among opinion leaders—a consensus first appearing in television news and later in public opinion—researchers generally interpret the association as part of a causal chain that results in real-world changes in public support for policies that are reported favorably in the broadcast or print media.[118] Recognizing this, claims-makers work diligently to garner media attention and favor.

Unfortunately, until just recently, most studies discussing a media effect on criminal justice policy have only alluded to it as a potential result of media consumption; they have left actual relationships unmeasured and unanalyzed. Historically, statements such as "Television viewing elicits irrational policy support, heavily tilted toward a law and order punitive orientation" have been asserted without any empirical evidence.[119] It has also been forwarded that heavy television viewing leads to increased public acceptance of police violence;[120] and that the incredible success rate of the entertainment media's crime fighters unrealistically raises viewers' expectations of police and the criminal justice system.[121]

When supporting evidence is provided, a good deal of it has been of an anecdotal or correlational nature. Anecdotal references have mentioned increased jury acquittals, more argumentative and hostile witnesses, influences on the way the police enforce the law and investigate crime, and influences on police recruits to hold false expectations and unrealistic attitudes about police work.[122]

The correlational data support these anecdotal effects. For example, the correlation between TV exposure and crime-and-justice policy support appears to be strong, particularly among adolescents.[123] Adolescents who are heavy viewers of TV crime shows are found to measure lower on knowledge of criminal justice processes, are disposed to support the law enforcement system, more highly value norm compliance, and favor crime control over due process policies.[124] Even students who achieve high grades, are heavy readers, and are aware that television content is unrealistic come to devalue due process considerations such as the protection of civil liberties. And despite the fact that most people know little about the criminal justice system, television crime show viewers learn nothing about the criminal justice system, and television viewing exacerbates a preexisting lack of criminal justice knowledge.[125] In addition, varying the content and style of a news story changes its effect on the public's support for crime control policies. Tabloid-style coverage creates the greatest support for harsher sentences, whereas summaries of court documents produces the least.[126] Not surprisingly, the predatory crime content that is most common contains claims about criminality that pro–crime control claims-makers can easily use to enhance crime control policies.

Particularly revealing and important is how the causes of crime are framed in the media. Two dichotomous presentations compete. The first construction is of societal causal responsibility, which includes references to economic conditions, discrimination, racial inequality, poverty, and cultural institutions. This causal explanation competes with individual causal responsibility involving character deficiencies (greed, mental disorders, laziness) or lack of individual skills (uneducated, untrained).[127] Because media portray crime almost exclusively in episodic terms—that is, reporting on a specific individual and a violent predatory criminal act—the cause of crime is largely framed in the media in the individual responsibility perspective. The construction of the cause of crime is dominated by the individual perspective, which forwards a stigmatizing nonredeemable portrait of criminals more often than a potentially salvable one.[128] Support for these claims about the causes of crime is particularly apparent among consumers who have limited alternate sources of crime and justice information. When people have a full spectrum of information resources, alternative and competing explanations of crime are more likely to be given credence and are more strongly argued.[129]

The result of this uneven competition can create public perceptions of crime and justice reality and general acceptance of claims about crime and justice that are far removed from real-world conditions. For example, Canadians, like U.S. citizens, believe that their courts are too lenient in sentencing robbers. When asked what percentage of convicted robbers should be sentenced to prison, however, over half give estimates lower than the 80 percent to 90 percent of convicted robbers that judges actually send to Canadian prisons. Thus people report feeling that their criminal justice system is not harsh enough—when they would instead be more lenient.[130] Despite the fact that the research discussed to this point does not prove causal relationships between media-based content and claims and support for specific crime-and-justice policies, such distorted reality constructions are commonly credited to the influence of the media.[131]

The search for firm evidence of a causal relationship between the media, claims-makers, and public policy has taken shape under a methodology termed an *ecological approach*, which combines case studies with public survey or justice system data analysis. In this approach the media are conceptualized not only as carriers of information and images but as direct claims-making actors in the politics of policy formation. In each local social, political, and cultural environment, the media are seen as helping to shape criminal justice policy by establishing ongoing relationships with other local claims-makers including policy makers, lobbyists, and public officials.[132] This conceptualization recog-

BOX 7.1 NRA Ads

Despite the lack of definite conclusions regarding the media's effects and mechanisms of influence, political and private lobby groups such as the National Rifle Association commonly use the media to try to influence the public's views on crime and justice.

Source: *Courtesy of The National Rifle Association of America, Washington, DC 20036*

nizes the media's role in the ecology of public policy and the fact that journalists oftentimes collaborate with officials and form symbiotic alliances between reporters and policy makers,[133] sometimes to the point of building official reaction into their stories.[134] The strength of this approach is its simultaneous recognition of the overt role of the media in policy development and its acknowledgment that differing local social, political, cultural, and historical conditions will make that role different in each actual case.

One of the earliest studies in this tradition, and one that revitalized the current study of justice and the media, was by Mark Fishman in 1978.[135] Fishman studied the role of the news media as claims-makers in creating the perception of a wave of crimes against the elderly in New York City. He reported that the end result of the news media theme coverage of crimes against the elderly was the creation of new enforcement squads, the reallocation of public resources, and the introduction of new legislation—all without any measurable increase in actual victimization of the elderly. The final constructed reality had no basis in any relevant empirical reality. A similar effect was noted in Britain regarding muggings.[136] In a third study, it was found that prosecutors' perceptions of both public and press opinion were important factors in their decision whether or not to prosecute pornography.[137] The prosecutor's estimation of pornography's position on the local citizens' agenda and the local press's agenda were two of the most significant predictors of whether or not a prosecutor reported having filed formal obscenity charges within the prior year. These findings support the conclusion that criminal justice officials tend to respond both to tangible media content and to what they believe to be local public and media opinion in determining their policy course.[138]

Researchers continue to explore the nature of the media–criminal justice policy relationship, and they have been able to report clear, positive connections between the two. The results of the ecological research, in particular, have established that the media can directly affect what actors in the criminal justice system do without having to first change the public's attitudes or agendas. Though establishing that causal relationships develop at least in some cases, the research has not been able to specify the general nature or prevalence of the relationships. The idiosyncratic nature of the media–justice policy relationship makes predicting the direction and magnitude of media influence in specific instances difficult. The difficulty arises because the media may themselves be claims-makers or serve as the voice of nonmedia claims, and claims-makers may employ the media in various ways, and because the media are as likely to affect criminal justice decision making indirectly as they are to directly influence crime and justice policy.[139] Therefore, conclusions regarding the importance of the media for crime and justice policy have remained tentative.

However, knowledge has advanced beyond the idea that the media have only minimal effects and the contention that the media's short attention span combined with the long-term gestation of most public policy preclude significant media effects. In the criminal justice system, the sometimes glacial legislative and appellate processes are counterbalanced by the daily stream of case-by-case decisions. Criminal justice policy and decision making are composed of both long-term legislative, regulatory, and administrative decisions and short-term individual case-level decisions.[140] In accordance, criminal justice policy is created in both long and short time periods and the media often significantly influence the policy process,[141] generating short-term bursts of activity by their focus and serving as one of a number of social steering mechanisms for long-term developments.[142]

The social and political ecologies in which the media exert their policy effects represent a complex and evolving reality. Among criminal justice system officials, response to the media can be either reactive or proactive—that is, they may react to what they have seen and heard in the media or act in anticipation of claims they expect to find in the media.[143] As the source of much news information, criminal justice policy makers and claims-makers also strongly influence the content of crime and justice news.[144] This ability has expanded as criminal justice agencies have become more adept at dealing with the media, developing public information and public relations offices, and beginning to employ claims-making marketing strategies with the public.[145] In the final analysis and from a practical standpoint, even if the media ultimately pay no attention to an issue, a criminal justice official may still act on the expectation that attention will be forthcoming. In effect, it is impossible—even if the media desires it—for the media to eschew any policy-making role in the criminal justice system.[146]

As it stands, the research indicates that among criminal justice officials, even more than among the public, the media significantly influence both policy development and support.[147] Effects are multidirectional, and the media content, the timing and presentation of the claims, and the characteristics and concerns of the general public, claims-makers, and the criminal justice policy makers at any particular time interact to determine the media's influence on criminal justice system policies.[148] Effects have been shown to range from broad, far-reaching policy crusades and criminal legislation to specific point influences on individual discretionary case decisions within the criminal justice system. In the end, media attention sometimes emerges as more important an influence on criminal justice activities than the legislation or policy initiative that its influence spurs.[149] The research difficulty is not in the media's lack of significant policy or social construction effects but in the difficulty of determining when these effects occur.

PROBLEMS IN DETERMINING MEDIA EFFECTS ON CRIMINAL JUSTICE POLICY

The research regarding the media and criminal justice policy has plateaued in an exploratory stage and neither the causal structure of the relationship nor useful generalizations about it have been forthcoming. This is particularly disappointing to criminal justice practitioners, as the media's influence is commonly recognized and the need to function in a media-influenced policy environment becomes increasingly pressing.[150] Determining the effects of the media on criminal justice policy is hindered in two ways.[151] Initially, the determination is burdened by a set of common social research concerns that are exacerbated in the media–criminal justice area. In addition, a set of research difficulties unique to the media–criminal justice policy relationship further retards research efforts.

The first set of difficulties involve the identification and measurement of relevant concepts[152] as well as *history* effects resulting from the media portrayal of external worldly events.[153] In addition, research difficulties associated with group versus individual levels of analysis are common in media-policy research. As with the *ecological fallacy* (the error of ascribing characteristics of a group to each group member or those of individual members to the group),[154] a number of media effects can be observed at the aggregate level even though their appearance and causal mechanisms cannot be predicted or understood at the individual level of analysis.[155] The study of highway fatalities offers a useful analogy here. Based on past trends, it is possible to make fairly accurate predictions of the number of highway deaths that will occur over a holiday—to say, for example, "Fifty to sixty people will die on the state highways this New Year's weekend." But no one can predict who those fifty to sixty persons will be, so it isn't possible to issue preemptive warnings telling the destined victims to stay home.

In the media–criminal justice area, this difficulty is best shown in the aggression research findings. Positive aggregate relationships between violent media content and viewer aggression are consistently found but researchers are not able to predict and therefore to fully understand effects at the individual level. Thus we may know that a certain proportion of individuals will behave aggressively after exposure to violent media, and we may even be able to fairly accurately predict the size of the proportion, but we cannot accurately predict which individuals will respond aggressively and which will not. It follows that the reason for this deficiency is not simply a lack of knowledge or measurement skill but rather that multiple sets of factors are involved in the generation of effects. Effects will vary not only from individual to individual, but for the same individual from media exposure to exposure. In practice, responses to media are related simultaneously to characteristics of the individual, characteristics of the media content, and characteristics of the exposure setting.

This aggregate-to-individual discrepancy also extends to the media and criminal justice policy area. In a similar fashion, the reactions of individual criminal justice decision makers to the media are the result of a three-pronged interaction between the media, the characteristics of the claims-makers and decision makers, and the characteristics of the setting. As found in other social behavior areas, the media's effects are most often indirect, filtered through personal social networks. Such effects are not usually predictable at the individual level or amenable to direct, short-term manipulation at the systematic level. Furthermore, because effects are often subtle, delayed, and hidden, rather than direct and planned, they often appear to be insignificant.

These common research problems are especially a concern when studying the relationship of the media to public policy because they ultimately present the researcher with three sets of potential effects. As the examples in Table 7.2 show, the media may actually be the cause of a criminal justice policy change (model A). Conversely, an external event may be the cause, while the media simply covers the event simultaneously with the policy change (model B)—or the media's coverage of an external event and the event may both be influencing criminal justice policy (model C).

Table 7.2 Media Criminal Justice Policy Relationship Models

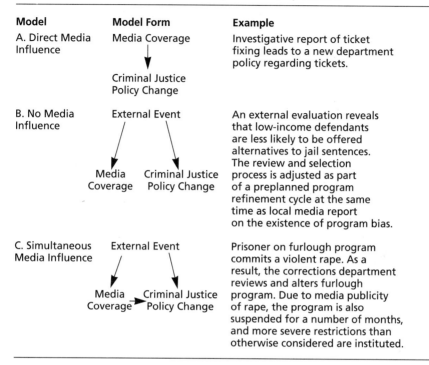

Model	Model Form	Example
A. Direct Media Influence	Media Coverage ↓ Criminal Justice Policy Change	Investigative report of ticket fixing leads to a new department policy regarding tickets.
B. No Media Influence	External Event ↙ ↘ Media Coverage / Criminal Justice Policy Change	An external evaluation reveals that low-income defendants are less likely to be offered alternatives to jail sentences. The review and selection process is adjusted as part of a preplanned program refinement cycle at the same time as local media report on the existence of program bias.
C. Simultaneous Media Influence	External Event ↙ ↘ Media Coverage → Criminal Justice Policy Change	Prisoner on furlough program commits a violent rape. As a result, the corrections department reviews and alters furlough program. Due to media publicity of rape, the program is also suspended for a number of months, and more severe restrictions than otherwise considered are instituted.

A researcher's task of sorting out the effects of the media from the effects of external events—and from the effects of the coverage of external events—is obviously difficult. Compounding these problems, another set of unique research problems arise from the novel manner in which the media are related to criminal justice policy. Not only can these relationships be unexpected and opposite to common-sense expectations, they can be anticipatory and precede media attention. Regarding unexpected effects, two types appear in the literature: systematic echo effects and counterproductive results.

An unexpected systematic effect is best shown by a rarely recognized news media coverage effect. Termed an *echo effect* in the research literature,[156] it was first described thirty years ago as the tendency for officials to treat defendants in unpublicized cases harshly if the press has been demanding such treatment for defendants in publicized cases.[157] Experimental evidence of echo effects from pretrial publicity on jurors has been found in a number of studies.[158] For example, a study of the processing of criminal cases prior to, during, and following a highly publicized case involving the sexual abuse of toddlers at a private day care center demonstrated an echo effect in operation.[159] Initial analysis showed marked increases in the number of filings of cases involving child victimization following the publicized case and an increase in the sentences of defendants adjudicated guilty. There were also indications of a second echo in the local system to national news coverage of a second day care sexual child abuse case involving a California day care center that broke about one year after the local story. The data reveal a jump in cases immediately following the local case and then another jump following the appearance of the California case. The existence of echo effects portend an influence spillover from the coverage of publicized criminal cases onto nonpublicized ones. Pervasive systematic media effects on a large number of unpublicized cases are likely, but this influence has not been generally recognized or adequately studied. To date, the courts and social science researchers have focused nearly exclusively on effects on cases that directly receive news coverage.

The second effect, counterproductive results, occurs in situations where the media are part of a new criminal justice policy initiative, usually involving a crime reduction goal. Media-based anticrime campaigns have sometimes been found to have effects opposite to the campaign goals. For example, early media-based antidrug campaigns have been described as resulting in increases in illegal drug experimentation by providing uninformed audience members with detailed drug use information.[160]

Collectively, echo and counterproductive effects underscore the idiosyncratic nature of the media–criminal justice social construction relationship. The relationship's unpredictability makes it difficult to determine the direction and magnitude of influence or to specify the mechanism through which the media's influence is being exerted. In addition to systematic and counterproductive effects, a third problem unique to this area makes such determinations even more difficult. Extremely rare for other social factors but not uncommon for the media, anticipatory effects seem to reverse the causal order of media attention and criminal justice policy change. In these situations, the effect on policy occurs before any measurable change in the media. The policy changes occur because criminal justice system officials can respond in a proactive manner to anticipated media coverage. In a similar fashion, offenders can respond to an announced criminal justice policy change even though no real-world changes have occurred.

Anticipatory effects are thus of two types. The first involves an effect on criminal justice policy makers; the second is an anticipatory effect on offender populations. Regarding the first type, criminal justice system personnel sometimes determine their policy course based on the local public and media opinion they expect to encounter. Therefore, even if the media pay no attention to an issue, an official may still act on the idea that attention might be forthcoming and initiate a new policy or fail to implement a requested policy in order to avoid expected negative media reaction. Referring to the three models in Table 7.2, this effect is a hybrid of model A, in which a criminal justice policy change occurs in an effort either to prevent media coverage or to align policy with expected coverage. In the first instance, a successful policy change cancels the coverage, and in the second, the proactive policy change could very well be in anticipation of coverage that might never have occurred, such as when the media's interest is diverted to other issues. In either case, because the media influence policy without any tangible coverage, the task of determining and studying a media policy effect is daunting. The difficulty is greater, but the problem is somewhat similar to that of determining how many crimes were not committed as a result of the possible deterrent effect of punishment.

As discussed in Chapter 6, offenders can also display a type of anticipatory reaction to the media through an announcement effect. Evoked in offender populations, this effect occurs when media publicity causes offender behavior changes in anticipation of a new criminal justice policy publicized in the media. This media-induced behavior effect will occur with or without an actual criminal justice policy change. Announcement effects will decline and dissipate over time. Their effects, however, interweave with effects from criminal justice policies and again make the separating of media coverage effects from those of the criminal justice policy both important and difficult: new criminal justice policies can (and have) been acclaimed as successful due to confusion of media announcement effects with criminal justice policy effects.[161] An error can be made by too quickly ascribing the media-induced change in behavior to a new criminal justice policy when sometimes it is only the announcement effect that has reduced offenses—the actual policy change having no effect.[162]

Counterproductive, echo, and anticipatory reactions add a unique level of difficulty to deciphering the relationship of the media and the criminal justice system. These media-related effects interweave with any criminal justice policy effects. Observed changes can be in anticipation of the media attention (as when prosecutors decide to increase DUI prosecutions to head off potential negative publicity), in anticipation of a policy being changed (as when prosecutors decide to pursue harsher sentences for drunk drivers due to the echo effect from a highly publicized DUI case), or due to a criminal justice policy change directly lobbied for by the media (as when DUI prosecutions increase due to a media investigatory series suggesting that lenient treatment for DUI offenders is common).

There is the real possibility of one anticipatory effect occurring to prevent a second anticipatory effect from occurring. In such a case, a preemptive decision to not change an established policy in favor of a new policy would occur so as to avoid the anticipated negative media coverage generated by the appearance and subsequent waning of an announcement effect of the (now rejected) new criminal justice policy. For example, a prosecutor sensitive to media dynamics may decide against launching a tougher but expensive DUI policy to avoid the problem of future negative coverage of the apparent loss of initial prosecutorial effectiveness that will occur when the media-generated announcement effect wanes. At that point, the new DUI policy, cast as suddenly failing to maintain its initial successful deterrent impact, results in the prosecutor being called to task. Sensing this pitfall, a prosecutor might well decide to forgo this or other new policies. For the researcher and the public, the recognition and delineation of the media's role in such a scenario would be Herculean. Indeed, based on the discussion thus far, confidently comprehending any effect of the media appears daunting, and it is perhaps surprising that the research has progressed as far as it has.

In the final analysis, then, the media must be viewed as both claim-carrying messengers and claims-making actors in the criminal justice policy arena. Journalists, programmers, and editors are part of the policy-forming process, sometimes initiating and sometimes responding to changes in criminal justice policies. Although it is clear that media effects occur, the studies of these effects have not yet identified the characteristics of decision makers who are likely to be sensitive to media attention (for example, it seems likely that those elected to office are more at risk of media influence, but no one has actually studied the point) or the situations in which criminal justice policy will be affected. Because of the highly idiosyncratic and interactive nature of the relationship between the media and the criminal justice decision-making process, it is unlikely that the effects of the media will be broadly predicted with confidence or described in widely generalizable propositions.

Summary: The Media and the Social
Construction of Crime-and-Justice Reality

Many diverse factors influence the social construction of criminality and criminal justice. On the basis of the existing evidence, the media cannot be forwarded as the primary factor, although their influence cannot be ignored. Given the limited media applications identified in the research on public communication campaigns, it is not surprising that strong and consistent relationships have not been found in the realm of crime and justice. Overall, the research findings indicate that the media do influence to various degrees the construction of crime-and-justice agendas, perceptions, and policies of media consumers, but not directly or simply. In general, the media appear to more directly influence factual perceptions of the world, such as consumers' estimations of the actual level of crime (especially when a consumer has few alternative sources of information about crime), than overall evaluations of social conditions or practices.

The media also appear to affect people's perceptions of newer issues more than their perceptions of long-standing problems, and perceptions of the larger world more than perceptions of local community conditions.[163] This is likely because the media-based claims about new issues and distant situations are less likely to be challenged by information from other sources such as personal experience. Thus the media appear to affect people's concern about crime as an issue independent of affecting their personal fear of victimization.[164] And people's judgments about the world, such as whether the world is generally bad or good and what should be done about crime, remain more influenced by personal experience, information from acquaintances, individual background, and local conditions than by media programming.[165] Within these limitations, the media do help construct crime-and-justice social reality and influence the formation of the social policies that reflect that social reality.

Further complicating and obscuring the relationship between the media and crime and justice, perceptions of crime and justice appear to be intertwined with other social perceptions. Several researchers have pointed out that crime-related attitudes are not determined solely by one's perception of the crime problem.[166] And if perceptions of crime are intricately related to broader perceptions of the world, it is unrealistic to expect that they would change solely in accordance with media presentations of crime. Instead, perceptions of crime and justice are part of a larger construction of the nature and health of society and not a unique, separate component.[167] The likelihood is that these broader media-influenced constructions combine with individual preexisting attitudes and experiences to influence the construction of each individual's crime-and-justice reality.

At present, the most plausible model of the relationship between the media and public perceptions is one in which causation is reciprocal and multidirectional.[168] The media emerge as a significant steering mechanism for long-term changes in attitudes regarding crime and justice.[169] A slowly growing body of evidence indicates that the media, sometimes directly but more often indirectly, affect the way audiences perceive, interpret, and behave toward the world by influencing their social construction of the reality of their world.

PROSPECTS FOR THE MEDIA'S SOCIAL REALITY OF CRIME AND JUSTICE

In the preceding chapters, we have moved from the origins of news and entertainment to the impact of media on public attitudes and policies. Reviewing the implications of those chapters, we have seen that by the late nineteenth century the "pre–mass media" media contained the same criminal stereotypes and causal explanations of crime found in today's media. And crime-related themes have been the most common plot element throughout the one-hundred-plus-year existence of U.S. commercial media. The image of justice that is most palatable and popular is the image that has been historically projected. The messages of the entertainment media conform to a law of opposites: The reality the media depict with regard to crime and justice is opposite to any objective measure of reality. Much of this is also true of news: Crime constitutes a constant, significant portion of the total news; criminals are normally constructed as either predatory street criminals or dishonest businesspeople and professionals; and the criminal justice system is shown as an ineffective, often counterproductive means of dealing with crime. In every category—crimes, criminals, crime fighters, the investigation of crime, arrests, case processing, and case dispositions—the media present a world of crime and justice that is not found in reality. The increased merging of the news and entertainment media means that the portraits of crime and justice in each will continue to be more alike than different. As a basic rule of thumb, both the news and entertainment media consistently take the least common crime or justice event and make it the most common crime or justice image.

The lack of realistic information in the media further mystifies and obscures criminality and the criminal justice system.[170] The media emphasize individual personality traits as the cause of crime and violent interdiction as its solution, showing a preference for crimes involving weapons or sophisticated technology.[171] They present criminality as an individual choice and imply that other social, economic, or structural explanations are irrelevant. Their frequent use of a vocabulary of force and terms like *crime fighter* and *war on crime* suggest to the public that crime must be fought rather than solved or prevented.[172] Media portrayals further instruct the public to fear others, for the criminal is not easily recognizable and is often found among the rich, powerful, or seemingly trustworthy. Cumulatively, these images tilt perceptions toward law enforcement and crime control constructions, for, ironically, although the criminal justice system is not shown favorably, the solutions to crime suggested involve expansion of the existing criminal justice system through harsher punishments and more law enforcement.

Despite being frequently at odds, the media and the courts react similarly to criminal events. Both want to gather information, control access to this information, construct a particular reality of the event, and present it to a specific audience. In addition, both have been pressured by the same social forces to be more open and accessible, to reveal their backstage news-gathering or case-processing procedures, and, sometimes reluctantly, to provide information to each other. Not surprisingly, when the courts use a proactive strategy such as closure to control their information and directly impinge on the activities of the media, the media respond with vigorous opposition. But though reactive, less restrictive mechanisms such as expanded voir dire are more popular, their effectiveness is questionable, and it is not clear when they should be used. On the media's part, they have worked to control their information by arguing that journalists have a constitutional right to "privileged conversations" with news sources and by lobbying for the passage of shield laws to legislatively ensure this protection. These efforts have intensified as the media have been more frequently pressed for information and reporters have been periodically forced to testify. Though the media have had successes, at this time their ability to avoid opening news files or testifying varies considerably from state to state and case to case.

Evidence for media behavioral effects, such as an increase in social aggression following exposure to violent visual media content, is clear in the laboratory but mixed in society. Though a cathartic effect has been discredited, debate continues about the extent to which the media may stimulate violence and the significance of such an effect. The research suggests—without conclusively proving—that we are a more aggressive society because of our mass media. However, social aggression is not necessarily criminal, nor is most crime aggressive in nature, and the media's influence on criminality, independent of its effect on aggressive behavior, has not often or adequately been explored. Aggregate crime rate studies suggest that the media may very well affect crime independently of violent content. In addition, evidence has suggested that the visual media may have more of a copycat or stimulation effect on property crime than on violent crime. One important exception to this generalization concerns sexually violent media content. There is increasing evidence that sexual violence against women need not be portrayed in explicit, X-rated media to have negative effects, and the influence of sexually violent media content on predisposed, hypermasculine males presents a clear danger.

The total available evidence suggests, and most reviewers agree, that the media do affect crime rates. But both the nature of the effect and its magnitude are undetermined. The research on media violence and pornography indicates that the media operate on pools of already-at-risk individuals, some unknown proportion of whom will have a mix of characteristics and circumstances that make them likely to respond with violence. The results are media-induced acts of aggression, sexual and otherwise, most likely induced through the short-term mechanism of modeling. The more heavily the consumer relies on the media for information about the world and the more predisposed the viewer is, the more likely the effect. Therefore, violence-prone children and the mentally unbalanced are especially at risk of aping media violence. When sex and violence are linked, hypermasculine males are most influenced. When the news media sensationalize crimes and make celebrities of criminals, people seeking notoriety imitate those crimes. And when successful crimes, in particular property crimes, are detailed either in print or in visuals, some criminals will emulate them. Only a small number of people appear to be significantly affected, but the media also slightly affect a larger, unknown portion of the general population, by fostering attitudes that support crime. Both attitudinal and behavioral effects by the media are therefore important influences on the total crime picture.

On the other side of the media social construction equation are media-based anticrime efforts. The available evaluations show these efforts to be effective means of disseminating information and to have an apparent ability to influence attitudes. However, their ability to significantly affect behavior has not been established. The media are not a panacea for crime, and though useful in specific areas, media-based anticrime programs are not likely to significantly reduce the overall crime rate. No program has empirically demonstrated a significant long-term and displacement-free effect on the crime rate. Still, the evaluations show that media-based anticrime programs can have significant immediate effects simply by having well-publicized starts. In fact, an announcement effect is normally the strongest effect found, and the prime difficulty for these programs is to maintain their immediate gains over a longer period of time. To use the media and media technology effectively to combat crime, planners must therefore allocate resources and effort to ensuring and maintaining real-world changes, such as changes in prosecution and sentencing practices, not just to publicizing a perceived change. Single-handedly, the media alone are as unable to deter criminal behavior as they are to criminalize individuals.

In regard to the use of the technology of the media in the criminal justice system, such use has become common in the presentation of physical evidence and testimony. But media technology has been used only in limited applications in creating permanent records and facilitating live proceedings. For most judicial personnel the processing and recording of brief, nontrial procedural steps and small portions of a regular trial is acceptable; anything more is resisted. Acceptance or rejection seems to depend on whether or not a crucial element of justice is felt to be lost because of the technology. For preliminary and short procedural steps, most participants feel that the integrity of the process is unaffected. With regard to longer, more significant, and more symbolic steps such as trials, concerns and resistance rise. As a law enforcement and judicial tool, the technology is in most cases efficient, and its use has been judged not to violate due process protections. Though initially promising in restricted uses, however, the technology's long-term effects on participants, on the decorum of the judicial system, and, ultimately, on the social construction of justice have not yet been fully assessed.

Lastly, by aiding in the construction of crime-and-justice reality, the media also subtly but significantly affect crime-and justice-policies. To varying degrees, they influence the agendas, perceptions, and policies of their consumers with regard to crime and justice. These media effects interact with other factors, are difficult to discern, and are difficult to counteract. Perceptions of crime and justice appear to be intertwined with other, broader perceptions of social conditions; therefore, it is not surprising that consistently strong relationships have not been found between the media and crime and justice public attitudes. In general, media portrayals of crime and justice appear to have most influence on people's factual perceptions, such as the amount of crime they believe to be occurring, and to have less direct influence on overall evaluations of social conditions or ideas about what should be done.[173]

Overall, the mass media are constant, subtle, and unpredictable agents with regard to crime and justice—beneficial if carefully used, but neither the magic cure nor the potent demon they are sometimes presented as. They cannot be ignored, and they should not be seen as uncontrollable. Where then do we stand in terms of a broad understanding of media and the social construction of a crime-and-justice reality?

Understanding Media and Crime-and-Justice Reality

A beginning point for addressing the media's role are three media, crime, and justice paradoxes.

- The media more often than not construct the criminal justice system and its people negatively and as ineffective. Yet the cumulative effect is support for more police, more prisons, and more money for the criminal justice system. (The media-constructed reality is that the system does not work but remains the best hope against crime.)

- Despite being portrayed as objective and chosen for its newsworthiness, crime news is routinely created and prepackaged by and for news agencies, which then present the crime news within established, stereotypic themes. (The public is encouraged to believe that crime news is representative and reflects the common nature of actual crime rather than the organizationally created product such news really is.)

■   As the technical capability to cover crime news has expanded, media organizations have conversely increasingly blurred the line between news
and entertainment. In the process, crime stories have become the mainstay of new hybrid news-and-entertainment or info-tainment programs.
(As the news media, led by the electronic media, have become more able
and willing to cover backstage events and expose new information, they
have also been spurred by competition to present these events and information in entertainment formats to maximize revenues.)

All three of these paradoxes reflect the continuing disparity between the
media-constructed reality of crime and justice and the actual social reality of
crime. This disparity has come about because the media have converged on a
single image of crime and justice, emphasizing it in news, entertainment, infotainment, and anticrime programming—an image of rampant, predatory criminality ineffectively checked by traditional criminal justice system methods.
And though the media, led by television, have increased their capability to
discover and deliver information about the world, both the print and the electronic media have moved instead toward greater reliance on created, prepackaged information, stereotypes, and entertainment-style content heavily
influenced by crime-and-justice claims-makers. As a result, the public receives
an image of crime and justice that is not only unnecessarily distorted but that
supports basically one anticrime policy. Enhanced crime control mechanisms
are advanced at the expense of due process protections and approaches that do
not rely on the criminal justice system.

Commercial, organizational, and cultural forces drive the media to construct and perpetuate this predatory crime-centered image. The media are
commercial businesses and must show a profit. Therefore they must compete
for consumers while keeping their production costs low. This makes them
conservative. They become reluctant to experiment with new content and
frequently copy content ideas from their competitors, resulting in news and
entertainment dominated by standard styles, themes, plots, content, and underlying claims and constructions. In addition, media agencies are organizations and must respond to organizational constraints such as deadlines and the
need to control resources and schedules.[174] These factors pressure the media to
apply their limited resources in established, safe ways. They thus continue to
produce updated versions of what has been produced and found socially acceptable in the recent past.

In determining what is socially acceptable with regard to crime and violence, cultural forces come into play. As a culture, depictions of predatory
criminals both entertain and comfort us. They entertain because they frighten
and provide glimpses of realities we are not likely to encounter. They comfort
because they relieve our social conscience for crime and violence by constructing crime as not due to social inequities, racism, or poverty—things society could be held responsible for and might address. The media's maddened,
greedy predators are criminals out of their own will, or maybe God's will, but
certainly not society's will. Such criminals, and with them the crime problem,

can therefore be guiltlessly eliminated. Together, the commercial, organizational, and cultural forces create a strong resistance to a different and broader construction of crime and justice in the media: the media resist because they cannot afford to seriously challenge the current construction, and we resist as consumers because we are more comfortable with the narrow picture.

The Future of Reality

As is found in much regarding the media and justice, however, not all signs point in the same direction. Running counter to the narrow construction of crime is the modern media's ability to expand our access to previously hidden criminal justice realms and thus to expand our crime-and-justice reality. Phrases such as *government in the sunshine* and *freedom of information* reflect government responses to a larger, media-driven social trend toward more open public institutions and enhanced scrutiny of public officials.[175] The two dominant social institutions, the media and the criminal justice system, play critical roles in this process, which can be understood as part of the general process of exposing more and more of the previously hidden backstage areas of society to the public.[176] In a hypermedia society, closed institutions and proceedings and secret information and sources are automatically viewed with suspicion and challenged. Ironically, in the face of these developments, the criminal justice system and the mass media remain among a handful of social institutions that still resist full, open access and struggle to keep their realities closed. Apparent throughout the preceding chapters, the results of this trend toward greater access are the revelation of previously hidden backstage events, the presentation of more graphic news and entertainment, the increased public tolerance of surveillance, the increased recording of judicial steps and interactions between the police and citizens, the proliferation of media trials, and the increased acceptance of media technology in more situations.

As the media have evolved, the distinction between front- and backstage social behaviors has blurred, and we now have only onstage and offstage behavior. That is, an event or an individual is either an object of media attention and subject to full exposure, or ignored by the media. For the media, the concepts of public and private have lost their meaning.[177] Any aspect of anything that is the focus of media attention is now open to news coverage and entertainment productions. In today's media-saturated society, to ensure privacy, one must be ignored. Like the highly visible British royal family, participants in high-profile criminal cases forfeit broader and broader areas of their lives to media scrutiny. We now have and follow closely celebrity crime and criminals constructed from the illegal acts of entertainment, political, and sports persons. Our vicarious entrance into the backstage private lives of the famous and unfortunate has also led to pseudosocial, media-based relationships with "media friends" whom we feel we know intimately and whose life developments we follow with personal interest. Many know Oprah Winfrey better than they know their neighbors. It has also led to a new form of murder and a new type of murder motive. In addition to murders committed by persons who know the victim and murders committed by strangers, there are now murders committed by persons who know the victim only through the media—the murder of John Lennon by Mark Chapman, for example. And there's a whole new phenomenon for the 1990s—some offenders (especially juveniles) have begun to videotape their own crimes, apparently in an effort to assure themselves of its reality.

With regard to crime and justice, as well as other social concerns, the critical issue is ultimately the media's role in the social construction of reality. Evidence is building that the media alter reality by affecting the ways in which the audience perceives, interprets, and behaves toward it. The question is no longer whether the media have a substantial impact or not, but how their impact will be felt. The most solid evidence indicates that the impact is indirect:

> Thus the media affects elections not so much by changing votes as by molding the images of reality that lead to vote decisions. They affect public policy not by forcing change but by channeling information that stimulates or stymies the efforts of political elites. They affect opinion not by changing minds but by shaping the political culture that makes certain opinions seem reasonable or defensible. They affect our social institutions not by calling for their preservation or destruction but by influencing our expectations and evaluations of their performance.[178]

These indirect effects cycle through the culture in media loops. In *media looping*, media content is extracted from one context or component of the media and reused and reframed in another.[179] It is not unusual for looping to result in new, ambiguous media realities. These looping effects are observed in both real events that are mediated such as the Rodney King beating and the Oklahoma City bombing and in created-for-media pseudo-events found in shows like *COPS*. A hyper-reality results in which the media-generated reality loops and interweaves with our unmediated personal reality. Bringing to mind Plato's "shadows on the cave wall," this harbingers a future where media images of other media images will construct the social reality and where crime and justice will be understood and experienced only through the reality mixing bowl of the mass media.

The future also involves the continued mass media merging of news and entertainment and the increased marketing of crime and justice. What effect these loops will have on the crime-and-justice gatekeeping process is less clear. The availability of video and new media technologies has already created the new genre of reality programming, which relies heavily on images of real crimes, criminal investigations, and criminal justice agency activities as fodder for entertainment programs.[180] It will be interesting to see what effect video in public hands has on the reporting of police violence and other types of crime news—as pictures invariably increase the newsworthiness of an event and as the videotaping of the Rodney King beating exemplifies. Whether the application of entertainment criteria to the selection of crime news has plateaued is not known, but there is no indication of its decline.

The media influence the real world of crime and justice by projecting a multimedia image of crime and justice that makes increasing the punitiveness of the real criminal justice system appear to be the only reasonable course. And in a cyclic effect, the actions of the real criminal justice system are compared and evaluated against the expectations and desires raised by the media criminal justice system. Ironically, one reason for the resistance to the use of media technology by the judiciary is that such uses conflict with the traditional, media-supported image of what a trial should be like.

The media and its technology shape our social world and meanwhile the media have become a world in themselves.[181] By the 1960s, children had grown up spending more time in the media reality than in a directly experienced reality. Today, a web of media-linked technology and products gives the media reality an enormous reach and impact. We cannot have some of the media forces for social change without having all or most of the forces. We cannot select uses for new media that advance old goals without altering the social systems out of which the goals developed. Hence we cannot use television to educate without altering the functions of reading and the structure of the family and the school.[182] And by extension, we cannot use the media in crime reduction and case processing or provide media access to new criminal justice arenas without also changing the reality of the criminal justice system.

To solve and prevent crimes the government must intervene in its citizens' lives. The media provide a means to do so in new ways, ways that are considered both more efficient and less obviously intrusive. The recent embracing of media technologies by the criminal justice system is a prime example. In practice, however, such applications cannot avoid opening up for view further-backstage areas of public life, criminal justice system operations, and interactions between police and citizens. In certain instances, such as patrol car cameras, which record police actions as much as citizen actions, this is seen as positive. In other instances, such as hidden police surveillance systems, it is not so clear.

Expansions of these technology-based systems will further depersonalize criminal justice. Adjudication within the criminal justice system is based on the principle of face-to-face interaction, particularly that an accused person is entitled to face his or her accusers. The extended use of media technologies, however, will mean a decline in live encounters between witnesses and defendants, police and the public, attorneys and their clients, judges and defendants, and jurors and all the previous groups. This process will be hastened as the technology becomes more economical, less obtrusive, and more approximate to live personal meetings. As with surveillance, as the general media have become pervasive and common, the public has become more accepting of an impersonal criminal justice system and the substitution of media technology for live encounters.

The development of interactive media further changes the relationship between media and users. Interactive media evolution has steadily moved the media experience closer to the direct personal experience. It has also changed the way people interact with each other, with less direct and face-to-face conversation but more face-to-face–like communication via media technology. A culture is developing where people interact less with people physically near them such as neighbors, and more with distant people via videophones, digital cameras, home computers, and other "being there" minimizing technology. The full effects on the social construction of crime-and-justice reality from these changes will become apparent only after such practices have been in place longer.

Regarding the negative effects of the entertainment and news media and their content, there is considerable doubt regarding an ability to institute change. The three parties who could act—the federal government, the mass media industry, and the audience—are unlikely to do so.[183] The government is an ineffective source of change; the industry has an economic interest in continuing its violent, criminogenic portrayals; and audience groups' desire and ability to organize and create change are questionable. And those at-risk audience members who are attracted to such portrayals and susceptible to their influence should not be expected to abstain voluntarily. Indeed, there is evidence that advisories regarding violent content attract aggressive children to violent programming rather than dissuade them from watching it.[184] Whether such social reactions as the negative perception of the O.J. Simpson trial coverage accompanied by simultaneous high ratings will effect any changes remains to be seen. It is thought to be doubtful.

Recommendations

What might we do with the knowledge we now possess? Not all the factors discussed in this book are good candidates for public intervention strategies, but some media influences on crime are amenable to intervention. It should be remembered, however, that family, neighborhood, and personality factors—ultimately more important than the media for generating crime—are not easily influenced by public actions. Media-related public policies are also important because the media also have subtle long-term influences on the family, neighborhood, and personality through indirect processes. Because most of our knowledge about the media and crime and justice is general rather than specific, existing public policies are also general, aimed largely at the general population rather than at specific at-risk groups.

As a primary research need, those populations who are most susceptible to having their social construction of crime-and-justice reality influenced by the media should be described. At present, their relative size and demographic composition is largely unknown. Better knowledge of these media-susceptible consumers and the situations and content that most influence them would allow more focused policies that specifically target these consumers. For example, educational debriefings have been found to be useful in reversing the negative attitudinal effects of pornography,[185] and some have proposed the development of preemptive educational media to debunk the pleasurable rape myth and other attitudinal effects.[186] It is further recommended that the curtailment of sexually violent material (regardless of its industry rating) that

---

BOX 7.2   The Future of Media, Crime and Justice on the Internet

---

Fugitive Is 1st of Most Wanted Caught in Computer Dragnet

WASHINGTON — For the first time, the FBI has nabbed one of its most-wanted fugitives thanks to the Internet.

Leslie Isben Rogge, who had been on the FBI's Ten Most Wanted list for six years, surrendered to U.S. authorities in Guatemala after his picture was seen on the Internet, the FBI said Sunday.

The bureau said this was the first time that listing the most-wanted fugitives on the Internet has led to a capture. Rogge's picture had been placed on the FBI's home page and was spotted by someone in Guatemala who had seen Rogge and alerted the authorities.

Guatemalan police launched a manhunt and Rogge, "feeling the intense pressure," turned himself in at the U.S. Embassy on Saturday, the FBI said.

Rogge, 56, escaped from federal custody in Idaho in 1985 after a conviction for armed robbery.

He also was wanted for bank robbery, transporting stolen property across state lines and wire fraud, the FBI said in a written statement. He was placed on the most-wanted list in 1990.

Police want Rogge in connection with a 1986 robbery in North Carolina and a 1991 robbery in Missouri.

He was flown to Miami to await a hearing today before a U.S. magistrate, the FBI said.

SOURCE: Associated Press

Florida Law Officers Seek Tips from Surfers— Online

TALLAHASSEE — Police agencies that made television a crime-fighting tool with shows such as *America's Most Wanted* are turning to cyberspace to improve their sleuthing.

The Internet can also be used to spread information and cast a wide net for leads, law enforcement agencies are finding. On Sunday, the FBI said it nabbed one of its most-wanted fugitives, Leslie Isben Rogge, thanks to the Internet.

Agencies are setting up a growing

---

portrays violence against women as pleasurable, rewarding, and acceptable for either the perpetrator or the victim be pursued as a public policy goal.

Additional basic methodological work must also be completed. In particular, the measurement of theoretical concepts in key areas must be refined. Although anecdotal, case studies are slowly filling the gap. When concept definitions and their measurements are agreed upon and validated, topologies, indexes, and scales can be developed and the search for generalizable findings will quicken. For example, a measurement of the density and quality of local media networks would allow the direct comparison of multiple communities in terms of the social and political characteristics of the media's role in crime-and-justice policy. Along these same lines, a coverage topology of heavily covered criminal trials has been offered but needs to be validated. The development of an index of prejudicial coverage would aid both research and the courts, and the validation of a scale of the perception of the reality of media content would improve empirical investigations.[187]

BOX 7.2   *Continued*

number of home pages where anyone with a computer and modem can check out fugitives from across the country, or read about unsolved murders in their area.

Some police agencies use a personal touch to lure net surfers, like the photo of a Pinellas County sheriff's deputy riding a surf board in full uniform.

"I like it. It adds personality to their (home) page," said Lisa Aaron, digital information director for the Florida Attorney General's Office.

In Florida, 17 sheriffs and 35 police departments have home pages that can be visited through Attorney General Bob Butterworth's online Citizen Safety Center. And the trend is international.

"Even a local sheriff can get their guys featured worldwide," said Dean Fletcher, a public affairs specialist for the FBI in Washington, D.C.

The FBI has had its Top 10 list of fugitives on the Internet since last year.

Many online pages carry crime prevention tips and a look at outlaws and unsolved mysteries.

St. Petersburg police have used the Internet since last year to try to identify a woman whose skeleton was found along Interstate 275.

Police have posted photos of her jewelry, a list of her clothes and an artist's sketch of what she probably looked like.

"Somewhere this girl has a mother," Detective Leonard Leedy said. "Or a friend, or someone who knew her."

Leading the Florida Department of Law Enforcement's online wanted list is Juan Jesus Fleitas, 31, a Cuban-born killer who tunneled out of Glades Correctional Institution with five other men last year in South Florida. He's the only one still free.

SOURCE: Associated Press. From the *Orlando Sentinel*, Monday, May 20, 1996, p. A-7.

It is safe to say that popular culture will remain a dominant social construction engine, so that influence in the popular culture realm will remain highly important. In that the crime-and-justice content of popular culture continues to be distorted and biased, the debunking of its content remains a crucial task.[188] This task is especially needed in the crime-and-justice area because of limited alternative information sources; it becomes increasingly necessary the further into the criminal system one looks. To the extent that the dynamics of the mass media define criminalization and the workings of the criminal law and criminal justice system, then the urgency of comprehending this process and the links between media content, public construction of crime and justice, and overall crime-and-justice policies is apparent.

In a consumerism-saturated country like the United States, hopelessness, bitterness, and disregard for moral values and law are heightened by a growing economic disparity. The mass media heighten the negative effects of economic disparities through the barrage of consumer messages in advertising and entertainment. The media also exacerbate the problems generated by a reckless American gun culture by portraying guns as glamorous, effective, omnipotent devices. Both effects add to the problem of crime and are sometimes publicly debated, but the debate about the media's social impact remains tightly focused on measuring and reviewing violent media content. Within this focus, the emphasis has been on counting violent acts rather than on exploring the context of violence in the media. Deciphering the media's moral and value messages about crime has been largely ignored, but recent studies have begun to examine content from this perspective.[189]

One policy goal therefore should be to reduce the glorification of crime and the graphic and gratuitous portrayal of violence; to portray crime and violence not as simple solutions but as distasteful last resorts with tragic, unanticipated consequences. Violence shown consistently as a generator of pain and suffering and not as a personal or social panacea could be positive media violence. Too often violence in the media is shown as an effective solution, and too often it is simply met by increased counterviolence. More research is also needed to identify precisely what content is at fault.[190] Such research could help the media industry improve programming without losing its audience, whereas the current research leads to an economically unacceptable policy focus on violent versus nonviolent programming. The media industry is more likely to voluntarily cooperate with suggestions that will not compromise the size of program audiences and profits.

Research into the long-term effects of violent, criminogenic, and pornographic media content should also be pursued. The cumulative and interactive effects of television, print, and other types of media have yet to be explored. In addition, more attention to how consumers interact with and use the media is needed. For example, do people learn specific facts about crime and justice through the media and then apply these facts in deciding what public policies to support? Or does their preference for or predisposition toward particular policies determine which crime-and-justice facts they cull and retain from the media? Although researchers agree that media effects operate at both an individual and systematic level in criminal justice, they do not agree on how and through what mechanisms they operate. A basic question continually debated is the causal position of the media. Does exposure to media precede or parallel certain behavior? Do the media cause changes in subjects or do predisposed individuals selectively seek out and attend to media content that supports their already established perceptions?

Competing Causal Models

As reflected in Figure 7.3, the conflicting arguments of the media as a primary cause versus a negligible cause of crime not only posit differing causal relations between the media and violence but imply vastly different public policies regarding the media as well. The *primary cause models* argue that a significant, direct linear relationship exists between media content and consumer behavior. The media, independent of other factors, directly cause var-

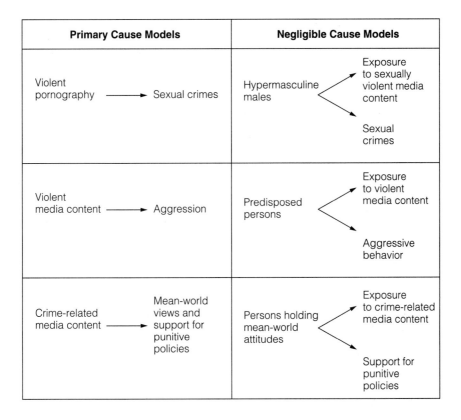

Primary Cause Models	Negligible Cause Models

FIGURE 7.3 Competing Models of the Media's Relationship to Sex Crimes, Aggression, and Support for Punitive Policies

ied social behaviors. If valid, these models indicate that strong intervention is necessary in the creation, content, and distribution of media.

The *negligible cause models* concede a statistical association between the media and violent behavior, but argue that the connection is due not to a causal relationship but to persons predisposed to certain behaviors seeking out particular types of media and concurrently behaving in ways similar to the behavior displayed in the media. As the relationship is associative and not causal, in these models policies targeted at the media will have no effect on social behavior and the media can be safely ignored.

Both sets of models inaccurately describe the media–social behavior relationship. As shown in Figure 7.4, the actual relationship is bi-directional and cyclical. In addition to predisposed people acting out their predispositions while seeking out supportive media, and media causing behavior to be modeled, the media play a role in the generation of predisposed people. As the made-for-TV movie industry exemplifies, in the relationship between violent media and violent behavior, real-world violence sometimes results in the creation of violent media. And by providing live models of violence and creating community and home environments that are more inured to and tolerant of violence, violent behavior also helps to create more violently predisposed individuals in society. Therefore, while the direct effect of media violence on social violence may not be initially large, its influence loops, recycles, and accumulates.[191]

Therefore, despite being only one of many factors rather than stand-alone causes, the media can not be ignored regardless of the level of their direct impact. Because crime is a pressing problem, even those factors that only modestly contribute to it are important. Exactly how and to what extent the media cause long-term changes in social behavior remains unknown, but it is clear that they play an important if not independent role. The media are one engine in the crime production process, working in combination with other more significant engines—as an overdrive or afterburner for crime and violence, if you will, increasing and exacerbating the crime production thrust of other social engines. Ethnic violence, racial strife, oppressive living conditions, violent cultural history, economic disparities, family destruction, and interpersonal violence are all more important for crime levels but are all subject to significant enhancement by the media. As with individuals, it seems that the media alone cannot criminalize a country—but once a country criminalizes its media through an emphasis on predatory and unrealistic portraits, a slow spiral of increased crime and tolerance for crime begins. For modern societies, the media set the expectations and moral boundaries for crime, guide the public policies, and steer the social construction of crime and justice reality.

CONCLUSION

In closing, the single most significant social effect of media content is not its direct generation of crime but its effect on our criminal justice policies. The fear and loathing we feel toward criminals is tied to our media-generated image of criminality. The media portray criminals as typically animalistic, vicious predators. This media image translates into a more violent society by influencing the way we react to all crime in America. We imprison at a much greater rate and make reentry into law-abiding society (even for our nonviolent offenders) more difficult than other advanced but less violent nations. The predator criminal image results in crime and justice policy based on the worst-case criminal and a constant ratcheting up of punishments for all offenders. In its cumulative effect, media coverage both provides violent models to emulate and justifies a myopic, harshly punitive public reaction to all offenders.

As our media-induced sensitivity to violent crime and perceptions of its growth are heightened, we have become nationally fixated on heightening and extending our capacity to punish in an attempt to reduce violence.[192] However, two social mechanisms are needed to reduce violence—the punishment of violent criminals and the rewarding of law-abiding, nonviolent be-

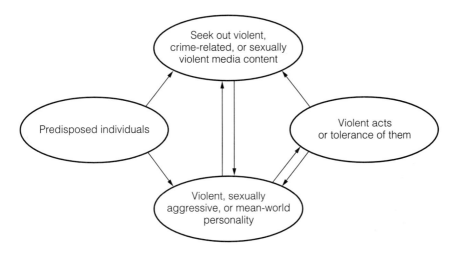

FIGURE 7.4 A Reciprocal Feedback Model

havior. Societies that are more successful in balancing the two mechanisms are also less violent. The emphasis on punishment coupled with the concentration of wealth in America has resulted in the degrading of the equally important social capacity to reward law-abiding behavior. By emphasizing one we have lamed and discredited the other. Nonmaterial rewards like good social status, an esteemed reputation, a clear conscience, being known as an honest, hardworking person, have all been losing their legitimacy—while material rewards for law-abiding lifestyles, like careers, comfortable incomes, and affordable goods are less generally available to our poorest and not surprisingly most crime-prone citizens.[193]

The most important observation running through this book is of the social construction competition that is ongoing. The ultimate competition is not for the construction of crime and justice but for influence over the mass media's social construction engine. If you influence the symbol-creating and symbol-defining engine of a society, you create the social reality of that society. And if a particular perspective of social reality gains control of a social construction engine, other constructions will never be truly competitive. The significance of the social construction of crime and justice is that it sets the stage for enhanced future access and influence on the media's social construction machinery. Winning a social construction contest puts one in a better position for future contests.

Crime is both a cultural and an individual product. The media are both reflections of the culture and engines in the cultural production process. Although they are not the sole or even the most powerful cause, the media are tied into the other crime-generating engines and their influence is compounded. The result of all these forces is a national character and resultant crime-and-justice reality that is individualistic, materialistic, and prone to violence. By encouraging us to ignore the sources of this reality, in the end the media function as much as a means of avoiding reality as a means of constructing it:

> The ritual of crime and punishment—in newspaper headlines and on television screens—has become America's great reality avoidance mechanism, its all sufficient substitute for knowledge and thought: let a scapegoat be found, let a culprit be punished, and the public relaxes, confident that the crisis has been surmounted.[194]

If we wish to change our socially constructed crime-and-justice reality, we cannot take on only one source of its genesis, the media—nor can we ignore them. For in media, crime, and justice, perceptions have a nasty habit of becoming reality.[195]

CHAPTER CONCEPTS

Public Communication Campaigns	Mainstreaming	Anticipatory Effects
Fear of Crime	Chronic Know-Nothings	Primary and Negligible Causal Models
Public and Media Agenda	Hypermasculinity	Interactive Media
History Effects	Mean-World View	Agenda Setting and Building
Hypodermic Needle Mechanism	Downward Comparison	Echo Effects
	Sexually Violent Media	

DISCUSSION QUESTIONS

1. Discuss a local criminal justice policy that has been influenced by news media coverage or a media-based lobby effort to pass crime-related legislation.

2. Survey students regarding their fear of crime and media usage and discuss their level of correlation. Discuss what factors might affect this relationship, such as age, race, favorite type of TV show, education, neighborhood crime level, or personal victimization history.

3. Discuss the future development of media and crime and justice and the impact of new media technology.

4. Discuss the implications of the increasing entertainmentization of crime-and-justice media.

5. Discuss how the media have influenced your social construction of crime-and-justice reality.

6. Do the mass media have too much influence on society? What

should be done in the area of crime and justice concerning the media?

7. What specific aspects or content of the media do you find most troubling?

8. How might criminologists from differing theoretical perspectives construct crime-and-justice entertainment or news to reflect their perspective?

Appendix I

Supreme Court Decisions

PRETRIAL PUBLICITY

The first modern Supreme Court case regarding pretrial publicity was *Sheppard* v. *Florida* (341 U.S. 50 [1951], 71 S. Ct. 549 [per curiam]), in which the Court reversed the conviction of two blacks for the rape of a young white woman. Contributing to the decision to reverse was the publication of a sheriff's statement that the defendants had confessed to the rape, though no confession was produced at the trial. The Court stated that the inherent difficulties of blacks in obtaining fair trials when accused of raping whites was compounded by the actions of the local press and law enforcement officers. The importance of this decision is that the Court implied that circumstances such as the publication of information about a confession are inherently prejudicial; that is, no actual evidence of juror prejudice had to be provided. In the Court's view, "The trial was but a legal gesture to register a verdict already dictated by the press and the public opinion which it generated" (341 U.S. 50 [1951]). The Court did not clearly state what conditions were necessary for inherent prejudice to exist, however, and over the following decade it was reluctant to accept unsubstantiated coverage effects as grounds for reversal (Jaffe 1965, p. 514). The Supreme Court has been reluctant to extend its position in *Sheppard* to consider other circumstances inherently prejudicial.

For example, *Stroble* v. *California* (343 U.S. 310 [1952]) involved the murder of a child to which the defendant initially confessed but subsequently pled innocent and went to trial. Details of the confession were released to the media and resulted in widespread publicity. Unlike in *Sheppard* in 1951, the confession was introduced in court as evidence. The Supreme Court refused to reverse this conviction, arguing that the defendant failed to prove prejudicial results from the publication of the information and that his claim of press-generated bias was thus unsubstantiated. In contrast to *Sheppard*, in which prejudice was presumed, in this case actual proof of prejudice was required (Dubnoff 1977, p. 93). In a similar decision in 1956, the Supreme Court in *United States ex rel. Darcy* v. *Handy, Warden* (351 U.S. 454 [1956]) declined to reverse the murder conviction of a defendant in a case where the trial judge was quoted in the local newspaper as saying that he couldn't see how the jury could have reached any decision but the one they had, for conviction and a sentence of death. He went on to comment that such decisions are the only hope of stemming the tide of crime (351 U.S. 454, 458). Again the Court ruled that the defense had failed to prove actual prejudice. A key in both cases for the Court is that the defense had failed to aggressively pursue the legal avenues available to mitigate prejudice, such as asking for changes of venue, using peremptory challenges, or requesting continuances. These decisions placed the onus on the defense in the 1950s not only to establish that the media had caused prejudice but to suggest and pursue remedies.

In *Marshall* v. *United States* (360 U.S. 310 [1959]), however, the Supreme Court abandoned the *Stroble* position for federal courts when it ruled that evidence or information that has been ruled inadmissible in court but that reaches the jury can be presumed to be prejudicial. The *Marshall* case involved the revelation to jurors that a defendant charged with unlawfully dispensing amphetamines had previously been found to be practicing medicine without a license. The trial judge had ruled the information inadmissible as evidence, but the jury had access to newspaper stories containing the information. The Supreme Court reversed, despite the fact that when queried by the trial judge, the jurors stated that they could reach a verdict solely on the evidence presented in court. The Court thus seemed to have established its first general rule regarding what is prejudicial and what is not in terms of media publicity: If the information is inadmissible as evidence and it reaches the jury, prejudice can be assumed to exist.

Since *Marshall*, the Court has held to its position that under certain circumstances the defense need not provide evidence of prejudice. It has not, however, provided clearer guidelines for recognizing such cases, stating only that in extreme or flagrant cases, prejudice is inherent—without defining extreme or flagrant. For example, in 1961, the Court reversed in *Irvin* v. *Dowd* (366 U.S. 717 [1961]), a case that it deemed had flagrant circumstances of prejudicial media pretrial publicity. The prosecutor announced to the press that the defendant had confessed, and there were press reports of prior convictions, confessions to other crimes, and an attempt to plead guilty. Ninety percent of the prospective jurors admitted holding an opinion concerning Irvin's guilt, Irvin used all his peremptory challenges, and, finally, of the seated jurors, eight admitted prior to the trial to believing that Irvin was guilty (Dubnoff 1977, pp. 94–95). A change of venue was granted but was limited by state statute to the next county, which had been exposed to the same coverage. The Court ruled that "such extraneous influences, in violation of the decencies guaranteed by our Constitution, are sometimes so powerful that an accused is forced, as a practical matter, to forgo trial by jury. . . . It is not requiring too much that petitioner be tried in an atmosphere undisturbed by so huge a wave of public passion" (366 U.S. at 730, 727–728). The Court did not specify which of the above factors were most important or what combination of factors would establish inherent prejudice but did establish in this case that review of voir dire is an acceptable method of determining if prejudice exists (Jaffe 1965, p. 515). In reaching this decision, however, the Court rejected the argument that a jury must be totally uninformed of a case and that because the public had received a large amount of information about a case, a conviction should be automatically reversed. The Court said, "It is not required, however, that the jurors be totally ignorant of the facts and issues involved. In these days of swift, widespread and diverse methods of communication, an important case can be expected to arouse the interest of the public in the vicinity, and scarcely any of those best qualified to serve as jurors will not have formed some impression or opinion as to the merits of the case" (366 U.S. at 722).

Subsequently, in *Rideau* v. *Louisiana* (373 U.S. 723, [1963]), the Court introduced the condition of "a fundamental fairness test" in reversing a conviction. Following his arrest, Rideau was filmed at the local jail in an "interview" with the local sheriff, during which Rideau confessed to a robbery, kidnapping, and murder. According to the Court, the television broadcast of the interview confession was prejudicial enough to require a change of venue order, and failure to move the trial made "any subsequent proceedings in the community so overwhelmingly prejudicial as to require a reversal." The Court considered Rideau's televised confessions—at which he pled guilty to murder—in a very real sense to constitute his trial (373 U.S. 726). In its decision, the Supreme Court attempted to help trial judges identify inherently prejudicial situations, mentioning "the truthfulness of news reporting," "if the accused is a prominent person in the community," or "if the case by its nature attracts attention," as factors useful for determining bias. Responsibility for protecting a defendant from prejudicial publicity remained the defense attorney's, however. The Court held that defense attorneys should seek gag or protective orders, should introduce proof of the danger of prejudice and focus attention on offending media, and in any appeals should establish the inherent prejudice of the publicity.

In 1966, in perhaps the best-known case in this area (its fame stems from the coverage it received and the movies and books produced about it, as well as the subsequent fame of the defense lawyer, F. Lee Bailey), the Court in *Sheppard* v. *Maxwell* (384 U.S. 333 [1966]) shifted the onus of requesting protection from prejudicial coverage and establishing prejudicial effects from defense attorneys to the trial judge (Carroll et al. 1986, p. 188). The Court declared the judge responsible for recognizing media-generated prejudice and pursuing means of controlling it. The *Sheppard* case involved a prominent Cleveland doctor who was accused of bludgeoning his pregnant wife to death. The coverage was intense and pervasive, beginning prior to indictment and continuing through the trial. In its review, the Supreme Court not only reversed the conviction, but suggested for the first time specific actions that trial judges should follow in controlling the effects of publicity. It also reaffirmed, however, that it is not the amount of publicity per se that results in reversal in a particular case, but whether or not the defendant in that case received a fair and impartial trial (see also *People* v. *Speck*, 41 Ill. 2d 177, 183, N. E. 2d 208, 212 [1968]). Therefore, massive coverage alone would not automatically be interpreted as prejudicial or ensure a reversal. The Court still refrained from stating a general rule for determining prejudice and left that determination to trial judges, only suggesting specific factors that the judges should be sensitive to. The *Sheppard* decision thus clearly signaled judges that measures have to be taken in certain cases whether counsel requests them or not, but did not indicate exactly when they should be taken. The Court's precise directions read as follows:

> When there is a reasonable likelihood that prejudicial news prior to trial will prevent a fair trial, the judge should continue the case until the threat abates, or transfer it to another county not so permeated with publicity. In addition, sequestration of the jury was something the judge should have raised sua sponte with counsel. If publicity during the proceedings threatens the fairness of the trial, a new trial should be ordered. . . . Neither prosecutors, counsel for the defense, the accused, court staff nor enforcement officers coming under the jurisdiction of the court should be permitted to frustrate its function. Collaboration between counsel and the press as to information affecting the fairness of a criminal trial is not only subject to regulation, but is highly censurable and worthy of disciplinary measures. (*Sheppard*, 384 U.S. 363 [1966])

Determining when a "reasonable likelihood" exists is left to each trial judge. In 1975, however, in *Murphy* v. *Florida* (421 U.S. 794 [1975]), the Court reaffirmed that only in extreme cases will inherent prejudice be accorded; it returned to its position that the burden of showing inherent prejudice usually falls on the defendant. In its ruling, the Court concluded that the "petitioner has failed to show that the setting of the trial was inherently prejudicial or that the jury selection process of which he complains permits an inference of actual prejudice." Having established the trial court judge's responsibility for recognizing and controlling the effects of publicity, the Supreme Court in the 1980s declined to review a number of trial court decisions and has consistently supported trial judges' assessments and decisions in this area.

PRIVACY

In *Melvin* v. *Reed* (112 Cal. App. 285 [1975]), the plaintiff was a former prostitute who had been tried for murder, acquitted, and thereafter reformed. Seven years later, a movie revealing her identity and detailing the facts of her story was released. The California Supreme Court allowed a civil suit to continue and supported the defendant's view that her privacy had been unnecessarily invaded. The court cited the passage of time and the lack of relevancy in identifying the defendant for the movie.

In 1971, in *Briscoe v. Reader's Digest Association* (4 Cal. 3d 529, 483 P.2d 34 [1971]), the California Supreme Court ruled on a similar case involving a plaintiff convicted in 1956 of truck hijacking and thereafter rehabilitated. The court acknowledged the importance of reporting crimes and judicial proceedings and even of identifying persons currently charged with crimes but ruled that reports of past crimes and past defendants were qualitatively different and that publicizing them served little independent public purpose.

However, in *Cox Broadcasting Corp. v. Cohn* (420 U.S. 469 [1975]), the U.S. Supreme Court ruled that the broadcasting corporation was not wrong in publishing the identity of the victim of a recent rape-murder, because the information was available to the public prior to the broadcast. The Court stated that although there is no broad media right under the First Amendment to the identities of crime victims, in this case, where the information was available in public court records, there was no invasion of privacy.

Subsequently, in 1977, in *Oklahoma Publishing Co. v. District Court* (555 P.2d 1286 [Okla. 1976], rev'd 97 S. Ct. 1045 [1977], per curiam), the Supreme Court again emphasized that information legally obtained in open court proceedings could be published. The case involved the publishing of the name and picture of an eleven-year-old murder suspect, both of which had been obtained during an open detention petition hearing. The judge moved to prohibit publication, but the Court held that the judge could not prohibit the publication of widely disseminated information obtained at court proceedings that are open to the public.

In regard to camera access, the Florida Supreme Court discussed the privacy issue in 1979 and ruled that Florida courts can allow cameras without defendants' consent. The court argued that a judicial proceeding is a public event that by its nature denies certain aspects of privacy and that there is no constitutionally recognized right to privacy in the context of courtroom proceedings (In re Petition of Post–Newsweek Stations, Florida, 370 So. 2d 764 at 799 [Fla.], app'l dismissed, 444 U.S. 976 [1979]). This position appears to be the one currently favored by the Supreme Court, which has deemed privacy only an interest and not an absolute right in judicial proceedings.

The question of prison inmates' right to privacy is still clouded. In 1978, in *Houchins v. KQED, Inc.* (438 U.S. 1, 5 n.2), Justice Warren Burger wrote that inmates in jails, prisons, or mental institutions retain certain fundamental rights of privacy. The limitations on this right for inmates have not been fully determined, however. Another criminal justice issue that touches on privacy, the courts, and the media is that of "postverdict interviews" with jurors (see Bacharach 1985; Sharp 1983). At issue is the proper scope of press interviews with jurors following a trial and verdict. The concern is that intensive interviews will undermine the integrity of the deliberation process and invade the personal privacy of the individual jurors. The courts have the right to prohibit the interrogation of jurors regarding their deliberations or reasons for a particular verdict; however, when such prohibitions are proper is not clear (Sharp 1983, p. 14).

CLOSURE, RESTRICTIVE, AND PROTECTIVE ORDERS

Closure Orders

The increase in closure orders ultimately resulted in the Supreme Court's decision in *Gannett Co.* v. *DePasquale* (443 U. S. 368 [1979]). The case involved the investigation of the disappearance of a Rochester, New York, man who appeared to have met a violent death. After a fair amount of publicity regarding the case, all major parties agreed to closure of a pretrial hearing. The media claimed a public right of access to criminal proceedings based on the right to a public trial provided in the Sixth Amendment. The Supreme Court, however, held that the public trial provision of the Sixth Amendment exists solely for the benefit of the defendant and does not confer any constitutional right of access on the media or the general public (Bell 1983, p. 1299). Even though the justices ruled against the media in this case, they did not clearly address the general issue of closure and failed to specify standards for the use of closure (Apfel 1980, pp. 461–467). A majority accepted the media's claim that members of the general public, and, by extension, the media, have a constitutional right to attend a pretrial hearing but did not agree that the right had precedence in this case. The article "Secret Court Watch" (1979, p. 17) discusses the issues at greater length. A majority of the justices disagreed that the trial judge must conduct a hearing before issuing a closure order. Rehnquist stated that if the parties agree to a closed proceeding the trial court need not advance any reason for declining to open a hearing to the public. Powell stated that the public and the media have a First Amendment right to be present at a pretrial suppression hearing and concluded that the trial judge must make specific findings of fact in a hearing attended by all interested parties before closing a courtroom (Apfel 1980, p. 470).

The Court addressed the rank of the right to trial access relative to a defendant's right to a fair trial in *Richmond Newspapers* v. *Virginia* (448 U.S. 555 [1980]). The *Richmond* case involved a defendant who was tried for murder four times over two years. At the fourth trial, the defense counsel moved that the trial be closed to the public. The prosecution did not oppose the motion, and the trial judge granted it. The judge's closure of the trial was seen as particularly significant, for it represented a break with prior Supreme Court rulings in which clear distinctions between pretrial and trial proceedings had been made (Apfel 1980, p. 472). Reviewing the closure, the Court ruled that the media and the public have a right of access to trials and that access cannot be closed arbitrarily and without cause (Bell 1983, p. 1300). The Court did not, however, give the media's right of access supremacy over the defendant's right to a fair trial (Marcus 1982, p. 262). Furthermore, the Court placed the burden of showing compelling evidence that media access would result in the loss of Sixth Amendment due process protections squarely on the party seeking closure. Also specified in the *Richmond Newspapers* decision was the rule that before a trial judge can exclude the public and press from a trial, he or she must determine that alternative means will not meet the goal of assuring the accused a fair trial. In reversing, the Court noted that "the trial judge made no findings to support closure; no inquiry was made as to whether alternative solutions would have met the need to ensure fairness" (448 U.S. 580–581 [1980]).

Restrictive Orders

In *Nebraska Press Association* v. *Stuart* (427 U.S. 539 [1976]), the judge presiding over a preliminary hearing for a sensational small-town murder trial ordered that no information concerning confessions or statements "strongly implicative" of the defendant could be published until a jury had been impaneled. The Supreme Court reversed the ban in this specific case but left open the possibility that future restrictive orders might be upheld in cases of "clear and present danger" and if alternative actions to neutralize pretrial publicity were ineffective or unfeasible. The Court ruled that in this case the state had not shown that alternatives to a restrictive order would have failed to protect the defendant's rights.

The position that restrictive orders are acceptable only in rare circumstances was soon reinforced in *Landmark Communications* v. *Virginia* (435 U.S. 829 [1978]) and in *Smith* v. *Daily Mail Publishing Co.* (443 U.S. 97 [1979]). Both Supreme Court decisions overturned lower court restrictive orders because of a lack of clear overriding need for such orders.

Protective Orders

The seminal case in this area is *Central South Carolina* v. *Martin* (431 F. Supp. 1182 [D. S. C.], modified, 556 F.2d 706 [4th Cir. 1977], cert. denied, 431 U.S. 928 [1978]), in which the trial court in 1978 prohibited any statements that might divulge prejudicial material not a matter of the public record. Upholding the order, a federal appeals court (the Supreme Court declined to review the case) ruled that protective orders are to be judged by the less strict standards of closure and are not equivalent to restrictive orders (Apfel 1980, p. 477). The current standard governing the proper use of protective orders is the perception of a "reasonable likelihood" that prejudicial effects will result from statements by participants. The Supreme Court has resisted applying the stricter standards of closure orders, which require that "clear and present danger" be established (Apfel 1980, p. 478) and has specified one significant limitation to the use of protective orders. In *U.S.* v. *Mandel* (408 F. Supp. 673 [D. Md. 1975]), the government petitioned for a protective order that would have included the defendant, Governor Mandel of Maryland. The Supreme Court ruled that the accused cannot be denied his right of free speech, even though other trial participants may be denied this right.

JUVENILE PROCEEDINGS

Juvenile proceedings have traditionally been recognized as unique within the system of justice. Confidentiality is arguably essential to the rehabilitative function of the juvenile court. However, the Supreme Court has sided with media access and publication rights in two cases referring to juvenile decisions. In *Oklahoma Publishing Co. v. District Court* (555 P.2d 1286 [Okla. 1976], rev'd 97 S. Ct. 1045 [1977], per curiam), the Court reversed a ban on dissemination of information obtained at a pretrial detention hearing about an eleven-year-old, holding that once information is made public, prior restraints may not be employed. In *Smith v. Daily Mail Publishing Co.* (443 U.S. 97 [1979]), the Court held that criminal penalties may not be applied to the publication without prior court approval of lawfully obtained information, in this case publication of the names of juvenile offenders.

JOURNALISTS' PRIVILEGE
AND PROTECTION OF SOURCES

The seminal Supreme Court decision with regard to the protection of news sources' identities is *Branzburg v. Hayes* (408 U.S. 665 [1972]). In rendering this ambiguous decision, the Court reviewed three separate cases (*Branzburg, in re Pappas,* and *United States v. Caldwell*), all focusing on the right of journalists to maintain secrecy about the identity of sources before grand jury proceedings. *Branzburg v. Hayes* (408 U.S. 665 [1972]) involved a reporter who, after assuring secrecy to sources, was subpoenaed to testify before a grand jury as to illegal drug activity. *In re Pappas* dealt with a reporter who refused to divulge to a grand jury events that had transpired inside Black Panther headquarters. In *United States v. Caldwell,* a *New York Times* reporter refused to testify before a federal grand jury about Black Panther activities.

The media requested that a reporter be exempt from appearing before a judicial proceeding unless the desired information was not available from another source and the need for the information was great enough to overcome First Amendment considerations, similar to the clear-and-present-danger rule forwarded in *Nebraska Press* for restrictive orders. The Court, however, concluded that public interest in effective law enforcement was sufficient to override burdens on the press caused by testifying (*Branzburg v. Hayes,* 408 U.S. 690–691). In rejecting the media's argument, the Court did suggest that a three-prong, case-by-case test—in which the interests of society in completing criminal investigations would be balanced against the need to maintain an independent press—would not be overruled if adopted at the state level (Bohrer and Ovelmen 1987). To meet the first requirement of this test, the reporter must have the information and the information must be clearly relevant to a specific offense. Second, the information must not be available elsewhere. Third, there must be a compelling and overriding need for the information. Application of the *Branzburg* decision has been varied. Some courts have simply concluded that no privilege exists, and some have narrowly limited the decision to grand jury proceedings. Most jurisdictions, though, have defined a qualified privilege that gives reporters the right to refuse to answer questions in situations that fail the three-part test outlined here (Kirtley 1990, p. 164; Pember 1987, p. 324). In practice, however, the privilege frequently fails in criminal cases.

From the media's perspective, the situation became even graver with the *Zurcher* v. *Stanford Daily Press* decision in 1978 (426 U.S. 547, reh'g denied, 439 U.S. 885 [1978]). The case involved a police search of the offices of the Stanford University student newspaper for photographs of a clash between police and student demonstrators. The police obtained a search warrant prior to conducting the search, but the paper argued that they should have obtained a subpoena, which would have required a judicial review and ruling prior to a search. The Supreme Court disagreed with the media and ruled that legally warranted searches of press files and offices were allowable. The media feared that such searches would greatly reduce their access to news sources, in that, potentially, any information given to a reporter, not just that which is eventually published, could be given up in future police searches of news files. Furthermore, fulfilling the media's fears, the number of police searches of newsrooms dramatically increased during the following decade. In response and somewhat countering this trend, the media lobbied for passage of the Federal Privacy Protection Act, which was enacted in 1980 and has reduced the threat of arbitrary newsroom searches at both the state and the national level. The Privacy Protection Act requires subpoenas in most cases and limits situations in which searches based on a simple warrant are allowed (Kirtley 1990, pp. 172–173; Pember 1987, pp. 340–341).

Appendix II

Research Summaries

LABORATORY STUDIES OF MOCK JURIES

Klein and Jess (1966) selected forty-eight male university sophomores and formed eight six-man juries to be exposed to prejudicial and nonprejudicial news stories a few days prior to a simulated trial. Jurors were sent a copy of a newspaper with a story planted on page one and were asked to listen to a radio news tape including a story on the case. Following the trials and a reading of the standard jury instruction, the juries were surreptitiously observed during their deliberations. The results indicated that the judge's instructions to disregard external material influenced three of the four juries with regard to considering evidence encountered outside the courtroom. However, in all the jury deliberations involving jurors exposed to prejudicial information, reference was made to such information, and one jury used that information despite the judge's instructions.

Simon (1966) had ninety-seven subjects drawn from a voter registration list listen to a forty-five-minute edited tape of a murder trial. The subjects were divided into two groups, one of which also read three sensational stories containing information about the defendant's prior record and the second of which read conservatively written stories. Simon reported that subjects who were exposed to the sensational stories were more likely to reach guilty verdicts, but that judicial instructions remedied these effects. However, the study did not include a no-instruction control, and participants were informed that the study regarded "the problem of trial publicity."

Tans and Chaffee (1966) used newspaper stories about crimes that differed in the severity of the crime reported and the type of prejudicial information disclosed. One hundred fifty subjects from various groups were asked to evaluate the suspects on seven–point scales measuring qualities including good–bad, guilty–innocent, young–old, dumb–smart, and honest–dishonest. Groups included a university extension class, a steel workers' wives' auxiliary, clerical and professional state capitol workers, participants in a conference on home care of the ill, attendees at a conference for publicity chairpeople of the League of Women Voters, and attendees at a PTA meeting. Analyzing the results for the guilty–innocent scale, the authors reported that a police report of a confession was the single most damaging piece of information and that there was a clear relationship between unfavorable news articles and average guilty ratings.

Wilcox and McCombs studied 120 subjects selected from a voter registration list and divided them into eight groups (Wilcox 1970, reporting on a study conducted in 1967 at the University of California, Los Angeles; the initial and unpublished report was titled "Crime Story Elements and Fair Trial/Free Press"). Each group was provided a newspaper story concerning the arrest of a murder suspect containing various combinations of information about confessions, evidence, or a prior criminal record. Reporting of a confession was the most prejudicial item, especially in combination with disclosure of a criminal record.

Hoiberg and Stires (1973) tested the response of 337 high school students to four pretrial publicity conditions, labeled high and low prejudgmental publicity and high and low heinous-crime publicity, with prejudgmental publicity implying guilt and heinous-crime publicity presenting vivid and dramatic descriptions of the crime. The subjects were randomly presented different versions of newspaper stories reflecting one of the four conditions of pretrial publicity and a fifteen-minute tape recording of a trial. They were then asked to rate on a 1-to-10 scale their certainty as to the guilt of the defendant. Only female students were found to be affected by the publicity: Those exposed to publicity that dramatized the heinousness of the crime were more certain of the defendant's guilt. Also, female students with low IQs who had been exposed to high prejudgmental publicity gave higher guilty scores than higher-IQ female students exposed to low prejudgmental publicity. Hoiberg and Stires concluded that pretrial publicity does not necessarily infringe on the right to a fair trial, but that certain types of information can influence certain jurors.

Sue and his colleagues (1974) sampled two groups—102 psychology undergraduates and 100 nonstudents—to examine the influence of pretrial publicity on verdicts and on the perceived strength of the prosecution and defense cases. Pretrial publicity was of two types—either damaging and relevant or damaging but irrelevant to the trial. Four factors were isolated: sex, the two types of pretrial publicity, and the judge's instructions to disregard. Subjects were given transcripts of the trial and newspaper accounts of the crime. The authors found that exposure to inadmissible evidence (the information that a gun found in the apartment had been identified by ballistics as having been used in the robbery) resulted in higher evaluations of the strength of the prosecutor's case and more guilty verdicts, but suggested that less damaging information had less effect. They concluded that relevant and damaging information has an adverse effect even when ruled inadmissible and even when the jurors are directed to disregard such evidence.

Padawer-Singer and Barton (1975a) used jurors from regular jury pools and found initial evidence that prejudicial newspaper clippings may compromise a juror's impartiality. However, in a follow-up study, Rottenberg (1976) reported that voir dire examinations—examinations to determine the competence of potential jurors—apparently reduce the effect of prejudicial reports on jurors.

Sohn (1976) had twenty-four subjects who were chosen to conform to juror characteristics sort forty-eight news stories typed on 3" by 5" cards into piles forming a continuum from most guilty to most innocent. The stories manipulated three variables: (1) the kind of crime—a felony or a misdemeanor; (2) the name of the accused—common or uncommon; and (3) the penalty for conviction—high or low. The only effect they found for the three variables was that some people tended to assume that suspects described in pretrial news stories were guilty if they were charged with committing a felony rather than a misdemeanor.

Greene and Loftus (1984) discussed two experiments examining the impact of highly publicized news events on decision making by mock jurors. In their first, serendipitous experiment, 168 students rendered verdicts after reading about a trial that involved eyewitness testimony. In the middle of the experiment, the local newspaper ran a prominent news story about a mistakenly identified innocent man as the offender in a serious crime. Those students who reached a decision after this story ran were less likely to convict a hypothetical defendant. In the second experiment, seventy-two citizens grouped according to whether or not they had read a *Reader's Digest* story about a mistakenly identified defendant were also asked to render verdicts in a hypothetical case. Those who had read the article were significantly less likely to convict than those who had not.

Davis (1986) studied twenty simulated juries (composed of undergraduate students enrolled in introductory psychology courses) that were exposed to either neutral or negative publicity about a case and then shown a videotape of the criminal trial either immediately or one week later. Analysis of the juries' verdicts showed no significant difference in conviction rates or in deliberation factors, and there was no evidence of damaging effects from prejudicial pretrial publicity. Davis concluded that the jury verdicts and individual juror measures revealed considerable resistance to the influence of prejudicial news, supporting earlier studies that found that juries are able and willing to put aside extraneous information and base their decisions on the evidence (p. 601).

Greene and Wade (1988; see also Greene 1990) reported two other experiments exploring the impact of general pretrial publicity on juror decision making in unrelated cases. Using sets of 120 and 140 undergraduate psychology students as mock jurors, Greene and Wade reported that in their first experiment, jurors who had read about a defendant who had been mistakenly identified and convicted were less likely to convict a defendant in an unrelated case than a control group or a group that had read about a series of heinous crimes. In their second experiment, they found a stronger effect when the pretrial publicity concerned a case that closely resembled the one being decided than when the two cases differed. They concluded that student jurors who are exposed to news stories about certain crimes and trials may use that information to decide wholly unrelated cases (1988, p. 132) and that attorneys involved in nonpublicized cases similar to ones receiving publicity should be concerned about possible biasing caused by the general pretrial publicity (1984, p. 219).

Kramer and his colleagues (1990) tested the remedial effects of deliberation, continuance, and judicial instructions with regard to two types of pretrial publicity—emotional and factual—on 617 residents chosen from a circuit court's jury rolls, with one group receiving judicial instructions regarding pretrial publicity and a control group not. Following a simulated written voir dire to identify biased jurors, juries were formed and shown a fifty-one-minute videotape of a trial. Kramer and his colleagues report that the instructions had no effect, that deliberation exacerbated the effect, and that continuances remedied the effect of factual but not of emotional publicity.

Dexter and Cutler (1991) and Dexter, Cutler, and Moran (1992) used sixty-eight college undergraduates in mock juries for a videotaped murder trial. They found that exposure to case-specific pretrial publicity one week earlier in the form of newspaper articles increased subsequent conviction rates and that an extended voir dire did not reduce the effects of the pretrial publicity.

FIELD STUDIES OF MOCK JURIES

Simon and Eimermann (1971) surveyed by telephone 130 registered voters a week prior to an actual murder trial. They found high levels of recognition and knowledge of the case (80 percent of the 130 respondents indicated that they had heard or read about the case) and pretrial sentiments favoring the prosecution (65 percent of those who had heard of the trial said that they favored the prosecution). However, approximately two-thirds of the respondents stated that evidence could change their views, that they could sit on a jury with an open mind, and that the defendants could receive a fair trial. In the actual case, one defendant pled guilty, and after a voir dire of 118 jurors and a two-week trial, a jury found the second defendant not guilty, indicating that real jurors can for the most part put aside extraneous information and base their decisions on the evidence presented at trial.

Riley (1973) surveyed by telephone people in three North Carolina cities regarding the murder of the family of a Green Beret captain. The cities included that of the scene of the crime and two probable change of venue sites. Riley found that approximately 23 percent of the 183 respondents across all three cities had prejudged the defendant guilty. He thus concluded that a change of venue or *venire* (the pool from which the jury would be drawn) would not be effective in reducing the influence of the media. In his view, "merely to publicize the fact that a person is suspected of a crime is enough to produce bias and prejudgment on the part of a great many people" (p. 17). But he also reported that roughly 70 percent of the respondents did not admit to prejudging the captain, indicating that despite heavy media publicity, the selection of an impartial jury would have been possible.

Robinson (1974) surveyed by telephone 103 subjects drawn from the phone directories of Oregon on the first day and again during the final week of the Watergate hearings, thereby providing a pre- and posthearing measurement of the influence of the publicity surrounding the hearings. The reported effect of publicity was to significantly increase knowledge and awareness of the Watergate case (nearly doubling in some categories); opinions regarding the guilt or involvement of the president however, changed little. There was an increase in the negative perception of politicians in general, though. Robinson concluded that even massive media coverage does not necessarily make for negative public attitudes.

Rollings and Blascovich (1977) gave written questionnaires to 438 introductory psychology students prior to and following the arrest of Patty Hearst, sampling their opinions as to her guilt and probable sentence if convicted, and the likelihood of conviction and probable sentence if the respondent were in Hearst's position. The authors found little influence from the pretrial publicity surrounding the arrest, in that responses to both surveys were similar.

Moran and Cutler (1991) surveyed 604 potential jurors after a year of local newspaper coverage regarding a marijuana smuggling case and a second 100 community members about a police officer's murder. In both surveys, knowledge of the case correlated with perceived guilt, but knowledge was not associated with a willingness to admit bias. The authors concluded that even moderate publicity can deprive a defendant of the presumption of innocence and that juror bias may not be revealed or admitted during normal jury selection procedures.

Notes

CHAPTER 1

1. Ferrell, forthcoming.

2. Ferrell, forthcoming, p. 337. See also Sasson 1995.

3. Descriptors of society as heavily media influenced include "postmodern society" (Denzin 1986), "postmodernism" (Jameson 1992), "the society of the spectacle" (Debord 1983), "the cinematic society" (Denzin 1995), and the "surveillance society" (Lyon 1994)—cited by Manning, forthcoming.

4. Graham and Gurr 1979.

5. Altheide 1984; Meyrowitz 1985.

6. Klain 1989.

7. DeFleur and Dennis 1985.

8. See, for example, Altheide and Snow 1979; Comstock 1980; Gerbner et al. 1980; Gorelick 1989; Humphries 1981; Murray 1980; and Newman 1990.

9. For example, the Canadian Sentencing Commission concluded: "The public . . . is forced to build its view of crime and justice on data which does not reflect reality" (1988, pp. 95–96, cited by Roberts and Doob 1990, p. 452). See also Gorelick 1989.

10. Bailey and Hale, forthcoming; Barber 1987; Bennack 1983; Graber 1980; Yankelovich et al. 1978.

11. The ideas included within a social construction of reality fall under the broad umbrella of the sociology of knowledge tradition. See, for example, Mannheim (1952, 1953) and Scheler (1926). For an extended discussion of social constructionism issues see Miller and Holstein (1991). Of course there are other theoretical approaches to study of the media. This text falls loosely within the effects and cultural ratification models. Howell (1982) identifies three approaches. The *effects model* seeks to identify the nature of media influence on attitudes and behaviors. The *uses model* focuses on the function of a media component—do viewers watch a particular program for emotional release or instruction? And the *cultural ratification* model looks at the political and power impact of the media. For an overview of these other perspectives see Bryant and Zillman (1994).

12. John Locke, *An Essay on Human Understanding*; David Hume, *A Treatise of Human Nature*; John Stewart Mill, *Utilitarianism*. Another perspective that is different from social constructionism and logical empiricism is phenomenology. (See, for example, Benedict Spinoza, *Ethica*; Immanuel Kant, *Critique of Pure Reason*; Friedrich Nietzsche, *Thus Spake Zarathustra*). Phenomenology adopts a perspective that knowledge depends on innate human processes. Humans have tendencies to think, categorize, and process information in particular ways and it is these tendencies, not features of the world, that are important for fashioning knowledge. Knowledge is thus independent of both social processes and events in the world.

13. Gergen 1985.

14. Simonds 1978, p. 19.

15. Scheler 1980, p. 23.

16. Stewart and Mickunas 1974.

17. Gergen 1985.

18. Spector and Kitsuse 1987, p. 6.

19. Ferrell and Sanders 1995; Newman 1990; Nevins 1995; Porsdam 1994.

20. Altheide 1984; Quinney 1970; Tuchman 1978.

21. Adoni and Mane 1984.

22. Of course, government propaganda efforts, puppet governments, and sociological concepts such as "false consciousness" all reflect more pernicious examples of the same deceptive process.

23. Adoni and Mane 1984, p. 327; see also media-dependency theory Ball-Rokeach and DeFleur 1976.

24. Cohen and Young 1981; Lichter 1988.

25. Altheide 1984.

26. Hans and Dee 1991, citing Lippmann 1922; Nimmo and Combs 1983; and Tuchman 1978.

27. Ericson 1991, p. 242.

28. Altheide 1984.

29. See Best 1991.

30. Best 1991, p. 327. Ibarra and Kitsuse (1993) identify five rhetorical styles used in the United States to argue about social problems such as crime. They identify calamity (catastrophic threat), entitlement (vulnerable group denied), endangerment (health or safety threat), loss (extinction of benefit), and unreason (manipulation of an uninformed, unaware group).

31. Barrile 1994; see also Gusfield 1989.

32. Ferrell, forthcoming.

33. Reinarman 1997.

34. Contrast with Agree et al. 1982; Curran and Seaton 1980; DeFleur and Dennis 1985; Ericson 1991; Lowery and DeFleur 1983; Marcuse 1972; Murdock and Golding 1977; and Quinney 1970—who collectively argue that the media merely uphold the status quo.

35. Sasson 1995, p. 10.

36. Sasson 1995. Sasson also notes that media violence as an explanatory framework for violent crime is held nearly as a consensus view among Americans.

37. Ferrell, forthcoming.

38. Becker 1963; Cohen 1972.

39. Best 1989, p. 190.

40. Adoni and Mane 1984, p. 326.

41. Bailey and Hale, forthcoming. See also Bortner 1984; Cohen and Young 1981; Gerbner et al. 1978, 1979, 1980; Hans 1990; Quinney 1970; Pfuhl 1992; Surette 1984a.

42. Pfuhl 1992, p. 510.

43. Bailey and Hale, forthcoming.

44. Best 1991.

45. Jenkins 1994.

46. See also Pfuhl 1992.

47. Surette 1996. Other examples of social construction applied to criminal justice include Barton and Gregg 1982; Bond-Maupin, Cavender, and Jurik

1996; Brownstein 1997; Cavender and Mulcahy, forthcoming; Ferrell 1993, forthcoming; Iyengar 1991; Orcutt and Turner 1993; Kappeler et al. 1993, chapters 4–5; Lowney and Best 1995; Nava 1988; Pfuhl 1992; Reinarman 1997; Reinarman and Levine 1995; Ross 1989; Sacco 1995; Tierney 1982; and Tunnell 1992.

48. See Packer 1968.

49. Tajgman 1981, p. 509.

50. The concepts of backstage and front-stage behavior originate in Erving Goffman's concepts of regions and region behavior (see Goffman 1959). Here, however, they are not used precisely as Goffman used them but have been adapted to reflect a change in style and focus in the media over the last forty years. Goffman's original concepts described individual face-to-face interactions rather than interpersonal behaviors portrayed and perceived through the media, but by extending and transforming his concepts, we are better able to understand and discuss the development of the relationship between the media and crime and justice (see Goffman 1959, 1967); for while Goffman's model of back- and front-region behaviors describes a static set of stages and is limited to face-to-face interactions, the principles implicit in it can be adapted to describe the changes in situations and behaviors brought about by new media (Meyrowitz 1985a, p. 46).

51. See McLuhan 1962, 1964; McLuhan and Fiore 1967.

52. Meyrowitz 1985b; Kurtz 1993.

53. Kurtz 1993.

54. Meyrowitz 1985a, p. 111.

55. Lichter (1988, p. 36) argues that the emergence of the national media is the single most influential factor in transforming the political process and the political culture of late-twentieth-century America (see also Dye and Zeigler 1986).

56. Boorstin 1961.

57. Meyrowitz 1985a, pp. 87, 319; see also Foucault 1977; Goffman 1961.

58. Meyrowitz 1985a, p. 310.

59. Katsh 1989.

60. Meyrowitz 1985a, p. 175.

61. Ericson 1991, 1995.

62. Ericson 1991, 1995.

CHAPTER 2

1. Everson 1964.

2. Sayes 1929, cited by Bailey and Hale, forthcoming.

3. Stark 1987, p. 236. A listing of the world's great literature would include many works in which the commission of a crime and its aftermath are central themes. Examples include Dostoyevski's *Crime and Punishment*; many of Shakespeare's plays, notably *Macbeth*; and Hawthorne's *The Scarlet Letter*.

4. Grenander 1976, p. 48.

5. Papke 1987; Stark 1987.

6. Stark 1987.

7. Papke 1987, p. 117.

8. Stark 1987, p. 237.

9. Papke 1987, p. 105.

10. Papke 1987, p. 108.

11. Papke 1987, p. 102.

12. Grenander 1976, p. 48; Stark 1987, p. 238.

13. Newman 1990, citing Neale 1980, p. 48.

14. Papke 1987, pp. 181–182.

15. Lynn 1979.

16. See Deming 1985; Knight 1980; Krutnik 1991; Mandel 1984; Thompson 1993; Winks 1988.

17. Hartsfield 1985, pp. 105–106; see also Papke 1987.

18. Stark 1987, p. 231; Tuska 1987, p. 1. See also Papke 1987, Chapter 6. For additional discussions see Winks 1988; Deming 1985; Knight 1980; Krutnik 1991; Mandel 1984; and Thompson 1993.

19. See Duncan 1990; Inge 1990; Jensen 1993; Mooney and Ferell 1989; Nyberg, forthcoming; Sabom 1993; Whitlark 1988; Williams 1994; Witek 1989.

20. See Cole 1996; Newman 1993; Nyberg, forthcoming; and Williams 1994.

21. Nyberg, forthcoming.

22. Armour 1980, p. xix.

23. Jowett and Linton 1980, pp. 68–69.

24. Armour 1980, p. xxi.

25. Jowett and Linton 1980, p. 68; see also Altheide and Snow 1979.

26. See Armour 1980, pp. xxiii–xxiv; Jowett and Linton 1980, pp. 69, 109; Shadoian 1977, p. 3.

27. Jowett and Linton 1980, p. 73.

28. See *Mutual Film Corporation* v. *Hodges* and *Mutual Film Corporation* v. *Industrial Commission of Ohio*. This protection did not come unto the Supreme Court's *Miracle* decision in the 1950s.

29. Jowett and Linton 1980.

30. Dombrink 1988, p. 56.

31. Jowett and Linton 1980, pp. 69, 71–72.

32. Jowett and Linton 1980, p. 75.

33. Rosow 1978.

34. Rosow 1978, p. 37.

35. Rosow 1978, pp. 11–21.

36. McArthur 1972; Rosow 1978.

37. Hartsfield 1985, p. 129.

38. Rosow 1978, p. xiv.

39. Also popular in the early 1920s was a secondary crime theme in which criminality was portrayed in the form of evil, twisted, satanic beings—perhaps reflecting the popularization of Freud's theories. This portrayal soon waned in popularity, however.

40. Rosow 1978, p. 174.

41. See Blumer 1933; Blumer and Hauser 1933; Charter 1933; Dale 1935a; Holaday and Stoddard 1933; Peterson and Thurstone 1933; and Shuttleworth

and May 1933; see also Chapter 3. For a summary discussion of the Payne Fund studies from a communications perspective, see Lowery and DeFleur 1983, Chapter 2.

42. See Hays 1932.

43. Stark 1987, p. 240.

44. See Stark 1987, p. 239, citing Fogelson 1977.

45. McArthur 1972, pp. 29–30, 46; Rosow 1978, pp. 253, 262–268.

46. Rosow 1978, p. 319.

47. Dominick 1978.

48. Stevens and Garcia 1980, pp. 97, 141, 143.

49. Stevens and Garcia 1980, p. 143.

50. See Lewis 1984; Pearl et al. 1982, vol. 2.

51. Maguire 1988.

52. Kubey and Csikszentmihalyi 1990.

53. Dominick 1978, p. 113.

54. Dominick's data reflect the programming on NBC, CBS, and ABC and varying definitions of "prime time." If the DuMont Network, which broadcast from 1948 to 1954, is included and varying definitions of crime-and-justice shows are taken into account, a peak in crime-related shows appears in the early 1950s (see Kania and Tankan 1987).

55. See also Dominick 1978, p. 113.

56. Cole 1996; Kania and Tanhan 1987; Stark 1987, p. 269.

57. Wilson and her colleagues (1997, pp. 136–137; see also Cole 1996) found that for 1994 and 1995, 57 percent of programs contain violence, with cable more likely and broadcast networks less likely. Nearly half the violence on television is portrayed as justified and realistic but not shown as graphic. Depictions of the consequences of violence are not shown in the majority of programming and only 4 percent of all programs with violence feature a strong antiviolence theme. She summarizes the results thusly: "the context of violence or the way in which it is portrayed does not differ substantially across channels or genres. Violence typically involves behavioral acts that are perpetrated by white males against other white males. Acts of aggression often are repeated and frequently involve guns. Violence is typically sanitized on television. It is rarely punished in the immediate context in which it occurs and it rarely results in observable harm to the victims. In fact, violence is often funny on television. The serious consequences of violence are frequently ignored."

58. See Gerbner 1980; Kania and Tanhan 1987; Lewis 1984.

59. Cole 1996; Wilson et al. 1997.

60. Cole 1996; Murray 1984; Peterson and Zill 1980; Wilson et al. 1997. Children's programming and cartoons have naturally been a prime cause of concern and remain so. In a recent assessment of television content, Jeffery Cole (1996) commented on certain Saturday morning programming as rarely discussing alternatives to violence and sending the message that fighting, if not fun, is at least the norm. It is true that people rarely die on Saturday morning, but it is not true that they rarely fight.

61. The most recent content analysis studies suggest that these non–broadcast network sources are significantly higher in crime and violent content. See for example Cole 1996; and Wilson et al. 1997. Currently there are more than seventy cable networks operating in the United States.

62. Everson 1964, p. xi.

63. Binder 1993; Gray 1989; Lynxwiler and De Corte 1995.

64. Brantley and Di Rosa 1994.

65. Ferrell, forthcoming.

66. Cole 1996.

67. Meyowitz 1985.

68. Cole 1996.

69. Cole 1996.

70. See Newman 1993.

71. See Anderson and Ford 1987; Calvert and Tan 1994; Cole 1995, 1996; Cooper and Mackie 1986; Dominick 1987; Funk and Buchman 1994; Graybill et al. 1987; Mechrabian and Wixen 1986; Patkin 1994; Saxe 1994; Schutte et al. 1988; Silvern and Williamson 1987; Skirrow 1986; and Winkel et al. 1987.

72. Irwin and Gross 1995.

73. Anderson and Ford 1987. Opposite conclusions are offered by Saxe (1994), who argues that a control and catharsis effect can be a benefit of violent game playing. He offers no empirical evidence to support his contention however.

74. See Altheide and Snow 1979; Jowett and Linton 1980; Meyrowitz 1985a; Papke 1987; Stark 1987; and Stevens and Garcia 1980.

75. See Carlson 1985; Dominick 1978; Estep and MacDonald 1984; and Gerbner 1976.

76. Cole 1996.

77. See Antunes and Hurley 1977; Bortner 1984; Graber 1980; Jones 1976; Pandiani 1978; and Sherizen 1978. For a general discussion of the types of violence portrayed as either instrumental (rational goal-oriented) versus expressive (explosive emotional acts) and their use in the entertainment media see Newman, forthcoming.

78. The 1969 National Commission on the Causes and Prevention of Violence found violent episodes in more than 80 percent of shows (National Commission on the Causes and Prevention of Violence 1969; see also Newman 1990).

79. See Estep and MacDonald 1984, p. 115; Lichter and Lichter 1983, p. 10; Maguire 1988, p. 175.

80. Lewis 1984; Lichter and Lichter 1983.

81. Garofalo 1981a; Maguire 1988.

82. See Dominick 1973; Estep and MacDonald 1983; Graber 1980; Hauge 1965; and Roshier 1981.

83. Estep and MacDonald 1984, pp. 122–123; Pandiani 1978.

84. Lichter and Lichter 1983, p. 30; Maguire 1988.

85. Lichter and Lichter 1983, p. 57; Maguire 1988.

86. See Carlson 1985, p. 50; Estep and MacDonald 1984, pp. 122–123; Gerbner and Gross 1976; and Maguire 1988.

87. Scheingold 1984, p. 63. See discussion of media and fear of crime in Chapter 7 also.

88. Carlson 1985, p. 117; Garofalo 1981a.

89. Culver and Knight 1979.

90. Dominick 1978, p. 116.

91. Hall, forthcoming.

92. Bortner 1984, p. 19, citing Parenti 1978, and Sennet and Cobb 1973.

93. Culver and Knight 1979; Lichter and Lichter 1983.

94. Bortner 1984, p. 19.

95. Culver and Knight 1979, p. 209; Dominick 1978, p. 117.

96. Arons and Katsh 1977.

97. Litcher and Litcher 1983.

98. Litcher and Litcher 1983 p. 45.

99. Lichter and Lichter 1983, pp. 51–52; Maguire 1988.

100. Rosow 1978, pp. 326–327; Shadoian 1977, p. 212.

101. Bortner 1984; Price et al. 1992; Stark 1987.

102. Price et al. 1992.

103. See Brenner 1989; Chase 1986; Lichter and Lichter 1983; Rosen 1989; and Stark 1987. Media lawyers who concentrated on practicing law enjoyed their highest popularity during the 1960s, a period when police shows were at their lowest level. By the late 1960s, police shows had regained their popularity and lawyer shows had declined (Stark 1987, p. 229).

104. Bailey et al. forthcoming.

105. Bailey et al. forthcoming.

106. Lichter and Lichter 1983, pp. 42, 44.

107. Stark 1987; Surette 1989.

108. Snow 1984.

109. Stark 1987, p. 229.

110. Stark 1987.

111. Stark 1987, p. 275.

112. See Brenner 1989; Rosen 1989.

113. Lichter and Lichter 1983; Stark 1987.

114. Brenner 1989; Rosen 1989.

115. Quoted in *TV Guide* May 25, 1985.

116. Schwartz 1989, p. 38.

117. Lichter and Lichter 1983, p. 29.

118. Cheatwood, forthcoming.

119. Cheatwood, forthcoming; Freeman, forthcoming; Zaner 1989.

120. Cheatwood, forthcoming; Freeman, forthcoming.

121. Zaner 1989, pp. 64–66.

122. See for example Hale, forthcoming and Bailey et al. forthcoming.

123. Carlson 1985; Dominick 1973, pp. 244–245.

124. Bortner 1984; Pandiani 1978.

125. Maguire 1988.

126. Bortner 1984, p. 19; Maguire 1988.

127. Culver and Knight 1979, pp. 207–209; Garofalo 1981a.

128. Newman 1993.

129. Rennie 1978.

130. Newman 1993, p. 315.

131. Bellah 1985.

132. Newman 1993.

133. Moynihan 1969.

134. Altheide and Snow 1979.

135. Gerbner et al. 1978, 1979, 1980; see also Chapter 7.

136. Rosow 1978, p. 319.

137. Grenander 1976, p. 55.

138. Greene and Bynum 1982; Stark 1987, p. 276.

139. Carlson 1985, pp. 52, 117; see also Bortner 1984.

140. Stark 1987, p. 282.

141. Bennett 1985; Sheley 1985.

142. Dershowitz 1985.

143. Dershowitz 1985; Johnson 1983.

144. Johnson 1983; Walker 1983.

145. Letkemann 1973; cited by Sherizen 1978, p. 221.

146. Bortner 1984; Lichter and Lichter 1983.

CHAPTER 3

1. Zillman and Wakshlag 1985.

2. Newspaper reports of crime are also accessible only to people who can read, eliminating concerns about direct effects on children (Heath and Gilbert 1996, p. 382).

3. Compare with Park 1940.

4. Chibnall 1980.

5. Drechsel 1983, p. 35, citing Shaaber 1929.

6. Chibnall 1980, p. 180.

7. Chibnall 1980, p. 183.

8. Chibnall 1980.

9. Papke 1987, p. 22

10. Black 1987, pp. 80–81.

11. Chibnall 1980, p. 190.

12. Deschel 1983, p. 41, citing Lee 1937. In 1733, for example, Boston papers reported the arrest, charging, trial, and sentencing of a young woman who had killed her illegitimate newborn (Drechsel 1983, p. 44). See also Friedman 1994.

13. Baker and Ball 1969, p. 16.

14. Bleyer 1927.

15. Quoted in Blayer 1927, p. 157.

16. Compare with Dreschel 1983; Papke, 1987.

17. Stevens and Garcia 1980, pp. 121–122.

18. Gordon and Heath 1981, p. 227; Sherizen 1978, p. 208.

19. Papke 1987, p. 35.

20. Bleyer 1927.

21. See Wilmer, 1859.

22. Drechsel 1983, p. 68.

23. Forrest 1892, p. 553.

24. The criticism is best exemplified by the efforts of Anthony Comstock in New York City.

25. Gorn 1992, pp. 1–2.

26. Gorn 1992, pp. 3–4.

27. See Chibnall 1981; Isaacs 1961; Sherizen 1978; and Terry 1984.

28. Hughes 1940, p. 23.

29. Papke 1987.

30. Baker and Ball 1969, pp. 20–21.

31. Lotz 1991, p. 23.

32. Desmond 1978; Snyder 1992, p. 195.

33. Papke 1987, p. 35.

34. Drechsel 1983, p. 49.

35. Papke 1987, p. 54.

36. Papke 1987.

37. Drechsel 1983, p. 68; Papke 1987, p. 54.

38. Drechsel 1983.

39. Drechsel 1983, pp. 53–54.

40. See Rothman 1971.

41. Papke 1987; compare Rothman 1971.

42. Stevens and Garcia 1980, p. 124.

43. DeFleur and Ball-Rokeach 1975, p. 84.

44. Altheide and Snow 1979.

45. Bortner 1984.

46. Cohen and Young 1981.

47. Cohen and Young 1981, pp. 17–18.

48. Cohen and Young 1981; Ericson et al. 1989.

49. Terry 1984.

50. Martens and Cunningham-Niederer 1985, p. 62; see also Pritchard 1985.

51. Ericson, Baranek, and Chan 1991.

52. Ericson, Baranek, and Chan 1991; Hall et al. 1981.

53. Wisehart (1922) makes a similar point early in the century.

54. Drechsel, 1983; Ericson, Baranek, and Chan 1991; Wisehart 1922.

55. Gans 1979, p. 284.

56. Drechsel 1983, pp. 12, 49, citing Sigal 1973, pp. 4–5.

57. Graber 1980.

58. Cohen and Young 1981, p. 22; see also Gelles and Faulkner 1978.

59. Cohen and Young 1981, pp. 22–23.

60. Roshier 1981.

61. Warr 1991, p. 14.

62. Jones 1976, p. 244.

63. Cohen and Young 1981, p. 23; Westin 1982.

64. Ericson et al. 1989.

65. Cohen and Young 1981.

66. Chibnall 1981; Tuchman 1973, 1978.

67. Ericson, Baranek, and Chan 1987, 1989, 1991; Gordon and Heath 1981; Roshier 1981; Sherizen 1978, p. 212.

68. Sacco and Kennedy 1996, p. 37.

69. Chermak 1995, p. 166.

70. See Chermak 1995, Chapter 2; Schlesinger et al. 1991, p. 411.

71. Cavender and Mulcahy (n.d.). See also Ericson et al. 1989, 1991; Tumber 1993; and Katz 1987.

72. Shoemaker 1991.

73. See Chibnall 1975, 1977; Ericson, Baranek, and Chan 1987, 1989, 1991; Isaacs 1961; Sherizen 1978; and Terry 1984.

74. Sherizen 1978.

75. Ericson, Baranak and Chan 1989; Chermak, forthcoming.

76. Chibnall 1981.

77. Ericson, Baranek, and Chan 1987, 1989, 1991; Chermak, forthcoming.

78. Curran 1989; Tumbo 1994.

79. Schlesinger et al. 1991, p. 403.

80. Schlesinger et al. 1991, p. 399.

81. Chermak, forthcoming.

82. Sacco and Kennedy 1996, p. 37.

83. Ross, forthcoming.

84. See Chibnall 1981; Gordon and Heath 1981; and Sherizen 1978.

85. Sherizen 1978, pp. 209–212.

86. Antunes and Hurley 1977.

87. Fedler and Jordan 1982.

88. See Fishman 1978; Hall et al. 1981; Roshier 1981; Ross, forthcoming; and Sherizen 1978.

89. Hall et al. 1981, p. 358; see also Galtung and Ruge 1981; contrast with Schlesinger et al. 1991, p. 404.

90. Fishman 1978, p. 536.

91. Fishman 1978, p. 537.

92. An early account of news media creating crime waves can be found in Steffens 1931, chapter 2, and Wisehart 1922. (Reprinted in 1968.)

93. Orcutt and Turner, 1993. See also Jensen et al. 1991; Nelson 1984; Reinarman and Levine 1989; and Voumvakis and Ericson 1984.

94. Chiricos, forthcoming; Fishman 1978.

95. See Bortner 1984; Cohen and Young 1981; Estep and Lauderdale 1980; Gorelick 1989; and Humphries 1981.

96. Measures include the percentage of total space or time allocated to coverage of individual crimes (Deutschmann 1959; Otto 1962; Stempl 1962), summary coverage of an issue, and story placement or prominence (Cirino 1972; Deutschmann 1959; Dominick 1978, pp. 110–112; Lowry 1971; Otto 1962; Roshier 1973, p. 33; Sherizen 1978, p. 208; Stempl 1962).

97. Jerin and Fields 1993; Lotz 1991.

98. See Dominick 1978, p. 108; Graber 1980, p. 24; Garofalo 1981a; Jerin and Fields 1995. Lotz (1991) found 30 percent for New York newspapers.

99. Chermak 1996; see also Sherizen 1978; Jerin and Fields 1995.

100. Cirino 1972; Graber 1980; Lowry 1971.

101. Graber 1980.

102. See Bortner 1984; Cirino 1972; Garofalo 1981a; Lowry 1971; Jerin and Fields 1995; Schlesinger et al. 1991; Terry 1984.

103. Studies have estimated that over 90 percent of citizens cite the media as their prime source of crime information. (See Canadian Sentencing Commission 1987; Fox 1995.)

104. Graber 1980; Haskins 1969; Sherizen 1978, p. 208; Swanson 1953.

105. Katz 1987, p. 67.

106. Katz 1987.

107. Katz 1987; Lotz 1991.

108. See Bortner 1984, p. 16; Cavender and Mulcahy, forthcoming; Cirino 1974; Ditton and Duffy 1983; Dominick 1978, p. 108; Esterle 1986; Fishman 1978; Graber 1980; Jerin and Fields 1995; Roshier 1973, p. 32; Soothill and Walby 1991; Sheley and Ashkins 1981.

109. Sheley and Ashkins 1981, pp. 499–500.

110. Graber 1980, pp. 39–40.

111. Graber 1980, p. 63.

112. See, for example, Websdale and Alvarez (forthcoming) regarding the reporting of domestic violence.

113. Graber 1980, p. 52.

114. Gordon and Riger 1989.

115. See Coleman 1974; Evans and Lundman 1983; Molotch and Lester 1981; Quinney 1970; Shaw 1990a, 1990b, 1990c; Sneed 1985, p. 56.

116. Cavender and Mulcahy (n.d.).

117. Barak 1994; Gottfredson and Hirschi 1990, p. 35; Sheley 1985.

118. Chermak, 1996; Davis 1951; Fishman 1978; Graber 1980, pp. 38–42; Jones 1976; Roshier 1981; Sheley and Ashkins 1981.

119. Terry 1984, p. 36; see also Roshier 1981; Sheley and Ashkins 1981.

120. Graber 1980; Sheley and Ashkins 1981.

121. Morash and Hale 1987; Evans and Lundman 1987.

122. Graber 1980, p. 58.

123. Gorelick 1989.

124. Chermak 1995.

125. Chermak 1995, p. 107.

126. Chermak 1995; Manby and Brown 1984; Meyers 1996.

127. Meyers 1994, 1996. Marian Meyers (1996, p. ix) describes the news coverage of violence against women thusly: "The predominant problems with news about violent crime against women—such as blaming the victim and reinforcing harmful cultural stereotypes and myths—lie not with individual journalists but with the social structures and values that deny male violence against women is a serious, systemic problem rooted in misogyny and patriarchy. By reflecting this cultural blindness, the news reinforces it."

128. Johnstone, Hawkins, and Michener 1994; Wilbanks 1984.

129. Graber 1980.

130. Graber 1980; Lotz 1991, p. 125.

131. Roberts and Doob 1990, p. 453, citing the Canadian Sentencing Commission 1988.

132. Iyengar 1991.

133. Sasson 1995 citing Carlson 1985.

134. Graber 1980, pp. 46, 74; compare Terry 1984, p. 36.

135. Gorelick 1989; Graber 1980, p. 45; Surette, forthcoming.

136. Graber 1980; Terry 1984.

137. Graber 1980, pp. 74–75, 80, 83.

138. Marsh 1991, p. 76.

139. Marsh 1991, p. 76.

140. Lotz (1995) found for New York papers greater coverage of corrections with stories of correctional policy, conditions, and celebrity inmates.

141. Cheatwood, forthcoming; Freeman, forthcoming; Turnbo 1994. For a discussion of the news media's role in prison riots and inmate negotiations, see Mahon and Laurence 1996.

142. Mahon and Laurence 1996; Schwartz 1989, p. 40; Turnbo 1994.

143. Cheatwood, forthcoming; Freeman, forthcoming. Mahon and Laurence (1996) also point out that the goals and posture of prisoners and terrorists toward the media are remarkably similar, especially in hostage situations. Both are seeking media attention and are struggling against more powerful authorities.

144. Cavender and Fishman, forthcoming; see also Cole 1996. Whitney and his colleagues (1997, p. 271) found that 38 percent of reality programs contained some visual violence and an additional 18 percent contained talk about violence.

145. See Ruel 1994; Tunnell, forthcoming; Whitney et al. 1997.

146. Whitney and his colleagues (1997, pp. 297–298) found police reality shows to be the most intense, visual, and violent reality programs with every show analyzed containing at least one violent sequence. Oliver (1994) found that reality-based law enforcement programs overreported violent crime and the proportion of solved crimes.

147. Licher and Amundson (1994) point out that reality programming differs from fictional programming in the narrative context in which sequential

stories are frequently unrelated, and in the manner of depicting violence through recreations, reporting, and oral descriptions.

148. Oliver and Armstrong 1995.

149. Cole (1996) has noted the successful emergence of television specials revolving around real and re-created footage of animals attacking and, in some cases, killing people.

150. A concrete example of the continuing blurring of news and entertainment is ABC's contract with Barbara Walters. ABC gave Barbara Walters a $1-million-per-year contract, with part of her salary to be paid by ABC News for anchor work and part to be paid by ABC Entertainment for her prime-time specials. See Westin 1982.

151. Acorn 1989.

152. Cavender (n.d.), p. 6.

153. Cavender (n.d.), p. 19.

154. Cavender (n.d.), p. 24.

155. For example, few programs provide an advisory or warning of violent content and fewer provide information about how violence or crime can be avoided (Whitney et al. 1997, p. 303; see also Manning, forthcoming).

156. As news and entertainment has blurred, so has news and advertising. Public relations firms regularly produce video news releases analogous to press releases that are high-production corporate ads aired as news ("Making News" 1991).

157. Drucker 1989.

158. See Pillsbury 1997, p. 20 n. 27; Surette 1989; Thaler 1994.

159. Comstock 1980. See also Friedman 1994.

160. Walker 1985, citing Friedman and Percival 1981; and Gottfredson and Gottfredson 1980.

161. Walker 1985, p. 17.

162. Hariman 1990, p. 18.

163. Hariman 1990, p. 23.

164. Brummett 1990, p. 179; Drucker 1989.

165. Brummett 1989, pp. 188-189.

166. Brummett 1990, p. 190.

167. Tunnell 1992.

168. Roshier 1981. p. 47.

169. Harper 1982, p. 78.

170. Barber 1987, pp. 112–114.

171. Surette 1989.

172. Papke (1987, p. 22) reports that similar themes existed in the 1830s. Popular pamphlets portrayed crime within two long-standing themes—the *rogue* (a semi-hero who commits property fraud) and the *fiend* (a diabolical, frenzied villain). This period saw the creation of a new theme—the *fiendish rogue*. An example from the early part of the century is the 1913 Leo Frank case. This case involved the strangulation of a fourteen-year-old female factory worker in Georgia. As was common in such cases, coverage was heavily biased against the defendant. An Atlanta paper was typical: "Our little girl—ours by the Eternal God! has been pursued to a hideous death and bloody grave by

this filthy, perverted Jew of New York." The commutation of Frank's sentence from death to life imprisonment led to the Georgia governor's being driven out of office. A year after his conviction, Frank was taken from a prison farm by a band of men, driven 125 miles to the scene of the murder, and lynched.

173. Terry 1984.

174. Ball 1981, p. 62.

175. Ball 1981, p. 62. See also Simonett 1966.

176. Compare with Constock 1980; Gerbner 1980.

177. Drucker 1989.

178. Drucker 1989, p. 305. Regarding the impact of a televised civil trial, Raymond (1992) reports that viewers became more knowledgeable about the judicial process while not becoming less confident about the courts.

179. Bain 1995.

180. See, for example, Barak 1995; Schmalleger 1996.

181. Handy 1995; Pillsbury 1997.

182. See, for example, Gaines 1995; Garvey 1995; Rosenblatt 1995; Whitaker 1995.

183. Walsh 1995. See also Pillsbury 1997.

184. Gelernter 1995.

185. Walsh 1995.

186. See, for example, Websdale and Alvarez (forthcoming) regarding coverage of homicide/suicides.

187. Compare with Graber 1980; Haskins 1969; Sherizen 1978; Swanson 1953.

188. Marsh 1991, p. 67; Tunnell, forthcoming.

189. *Sourcebook of Criminal Justice Statistics—1994.* Table 2.24. Attitudes toward whether selected influences contribute to violence.

190. *Sourcebook of Criminal Justice Statistics—1994.* Table 2.25. Attitudes toward why the United States has more homicides and violent deaths than other countries.

191. *Sourcebook of Criminal Justice Statistics—1994.* Table 2.108. Attitudes toward the impact of crime coverage by local television news.

192. Graber 1980, p. 83; see also Chapter 4.

193. Sasson 1995.

194. Lotz 1991, Chapter 6.

195. Barrile 1984; Graber 1980, p. 73; Sasson 1995. Historically Wisehart ([1922] 1968) also notes the punitive effect of crime news coverage.

196. Sasson 1995.

197. Compare with Barrile 1984; Gorelick 1989; Sasson 1995.

198. Bennett, Wesley, and Triplett, forthcoming.

199. Avery 1989; Bennett, Wesley, and Triplett, forthcoming; Cheatwood, forthcoming; Freeman, forthcoming.

200. Chiricos, forthcoming. See also Fishman 1978; Graber 1980; Hall et al. 1981.

201. Lofton 1966, p. 138. Wisehart (1922) also makes references to echolike effects from media coverage.

202. Kaplan and Skolnick 1982, pp. 467-468.

203. See Greene and Loftus 1984; Greene and Wade 1988; Kaplan and Skolnick 1982; Loften 1966; Radin 1964; Surette 1989.

204. Katz 1987, p. 60.

205. O'Keefe and Reid 1990; Randall et al. 1988.

206. Snow 1984.

207. Barber 1987, p. 113; Gerbner 1980; Katz 1987.

208. See for example, Cashman and Fetter 1980.

209. Israel et al. 1972.

210. Comments from *All Things Considered.* 5/13/96. Pugh Research Center for People and the Press.

211. Katz 1987, p. 60.

212. Bergman 1971; Gorelick 1989.

213. Bortner 1984; Gorelick 1989.

214. See Barrile 1984; Gorelick 1989; Hennigan et al. 1982; Reiner 1985; Surette 1985b.

215. Surette 1994.

216. Surette 1992; Ball 1981.

217. Gans 1988; and Bullah et al. 1985.

218. Cavender and Mulcahy, n.d., p. 4.

219. See Gerbner 1980; Randall et al. 1988; Reiner 1985; Zucker 1978.

220. See Rosenberg 1990.

221. Cohen and Young 1981.

222. See Fishman 1978; Hall et al. 1981; Pritchard 1986.

CHAPTER 4

1. *United States* v. *Burr,* 25 F. Cas. 49, 49 [C.C.D. Va. 1807] [No. 14692g] cited by Marcus 1982, p. 237.

2. Baker and Ball 1969, p. 11; Blasi 1971, p. 233.

3. Salas 1984.

4. Yankelovich et al. 1978.

5. Altheide 1984.

6. Altheide 1984; Bennett et al. 1983.

7. Altheide 1984; see also Chapter 3.

8. Flynn 1993; Minow and Cate 1991.

9. Hoiberg and Stires 1973; Kramer et al. 1990; Simon 1966.

10. Pember 1987, pp. 364–366.

11. American Bar Association 1978; Siebert et al. 1970.

12. *Patton* v. *Yount,* 104 S. Ct. 2885 [1984].

13. *Murphy* v. *Florida,* 421 U. S. 794 [1975].

14. *People* v. *Taylor,* Ill. Sup. Ct., No. 58258 [1984].

15. *United States* v. *Faul,* 8th Cir. [1984].

16. *Rideau* v. *Louisiana,* 373 U. S. 723 [1963].

17. Apfel 1980, p. 446; Moran and Cutler 1991.

18. Tanick and Shields 1985.

19. *United States* v. *Burr*, 25 F. Cas. 49, 49 [C.C.D. Va. 1807] [No. 14692g]. See also Flynn 1993.

20. Flynn 1993; Jaffe 1965, p. 519.

21. Flynn 1993.

22. Dubnoff 1977, p. 97; interview with Jane Kirtley 9/5/96 Executive Director Reporters Committee for Freedom of the Press.

23. Dubnoff 1977, p. 98.

24. Apfel 1980, pp. 445, 449.

25. See Moran and Cutler 1991; Pember 1987, p. 366; Rollings and Blascovich 1977, p. 60; Simon 1977, pp. 520–521.

26. Compare with Buddenbaum et al. 1981, p. 5; Pember 1987, p. 367.

27. Carroll et al. 1986, pp. 194–195; Dexter, Cutler and Moran 1992; Kramer and Kerr, 1989; Kramer et al. 1990; Moran and Cutler 1991.

28. Moran and Cutler 1991.

29. Greene and Loftus 1984; Greene and Wade 1988.

30. See Chapter 3, also Surette 1989.

31. Cited by Levine 1987, pp. 17–19, n.2.

32. Levine and Bussian 1987, p. 1.

33. Generally, privacy concerns truthful articles. If the information published is false, the appropriate legal vehicle would be a libel action, in which the libeled individuals would sue the media for distributing false, defamatory information about them (Levine 1987, p. 11). Defamation includes both libel (a written defamation) and slander (an oral defamation). The law is also seen as a means of ensuring that the press remain accountable. Although the laws against defamation are complex, certain basic principles prevail. Unlike criminal actions, civil libel suits lay the burden of proof on the plaintiff, who must prove four elements: (1) that the libelous communication was published, (2) that the plaintiff was identified in the communication, (3) that the communication is defamatory in some way, and (4) that the libelous matter was published out of neglect or disregard or carelessness. The last element is usually the hardest to prove. For a full discussion of these issues with a review of cases, see Pember 1987.

34. Levine 1987, p. 11.

35. *Privacy Exemption Surmountable* 1985, pp. 33–35.

36. Spaniolo and Terilli 1987, p. 10.

37. See *Private Exemption Surmountable* 1985, pp. 34–35.

38. Pember 1987, p. 304.

39. Spaniolo and Terilli 1987, p. 23.

40. *Private Exemption Surmountable* 1985, p. 33.

41. Spaniolo and Terilli 1987, pp. 22–23.

42. Apfel 1980, p. 439.

43. See *Pell* v. *Procunier* (94 S. Ct. 2800 [1974]); *Saxbe* v. *Washington Post* (94 S. Ct. 2811 [1974]). In *Nixon* v. *Warner Communications* (435 U. S. 591 [1978]), in which the media sought access to Richard Nixon's Oval Office tapes, the Court refused the media access stating, "The First Amendment generally grants the press no right to information about a trial superior to that of the general public" (435 U. S. at 609). The media were denied access to trial evidence including exhibits not yet admitted into evidence, transcripts of bench conferences held *in camera*—that is, in private—written communication between the jury and the judge, lists of names and addresses of jurors, and grand jury testimony.

44. State Prisons Clamp Down on Prisoner Interviews 1996, pp. 5–6; Prison Ban on Media Interviews Upheld 1996, pp. 40–41. See also *United States* v. *Gurney* (558 F.2d 1202 [5th Cir. 1977], cert. denied sub nom.; *United States* v. *Gurney et al. Miami Herald Pub. Co. et al.*); *Sidebottom* v. *Schriro*, 927 F.Supp. 1221 (May 1996); Kirtley 1996b. See also Martin and Sussman (1993) for a discussion of prisoner and journalist censorship within the federal corrections system.

45. DeSilva 1984, p. 43; See Ban on Naming Rape Victims Unconstitutional 1992.

46. Barber 1987, p. 35.

47. *Florida* v. *Globe Communications Corp.* 1991. See also Ban on Naming Rape Victims Unconstitutional 1992.

48. Quoted by Kaplan and Skolnick 1982, pp. 563–564.

49. *Trials by Media* 1984, p. 4.

50. Barber 1987, p. 115.

51. Snow 1984; Surette 1996.

52. See Marcus 1982, p. 276; see also *State* v. *Hauptmann*, 115 N.J.L. 412 [1935] cert. denied, 296 U.S. 649 [1935].

53. 62 A.B.A. Rep, 1134–1135 (1937) cited by Kirtley 1995.

54. *Estes* v. *Texas*, 381 U. S. 532 (1965). Texas financier Billie Sol Estes was accused of a salad-oil swindle. The case was important in Texas due to Estes's political associations. Cameramen crowded into a tiny courtroom with their cameras and seriously disrupted the proceedings. After a trial of great notoriety, which was televised despite his objection, Estes appealed his conviction, arguing that the presence of television cameras denied him a fair trial. The Supreme Court agreed and reversed the decision. *Chandler* v. *Florida*, 101 S. Ct. 802 (1981).

55. *Estes* v. *Texas*, 381 U.S. at 535–536.

56. *Estes* v. *Texas*, 381 U.S. at 538 and 544.

57. Lawyers Aren't Convinced That TV Belongs in Courtroom 1979, cited in Marcus 1982, p. 278.

58. *Chandler* v. *Florida* (101 S. Ct. 802 [1981].) Florida policeman Noel Chandler was tried and convicted with another police officer for a series of burglaries. The case received a large amount of regional media attention and was televised over Chandler's objection as part of a Florida pilot program for televising judicial proceedings. The Supreme Court held that if other constitutional due process guarantees are met, a state could provide for television coverage of a criminal trial over the objection of defendants.

59. Nesson and Koblenz 1981, pp. 408–409; see also Thaler 1994.

60. Bennett, Feldman, and Feldman 1983.

61. Altheide 1984.

62. Compare with Altheide 1984; Barber 1987; Tajgman 1981.

63. Kirtley 1995, p. 367.

64. Marcus 1982, p. 286.

65. See Nesson and Koblenz 1981; Tajgman 1981.

66. *United States* v. *Hastings* 695 F.2d (11th Cir. [1983]), cert. denied, sub nom. *Post-Newsweek Stations* v. *United States*_461 U.S. 931 (1983).

67. *First, Sixth Amendments Permit Ban on Televising Federal Trials* 1983, pp. 2339–2340.

68. See Haas 1988; Johnson 1994; Lancaster 1984; Padden 1985; Raymond 1992.

69. Barber 1987; Johnson 1994. See also Kirtley 1995.

70. Kirtley 1995.

71. Kirtley 1995, p. 380; Johnson 1994.

72. See Barber 1987; Borgida et al. 1990; Gerbner 1980; Surette 1989.

73. Examples include the Los Angeles riots following the not guilty verdict for the police officers involved in the Rodney King beating; the Miami riots following the acquittal of police officers charged in the beating death of a black motorist, Edward McDuffie; and the acquittal of police officer William Lozano in the shooting death of a black motorcyclist.

74. See Barber 1987; Raymond 1992; and Surette 1989.

75. Meyrowitz, 1985.

76. Dubnoff 1977, p. 91.

77. Compare Carroll et al. 1986.

78. Foucalt 1977; Meyrowitz 1985a.

79. Pember 1987, p. 358.

80. *Gannett Co.* v. *DePasquale,* 443 U.S. 368 [1979]; see Appendix I.

81. Apfel 1980, p. 467; Pember 1987, p. 390; *Secret Court Watch*, 1979, pp. 17–23.

82. In *Richmond Newspapers* v. *Virginia* (448 U.S. 555 [1980]).

83. In *Press-Enterprise* v. *Riverside Superior Court* (Sup. Ct. 106 S. Ct. 2735 [1984]); see also 106 S. Ct. 2735 [1986].

84. Pember 1987, p. 395.

85. See Apfel 1980, pp. 455–458; Bell 1983, pp. 1310–1315; *Trial Court May Order Trial Proceedings Closed* 1985, p. 180, citing *In re Knight Pub. Co.*, 743 F. 2d 231 (4th Cir. 1984); and *Press-Enterprise* v. *Riverside Superior Court*, 104 S. Ct. 819 (1984).

86. Kirtley 1996a.

87. Interview with Jane Kirtley, Executive Director Reporters Committee for Freedom of the Press, 9/5/96. See also *Secret Court Watch* 1979, *News Media and the Law* (1979) vol. 3, no. 4, pp. 17–23.

88. Jacobs 1980, p. 685.

89. *Nebraska Press Association* v. *Stuart*, 427 U.S. 539 [1976]; see also Jacobs 1980, p. 686.

90. *Sheppard* v. *Maxwell*, 384 U. S. 333 [1966].

91. *Nebraska Press Association* v. *Stuart*, 427 U.S. 539 [1976].

92. Apfel 1980, pp. 456–459.

93. Apfel 1980, p. 449; see also Dulaney 1968, pp. 51–52, 59.

94. Interview with Jane Kirtley, 9/15/96, Executive Director Reporters Committee for Freedom of the Press.

95. Apfel 1980, p. 483; Carroll et al. 1986, pp. 187–189; Flynn, 1993.

96. Kramer et al. 1990.

97. Apfel 1980, p. 452.

98. Carroll et al. 1986, p. 192; Kerr et al, 1991; Siebert et al. 1970.

99. Carroll et al. 1986, p. 194; see also Dexter and Cutler 1991; Dexter, Cutler, and Moran 1992; Flynn 1993, pp. 871–875; Kerr et al. 1991; Kramer et al, 1990; Krauss and Bonora 1983; Minnow and Cate 1991; Zeisel and Diamond 1978.

100. Dexter, Cutler, and Moran 1992; Hans and Vidmar 1986; Hans and Dee 1991.

101. Apfel 1980, p. 451; Pember 1987, p. 373.

102. Flynn 1993.

103. Flynn 1993, p. 878.

104. Kramer et al. 1990.

105. See Dulaney 1968, p. 93; see also Friendly and Goldfarb 1967.

106. See Hans and Vidmar 1986; Vidmar and Judson 1981; Tanick and Shields 1985.

107. *People* v. *Taylor* (Ill. Sup. Ct., No. 58258 [1984]), cited in *Jurors' Knowledge of Lie Detector Test Raises Presumption of Partiality* 1984.

108. *United States* v. *Faul* (8th Cir. 1984).

109. *Publicity Didn't Require Change for Federal Defendants* 1984, pp. 2140–2141.

110. Cotsirilos and Philipsborn 1986.

111. Pember 1987, p. 385.

112. Jaffe 1965; Pember 1987.

113. Flynn 1993, p. 878.

114. Ebbesen 1987; Horowitz and Willging 1984; Pember 1987, p. 374; van Dyke 1977.

115. See Carroll et al. 1986, p. 184; Sue, Smith, and Pedroza, 1975; Thompson, Fong, and Rosenhan, 1981.

116. See Dexter, Cutler, and Moran, 1992; Jones 1987; Klein and Jess 1966; Kramer et al. 1990; Marshall 1983; Padawer-Singer and Barton 1975a, 1975b; Padawer-Singer et al. 1974; Sue et al. 1974; Tans and Chaffee 1966; Thompson et al. 1981. For a review, see Hans and Vidmar 1986.

117. *Patton* v. *Yount*, 104 S. Ct. 2885 [1984]; *Murphy* v. *Florida*, 421 U.S. 794 [1975]; *People* v. *Taylor*, Ill. Sup. Ct., No. 58258 [1984]; *United States* v. *Faul*, [8th Cir. 1984]; *Rideau* v. *Louisiana*, 373 U.S. 723 [1963].

118. *Pretrial Publicity—Habeas Corpus* 1984, p. 2366.

119. *State* v. *Kirkland,* Mont. Sup. Ct. [1979].

120. *State* v. *Kirkland,* Mont. Sup. Ct., 11/21/79. Cited in Fair Trial—Free Press—Exposure to Prejudicial News. *Criminal Law Reporter* 26, pp. 2279–2280.

121. Jaffe 1965, pp. 506–507, 524; Pember 1987, p. 358.

122. See Carroll et al. 1986, p. 195; Kramer et al. 1990; Kerr et al. 1990; Moran and Cutler, forthcoming; Thompson et al. 1981.

123. Compare Hans and Vidmar 1992; Kramer et al. 1990.

124. Gerald 1983.

125. Franklin 1964, p. 69.

126. Steigleman 1971, pp. 196–197.

127. Compare Blasi 1971.

128. Interview with Jane Kirtley, 9/5/96, Executive Director of the Reporters Committee for Freedom of the Press. See also *U.S.* v. *Cutler*, 6 f.3d67 (2nd Cir. 1993) and *Jankovics* v. *U.S.*, 22 F.3d 1091 (2d Cir. 1994).

129. Kirtley 1990, p. 164.

130. Kirtley 1990; *State Shield Laws: Do They Work?* 1982, pp. 31–33. The questionable effectiveness of shield laws is shown in the case of *In re Farber* (394 A.2d 330 [1978]), in which the New Jersey high court ruled that the state's shield law must yield to the due process rights of a murder defendant. Farber, a *New York Times* reporter, was ordered to turn over his investigation notes and information about the case. The Supreme Court declined to review the case.

131. *State Shield Laws: Do They Work?* 1982, pp. 31–33.

132. Kennedy 1985, pp. 44–45.

133. Steigleman 1971, pp. 201–202; see also Van Alstyn 1977.

134. Interview with Jane Kirtley, 9/15/96, Executive Director of Reporter's Committee for Freedom of the Press. The last appealed case to seriously consider the limits of privilege conversation was a lower court decision in *U.S.* v. *Cutler*, 6 F.3d 67 (2d Cir. 1993). The Supreme court has steadfastly refused to hear new cases on the issue.

135. See Fair Trial—Free Press—Reporter's Privilege 1983, p. 2428, citing *United States* v. *Burke,* 700 F. 2d [1983] cert. denied, 104 S. Ct. 72 [1983]; Major Setback for the News Media 1983, p. 9; Confidential Sources and Information 1989.

136. See Garner 1987; see also Wise 1986.

137. Dulaney 1968; Garner 1987.

138. Drechsel 1985, p. 389.

139. *Police Adopt Media Guidelines* 1985, pp. 31–32.

140. See Barber 1987; Gerbner 1980; Surette 1989; see also Chapter 3.

141. Garner 1987; Schwartz 1989.

142. Garner 1987; Schwartz 1989.

143. Pember 1987, p. 400.

144. Curran 1989; Garner 1987; Schwartz 1989; Surette 1995a.

145. See for example Kurtz, 1993; Mayer 1987; Westin 1982.

146. Salas 1984.

147. Tajgman 1981.

148. See, for example, State Prisons Clamp Down on Prisoner Interviews 1996, p. 5; Kirtley 1996b.

CHAPTER 5

1. W. I. Thomas cited by Fenton 1910, p. 491.

2. See Lowery and DeFleur 1983; Nyberg forthcoming; Wertham 1954.

3. Cited by Cole 1996. The first study about the violent content of television was published in 1961: *Television in the Lives of Our Children* by Wilbur Schram, Jack Lyle, and Edwin Parker.

4. U.S. Senate Judiciary Committee on Juvenile Delinquency 1969, p. 7.

5. *Sourcebook of Criminal Justice Statistics—1994.* Table 2.108. Attitudes toward the impact of crime coverage by local television news.

6. *Sourcebook of Criminal Justice Statistics—1994.* Table 2.24. Attitudes toward whether selected influences contribute to violence. In addition, 38 percent feel the video games contribute a lot and 35 percent feel that television news contributes a lot to social violence.

7. *Sourcebook of Criminal Justice Statistics—1994.* Table 2.25. Attitudes toward why the United States has more homicides and violent deaths than other countries.

8. *Sourcebook of Criminal Justice Statistics—1994.* Table 2.111. Attitudes toward relationship between violence on television and crime.

9. *Sourcebook of Criminal Justice Statistics—1994.* Table 2.107. Attitudes toward violence on television.

10. National Commission on the Causes and Prevention of Violence 1969, vol. 9, p. 356; see also Bailey and Hall, forthcoming; Barber 1987; Bennack 1983; Graber 1980; Yankelovich et al. 1978.

11. Israel et al. 1972, pp. 99–100.

12. Andison 1977, citing Baldwin and Lewis 1972, p. 349.

13. National Commission on the Causes and Prevention of Violence 1969, pp. 169–170.

14. The three primary harmful effects associated with viewing television violence are learning aggressive attitudes and behaviors, becoming desensitized to real-world violence, and developing an unrealistic fear of being a victim of violence (Wilson et al. 1997, p. 5).

15. National Institute of Mental Health 1982, pp. 38–39. See also Bandura 1994.

16. Wilson et al. 1997, p. 144.

17. Bandura 1994; see also Pearl 1984. Wilson and her colleagues (1997, p. 144) link the desensitization effect of television content to repeated acts of violence found in more than half of the violent interactions shown and to the substantial portion of violent scenes involving humor, which are seen as trivializing violence.

18. See, for example, Bandura, Ross, and Ross 1961, 1963.

19. See Comstock et al. 1978, for a review.

20. Natural field experiments typically take advantage of a planned introduction of television to a previously unexposed population. This allows both a pretelevision and posttelevision comparison of the new television group and comparisons with similar but still nonexposed other groups. Although rare because of the unique circumstances necessary and by definition confined to nonmainstream populations, these studies report significant increases in aggressive behavior for children who watched a lot of television in the new-television populations. See, for example, Granzberg 1980; Williams 1986.

21. Lefkowitz et al. 1971.

22. Milavsky et al. 1982b.

23. Personal aggression toward others, aggression against a teacher (rudeness or unruliness), property aggression (theft and vandalism), and delinquency (serious or criminal behaviors).

24. See Huesmann and Eron 1982, 1983.

25. National Institute of Mental Health 1982, pp. 36–37.

26. See Brannigan 1987; Brannigan and Kapardis 1986; Feshbach and Singer 1971; Freedman 1984; Howitt and Cumberbatch 1975; Milavsky et al. 1982a; Mould 1988; Wurtzel and Lometti 1984a, 1984b.

27. Wurtzel and Lometti 1984a, 1984b.

28. Wurtzel and Lometti 1984a, 1984b.

29. Cook, Kendzierski, and Thomas 1983.

30. See Gottfredson and Hirschi 1990, citing Eron 1987, p. 440.

31. Andison 1977.

32. Andison 1977, p. 321.

33. Howitt and Cumberbatch 1975; Milavsky et al. 1982a; Wurtzel and Lometti 1984a, 1984b.

34. Cook, Kendzierski, and Thomas 1983, pp. 180–182.

35. See Brannigan 1987; Brannigan and Goldenberg 1987; Brannigan and Kapardis 1986; Fisher and Barak 1991; Fisher and Grenier 1994; Mould 1988; Nemes 1992.

36. Demare et al. 1988.

37. Demare et al. 1988, p. 150.

38. See Fisher and Grenier 1994 and Linz 1989 for discussions.

39. Imrich, Mullin, and Linz 1990. A contrary study was conducted by Marshall (1988). Contrary to other reports, Marshall found that rapists and child molesters whose victims were not related to them reported significantly greater use of sexually explicit materials than either incest perpetrators or nonoffender controls. Rapists and child molesters also report frequent use of these materials while preparing to commit an offense. Because of the retrospective, self-reported nature of Marshall's data, however, it is impossible to determine whether exposure to sexually explicit materials contributes to sexually deviant behavior, or whether these offenders seek out this material after their deviant orientations are established. Similar results are reported by Carter et al. 1987, 1988. See also Garcia 1986; Goldstein 1973; Langevin et al. 1988.

40. Donnerstein and Berkowitz 1981; Malamuth 1983, 1986; Malamuth and Ceniti 1986.

41. Malamuth 1986.

42. Fisher and Barak 1991; Quinsey et al. 1993, 1995.

43. Malamuth, Check, and Briere 1986.

44. Cook, Kendzierski, and Thomas 1983.

45. See, for example, Heath, Bresolin, and Rinaldi 1989; Wilson et al. 1997.

46. See Andison 1977; Comstock 1983; Comstock and Fisher 1975; Comstock and Lindsey 1975; Comstock et al. 1978; Garofalo 1981b; Lewis 1984; Murray 1980; National Institute of Mental Health 1982; Phillips 1982a, 1982b. Federman (1997, p. 2) states that television violence has been recognized as a significant factor contributing to violence and aggressive antisocial behavior by an overwhelming majority of the scientific community, including such organizations as the American Psychological Association, the American Medical Association, the Surgeon General's Advisory Committee on Television and Behavior, and the National Institute of Mental Health.

47. See Andison 1977; Berkowitz 1964, 1969, 1970; Berkowitz, Corwin, and Heironimus 1963; Berkowitz and Geene 1966; Berkowitz and Rawlings 1963; Garofalo 1981b; Greene and Bynum 1982; Hennigan et al. 1982; Tannenbaum and Zillman 1975; Watt and Krull 1978.

48. Federman 1997.

49. Federman 1997; Wilson et al. 1997.

50. Comstock 1983, pp. 255–256.

51. National Institute of Mental Health 1983 pp. 89–90.

52. Cook, Kendzierski, and Thomas 1983, pp. 191–192.

53. Andison 1977; Comstock 1980; Huesmann 1982; Murray 1980; National Institute of Mental Health 1982; Wood, Wong, and Chachere 1991.

54. Cook, Kendzierski, and Thomas 1983, Freedman 1984; Lewis 1984; Milavsky et al. 1982a; Wilson and Herrnstein 1985.

55. See Leifer and Roberts 1972; see also Collins 1973.

56. See, for example, Wilson et al. 1997.

57. National Institute of Mental Health 1982, pp. 89–90.

58. Wilson and Herrnstein 1985, p. 346.

59. Comstock 1980, p. 258.

60. Phillips 1982a, p. 388.

61. Cole 1996; Federman 1997.

62. Rosenthal 1986; Wood, Wong, and Chachere 1991.

63. See Bandura 1994; Comstock et al. 1978; Lewis 1984; Liebert, Neale, and Davidson 1973; National Commission on the Causes and Prevention of Violence, vol. 9 and 9a, 1969, p. 276; Parke et al. 1977; Pearl et al. 1982, p. 6; Wilson et al. 1997, p. 22; Wood, Wong, and Chachere 1991.

64. See Bandura 1968; Drabman and Thomas 1974; Husemann 1982, p. 132; Molitor and Hirsch 1994.

65. Wilson and Herrnstein 1985, p. 343.

66. Wilson and Herrnstein 1985.

67. Hennigan et al. 1982.

68. Hennigan et al. 1982, p. 461.

69. Hennigan et al. 1982, p. 474.

70. Hennigan et al. 1982, p. 475; see also Berkowitz and Macaulay 1971; Jarowitz (1979) credits TV with fostering race riots and especially looting.

71. Dominick 1978. See also Haskins 1969; Payne 1974; Payne and Payne 1970.

72. See Donnerstein, Linz, and Penrod 1987; Malamuth and Donnerstein 1984; U.S. Department Of Justice 1986; U.S. Surgeon General 1987 for reviews.

73. See Donnerstein 1980; English 1980; Eysenck and Nias 1978; Fisher and Grenier 1994; Gray 1982; Linz 1989; Malamuth and Donnerstein 1984; Malamuth, Haber and Feshback 1980a.

74. Goldstein 1973; Goldstein et al. 1972.

75. Kutchinsky 1972.

76. See, for example, Greek and Thompson (1992) for a discussion of religious group reactions to these reports.

77. *Sourcebook of Criminal Justice Statistics—1994.* Table 2.113. Attitudes toward pornographic material leading to rape. See also Greek and Thompson 1992.

78. Court 1976, p. 153.

79. See Cline 1974; Dienstbier 1977; Russell 1988; Wills 1977.

80. Donnerstein 1980; Donnerstein and Berkowitz 1981; Greek and Thompson 1992; Sommers and Check 1987; Russell 1988.

81. Donnerstein and Linz 1986; Malamuth and Donnerstein 1984.

82. Check and Guloien 1989; Demare, Briere, and Lips 1988.

83. Donnerstein and Berkowitz 1981.

84. In one content review conducted in the 1970s, the "rape myth" was found to be a plot feature in one-third of adult books (see Smith 1976). Typically, in these books, a woman would be forced to participate in an initially unwanted sexual act that begins with the woman protesting, but ends with the woman pleading for more sex, her passion apparently unleashed by force (Donnerstein and Berkowitz 1985; Intons-Peterson et al. 1989; Malamuth and Check 1981; Malamuth, Haber, and Feshbach 1980.)

85. Donnerstein and Linz 1984, 1986; Garcia, 1986; Malamuth and Check 1981.

86. Baron and Straus 1989; Donnerstein and Linz 1986b; Donnerstein, Linz, and Pound 1987; Gray 1982; Imrich, Mullin, and Linz 1990; Malamuth and Donnerstein 1984; Padgett, Brislin-Strutz, and Neal 1989; compare with Fisher and Grenier 1994; Demare et al. 1993.

87. Comstock 1983, p. 254.

88. See Baron and Straus 1984, 1985, 1986; however, compare with Gentry 1991 and Baron 1990.

89. Gentry 1991.

90. Imrich, Mullin, and Linz 1990, p. 116.

91. Donnerstein and Berkowitz 1981; Malamuth and Ceniti 1986.

92. Malamuth and Donnerstein 1984, p. 4; see also Condron and Nutter 1988; Fisher and Grenier 1994.

93. Bowen 1987; Kutchinsky 1972, 1985, 1991.

94. See Donnerstein and Linz 1986a; Imrich, Mullin, and Linz 1990; Malamuth, Haber, and Feshbach 1980; Nemes 1992.

95. See Bowen 1987; Donnerstein 1984; Donnerstein and Linz 1986a; Gray 1982; Imrich, Mullin, and Linz 1990.

96. See Brannigan 1987; Brannigan and Goldenberg 1987; Brannigan and Kapardis 1986; Fisher and Grenier 1994; Fisher and Barak 1991; Mould 1988.

97. Compare with Bowen 1987; Russell 1988; Sommers and Check 1987; Weis and Borges 1973.

98. Fisher and Grenier 1994; Hawkins and Zimring 1988.

99. Donnerstein and Linz 1986a and 1986b, p. 606, citing Donnerstein and Berkowitz 1985 and Malamuth and Check 1983.

100. See Demare et al. 1993; Donnerstein and Linz 1986a, p. 607; see also Imrich, Mullin, and Linz 1990; Linz et al. 1984, 1988.

101. See Donnerstein and Linz 1986a, p. 611; Imrich, Mullin, and Linz 1990, p. 120; Intons-Peterson et al. 1989; Malamuth and Check 1983. There is some evidence that the production of violent pornography increased during the 1970s (Malamuth and Spinner 1980; Smith 1976) and abated in the 1980s (Scott 1985; Scott and Cuvelier 1987; Palys 1986). The research that tries to quantify whether the levels are high or low directly conflict (see Fisher and Grenier 1994 for a discussion).

102. The Internet has raised new concerns over access to pornography but its effects have just begun to be examined. See Mehta and Plaza 1994.

103. Paladin's catalog, for example, lists the following basic crime instruction manuals: *Gunrunning for Fun and Profit; Expedient Hand Grenades; Improvised Explosives: How to Make Your Own; New I.D. in America; The Complete Book of International Terrorism; How to Kill* (6 volumes); *The Perfect Crime and How to Commit It;* and *Hitman,* a manual that resulted in an unsuccessful civil suit against the publisher. See Kirtley 1996c.

104. Bleyer 1927 p. 157, quoting the *New York Evening Post,* June 6, 1828.

105. Papke 1987, pp. 171–172.

106. Motion Picture Producers and Distributors of America cited by Cole 1996.

107. Kirtley 1996c, p. 51. In a 1989 case, the producer of a violent movie and the theater that showed it were held not liable for the death of a youth in a gang fight after the assailant saw the film *Warriors* twice. The Massachusetts Supreme Court held that the film did not incite the attacker, rejecting a claim that the assailant was imitating a scene from the film during the attack and that the theater displayed negligence in showing the film after learning of violent incidents at other theaters. "Although the film is rife with violent scenes, it does not at any point exhort, urge, entreat, solicit, or overtly advocate or encourage unlawful or violent activity on the part of viewers," the court said.

Yakubowicz v. *Paramount Pictures*; see also Violent Movie Didn't Cause Youth's Death 1989. More recently, the publishers of a manual containing instructions on how to commit murder were sued by the families of murder victims who were killed by a man following the directions laid out in the text. Their claims against the publisher were denied. See *Rice* v. *Paladin Enterprises, Inc. No. AW 95–3811, 24 Med.L.Rptr 2185 (D. Md 1996)*. The court ruled that the publisher must have intended for the reader to commit murder immediately after reading the book. Because the killings did not happen for more than a year afterward, they could not be characterized as a command to immediately murder the three victims. See also "Hit Man Manual" Protected by First Amendment (1996) for discussion.

108. Cited by Kirtley 1996c, p. 51.

109. Snow 1984, p. 217.

110. Hans and Slater 1983; Snow 1984.

111. Snow 1984.

112. Snow 1984, p. 226; Cramer 1994.

113. See Berkowitz et al. 1978; Eysenck and Nias 1978; Siegel 1974; Toplin 1975.

114. Cook, Kendzierski, and Thomas 1983.

115. See Bollen and Phillips 1982; Gould and Shaffer 1986; Phillips 1974, 1977, 1978, 1979, 1980, 1982a, 1982b; Phillips and Carstensen 1986, 1988; Phillips and Paight 1987; Stack 1987a.

116. See Gould and Shaffer 1986; Ostroff and Boyd 1987; Ostroff et al. 1985; Phillips 1982b; Phillips and Paight 1987; Schmidtke and Hafner 1988.

117. Goethe 1774.

118. Phillips 1974; Phillips and Carstensen 1986.

119. Gould and Shaffer 1986.

120. Lesyna and Phillips 1989.

121. See Bollen and Phillips 1982; Phillips and Bollen 1985; Phillips and Carstensen 1986.

122. See Baron and Reiss 1985; Berman 1988; Kessler and Stipp 1984; Kessler et al. 1988; Platt 1987; Williams et al. 1987.

123. Phillips 1983. Phillips and Hensley (1984) subsequently reported evidence that homicide appears to increase when violence is rewarded in the media (for example, in prize fights) and decreases or is deterred when it is punished through stories of successful murder trials and executions. However, in a study that examined monthly homicide rates and television publicity, Bailey (1990) reported that homicide rates are not related to either the amount or type of execution publicity. Television news coverage, at least, was not found to deter future murders or, through a brutalization effect on society, to promote future killings.

124. See Comstock 1983; Pease and Love 1984b; Schmid and de Graaf 1982; Wilson and Herrnstein 1985.

125. Comstock 1983, p. 252.

126. Pease and Love 1984b; Surette 1990b.

127. Comstock 1980, p. 131.

128. Milgram and Shotland 1973. See also Turner and Fern 1978 cited by Cole 1996.

129. See also Comstock 1980; Dominick 1978; Greene and Bynum 1982; Huesmann 1982, p.132; Lewis 1984; National Commission on the Causes and Prevention of Violence, vol. 9 1969, pp. 376–378.

130. See Comstock 1980, p. 138; Pease and Love 1984b; Surette 1990b; Heller and Polsky 1976.

131. Heller and Polsky 1976, pp. 151–152.

132. Hendrick 1977.

133. Pease and Love 1984a.

134. Compare with Schmid and de Graaf 1982.

135. Cressey 1938.

136. Cressey 1938 p. 517, cited by Thrasher 1949, p 199.

137. Tarde 1912.

138. Bassiouni 1981; Livingstone 1982; Schmid and de Graaf 1982.

139. Pease and Love 1984b.

140. Berkowitz 1984, p. 414.

141. Hennigan et al. 1982.

142. Heller and Polsky 1976; Hendrick 1977.

143. Berkowitz 1984. See also Bandura, 1994.

144. Berkowitz 1984, p. 414; Jo and Berkowitz 1994.

145. Jo and Berkowitz 1994, p. 45.

146. Jo and Berkowitz 1994, p. 46.

147. Rogers and Dearing 1988, p. 568; see also Fiske and Taylor 1984, p. 231; Iyengar and Kinder 1987.

148. Mazur 1982.

149. See also Comstock 1980, p. 131.

150. See Bandura 1994 for a general discussion of the media's social construction role in influencing human behavior through observational learning.

151. Bandura, 1994, p. 62; Meyrowitz 1985a.

152. Report of the U.S. Task Force on Disorders and Terrorism, 1976, p. 9.

153. Hickey 1976, p. 10.

154. Weimann and Winn 1994, p. 47. See also Mahan and Lawrence 1996.

155. Weimann and Winn 1994, p. 91.

156. Weimann and Winn 1994, p. 57.

157. Weimann and Winn 1994, p. 31.

158. Schmid and de Graaf 1982, p. 51.

159. Crenshaw 1981; Poland 1988, p. 45.

160. *Minimanual of the Urban Guerrilla* (n.d., cited by Alexander 1979, p. 161)

161. Alter 1985.

162. Jenkins 1975, p. 4; Iyengar 1991; Schmid and de Graaf 1982, p. 69; Weimann 1991.

163. Nimmo and Combs 1990, pp. 46–48; Weimann 1991.

164. Livingstone 1982, p. 62.

165. Termed a contagion effect in the literature on terrorism. Bassiouni 1981, p. 18; Johnson 1978; Schmid and de Graaf 1982, pp. 117–119.

166. Poland 1988, p. 47.

167. Bassiouni 1981, p. 18; Schmid and de Graaf 1982.

168. Poland 1988.

169. Iyengar 1991; Schmid and DeGraaf 1982; Weimann 1983; Weimann and Winn 1994.

170. Bassiouni 1981, p. 25.

171. Mazur 1982, p. 407.

172. Livingstone 1982, p. 71; see also Schmid and de Graaf 1982, pp. 128–136.

173. Bassiouni 1979, p 19.

174. Schmid and DeGraaf 1982. The same potential for interference in prison riot and hostage situations has been documented by Mahan and Lawrence 1996.

175. Grabosky and Wilson 1989.

176. Mayer 1987.

177. Grabosky and Wilson 1989.

178. Quoted by Church 1982, p. 27.

179. Grabosky and Wilson 1989.

180. Wilson and Herrnstein 1985, p. 339.

181. Boorstin 1961.

CHAPTER 6

1. The principle has also been extended to the Internet. In May 1996, the FBI for the first time captured one of its most-wanted fugitives due to the listing of a picture on the Internet. See Fugitive Is 1st of Most Wanted Caught in Computer Dragnet 1996 and Florida Law Officers Seek Tips from Surfers—Online 1996.

2. McLynn 1989, p. 34; see also Black 1987.

3. Braithwaite 1989; Braithwaite and Mugford 1994 (cited by Bennett et al., forthcoming). Unfortunately, the media are also described as more frequently engaged in disintegrative shaming, which does not reduce but instead encourages recidivism.

4. See Himmelwitt 1980; Kaplan and Baxter 1982; Murray and Clarke 1980; Rushton 1976a, 1976b.

5. See Hovland et al. 1949; Hyman and Sheatsley 1947; Janis and Feshbach 1953; Klapper 1960; Star and Hughes 1950.

6. See Douglas, Westley, and Chaffee 1970; Flay 1986; Mendelsohn 1973; Robinson 1972; Rogers 1973; Rosenstock 1960.

7. See, for example, Salcedo et al. 1974.

8. Rushton 1982b, p. 255.

9. See Collins 1973, 1975; Cosgrove and McIntyre 1974; Fox et al. 1977; Friedrich and Stein 1975; Stein and Friedrich 1972; Stein et al. 1973.

10. See Ball and Bogatz 1970; Coates et al. 1976; Lesser 1974; Palmer 1973.

11. Ball and Bogatz 1970; CBS 1974; Coates et al. 1976; Lesser 1974; Noble 1983; Palmer 1973; Roberts et al. 1974; Rubinstein et al. 1974; Rushton 1982a; Sprafkin et al. 1975; Teuchman and Orme 1981.

12. Rushton 1982a, vol. 1, p. 51.

13. Heller and Polsky 1976, p. 290.

14. Cook, Kendzierski, and Thomas 1983, p. 167.

15. National Institute of Mental Health 1982, vol. 1, p. 90.

16. Another question is whether or not prosocial media efforts are commercially viable. Probably not. *Sesame Street, Mister Rogers' Neighborhood,* and *The Electric Company* have not been copied by any commercial networks and many of the commercial prosocial programs developed in the seventies have been dropped.

17. See Lindesmith 1965.

18. Schemling and Wotring 1976, 1980.

19. Hanneman and McEwen 1973, p. 329.

20. Pierce and Bowers 1979.

21. Pierce and Bowers 1979, p. 92.

22. Ross et al. 1970.

23. Campbell and Ross 1968. See also Nienstedt 1990 and West et al. 1989 for recent studies that provide empirical evidence of announcement effects.

24. Bailey and Peterson 1989, 1990; Bailey 1990.

25. Bailey and Peterson 1989, 1990; Bailey 1990.

26. Black 1988; O'Keefe et al. 1996.

27. O'Keefe et al. 1996.

28. See Black 1988.

29. See American Association of Advertising Agencies 1990.

30. Biocca et al. 1997.

31. Biocca et al. 1997, p. 415.

32. Biocca et al. 1997, p. 415.

33. Rogers and Storey 1987. See also Weinstein 1987.

34. O'Keefe and Reid 1996 and 1990, citing Bureau of Justice Statistics 1986; Greenberg 1987; O'Keefe and Reid-Nash 1987b; Sacco and Silverman 1981; Skogan and Maxfield 1981.

35. O'Keefe and Reid 1990, O'Keefe et al. 1996. The second describes a *Let's Not Give Crime a Chance* campaign in Canada. The Canadian program consisted of a two-stage media campaign in the province of Alberta in 1978. An analysis of pre- and postcampaign surveys showed that, as in the U.S. campaign, many people recognized the campaign messages. But in contrast to the McGruff program, the Canadian project reported little impact on respondents' attitudes toward crime prevention and, incredibly, found a slight decrease in crime preventive behaviors after the campaign. The evaluators concluded that though a large number of Albertans were exposed to the campaign, a considerably smaller number saw the campaign themes and messages as salient, and only a negligible number altered their behavior in response—apparently in the wrong direction. See Sacco and Silverman 1981, p. 198. Other previous programs include a 1978 anti–auto theft program in Spokane, Washington, which used television to teach theft prevention techniques to the public. Another program, associated with a Minnesota Crime Watch effort, was aimed at general crime prevention and a limited evaluation reported some success (see White et al. 1975).

36. See O'Keefe et al. 1996 for a review.

37. O'Keefe et al. 1996; O'Keefe and Mendelsohn 1984. The first evaluation consisted of a one-time national survey of 1,200 adults conducted in 1981 and a pre- and postcampaign survey of three U.S. cities—Buffalo, Denver, and Milwaukee. The second is based on a national survey of 1,500 adults conducted in 1992.

38. O'Keefe et al. 1996, p. 105.

39. O'Keefe et al. 1996, p. 105. Up from only 8 percent in 1981 (Tyler 1984).

40. See O'Keefe 1985b; O'Keefe and Reid 1990; Riley and Mayhew 1980; Tyler and Cook 1984; Tyler and Lavrakas 1985.

41. O'Keefe et al. 1996, p. 121.

42. O'Keefe et al. 1996.

43. Janis and Feshbach 1953.

44. Boster and Mangeau 1984. See Dillard et al. 1996 and Higbee 1969, for a review of the research from 1953 to 1968.

45. Higbee 1969, p. 440; Ray and Wilkie 1970.

46. Burnett and Oliver 1979; Kohn et al. 1982; see also Berkowitz and Cummingham 1966.

47. Wheatley 1971.

48. See Black 1988; O'Keefe et al. 1996—the McGruff campaign has not been associated with measurable increases in fear of crime, for example.

49. Biocca et al. 1997; Devine and Hirt 1989; McGuire 1989; Roberts and Grossman 1990.

50. Black 1988; O'Keefe et al. 1996.

51. Sacco and Silverman 1982, p. 258, citing Klapper 1960.

52. See O'Keefe et al. 1996; Sacco and Silverman 1982.

53. Pfau and Parrott 1993; Schultz and Barnes 1995.

54. Flora et al. 1989; O'Keefe et al. 1996; Rogers and Storey 1987.

55. Rosenbaum 1988; Bursik and Grasmick 1993.

56. O'Keefe et al. 1996.

57. O'Keefe et al. 1996; McGruff Campaign Team, n.d.

58. Also known as crime alert, crime solvers, silent witness, or crime line. See Lavrakas et al. 1990; Rosenbaum et al. 1989; and O'Keefe and Reid 1990.

59. Rosenbaum et al. 1986, p. 110.

60. Schlesinger et al. 1991, p. 408.

61. Rosenbaum et al. 1986, p. 34, 1989, p. 417.

62. Nelson 1989.

63. Rosenbaum and Lurigio 1985; Rosenbaum et al. 1986, p. 36.

64. Author's interview with the chair of the Crime Stoppers, Media Relations Committee, Dade County, Fla., February 5, 1983.

65. Case Reviews Support Crime Stoppers 1986, p. 7; *United States* v. *Debango* (780 F.2d 81 {D.C. Cir. 1986]); and *United States* v. *Zamora* (784 F. 2d 1025 [10th Cir. 1986]); and *United States* v. *Briley* (726 F. 2d 1301 [8th Cir. 1984]).

66. Rosenbaum et al. 1986, p. 34; 1989.

67. Rosenbaum and Lurigio 1985, p. 61; Program advocates argue that the programs are targeted at people unlikely to cooperate or become involved without a monetary incentive. There is also fear that reenacts of crimes will encourage false testimony and prejudice witnesses' testimony and trial juries.

68. See Marx 1985; Paulin 1988; Rosenbaum and Lurigio 1985, pp. 60–61; Rosenbaum et al. 1989; Surette 1986.

69. Marx 1985, p. 21.

70. Pfuhl 1992, p. 512.

71. Pfuhl 1992, p. 513.

72. An assessment of one program, based on a review of its "crime of the week" and "most wanted" cases for the first two years of operation, revealed that in terms of the types of crime portrayed, violent crime dominated. Nonviolent crimes were rarely portrayed, and homicide was the single most popular crime shown. On the whole, the program portrayed criminality as an attribute of a young, violent, dangerous class of criminals composed mostly of minorities. Crime was portrayed as largely stranger-to-stranger, injurious or fatal encounters in which handguns played a dominant role. See Surette 1986.

73. Pfuhl 1992, p. 519.

74. Bortner 1984; Rosenbaum and Lurigio 1985, p. 61.

75. Bortner 1984.

76. See Culver and Knight 1979; Dominick 1978; Estep and MacDonald 1984.

77. Rosenbaum and Lurigio 1985.

78. Lavrakas et al. 1990; Rosenbaum et al. 1986, p. 109.

79. Lavrakas et al. 1990.

80. Lavrakas et al. 1990.

81. Pfuhl 1992, p. 519, n. 14.

82. Newman 1972, 1975, 1976; see also Jacobs 1961.

83. Milander and Power 1995.

84. Bartlett 1992.

85. Marx 1985, p. 23; Surette 1985a.

86. Surette 1985a, p. 79. See also Salamone 1997.

87. Mayhew et al. 1979.

88. Marx 1985, p. 21.

89. Surette 1985a.

90. Surette 1988.

91. Reppetto 1974.

92. Mayhew et al. 1979.

93. Mayhew et al. 1979, pp. 25–26, 28.

94. See Surette 1985a, 1988.

95. Surette 1985a, p. 83.

96. Long 1995; Sander 1993.

97. Valentine 1997.

98. Sander 1993; Surette 1985a; Valentine 1997.

99. Sechrest et al. 1990, citing Rubinstein 1973, p. 20.

100. See *New York* v. *Class,* U.S. 106 S. Ct., 960 [1986]. In a 1990 decision, *Penn.* v. *Munk* (110 S.Ct. 2714 [1990]), the Supreme Court concluded that the *Miranda* ruling allows the courtroom use of videotaped responses to routine booking questions asked before the Miranda warning has been given.

101. Sechrest et al. 1990.

102. Sechrest et al. 1990.

103. Grant 1987 1990.

104. Grant (1987) did not measure the opinions of those actually interviewed, so their perceptions are unknown.

105. Mayhew and his colleagues 1979, p. 12.

106. See *Broddie* v. *ABC,* 881 F.2d 1318 [11th Cir. 1989].

107. It has also been argued that mass media attention on political elites allows for the surveillance of the powerful by the public and could therefore have positive democratizing effects. It does not because of the limits on the influence on agenda-setting by the public (see Mathiesen 1987; Seaman 1992).

108. Surette 1988 1990a.

109. Surette 1988.

110. See *State* v. *Hauptmann,* 115 N. J. L. 412 [1935]; *Estes* v. *Texas,* 381 U.S. 532 [1965]; Chapter 7.

111. See Benowitz 1974, pp. 86–88; Brakel 1974, p. 956; Burt 1978, p. 66; Greenwood et al. 1978, p. 27; Kosky 1975, p. 231; Lieberman 1976, p. 89; Monteleone 1982; Murray 1978; Salvan 1975, p. 225.

112. Benowitz 1974, p. 86.

113. Joseph 1982.

114. Coleman 1977, p. 2; see also Joseph 1986.

115. Dombroff 1981.

116. Doret 1974.

117. Joseph 1986, p. 61.

118. Cited by Greenwood et al. 1978, p. 27.

119. See Benowitz 1974, pp. 86–88; Brakel 1975, p. 956; Burt 1978, p. 66; Greenwood et al. 1978, p. 27; Kosky 1975, p. 231; Lieberman 1976, p. 89; Monteleone 1982; Murray 1978; Salvan 1975, p. 225.

120. Murray 1978.

121. Coleman 1977.

122. Salvan 1975.

123. Rypinski 1982.

124. Rypinski 1982, p. 72.

125. Doret 1974; Shutkin 1973.

126. Benowitz 1974, p. 90.

127. Brakel 1975, p. 957.

128. Doret 1974, p. 244.

129. Doret 1974, p. 252.

130. See Boster et al. 1978; Hocking et al. 1978; Kaminski et al. 1978; Miller 1976; Miller and Fontes 1979a, 1979b; Miller and Siebert 1974, 1975.

131. Miller and Fontes 1979b, p. 207. Miller and Fontes (1979a, p. 100) also found that jurors retain more information from black-and-white videos, but that color videotape enhances the credibility of a

witness, raising an unresolved dilemma: Should the courts select a system that seems to enhance witness image (color) or one that enhances jurors' retention of information (black-and-white)? In practice, the tendency has been to go with color, because it is felt to be more realistic and, despite the contrary evidence, better able to sustain jurors' attention.

132. Miller and Fontes 1979a, p. 100.

133. See also Miller and Siebert 1974, 1975; contrast with Junke et al. 1979.

134. Brakel 1975.

135. See Hartman 1978.

136. See *Craig* v. *Maryland,* U.S. 836 (1990); Cullen 1993; Shutkin 1973, pp. 391, 497.

137. Levine 1992.

138. See Brakel 1975; Doret 1974; Farmer et al. 1976; Kosky 1975; Shutkin 1973.

139. Burt 1978; Kosky 1975; Weiss 1982, p. 64. Benowitz (1974, p. 86) has noted that court reporters are not unequivocally opposed to the use of videotape equipment in the courtroom: "Under the leadership of the National Shorthand Reporter's Association, they have examined objectively the possible applications of this new tool, have been pioneers in the use of videotape where applicable and desirable, and have arrived at the conclusion that in certain areas of litigation, a marriage between court reporters and VTR will better serve the judicial process."

140. Brakel 1975, p. 957; Burt 1978; Coleman 1977; Greenwood et al. 1978, p. 27; Kosky 1975, pp. 231, 232–235.

141. Coleman 1977, citing Madden 1969.

142. Kosky 1975.

143. Coleman 1977, pp. 13–14.

144. Hewitt 1990, 1992.

145. See McCrystal 1978, p. 251.

146. Coleman 1977.

147. Shutkin 1973, pp. 363–364.

148. Kosky 1975. See also McCrystal 1976, 1978, pp. 253–254; Miller and Fontes 1979a, p. 92; Murray 1978, pp. 260–261; Coleman 1977, citing Bermant et al. 1975; "How Jurors Feel about Videotaped Trials," 1980; Shutkin 1973.

149. See also Brakel 1975; Doret 1974; Shutkin 1973.

150. Brakel 1975, pp. 957, 958; see also Shutkin 1973, p. 391.

151. Doret 1974, p. 256; Kosky 1975.

152. See O'Neill 1990; Surette 1988.

153. Doret 1974.

154. Surette and Terry 1984. The first live video-facilitated proceeding was most likely a bail bond hearing in Cook County (Illinois) Circuit Court in 1972. In 1975 an appellate case was argued via picture-phone service between Washington, D.C., and New York (Weis 1977). See also Philadelphia's Popular Police Station 1979, p. 1; New York City 1983, p. 21; Rockwell 1983.

155. The Chicago Seven were anti–Vietnam War protesters charged with conspiracy to incite a riot at the 1968 Democratic National Convention.

156. *Illinois* v. *Allen*, 90 S. Ct. 1057 [1970].

157. *Craig* v. *Maryland*, 89 U.S. 478 [1990] [Md. Ct. App. 1989].

158. See Surette and Terry 1984.

159. The realignment of communication channels and changes in behavior and attitudes seldom occur simultaneously (Lipetz 1980).

160. Benowitz 1974; Brakel 1975; Burt 1978; Hartman 1978; Kosky 1975.

161. Hartman 1978, pp. 256–257; see also Doret 1974, p. 245; Monteleone 1982, p. 863.

162. Compare with Casper 1978.

163. Dinitz 1987.

164. Compare with Jeffery 1990.

CHAPTER 7

1. Zucker 1978, p. 239.

2. Wisehart (1922) provides a good historical discussion of the concern with the media's effects in the administration of justice. See also Stroman and Seltzer 1985, p. 34.

3. Canadian Sentencing Commission 1987; Dominick 1978, p. 106; Greenberg 1969.

4. Canadian Sentencing Commission 1987; Graber 1979; Tunnell 1992.

5. Compare with Barber 1987; Lewis 1984; Stroman and Seltzer 1985, p. 340.

6. O'Keefe and Reid 1990, citing Rogers and Storey 1987, p. 539.

7. Paisley 1981.

8. Atkin 1979, p. 655; Lazarsfeld et al. 1948; Merton 1946.

9. See Katz and Lazarsfeld 1955.

10. Hyman and Sheatsley 1947.

11. Hyman and Sheatsley 1947, p. 413.

12. See Hyman and Sheatsley 1947; Janis and Feshbach 1953; Klapper 1960; Star and Hughes 1950.

13. Atkin 1979, p. 656; Salcedo et al. 1974, p. 91.

14. Mendelsohn 1973, p. 50.

15. Mendelsohn 1973; Robinson 1972; Rogers 1973; Zucker 1978. See also Pfau and Parrott 1993; Schultz and Barnes 1995.

16. See McLuhan 1962, 1964; Meyrowitz 1985a.

17. See Herrnstein and Murray 1995.

18. Atkin 1979, p. 655. See also Pfau and Parrott 1993; Schultz and Barnes 1995.

19. O'Keefe 1971, p. 243.

20. O'Keefe and Reid 1990, p. 215; Rogers and Storey 1987.

21. O'Keefe et al. 1996, p. 18; Page et al. 1987; Schultz and Barnes 1995.

22. See Katz and Lazarsfeld 1955; Robinson 1976.

23. Zucker 1978, p. 226.

24. O'Keefe et al. 1996, p. 18; Tyler 1984.

25. Entman 1989; MacKuen, 1984.

26. See Lasorsa and Wanta 1990; see also McLeod et al. 1974; Protess et al. 1985, p. 30, 1991.

27. Doppelt and Manikas 1990, p. 132.

28. Doppelt and Manikas 1990, p. 134; see also Erbing et al. 1980; Rogers and Dearing 1988.

29. Molotch et al. 1987; see also Protess et al. 1991; Pritchard 1992; Salwin 1986.

30. See Shaw and McCombs 1977.

31. Page et al. 1987, citing Katz and Lazarsfeld 1955. See also Cook, Kendzierski, and Thomas 1983; Cook, Tyler, et al. 1983; Faunkhouser 1973; Iyengar et al. 1982; Leff et al. 1986; MacKuen 1981, 1984; McCombs and Shaw 1972; Pritchard 1992; and Protess et al. 1991.

32. Lasorsa and Wanta 1990.

33. Murray 1980, pp. 48–49; see also Fishman 1978; Hall et al. 1981.

34. See McCombs and Weaver 1973; Rogers and Dearing 1988; Weaver 1980; Yagoda and Dozier 1990.

35. See Cook, Tyler, et al. 1983; Graber 1980, 1989; Protess et al. 1985; Swanson 1988.

36. See Cook, Tyler, et al. 1983; Leff et al. 1986; Protess et al. 1987, 1991.

37. Lang and Lang 1983; Protess et al. 1991.

38. Doppelt and Manikas 1990; Graber 1989; Lang and Lang 1983; Protess et al. 1991.

39. Doppelt and Manikas 1990, p. 133, citing Noelle-Neumann 1983; Roberts and Bachen 1981.

40. Doppelt and Manikas 1990, p. 134, citing Graber 1989; Gordon and Riger 1989; Pritchard 1986.

41. Gordon and Heath 1981, pp. 228–229. Wisehart (1922) reported a strong media effect on public opinion regarding justice and the setting of the crime-and-justice agenda.

42. Cohen and Young 1981.

43. Stinchcombe et al. 1980.

44. Gordon and Riger 1989; Reiner 1985.

45. Doppelt and Manikas 1990; see also Hughes 1987.

46. See Gerbner and Gross 1976, 1980; Gerbner et al. 1978, 1979, 1980, 1994.

47. Carlson 1985, p. 7.

48. Gerbner and Gross 1976, p. 179.

49. See, for example, Hirsch 1980, 1981.

50. Gerbner et al. 1980.

51. Gerbner and Gross 1976, p. 176.

52. Gerbner and Gross 1980, p. 156.

53. See Cook, Tyler, et al. 1983; Hirsch 1980, 1981; Hughes 1980; Sacco 1982.

54. Carlson 1985, pp. 135, 191; Coleman 1993; Gomme 1986; Heath and Petraitis 1987; Wober 1978.

55. See Bandura 1968; Drabman and Thomas 1974; Gordon and Heath 1981; Hans and Dee 1991;

Huesmann 1982, p. 132; Jarhnig et al. 1981; Molita and Hirsch 1994; O'Keefe 1984; O'Keefe and Reid-Nash 1987a; Roberts and Doob 1990; Sheley and Ashkins 1981; Stalans and Diamond 1990; Treevan and Hartnagel 1976. For reviews, see also National Institute of Mental Health, 1982, pp. 38–39; O'Keefe and Reid 1990.

56. Compare with Lichter 1988, p. 38.

57. Doob and MacDonald; see Sacco 1982; see also Skogan and Maxfield 1981.

58. Heath and Gilbert 1996. See also Garofalo 1981a; Schlesinger et al. 1991; Skogan 1984; and Wilson et al. 1997 for reviews.

59. Williams and Dickerson 1993, p. 34; see also Skogna and Maxfield (1981), who discuss vulnerability to attack; Hirsch (1980), who found none of the expected cultivation effects postulated by Gerbner in groups highly victimized in 1970s television drama (women, older women and blacks); and Heath and Petraitis (1987), who found associations only for males.

60. Warr 1991.

61. There are two separate literatures on fear of crime, one of which hardly mentions the media and the other scarcely mentions anything else (Schlesinger et al. 1991, p. 416).

62. See for example Wilson et al. 1997, p. 18. In their content study of television, Wilson and her colleagues (p. 145) found that nearly 75 percent of television violence scenes do not show the perpetrator being punished. They note that research indicates that violence shown as unpunished is significantly more likely to generate fear among viewers. They further note that the majority of televised violent acts are unjustified (undeserved or targeted against innocents) and also involve repeated acts of violence, both factors related to increased fear in viewers.

63. Chiricos et al. 1996, p. 7.

64. Heath and Gilbert 1996.

65. Wilson et al. 1997.

66. Potter 1986.

67. Bryant et al. 1981; Gunter 1987; Tamborini et al. 1984, Wakshlag 1983; Zillman and Wakshlag 1985.

68. Bryant, Carveth, and Brown 1981 cited by Wilson et al. 1997.

69. Gomme 1986, and Skogan and Maxfield 1981, found no relationship while Gebotys et al. 1988; Gordon and Heath 1981; Heath 1984; Liska and Baccaglini 1990; Smith 1984; and Williams and Dickinson 1993 did find one. See Heath and Gilbert 1996 for a general discussion.

70. Gordon and Heath 1981.

71. Heath 1984.

72. Heath 1984; Liska and Baccaglini 1990; Williams and Dickinson 1993.

73. Heath 1984.

74. Schlesinger et al. 1991, p. 415; see also Williams and Dickinson 1993.

75. Heath 1984, p. 274.

76. Heath 1984, pp. 264–265; Liska and Baccaglini 1990; for a discussion of this process in the nineteenth-century frontier, see Einstadter 1979.

77. Potter 1996.

78. Tamborini et al. 1984, Wakshlag et al. 1983; Zillman and Wakshlag 1985.

79. Heath and Gilbert 1996.

80. Perse et al. 1994.

81. Heath and Gilbert 1996, p. 384.

82. Sparks and Ogles 1990.

83. Heath and Petraitis 1987.

84. Zillman and Wakshlag 1985.

85. Chiricos et al. 1996.

86. Chiricos et al. 1996, pp. 17–19.

87. Gunter 1987, p. 61.

88. See, for example, Barrile 1984; Carlson 1985; Marks 1987; Sparks and Ogles 1990; Surette 1985b; and Tyler 1980; compare with Bennack 1983; Robinson 1976.

89. Imrich, Mullin, and Linz 1990; see also discussion in Chapter 5; Demare et al. 1988, 1993; Linz 1989; Nemes 1992; compare with Fisher and Grenier 1994.

90. Demare et al. 1993; Imrich, Mullin, and Linz 1990; Nemes 1992.

91. Imrich, Mullin, and Linz 1990. See also Fisher and Grenier 1994.

92. Malamuth, Haber, and Feshback 1980.

93. Weaver 1987. Other relevant research includes studies by Check and Guloien 1989; Demare et al. 1988, 1993; Donnerstein 1984; Intons-Peterson et al. 1989; Krafka 1985; Linz et al. 1988; Malamuth 1981, 1983, 1986; Malamuth and Ceniti 1986; Malamuth and Check 1980, 1981, 1983, 1985; Malamuth, Check, and Briere 1986; Malamuth and Donnerstein 1982, 1984; Malamuth, Haber, and Feshbach 1980; Malamuth, Heim, and Feshbach 1980; Malamuth and Spinner 1980; McKenzie-Mohr and Zanna 1990; Nutter 1988; Padgett and Brislin-Slutz 1989; Zillman and Bryant 1982.

94. Imrich, Mullin, and Linz 1990, p. 115.

95. Fisher and Grenier 1994; Demare et al. 1993; Nemes 1992.

96. Demare et al. 1988, 1993; Imrich, Mullin, and Linz 1990.

97. Malamuth and Briere 1986, p. 89.

98. See Gray 1982.

99. Sommers and Check (1987) found that the presence and use of pornography to be higher among the partners of battered women and associated with greater use of sexual aggression.

100. Fisher and Grenier 1994; Imrich, Mullin, and Linz 1990.

101. Fisher and Grenier 1994.

102. Brannigan and Goldenberg, 1987; Demare et al. 1988; Fisher and Barak 1991; Fisher and Grenier 1994; Linz, Donnerstein, and Penrod 1988; Malamuth and Ceniti 1986; Malamuth, Haber, and Feshbach 1980.

103. In a study to explore this possibility among imprisoned males, Fisher (1989) explored the impact of the mass media on the sex role attitudes of men incarcerated in a maximum-security prison. He reported that increased radio and television exposure is

associated with more egalitarian attitudes about sex roles. Fisher suggested that providing televisions in cells could have a rehabilitative effect and aid in a prisoner's reentry into society. In a correlated study Baron (1990) found that states with higher circulations of soft-core pornographic magazines also tended to have more gender equity.

104. Garcia 1986, p. 384. See also Fisher and Grenier 1994; Linz 1989.

105. Roberts and Grossman 1990.

106. Petty and Priester 1994, p. 115.

107. Drew and Weaver 1990; Fisher and Grenier 1994; Petty and Priester 1994.

108. See Hawkins and Pingree 1981; O'Keefe 1984; Slater and Elliott 1982.

109. See Chapter 2 discussion.

110. Chiricos et al. 1996; O'Keefe and Reid 1990, p. 220.

111. Smith 1984; see also Warr 1980.

112. Schlesinger et al. 1991.

113. O'Keefe and Reid 1990, p. 220.

114. Schlesinger et al. 1991, p. 412.

115. For example, Anne Heinz (1985 citing Lang and Lang 1983) found after a study of ten U.S. cities that newspaper editors and publishers are central parts of municipal criminal justice policy processes. See Duffee 1980, Elias 1986, and Scheingold 1984 for general discussions.

116. Protess et al. 1991; Pritchard 1992.

117. Page et al. 1987.

118. Page et al. 1987, p. 31; other research by Hallin 1984; McClosky and Zaller 1984; and Noelle-Neumann 1974, 1980 suggests a similar relationship.

119. Pandiani 1978, p. 455.

120. Gerbner 1976; Culver and Knight 1979.

121. Culver and Knight 1979; Estep and MacDonald 1984.

122. Stark 1987, pp. 257–258, 267.

123. See Barrile 1984; Carlson 1985; Marks 1987; Roberts and Doob 1990; Roberts and Edwards 1989; Surette 1985b.

124. Carlson 1985, p. 189.

125. Carlson 1985, pp. 116, 118.

126. Doob and Roberts 1988; Roberts and Doob 1990; and Roberts and Edwards 1989.

127. Iyengar 1991, p. 29.

128. Bennett et al. forthcoming.

129. Sasson 1995, pp. 129–130. Sasson argues (p. 163) that a diversity of resources is important because it allows the integrating of personal and cultural knowledge and the combining of the impact of firsthand experience with confidence to generalize one's own experience to the experiences of others.

130. Doob and Roberts 1988, p. 132.

131. Doob and Roberts 1988, 1990.

132. Doppelt and Manikas 1990; Protess et al. 1985.

133. Protess et al. 1991; Schlesinger et al. 1991.

134. Molotch et al. 1987, p. 39.

135. Fishman 1978. See discussion in Chapter 2 also.

136. Hall et al. 1981; Both the Hall and Fishman studies are further described in Chapter 3.

137. Pritchard et al. 1987.

138. Pritchard et al. 1987, p. 396; other research by Cook and his colleagues (Cook, Tyler, et al. 1983) and Pritchard 1986 reported similar findings.

139. Doppelt and Manikas 1990; Jacob and Lineberry 1982.

140. Doppelt 1990. That is, criminal justice policy is ultimately determined both by ad hoc decisions made by criminal justice personnel and offenders regarding individual crimes and cases, and by systemwide decisions that affect entire classes of offenses and cases. See, for example, Blumberg 1967; Cole 1970; Feeley 1982; Goldstein 1980; Lipsky 1971; and Packer 1968. Systemwide decisions can be conceived of as policy formation decisions and incorporate the most common idea of policy, the laws, rules, and regulations of the system. Individual decisions regarding cases and crimes can be thought of as policy implementation decisions whose cumulative effects result in criminal justice policy in practice or how the laws, rules, and regulations are actually applied in the field.

141. Doppelt and Manikas 1990, p. 139.

142. Surette 1996.

143. Doppelt and Manikas 1990.

144. Schlesinger et al. 1991, p. 401.

145. Schlesinger et al. 1991, p. 403.

146. Drechsel 1983, p. 14.

147. Cook, Tyler, et al. 1983; Gilberg et al. 1980; Pritchard 1986; Pritchard et al. 1987.

148. See Ettema et al. 1989; Lang and Lang 1983; Molotch et al. 1987.

149. Nienstedt 1990; see also Campbell 1969; Campbell and Ross 1968; Mayhew et al. 1979; Ross et al. 1970.

150. See Altheide and Snow 1991; Dye 1985; and Lichter 1988 for discussions.

151. For a discussion see Surette 1991.

152. See Anderson et al. 1985, 1986; Bechtel et al. 1972 for discussions.

153. Surette 1995b.

154. For example, a group of all-stars will not always be a successful team, and not all the members of a highly innovative productive group will be themselves highly innovative and productive as individuals.

155. See Russell (1988) for a discussion regarding this issue applied to the question of pornography and sexual crime.

156. See Surette 1989, 1992a. See Chapter 3 also.

157. Lofton 1966, p. 138; Kaplan and Skolnick 1982, pp. 467–468.

158. Greene and Loftus 1984 and Greene and Wade 1988 both reported that exposure to publicity that questions the accuracy of eyewitnesses influences decisions in later nonpublicized cases. In their research the effect was a reduction in guilty pleas, or a lenient

echo effect on mock jurors. See also Loften 1966; Kaplan and Skolnick 1982; Radin 1964; Surette 1989.

159. Surette 1993.

160. Leukefeld 1991.

161. Neinstedt 1990.

162. See Campbell and Ross 1968; Nienstedt 1990, Surette 1985.

163. Cook, Tyler, et al. 1983, p. 174.

164. See Gordon and Heath 1981; Skogan and Maxfield 1981; Tyler 1984.

165. See Comstock 1980; Doob and MacDonald 1979; Sacco 1982; Surette 1984b.

166. See Furstenberg 1971; Garofalo and Laub 1978; Lotz 1979; Sacco 1982; Smith 1984; Wilson 1975.

167. Sacco 1982, p. 490.

168. See Cook, Tyler, et al. 1983; Graber 1980, pp. 119–122; Sacco 1982; Smith 1984.

169. Graber 1980.

170. Dominick 1978; Estep and MacDonald 1984.

171. Culver and Knight 1979, pp. 207–209; Garofalo 1981a.

172. Gorelick 1989, p. 429.

173. Cook, Kendzierski, and Thomas 1983, p. 174.

174. Scott and Hart 1979.

175. Mathiesen 1987.

176. Mathiesen 1987.

177. This media intrusiveness has cycled back onto the media with current media actively involved in analyzing themselves and exposing their own backstage processes. See, for example, the cable television program *Reliable Sources* on CNN.

178. Lichter 1988, p. 40.

179. Manning, forthcoming.

180. Cavender and Fishman, forthcoming.

181. Rushkoff 1994.

182. Meyrowitz 1985a, p. 319.

183. Comstock 1983.

184. Cantor and Harrison 1997, p. 409.

185. See Malamuth and Check 1983.

186. Donnerstein and Linz 1986, p. 611; Imrich, Mullin, and Linz 1990.

187. See Carlson 1985; Surette 1989, 1992b.

188. Barak 1995.

189. Cole (1995, 1996) provides a contrary example to this history.

190. Belson 1978.

191. Manning forthcoming; Rosenthal 1986.

192. Construction projects to increase the number of prison cells have cost between $3 and $3.5 billion a year for several years. The nation spends about $21 billion annually to run prisons and jails (Irwin and Austin 1994, p. 13).

193. Murray 1984.

194. Powers 1990, p. G8.

195. For a discussion of changes in the reality of criminal justice to accommodate perceptions of criminal justice see Kappler, Blumberg, and Potter 1996

References

Acorn, L. 1989. Crime in Prime Time: New Shows Capture Audiences. *Corrections Today* February, pp. 44, 46, 54.

Adoni, H., and Mane, S. 1984. Media and the Social Construction of Reality: Toward an Integration of Theory and Research. *Communication Research* 11:323–340.

Agree, W., Ault, P., and Emery, E. 1982. *Introduction to Mass Communications*. New York: Harper-Collins.

Akers, R. 1985. *Deviant Behavior: A Social Learning Approach*. Belmont, Calif.: Wadsworth.

Alexander, Y. 1979. Terrorism and the Media: Some Considerations. In *Terrorism: Theory and Practice*, edited by Y. Alexander, D. Carlton, and P. Wilkinson. Boulder, Colo.: Westview Press.

Alter, J. 1985. The Network Circus. *Newsweek*, July 8, p. 21.

Altheide, D. 1984. TV News and the Social Construction of Justice: Research Issues and Policy. In *Justice and the Media*, edited by R. Surette. Springfield, Ill.: Thomas, pp. 292–304.

Altheide, D., and Snow, R. 1979. *Media Logic*. Thousand Oaks, Calif.: Sage.

Altheide, D., and Snow, R. 1991. *Media Worlds in the Postjournalism Era*. Hawthorne, N.Y.: Aldine de Gruyter.

American Association of Advertising Agencies. 1990. *What We've Learned About Advertising from the Media-Advertising Partnership for a Drug-Free America*. Pamphlet. New York: Author.

American Bar Association. 1937. Canons of Judicial Ethics, No. 35. Reprinted in *ABA Reporter* 62:1123, 1134–1135.

American Bar Association. 1978. *Standards Relating to the Administration of Criminal Justice, Fair Trial and Free Press*. Chicago: Author.

Anderson, C., and Ford, C. 1987. Affect of the Game Player: Short-Term Effects of Highly and Mildly Aggressive Video Games. *Personality and Social Psychology Bulletin* 12:390–402.

Anderson, D., Lorch, E., Field, D., Collins, P., and Nathan, J. 1985. Estimates of Young Children's Time with Television: A Methodological Comparison of Parent Reports with Time-Lapse Video Home Observation. *Child Development* 56:1345–1357.

Anderson, D., Lorch, E., Field, D., Collins, P., and Nathan, J. 1986. Television Viewing at Home: Age Trends in Visual Attention and Time with TV. *Child Development* 57:1024–1033.

Andison, F. 1977. TV Violence and Viewer Aggression: A Review of Study Results, 1956–1976. *Public Opinion Quarterly* 41:314–331.

Antonovich, M., Prospter, R., Olson, K., and Krott, C. 1987. *Video Arraignment Pilot Project Glendale Municipal Court—Year End Report*. Glendale, Calif.: The Municipal Court Glendale Judicial District.

Antunes, G., and Hurley, P. 1977. The Representation of Criminal Events in Houston's Two Daily Newspapers. *Journalism Quarterly* 54:756–760.

Apfel, D. 1980. Gag Orders, Exclusionary Orders, and Protective Orders: Expanding the Use of Preventive Remedies to Safeguard a Criminal Defendant's Right to a Fair Trial. *American University Law Review* 29:439–484.

Armour, R. 1980. *Film*. Westport, Conn.: Greenwood Press.

Arons, S., and Katsh, E. 1977. How TV Cops Flout the Law. *Saturday Review* March 19, pp. 11–19.

Atkin, C. 1979. Research Evidence on Mass Mediated Health Communication Campaigns. In *Communication Yearbook*, Vol. 3, edited by D. Nimmo. New Brunswick, N.J.: Transaction Books, pp. 655–668.

Audio-Visual Coverage on Trial in States. 1988. *News Media and the Law* 12:48–50.

Avery, D. 1989. Corrections: The Hard Sell. *Corrections Today* 51:6.

Bacharach, R. 1985. Posttrial Juror Interviews by the Press: The Fifth Circuit's Approach. *Washington University Law Quarterly* 62:783–788.

Bailey, F., and Hale, D., eds. forthcoming. *Popular Culture, Crime, and Justice*. Belmont, Calif.: Wadsworth.

Bailey, F., Pollock, J., and Schroeder, S. forthcoming. The Best Defense: Images of Female Attorneys in Popular Films. In *Popular Culture, Crime, and Justice*, edited by F. Bailey and D. Hale. Belmont, Calif.: Wadsworth.

Bailey, W. 1990. Murder, Capital Punishment and Television: Execution Publicity and Homicide Rates. *American Sociological Review* 55:628–633.

Bailey, W., and Peterson, R. 1989. Murder and Capital Punishment: A Monthly Time-Series Analysis of Execution Policy. *American Sociological Review* 54:722.

Bailey, W., and Peterson, R. 1990. Capital Punishment and Non-Capital Crimes: A Test of Deterrence, General Prevention, and System-Overload Arguments. *Albany Law Review* 54: 681–707.

Bain, G. 1995. The Criminal Trial as a Sport Spectacle. *Maclean's* 108 (Feb. 20.): 55.

Baker, R., and Ball, S. 1969. *Mass Media and Violence: A Report to the National Commission on the Causes and Prevention of Violence*. Vol. ix. Washington, D.C.: U.S. Government Printing Office.

Baldwin, J., and Lewis, C. 1972. Violence in Television: The Industry Looks at Itself. In *Television and Social Behavior*. Vol. 1. *Media Content and Control. Report of the Surgeon General's Scientific Advisory Committee on Television and Behavior*, edited by G. Comstock and E. Rubinstein. Washington, D.C.: National Institute of Mental Health, pp. 290–373.

Ball, J., and Bogatz, G. 1970. *The First Year of "Sesame Street": An Evaluation*. Princeton, N.J.: Educational Testing Service.

Ball, M. 1981. *The Promise of American Law*. Athens: University of Georgia Press.

Ball-Rokeach, S. J., and DeFleur, M. 1976. A Dependency Model of Mass Media Effects. *Communication Research* 14(1).

Ball-Rokeach, S., Rokeach, M., and Grube, J. 1984. *The Great American Values Test: Influencing Behavior and Belief through Television*. New York: Free Press.

Ban on Naming Rape Victims Unconstitutional. 1992. *News Media and the Law* 10(1):19–20.

Bandura, A. 1965. Influence of Models' Reinforcement Contingencies on the Acquisition of Imitative Responses. *Journal of Personality and Social Psychology* 1:589–595.

Bandura, A. 1968. What TV Violence Can Do to Your Child. In *Violence and the Mass Media*, edited by O. M. Larson. New York: HarperCollins, pp. 123–130.

Bandura, A. 1969. *Principles of Behavior Modification*. Austin, Tex.: Holt, Rinehart & Winston.

Bandura, A. 1971. *Social Learning Theory*. Morristown, N.J.: General Learning Press.

Bandura, A. 1973. *Aggression: A Social Learning Analysis*. Englewood Cliffs, N.J.: Prentice Hall.

Bandura, A. 1977. *Social Learning Theory*. Englewood Cliffs, N.J.: Prentice Hall.

Bandura, A. 1994. Social Cognitive Theory of Mass Communication. In *Media Effects Advances in Theory and Research*, edited by J. Bryant and D. Zillman. Hillsdale, N.J.: Erlbaum.

Bandura, A., Ross D., and Ross, S. A. 1961. Transmission of Aggression through Imitation of Aggressive Models. *Journal of Abnormal and Social Psychology* 63:575–582.

Bandura, A., Ross, D., and Ross, S. A. 1963. Imitation of Film: Mediated Aggressive Models. *Journal of Abnormal and Social Psychology* 66:3–11.

Barak, G., ed. 1995. *Media, Process, and the Social Construction of Crime*. New York: Garland.

Barak, G., ed. 1997. *Representing O.J.: Murder, Criminal Justice, and Mass Culture*. Albany, N.Y.: Harrow and Heston.

Barber, S. 1987. *News Cameras in the Courtroom*. Norwood, N.J.: Ablex.

Barlow, M., Barlow, D., and Chiricos, T. 1995. Economic Conditions and Ideologies of Crime in the Media: A Content Analysis of Crime News. *Crime and Delinquency* 41:3–19.

Baron, J., and Reiss, P. 1985. Same Time Next Year: Aggregate Analyses of the Mass Media and Violent Behavior. *American Sociological Review* 47:802–809.

Baron, L. 1990. Feminist Perspectives on Sexuality. *Journal of Sex Research* 27:363–380.

Baron, L., and Straus, M. 1984. Sexual Stratification, Pornography, and Rape in the United States. In *Pornography and Sexual Aggression*, edited by N. Malamuth and E. Donnerstein. New York: Academic Press, pp. 185–209.

Baron, L., and Straus, M. 1985. *Legitimate Violence, Pornography, and Sexual Inequality as Explanations for State and Regional Differences in Rape.* Unpublished manuscript, Yale University.

Baron, L., and Straus, M. 1986. *Rape and Its Relations to Social Disorganization, Pornography, and Sexual Inequality in the United States.* Unpublished manuscript, Yale University.

Baron, L., and Straus, M. 1989. *Four Theories of Rape in American Society.* New Haven: Yale University Press.

Barrile, L. 1984. Television and Attitudes about Crime: Do Heavy Viewers Distort Criminality and Support Retributive Justice? In *Justice and the Media,* edited by R. Surette. Springfield, Ill.: Thomas, pp. 141–158.

Barrile, L. 1994. Review of "Using Murder: The Social Construction of Serial Homicide." *Journal of Criminal Justice and Popular Culture* 2(4):87–93.

Bartlett, A. 1992. Smile When You Run That Red Light. *Miami Herald,* July 9: 1A, 17A.

Barton, R., and Gregg, R. 1982. Middle East Conflict as a TV News Scenario: A Formal Analysis. *Journal of Communication* 32(2):172–185.

Bassiouni, M. 1979. Prolegomenon to Terror Violence. *Creighton Law Review* 12:745–752.

Bassiouni, M. 1981. Terrorism, Law Enforcement, and the Mass Media: Perspectives, Problems, Proposals. *Journal of Criminal Law and Criminology* 72:1–51.

Bechtel, R., Achelpohl, C., and Akers, R. 1972. Correlates between Observed Behavior and Questionnaire Responses on Television Viewing. In *Television and Social Behavior.* Vol. 4. *Television in Day-to-Day Life: Patterns of Use,* edited by E. A. Rubinstein, G. Comstock, and J. Murray. Washington, D.C.: U.S. Government Printing Office, pp. 274–344.

Becker, H. 1963. *Outsiders.* New York: Free Press.

Becker, T. 1971. *Political Trials.* New York: Bobbs-Merrill.

Bell, B. 1983. Closure of Pretrial Suppression Hearings: Resolving the Fair Trial/Free Press Conflict. *Fordham Law Review* 51:1297–1316.

Bellak, R., Madsen, R., Sullivan, W., Swidler, A., and Tipton, S. 1985. *Habits of the Heart.* Berkeley: University of California Press.

Belson, W. 1978. *Television Violence and the Adolescent Boy.* Westmead, England: Saxon House, Teakfield.

Bennack, F. 1983. *The American Public, the Media and the Judicial System: A National Survey on Public Awareness and Personal Experience.* New York: Hearst.

Bennett, G. 1985. TV's Crime Coverage Is Too Scary and Misleading. *TV Guide* January 5, pp. 14–15.

Bennett, K., Johnson, W., and Triplett, R. forthcoming. The Role of the Media in Reintegrative Shaming: A Content Analysis. In *Popular Culture, Crime and Justice,* edited by F. Bailey and D. Hale. Belmont, Calif.: Wadsworth.

Bennett, W., Feldman, L., and Feldman, M. 1983. *Reconstructing Reality in the Courtroom.* New Brunswick, N.J.: Rutgers University Press.

Benowitz, H. A. 1974. Legal Applications of Videotape. *Florida Bar Journal* 48:86–91.

Berger, P., and Luckmann, T. 1967. *The Social Construction of Reality.* New York: Anchor Books.

Bergman, A. 1971. *We're in the Money.* New York: HarperCollins.

Berkowitz, L. 1964. Aggressive Cues in Aggressive Behavior and Hostility Catharsis. *Psychological Review* 71:104–122.

Berkowitz, L., ed. 1969. Roots of Aggression: A Re-Examination of the Frustration-Aggression Hypothesis. New York: Atherton Press.

Berkowitz, L. 1970. Experimental Investigations of Hostility Catharsis. *Journal of Consulting and Clinical Psychology* 31:1–7.

Berkowitz, L. 1984. Some Effects of Thoughts on Anti- and Prosocial Influences of Media Events: A Cognitive-Neoassociation Analysis. *Psychological Bulletin* 95:410–417.

Berkowitz, L., and Alioto, J. 1973. The Meaning of an Observed Event as a Determinant of Its Aggressive Consequences. *Journal of Personality and Social Psychology* 28:206–217.

Berkowitz, L., and Cummingham, D. 1966. The Interest Value and Reliance on Fear Arousing Communications. *Journal of Abnormal and Social Psychology* 4:138–147.

Berkowitz, L., and Geen, R. 1966. Film Violence and the Cue Properties of Available Targets. *Journal of Personality and Social Psychology* 3:525–530.

Berkowitz, L., and Geen, R. 1967. Stimulus Qualities of the Target of Aggression: A Further Study. *Journal of Personality and Social Psychology* 5:364–368.

Berkowitz, L., and Macaulay, J. 1971. The Contagion of Criminal Violence. *Sociometry* 34:238–260.

Berkowitz, L., and Rawlings, E. 1963. Effects of Film Violence on Inhibitions against Subsequent Aggression. *Journal of Abnormal and Social Psychology* 66:405–412.

Berkowitz, L., Corwin, R., and Hieronimus, M. 1963. Film Violence and Subsequent Aggressive Tendencies. *Public Opinion Quarterly* 27:217–229.

Berkowitz, L., Parke, R., Leyens, J., West, S., and Sebastian, R. 1978. Experiments on the Reactions of Juvenile Delinquents to Filmed Violence. In *Aggression and Antisocial Behavior in Childhood Adolescence,* edited by L. A. Hersov and M. Berger. New York: Pergamon Press, pp. 59–72.

Berman, A. 1988. Fictional Depiction of Suicide in Television Films and Imitation Effects. *American Journal of Psychiatry* 145:982–986.

Berman, R. 1987. *How Television Sees Its Audience.* Thousand Oaks, Calif.: Sage.

Bermant, G., Chappell, D., Crockett, G., Jacoubovitch, M., and McGuire, M. 1975. Jury Responses to Prerecorded Videotaped Trial Presentations in California and Ohio. *Hastings Law Journal* 26:975.

Best, J. 1989. *Images of Issues: Typifying Contemporary Social Problems.* Hawthorne, N.Y.: Aldine de Gruyter.

Best, J. 1991. "Road Warriors" on "Hair-trigger Highways": Cultural Resources and the Media's Construction of the 1987 Freeway Shootings Problem. *Sociological Inquiry* 61:327–345.

Best, J. 1995. *Images of Issues: Typifying Contemporary Social Problems.* Hawthorne, N.Y.: Aldine de Gruyter.

Binder, A. 1993. Constructing Racial Rhetoric: Media Depictions of Harm in Heavy Metal and Rap Music. *American Sociological Review* 58:753–767.

Biocca, F., Brown, J., Shen, F., Bernhardt, J., Batista, L., Kemp, K., Makris, G., West, M., Lee, J., Straker, H., Hsiao, H., and Carbone, E. 1997. Assessment of Television's Anti-Violence Messages: University of North Carolina, Chapel Hill Study. In *National Television Violence Study.* Vol. 1. Thousand Oaks, Calif.: Sage.

Black, G. 1988. *Changing Attitudes toward Drug Use: Executive Summary and Statistical Report.* Rochester, N.Y.: Partnership for a Drug-Free America.

Black, J. 1987. *The English Press in the Eighteenth Century.* Philadelphia: University of Pennsylvania Press.

Blasi, V. 1971. The Newsman's Privilege: An Empirical Study. *Michigan Law Review* 70:229–284.

Bleyer, W. 1927. *Main Currents in the History of American Journalism.* Boston: Houghton Mifflin.

Blumberg, A. 1967. The Practice of Law as a Confidence Game: Organization Co-Optation of a Profession. *Law and Society Review* 1:15–39.

Blumer, H. 1933. *The Movies and Conduct.* New York: Macmillan.

Blumer, H., and Hauser, P. 1933. *Movies, Delinquency, and Crime.* New York: Macmillan.

Bohrer, S., and Ovelmen, R. 1987. Judicial Access: The Reporter's Right of Access to the Judicial System and Qualified Privilege from Compelled Testimony Relating to Newsgathering. In *The Reporter's Handbook.* Tallahassee: Florida Bar Association.

Bollen, K. A., and Phillips, D. 1982. Imitative Suicides: A National Study of the Effects of Television News Stories. *American Sociological Review* 47:802–809.

Bond-Maupin, L., Cavender, G., and Jurik, N. 1996. *The Construction of Gender in Reality Crime.* Unpublished manuscript, School of Justice Studies, Arizona State University, Tempe.

Boorstin, D. 1961. *The Image.* New York: Harper-Collins.

Borgida, E., DeGono, K., and Buckman, L. 1990. Cameras in the Courtroom: The Effects of Media Coverage on Witness Testimony and Juror Perceptions. *Law and Human Behavior* 14:489–509.

Bortner, M. A. 1984. Media Images and Public Attitudes toward Crime and Justice. In *Justice and the Media*, edited by R. Surette. Springfield, Ill.: Thomas, pp. 15–30.

Boster, F. J., and Mongeau, P. A. 1984. Fear-Arousing Persuasive Messages. In *Communication Yearbook*, Vol. 8, edited by R. Bostrum. Thousand Oaks, Calif.: Sage, pp. 330–375.

Boster, F. J., Miller, G. R., and Fontes, N. E. 1978. Videotape in the Courtroom: Effects in Live Trials. *Trial* 14:49–51, 59.

Bowen, N. 1987. Pornography: Research Review and Implications for Counseling. *Journal of Counseling and Development* 65:345–350.

Boyatzis, C., Matillo, G., and Nesbitt, K. 1995. Effects of "The Mighty Morphin Power Rangers" on Children's Aggression with Peers. *Child Study Journal* 25:45–55.

Brady, J. 1983. Fair and Impartial Railroad: The Jury, the Media and Political Trials. *Journal of Criminal Justice* 11:241–263.

Braithwaite, J. 1989. *Crime, Shame and Reintegration.* Cambridge: Cambridge University Press.

Braithwaite, J., and Mugford, S. 1994. Conditions of Successful Reintegration Ceremonies: Dealing with Juvenile Offenders. *British Journal of Criminology* 34:139–171.

Brakel, S. J. 1975. Videotape in Trial Proceedings: A Technological Obsession? *American Bar Association Journal* 61:956–959.

Brannigan, A. 1987. Is Obscenity Criminogenic? *Society* 24:12–19.

Brannigan, A., and Goldberg, S. 1987. The Study of Aggressive Pornography: The Vicissitudes of Relevance. *Critical Studies in Mass Communication* 4:262–283.

Brannigan, A., and Kapardis, A. 1986. The Controversy over Pornography and Sex Crimes: The Criminological Evidence and Beyond. *Australian and New Zealand Journal of Criminology* 19:259–284.

Brantley, A., and DiRosa, A. 1994. Gangs, A National Perspective. *FBI Law Enforcement Bulletin* 63:1–6.

Breman, P. 1977. Television's Dilemma: Stay on the Air or Bail Out? *Quill* March, pp. 8–9.

Brenner, L. 1989. Attention, Arnie Becker: Your Motions in Courtrooms—Not Bedrooms—Would be More Help. *TV Guide* June 17, pp. 10–14.

Brodsky, S. 1976. Sexual Assault: Perspectives on Prevention and Assailants. In *Sexual Assault*, edited by M. Walker and S. Brodsky. Lexington, Mass.: Heath, pp. 1–7.

Brody, W. 1990. *Communication Tomorrow.* New York: Praeger.

Brooks, T., and Marsh, E. 1985. *Complete Directory to Prime Time Network TV Shows, 1946–Present.* 3rd ed. New York: Ballantine.

Brown, S. H. 1980. *Video Arraignment Statistics.* Interoffice memorandum from Judge Seymore Brown, chief municipal judge, to Lloyd W. Zook, court administrator, Las Vegas, Nev., March 21.

Brownstein, H. 1997. *The Rise and Fall of a Violent Crime Wave: Crack Cocaine and the Social Construction of a Crime Problem.* Albany, N.Y.: Harrow and Heston.

Brummett, B. 1990. Mediating the Laws: Popular Trials and the Mass Media. In *Popular Trials,* edited by R. Hariman. Tuscaloosa: University Of Alabama Press, pp. 179–193.

Bryant, J., and Zillman, D., eds. 1994. *Media Effects: Advances in Theory and Research.* Hillsdale, N.J.: Erlbaum.

Bryant, J., Carveth, R., and Brown, D. 1981. Television Viewing and Anxiety: An Experimental Examination. *Journal of Communication* 31:106–119.

Buddenbaum, J., Weaver, D., Holsinger, R., and Brown, C. 1981. *Pretrial Publicity and Juries: A Review of Research.* Research Report No. 11. Bloomington: Center for New Communications, Indiana University.

Bullah, R., Madsen, R., Sullivan, W., Swidler, A., and Tipton, S. 1985. *Habits of the Heart.* Los Angeles: University of California Press.

Bureau of Justice Statistics. 1986. *Crime Prevention Measures.* Washington, D.C.: U.S. Department of Justice.

Burnett, J., and Oliver, R. 1979. Fear Appeal Effects in the Field: A Segmentation Approach. *Journal of Marketing Research* 16:181–190.

Bursik, H., and Grasmick, R. 1993. *Neighborhoods and Crime.* San Francisco: New Lexington Press.

Burt, L. W. 1978. The Case against Courtroom TV. *Trial* 12:62–63, 66.

Calvert, S. L., and Tan, S. L. 1994. Impact of Virtual Reality on Young Adults' Physiological Arousal and Aggressive Thoughts: Interaction Versus Observation. *Journal of Applied Developmental Psychology* 15:125–139.

Campbell, D. 1969. Reforms as Experiments. *American Psychology* 24:409–429.

Campbell, D., and Ross, L. 1968. The Connecticut Crackdown on Speeding. *Law and Society Review* 3:33–53.

Canadian Sentencing Commission. 1987. *Sentencing Reform: A Canadian Approach.* Ottawa, Ontario: Ministry of Supply and Services, Canada.

Canadian Sentencing Commission. 1988. *Sentencing in the Media: A Content Analysis of English-Language Newspapers in Canada.* Research reports of the Canadian Sentencing Commission. Ottawa: Department of Justice, Canada.

Cantor, J., and Harrison, K. 1997. Ratings and Advisories for Television Programming: University of Wisconsin, Madison Study. In *National Television Violence Study,* Vol. 1. Thousand Oaks, Calif.: Sage, pp. 361–412.

Carlson, J. 1985. *Prime Time Law Enforcement.* New York: Praeger.

Carroll, J., Kerr, N., Alfini, J., Weaver, F., MacCoun, R., and Feldman, V. 1986. Free Press and Fair Trial: The Role of Behavioral Research. *Law and Human Behavior* 10:187–201.

Carter, D., Prentky, R., Knight, R., and Vanderveer, P. 1987. Use of Pornography in the Criminal and Developmental Histories of Sexual Offenders. *Journal of Interpersonal Violence* 2:196–211.

Case Reviews Support Crime Stoppers. 1986. *The Caller* May, p. 7.

Cashman, V., and Fetter, T. 1980. *State Courts: Options for the Future.* Williamsburg, Va.: National Center for State Courts.

Casper, J. 1978. *Criminal Courts: The Defendant's Perspective.* Washington, D.C.: Law Enforcement Assistance Administration, Department of Justice, National Institute of Law Enforcement and Criminal Justice.

Cavender, G. (n.d.). *In the Shadow of Shadow: Television Reality Crime Programming.* Unpublished manuscript, Arizona State University, Tempe.

Cavender, G. 1981. Scared Straight: Ideology and the Media. *Journal of Criminal Justice* 34:430–441.

Cavender, G., and Fishman, M. forthcoming. *Reality Programming: The New Crime News.*

Cavender, G., and Mulcahy, A. (n.d.). *Trial by Fire: Media Constructions of Corporate Deviance.* Unpublished manuscript, Arizona State University, Tempe.

CBS. See Columbia Broadcasting System.

Chaffee, S. 1975. *Political Communication: Enduring Issues for Research.* Thousand Oaks, Calif.: Sage.

Channel 9 Shows Chase, Cuts Off Soap. 1995. *Orlando Sentinel* Wednesday, October 25, p. A-2.

Charter, W. 1933. *Motion Pictures and Youth: A Summary.* New York: Macmillan.

Chase, A. 1986. Lawyers and Popular Culture: A Review of Mass Media Portrayals of American Attorneys. *American Bar Association Research Journal* 2:281–300.

Cheatwood, D. forthcoming. Prison Movies: Films About Adult, Male, Civilian Prisons: 1929–1995. In *Popular Culture, Crime, and Justice,* edited by F. Bailey and D. Hale. Belmont, Calif.: Wadsworth.

Check, J., and Guloien, T. 1989. Reported Proclivity for Coercive Sex Following Repeated Exposure to Sexually Violent Pornography, Nonviolent Dehumanizing Pornography, and Erotica. In *Pornography: Research Advances and Policy Considerations,* edited by D. Zillman and J. Bryant. Hillsdale, N.J.: Erlbaum, pp. 159–184.

Chermak, S. 1994. Body Count News: How Crime Is Presented in the News Media. *Justice Quarterly* 11:561–582.

Chermak, S. 1995. Crime in the News Media: A Refined Understanding of How Crimes Become News. In *Media, Process, and the Social Construction of Crime*, edited by G. Barak. New York: Garland, pp. 95–129.

Chermak, S. forthcoming. Police, Courts, and Corrections in the News. *Popular Culture, Crime, and Justice*, edited by F. Bailey and D. Hale. Belmont, Calif.: Wadsworth.

Chibnall, S. 1975. The Crime Reporter: A Study in the Production of Commercial Knowledge. *Sociology* 9:49–66.

Chibnall, S. 1977. *Law and Order News*. London: Tavistock.

Chibnall, S. 1980. Chronicles of the Gallows: The Social History of Crime Reporting. In *The Sociology of Journalism and the Press*, edited by H. Christian. Lanham, Md.: Rowman & Littlefield, pp. 179–217.

Chibnall, S. 1981. The Production of Knowledge by Crime Reporters. In *The Manufacture of News*, edited by S. Cohen and J. Young. Thousand Oaks, Calif.: Sage, pp. 75–97.

Chiricos T., Eschholz S., and Gertz M. 1996. *News and Fear of Crime: Toward an Identification of Audience Effects*. Unpublished revised version of paper presented at the Annual Meeting of the American Society of Criminology, Boston, November 15, 1995.

Chiricos, T. forthcoming. Moral Panic as Ideology: Drugs, Violence, Race and Punishment in America. In *Race and Criminal Justice: A Further Look*, edited by M. Lynch and E. B. Patterson. Albany, N.Y.: Harrow and Heston.

Church, G. 1982. Copy Cats Are on the Prowl. *Time* November 15, p. 27.

Cirino, R. 1972. *Don't Blame the People*. New York: Vintage Books.

Cirino, R. 1974. *Power to Persuade*. New York: Bantam Books.

Cline, V., ed. 1974. *Where Do You Draw the Line?* Provo, Utah: Brigham Young University Press.

Coates, B., Pusser, H., and Goodman, I. 1976. The Influence of "Sesame Street" and "Mister Rogers' Neighborhood" on Children's Social Behavior in the Preschool. *Child Development* 47:138–144.

Cohen, B. 1963. *The Press and Foreign Policy*. Princeton, N.J.: Princeton University Press.

Cohen, D. A. 1993. *Pillars of Salt, Monuments of Grace: New England Crime Literature and the Origins of Popular American Culture, 1674–1860*. New York: Oxford University Press.

Cohen, S. 1972. *Folk Devils and Moral Panics*. London: MacGibbon and Kee.

Cohen, S., and Young, J., eds. 1981. *The Manufacture of News*. Thousand Oaks, Calif.: Sage.

Cohn, A. 1980. A Social Psychologist Views "Scared Straight!": Discussion. In *Forensic Psychology and Psychiatry*, edited by F. Wright, C. Bahn, and R. Rieber. New York: Academy of Sciences.

Cole, G. 1970. The Decision to Prosecute. *Law and Society Review* 4:313–343.

Cole, J. 1995. *The UCLA Television Violence Monitoring Report*. Los Angeles: UCLA Center for Communication Policy.

Cole, J. 1996. *The UCLA Television Violence Monitoring Report*. Los Angeles: UCLA Center for Communication Policy.

Coleman, G. V. 1977. *The Impact of Video Use on Court Function: A Summary of Current Research and Practice*. Washington, D.C.: Federal Judicial Center.

Coleman, J. 1974. *Power and the Structure of Society*. New York: Norton.

Collins, W. A. 1973. Effect of Temporal Separation between Motivation, Aggression, and Consequences: A Developmental Study. *Developmental Psychology* 8:215–221.

Collins, W. A. 1975. The Developing Child as a Viewer. *Journal of Communication* 25:215–221.

Columbia Broadcasting System (CBS). 1974. *A Study of Messages Received by Children Who Viewed an Episode of "Fat Albert and the Cosby Kids."* New York: CBS Office of Social Research.

Comstock, G. 1980. *Television in America*. Thousand Oaks, Calif.: Sage.

Comstock, G. 1983. Media Influences on Aggression. In *Prevention and Control of Aggression*, edited by A. Goldstein and L. Krasner. Elmsford, N.Y.: Pergamon Press, pp. 241–272.

Comstock, G., and Fisher, M. 1975. *Television and Human Behavior: A Guide to Pertinent Scientific Literature*. Santa Monica, Calif.: Rand.

Comstock, G., and Lindsey, G. 1975. *TV and Human Behavior: The Research Horizon, Future and Present*. Santa Monica, Calif.: Rand.

Comstock, G., Chaffee, S., Katzman, N., McCombs, M., and Roberts, D. 1978. *Television and Human Behavior*. New York: Columbia University Press.

Condron, M., and Nutter, D. 1988. A Preliminary Examination of the Pornography Experience of Sex Offenders, Paraphiliacs, Sexual Dysfunction Patients, and Controls Based on Meese Commission Recommendations. *Sex Marital Therapy* 14:285–298.

Confidential Sources and Information. 1989. Washington, D.C.: Reporters' Committee for Freedom of the Press.

Cook, T., Kendzierski, D., and Thomas, S. 1983. The Implicit Assumptions of Television Research: An Analysis of the 1982 NIMH Report on Television and Behavior. *Public Opinion Quarterly* 47:161–201.

Cook, T., Tyler, T., Goetz, E., Gordon, M., Protess, D., Leff, D., and Molotch, H. 1983. Media and Agenda Setting: Effects on the Public, Interest Group Leaders, Policy Makers, and Policy. *Public Opinion Quarterly* 47:16–35.

Cooper, H. 1976. Terrorism and the Media. *Chitty's Law Journal* 24:226–232.

Cooper, J., and Mackie, D. 1986. Video Games and Aggression in Children. *Journal of Applied Social Psychology* 16:726–744.

Corne, S., Briere, J., and Esses, L. 1992. Women's Attitudes and Fantasies about Rape as a Function of Early Exposure to Pornography. *Journal of Interpersonal Violence* 7:454–461.

Cornen, A., and Van Dijk, J., eds. 1978. Public Opinion on Crime and Criminal Justice. In *Collected Studies in Criminological Research*. Vol. XVII. Strasbourg Cedex, France: Council of Europe.

Cosgrove, M., and McIntyre, C. 1974. *The Influence of "Mister Rogers' Neighborhood" on Nursery School Children's Prosocial Behavior*. Paper presented at the meeting of the Southeastern Regional Society for Research in Child Development, Chapel Hill, N.C.

Cotsirilos, J., and Philipsborn, J. 1986. A Change of Venue Roadmap. *The Champion* July, pp. 8–15.

Court, H. 1976. Pornography and Sex-Crimes: A Re-evaluation in the Light of Recent Trends around the World. *International Journal of Criminology and Penology* 5:129–157.

Courtney, T. 1992. *Early Adolescent Males' Use of Comic Book Super Heroes as Ego Ideals*. Unpublished master's thesis, Smith College School for Social Work, Northampton, Mass.

Cramer, C. 1994. Ethical Problems of Mass Murder Coverage in the Mass Media. *Journal of Mass Media Ethics* 9(1):26–42.

Crenshaw, M. 1981. The Causes of Terrorism. *Comparative Politics* 13:374–396.

Cressey, P. 1938. The Motion Picture Experience as Modified by Social Background and Personality. *American Sociological Review* 11:517.

Crime Stoppers International, Inc. Web site. URL: http://www.c-s-i.org.

Cullen, T. 1993. *Maryland* v. *Craig*: The Collision of Policy and History. *New England Journal on Criminal and Civil Confinement* 19:141–173.

Culver, J., and Knight, K. 1979. Evaluative TV Impressions of Law Enforcement Roles. In *Evaluating Alternative Law Enforcement Policies*, edited by R. Baker and F. Mayer. San Francisco: New Lexington Press, pp. 201–212.

Cumberbatch, G., and Beardsworth, A. 1976. Criminals, Victims, and Mass Communications. In *Victims and Society*, edited by E. C. Viano. Washington, D.C.: Visage Press, pp. 72–90.

Curran, J. 1989. A Priority for Parole: Agencies Must Reach Out to the Media and the Community. *Corrections Today* February, pp. 30, 32, 34.

Curran, J., and Seaton, J. 1980. *Power without Responsibility*. London: Fontana.

Dale, E. 1935. *Children's Attendance at Motion Pictures*. New York: Macmillan.

Davis, F. 1951. Crime News in Colorado Newspapers. *American Journal of Sociology* 57:325–330.

Davis, R. 1986. Pretrial Publicity, the Timing of the Trial, and Mock Jurors' Decision Processes. *Journal of Applied Social Psychology* 16:590–607.

Davison, W. P. 1983. The Third Person Effect in Communication. *Public Opinion Quarterly* 65:299–306.

De Silva, B. 1984. The Gang-Rape Story. *Columbia Journalism Review* May-June, pp. 42–44.

Debord, G. 1983. *Society as a Spectacle*. Detroit: Red and Black Books.

DeFleur, M., and Ball-Rokeach, S. 1975. *Theories of Mass Communication*. 3rd ed. New York: D. McKay.

DeFleur, M., and Dennis, E. 1985. *Understanding Mass Communication*. Boston: Houghton Mifflin.

Demare, D., Briere, J., and Lips, H. 1988. Violent Pornography and Self-Reported Likelihood of Sexual Aggression. *Journal of Research in Personality* 22:140–153.

Demare, D., Briere, J., and Lips, H. 1993. Sexually Violent Pornography, Anti-Women Attitudes, and Sexual Aggression: A Structural Equation Model. *Journal of Research in Personality* 27:285–300.

Deming, C. 1985. *Hill Street Blues* as Narrative. *Critical Studies in Mass Communication* 2:1–22.

Denzin, N. 1986. Postmodern Social Theory. *Sociological Theory* 4:194–204.

Denzin, N. 1995. *The Cinematic Society*. Thousand Oaks, Calif.: Sage.

Dershowitz, A. 1985. These Cops Are All Guilty. *TV Guide* May 25, pp. 4–7.

Desmond, R. 1978. *The Information Process: World News Reporting in the Twentieth Century*. Iowa City: University of Iowa Press.

Deutschmann, P. 1959. *Front Page Content of Twelve Metropolitan Dailies*. Cincinnati: Scripps-Howard Research Center.

Devine, P. G., and Hirt, E. R. 1989. Message Strategies for information Campaigns: A Social Psychological Analysis. In *Information Campaigns: Balancing Social Values with Social Change*, edited by C. Salmon. Thousand Oaks, Calif.: Sage, pp. 229–258.

Dexter, H., and Cutler, B. 1991. *In Search of the Fair Jury: Does Extended Voir Dire Remedy the Prejudicial Effects of Pretrial Publicity?* Paper presented at the American Psychological Association Meeting, August, San Francisco.

Dexter, H., Cutler, B., and Moran, G. 1992. A Test of Voir Dire as a Remedy for the Prejudicial Effects of Pretrial Publicity. *Journal of Applied Social Psychology* 22:819–832.

Dienstbier, R. 1977. Sex and Violence: Can Research Have It Both Ways? *Journal of Communication* 27:176–188.

Dillard, J. P., Plotnick, C. A., Godbold, L. C., Freimuth, V. S., and Edgar, T. 1996. The Multiple Affective Outcomes of AIDS PSAs: Fear Appeals Do More Than Scare People. *Communication Research* 23(1):44–83.

Dinitz, S. 1987. Coping with Deviant Behavior through Technology. *Criminal Justice Research Bulletin* 3:1–15.

Ditton, J., and Duffy, J. 1983. Bias in the Newspaper Reporting of Crime News. *British Journal of Criminology* 23:159–165.

Dombrink, J. 1988. Organized Crime Gangsters and Godfathers. In *Controversial Issues in Crime and Justice*, edited by J. Scott and T. Hirschi. Thousand Oaks, Calif.: Sage, pp. 54–75.

Dombroff, M. 1981. Videotapes Enter the Picture as Demonstrative Evidence Tool. *National Law Journal* November 23, pp. 24–25.

Dominick, J. 1973. Crime and Law Enforcement on Prime-Time Television. *Public Opinion Quarterly* 37:241–250.

Dominick, J. 1978. Crime and Law Enforcement in the Mass Media. In *Deviance and Mass Media*, edited by C. Winick. Thousand Oaks, Calif.: Sage, pp. 105–128.

Dominick, J. R. 1987. Videogames, Television Violence, and Aggression in Teenagers. *Journal of Communication* 34:136–147.

Donnerstein, E. 1980. Pornography and Violence Against Women. *Annals of the New York Academy of Science* 347:277–288.

Donnerstein, E. 1984. Pornography: Its Effects on Violence against Women. In *Pornography and Sexual Aggression*, edited by N. Malamuth and E. Donnerstein. New York: Academic Press, pp. 53–81.

Donnerstein, E., and Berkowitz, L. 1981. Victims' Reactions in Aggressive Erotic Films as a Factor in Violence against Women. *Journal of Personality and Social Psychology* 41:710–724.

Donnerstein, E., and Berkowitz, L. 1985. *Role of Aggressive and Sexual Images in Violent Pornography.* Unpublished manuscript.

Donnerstein, E., and Linz, D. 1984. Sexual Violence in the Media: A Warning. *Psychology Today* January, pp. 14–15.

Donnerstein, E., and Linz, D. 1986a. Mass Media Sexual Violence and Male Viewers. *American Behavioral Scientist* 29:601–618.

Donnerstein, E., and Linz, D. 1986b. The Question of Pornography. *Psychology Today* 20:56–59.

Donnerstein, E., Linz, D., and Penrod, S. 1987. *The Question of Pornography.* New York: Free Press.

Donnerstein, E., Slaby, R. and Eron, L. 1994. The Mass Media and Youth Violence. In *Violence and Youth: Psychology's Response*, Vol. 2, edited by J. Murray, E. Rubinstein, and G. Comstock. Washington, D.C.: American Psychological Association, pp. 219–250.

Doob, A., and MacDonald, G. 1979. Television Viewing and Fear of Victimization: Is the Relationship Causal? *Journal of Personality and Social Psychology* 37:170–179.

Doob, A., and Roberts, J. 1988. Public Punitiveness and Public Knowledge of the Facts: Some Canadian Surveys. In *Public Attitudes to Sentencing Surveys from Five Countries*, edited by N. Walker and M. Hough. Grower-Brookfield, USA, pp. 111–133.

Doppelt, J., and Manikas, P. 1990. Mass Media and Criminal Justice Decision Making. In *The Media and Criminal Justice Policy*, edited by R. Surette. Springfield, Ill.: Thomas, pp. 129–142.

Doret, D. M. 1974. Trial by Videotape: Can Justice Be Seen to Be Done? *Temple Law Quarterly* 47:228–268.

Douglas, D., Westley, B., and Chaffee, S. 1970. An Information Campaign That Changed Community Attitudes. *Journalism Quarterly* 47:479–487.

Drabman, R. S., and Thomas, M. J. 1974. Does Media Violence Increase Children's Toleration of Real-Life Aggression? *Developmental Psychology* 10:418–421.

Drachman, V. 1992. Entering the Male Domain: Women Lawyers in the Courtroom in Modern American History. *Massachusetts Law Review* 77:44–50.

Drechsel, R. 1983. *News Making in the Trial Courts.* White Plains, N.Y.: Longman.

Drechsel, R. 1985. Judges' Perceptions of Fair Trial-Free Press Issue. *Journalism Quarterly* 62:388–390.

Drew, D., and Weaver, D. 1990. Media Attention, Media Exposure, and Media Effects. *Journalism Quarterly* 67:740–748.

Drucker, S. J. 1989. The Televised Mediated Trial: Formal and Substantive Characteristics. *Communication Quarterly* 37:305–318.

Dubnoff, C. 1977. Pretrial Publicity and Due Process in Criminal Proceedings. *Political Science Quarterly* 92:89–110.

Duffee, D. 1980. *Explaining Criminal Justice.* Cambridge, Mass.: Oelgeschlager, Gunn & Hain.

Dulaney, W. 1968. *An Assessment of Some Assertions Made Relative to the Fair Trial and Free Press Controversy.* Unpublished Ph.D. dissertation, Northwestern University, Evanston, Ill.

Duncan, R. 1990. *Panel Analysis: A Critical Method for Analyzing the Rhetoric of Comic Book Form.* Unpublished Ph.D. dissertation, Louisiana State University, Baton Rouge.

Dye, T. R. 1985. *Understanding Public Policy.* 5th ed. Chapter 1, 13. Englewood Cliffs, N.J.: Prentice Hall.

Dye, T., and Zeigler, H. 1986. *American Politics in the Media Age.* Pacific Grove, Calif.: Brooks/Cole.

Ebbesen, E. 1987. Affidavit in *People v. Rubio*, Superior Court of the State of California, Solano County, No. C21691.

Edgar, P. 1977. *Children and Screen Violence.* St. Lucia, Australia: University of Queensland Press.

Einstadter, W. 1979. Crime News in the Old West: Social Control in a Northwestern Town, 1887–1888. *Urban Life* 8:317–334.

Eisenberg, G. 1980. Children and Aggression after Observed Film Aggression with Sanctioning Adults. In *Forensic Psychology and Psychiatry*, edited by F. Wright, C. Bahn, and R. Rieber. New York: Academy of Sciences, pp. 304–317.

Eisenstein, J., and Jacobs, H. 1977. *Felony Justice: An Organizational Analysis of Criminal Courts*. New York: Little, Brown.

Ekman, P., Liebert, R., Friesen, W., Harrison, R., Zlatchin, C., Malmstrom, E., and Baron, R. 1972. Facial Expressions of Emotion while Watching Televised Violence as Predictors of Subsequent Aggression. In *Television and Social Behavior*. Vol. 5. *Television's Effects: Further Explorations*. Report of the Surgeon General's Scientific Advisory Committee on Television and Behavior, edited by G. Comstock, E. Rubinstein, and J. Murray. Washington, D.C.: U.S. Government Printing Office, pp. 22–58.

Elias, R. 1986. *The Politics of Victimization*. New York: Oxford University Press.

Elias, R. 1994. Official Stories: Media Coverage of American Crime Policy. *Humanist* 54:3–8.

Ellis, P., and Sekyra, F. 1972. The Effect of Aggressive Cartoons on the Behavior of First-Grade Children. *Journal of Psychology* 81:37–43.

English, D. 1980. The Politics of Porn. *Mother Jones* April, pp. 20–23.

Entman, R. 1989. How the Media Affect What People Think: An Information Processing Approach. *Journal of Politics* 51: 347–370.

Epstein, A. 1990. Ruling Allows TV Testimony in Child-Abuse Cases. *Tallahassee Democrat* June 28, pp. 1A, 4A.

Erbring, L., Goldenberg, E., and Miller, A. 1980. Front-Page News and Real-World Clues: A New Look at Agenda-Setting by the Media. *American Journal of Political Science* 24:16–49.

Ericson, R. 1991. Mass Media, Crime, Law, and Justice. *British Journal of Criminology* 31:219–249.

Ericson, R., ed. 1995. *Crime and the Media*. Brookfield, USA: Dartmouth.

Ericson, R., Baranek, P., and Chan, J. 1987. *Visualizing Deviance*. Toronto: University of Toronto Press.

Ericson, R., Baranek, P., and Chan, J. 1989. *Negotiating Control: A Study of News Sources*. Toronto: University of Toronto Press.

Ericson, R., Baranek, P., and Chan, J. 1991. *Representing Law and Order: Crime, Law, and Justice in the News Media*. Toronto: University of Toronto Press.

Eron, L. 1987. The Development of Aggressive Behavior from the Perspective of a Developing Behaviorism. *American Psychology* 42: 435–442.

Estep, R., and Lauderdale, P. 1980. The Bicentennial Protest: An Examination of Hegemony in the Definition of Deviant Activity. In *A Political Analysis of Deviance*, edited by P. Lauderdale. Minneapolis: University of Minnesota Press.

Estep, R., and Macdonald, P. 1984. How Prime-Time Crime Evolved on TV, 1976–1983. In *Justice and the Media*, edited by R. Surette. Springfield, Ill.: Thomas, pp. 110–123.

Esterle, J. 1986. Crime and the Media. *Jericho* 41:5, 7.

Ettema, J., Protess, D., Leff, D., Miller, P., Doppelt, J., and Cook, F. 1989. *Agenda-Setting as Politics: A Case Study of the Press-Public-Policy Connection at the Post-Modern Moment*. Paper presented at the Association for Education in Journalism and Mass Communication Convention, June, Washington, D.C.

Eunkyung, J., and Berkowitz, L. 1994. A Priming Effect Analysis of Media Influences: An Update. In *Media Effects*, edited by J. Bryant and D. Zillman. Hillsdale, N.J.: Erlbaum.

Evans, S., and Lundman, R. 1983. Newspaper Coverage of Corporate Price-Fixing. *Criminology* 21:529–541.

Everson, W. 1964. *The Bad Guys: A Pictorial History of the Movie Villain*. New York: Citadel Press.

Everson, W. 1972. *The Detective in Film*. New York: Citadel Press.

Eysenck, H., and Nias, D. 1978. *Sex, Violence and the Media*. New York: HarperCollins.

Fair Trial—Free Press—Reporter's Privilege. 1983. *Criminal Law Reporter* 32:24–28.

Farmer, L., Williams, G., Lee, R., Cundick, B., Howell, R., and Rooker, C. 1976. Juror Perceptions of Trial Testimony as a Function of the Method of Presentation. In *Psychology and the Law*, edited by C. Nemeth and N. Vidmar. Lexington, Mass.: Heath, pp. 209–238.

Faunkhouser, G. 1973. The Issues of the Sixties: An Exploratory Study in the Dynamics of Public Opinion. *Public Opinion Quarterly* 37:63–75.

Federman, J. 1997. Introduction. In *National Television Violence Study*, vol 1. Thousand Oaks, Calif.: Sage, pp. 1–2.

Fedler, F., and Jordan, D. 1982. How Emphasis on People Affects Coverage of Crime. *Journalism Quarterly* Autumn: 474–478.

Feeley, M. 1982. Plea Bargaining and the Structure of the Criminal Process. *Justice System Journal* 7:338–355.

Fenton, F. 1910. The Influence of Newspaper Presentations upon the Growth of Crime and Other Anti-Social Activity. *American Journal of Sociology* 7:342–371, 538–564.

Ferrell, J. 1993. *Crimes of Style*. Boston: Northeastern University Press.

Ferrell, J. forthcoming. Criminalizing Popular Culture. In *Popular Culture, Crime and Justice*, edited by F. Bailey and D. Hale. Belmont, Calif.: Wadsworth.

Ferrell, J., and Sanders, C. R. 1995. *Cultural Criminology*. Boston: Northeastern University Press.

Feshbach, S. 1972. Reality and Fantasy in Filmed Violence. In *Television and Social Behavior*. Vol: 2. *Television and Social Learning*, edited by J. Murray, G. Comstock, and E. Rubinstein. Washington, D.C.: U.S. Government Printing Office, pp. 318–345.

Feshbach, S., and Singer, R. D. 1971. *Television and Aggression: An Experimental Field Study*. San Francisco: Jossey-Bass.

Finchenauer, J. 1979. *Juvenile Awareness Project: An Evaluation Report.* New Brunswick, N.J.: Rutgers University School of Criminal Justice.

Finchenauer, J. 1980. "Scared Straight!" and the Panacea Phenomenon: Discussion. In *Forensic Psychology and Psychiatry,* edited by F. Wright, C. Bahn, and R. Rieber. New York: Academy of Sciences.

First, Sixth Amendments Permit Ban on Televising Federal Trials. 1983. *Criminal Law Reporter* 32:2339–2240.

Fisher, G. 1989. Mass Media Effects on Sex Role Attitudes of Incarcerated Men. *Sex Roles* 20:191–203.

Fisher, W., and Barak, A. 1989. Sex Education as a Corrective: Immunizing against Possible Effects of Pornography. In *Pornography: Recent Research, Interpretations, and Policy Considerations,* edited by D. Zillman and J. Bryant. Hillsdale, N.J.: Erlbaum, pp. 289–320.

Fisher, W., and Barak, A. 1991. Pornography, Erotica, and Behavior: More Questions Than Answers. *International Journal of Law and Psychiatry* 14:65–83.

Fisher, W., and Grenier, G. 1994. Violent Pornography, Antiwoman Thoughts, and Antiwoman Acts: In Search of Reliable Effects. *Journal of Sex Research* 31:23–38.

Fishman, G., and Weimann, G. 1985. Presenting the Victim: Sex-Based Bias in Press Reports on Crime. *Justice Quarterly* 2:491–503.

Fishman, M. 1978. Crime Waves as Ideology. *Social Problems* 25:531–543.

Fiske, J. 1994. *Media Matters.* Minneapolis: University of Minnesota Press.

Fiske, S., and Taylor, S. 1984. *Social Cognition.* Reading, Mass.: Addison-Wesley.

Flay, B. R. 1986. *Mass Media and Smoking Cessation.* Paper presented at the annual convention of the International Communication Association, May, Chicago.

Flora, J. A., Maccoby, N., and Farquhar, J. W. 1989. Communication Campaigns to Prevent Cardio-vascular Disease: The Stanford Community Studies. In *Public Communication Campaigns,* 2nd ed., edited by R. Rice and C. Atkins. Thousand Oaks, Calif.: Sage, pp. 233–252.

Florida Law Officers Seek Tips from Surfers—Online. *Orlando Sentinel,* May 20:A-7.

Flynn, J. 1993. Prejudicial Publicity in Criminal Trials: Bringing *Sheppard* v. *Maxwell* into the Nineties. *New England Law Review* 27:857–882.

Fogelson, R. 1977. *Big City Police.* Cambridge, Mass.: Harvard University Press.

Forrest, W. 1892. Trial by Newspapers. *American Criminal Law Magazine* 14:553.

Fosdick, R., Pound, R., and Frankfurter, F. 1922. *Criminal Justice in Cleveland,* edited by R. Pound and F. Frankfurter. Montclair, N.J.: Patterson Smith.

Foucalt, M. 1977. *Discipline and Punish: The Birth of the Prison.* Translated by A. Sheridan. New York: Vintage Books.

Fox, K. 1995. *Changes in the Estimation of Violent Crime and Media Influence.* Unpublished thesis, University of New Brunswick–Saint John, Canada.

Fox, S., Stein, A., Friedrich, L., and Kipnis, D. 1977. *Prosocial Television and Children's Fantasy.* Paper presented at the Biennial Meeting of the Society for Research in Child Development, March, New Orleans.

Franklin, B. [1771–1789] 1964. *The Autobiography of Benjamin Franklin.* New Haven, Conn.: Yale University Press.

Freedberg, S., and Holzman, T. 1984. Benson Is Hottest Show in Town. *Miami Herald* August 4, pp. 1A, 5A.

Freedman, J. 1984. Effect of Television Violence on Aggressiveness. *Psychological Bulletin* 96:227–246.

Freeman, R. 1996. *The Correctional Officer as Villain and the Inmate as Hero: How the Print Media and Corrections Perpetuate Hollywood Stereotyping.* Paper presented at the March, 1996, annual meeting of the Academy of Criminal Justice Sciences in Las Vegas, Nevada.

Freeman, R. forthcoming. Public Perception and Corrections: Correctional Staff as Smug Hacks. *Popular Culture, Crime, and Justice,* edited by F. Bailey and D. Hale. Belmont, Calif.: Wadsworth.

Friedman, L. 1994. *Crime and Punishment in American History.* New York: Basic books.

Friedman, L., and Percival, R. 1981. *The Roots of Justice: Crime and Punishment in Alameda County, California, 1870–1910.* Durham: University of North Carolina Press.

Friedrich, L., and Stein, A. 1975. Prosocial Television and Young Children: The Effects of Verbal Labeling and Role Playing on Learning and Behavior. *Child Development* 46:27–38.

Friendly, A., and Goldfarb, R. 1967. *Crime and Publicity: The Impact of News on the Administration of Justice.* New York: Twentieth Century Fund.

Fugitive Is 1st of Most Wanted Caught in Computer Dragnet. 1996. *Orlando Sentinel* May 20, p. A-7.

Funk, J., and Buchman, D. 1994. *Video Games and Children: Are There "High Risk" Players?* Paper presented at the International Conference on Violence in the Media, St. John's University, Oct. 3 and 4, New York.

Furstenberg, F. 1971. Public Reactions to Crime in the Streets. *American Scholar* 40:601–610.

Gailey, C. W. 1993. Mediated Messages: Gender, Class, and Cosmos in Home Video Games. *Journal of Popular Culture* 27:81–97.

Gaines, S. 1995. O.J. Simpson, Mark Fuhrman, and the Moral "Low Ground" of Ethnic/Race Relations in the United States. *Black Scholar* 25:46–48.

Galtung, J., and Ruge, M. 1981. Structuring and Selecting News. In *The Manufacture of News,* edited by S. Cohen and J. Young. Thousand Oaks, Calif.: Sage, pp. 52–63.

Gans, H. 1979. *Deciding What's News*. New York: Pantheon.

Gans, H. 1988. *Middle American Individualism*. New York: Free Press.

Garcia, L. 1986. Exposure to Pornography and Attitudes about Women and Rape: A Correlational Study. *Journal of Sex Research* 22:378–385.

Garner, G. 1987. *Chief, The Reporters are Here!* Springfield, Ill.: Thomas.

Garofalo, J. 1981a. Crime and the Mass Media: A Selective Review of Research. *Journal of Research in Crime and Delinquency* 18:319–350.

Garofalo, J. 1981b. The Fear of Crime: Causes and Consequences. *Journal of Criminal Law and Criminology* 72:839–859.

Garofalo, J., and Laub, J. 1978. The Fear of Crime: Broadening Our Perspective. *Victimology* 3:242–253.

Garvey, J. 1995. Race and the Simpson Verdict. *Commonwealth* 122:6.

Gebotys, R., Roberts, J., and DasGupta, B. 1988. News Media Use and Public Perceptions of Crime Seriousness. *Canadian Journal of Criminology* 30:3–16.

Geen, R. 1968. Effects of Frustration, Attack and Prior Training in Aggressiveness upon Aggressive Behavior. *Journal of Personality and Social Psychology* 9:316–321.

Geen, R., and Berkowitz, L. 1967. Some Conditions Facilitating the Occurrence of Aggression after the Observation of Violence. *Journal of Personality* 35:666–676.

Geen, R., and Stonner, D. 1972. Content Effects in Observed Violence. *Journal of Personality and Social Psychology* 25:145–150.

Gelernter, D. 1995. The Real Story of Orenthal James. *National Review* October 9, pp. 45–47.

Gelles, R., and Faulkner, R. 1978. Time and Television News Work. *Sociological Quarterly* 19:89–102.

Gentry, C. S. 1991. Pornography and Rape: An Empirical Analysis. *Deviant Behavior* 12: 277–288.

Gerald, E. J. 1983. *News of Crime, Courts, and Press in Conflict*. Westport, Conn.: Greenwood Press.

Gerbner, G. 1976. *Television and Its Viewers: What Social Science Sees*. Santa Monica, Calif.: Rand.

Gerbner, G. 1980. Trial by Television: Are We at the Point of No Return? *Judicature* 63:416–426.

Gerbner, G., and Gross, L. 1976. Living with Television: The Violence Profile. *Journal of Communication* 26:173–199.

Gerbner, G., and Gross, L. 1980. The Violent Face of Television and Its Lessons. In *Children and the Faces of Television*, edited by E. Palmer and A. Dorr. New York: Academic Press, pp. 149–162.

Gerbner, G., Gross, L., Jackson-Beeck, M., Jeffries-Fox, S., and Signorielli, N. 1978. Cultural Indicators: Violence Profile No. 9. *Journal of Communication* 29:176–207.

Gerbner, G., Gross, L., Morgan, M., and Signorielli, N. 1980. The Mainstreaming of America: Violence Profile No. 11. *Journal of Communication* 30:10–29.

Gerbner, G., Gross, L., Morgan, M., and Signorielli, N. 1994. Growing Up with Television: The Cultivation Perspective. In *Media Effects*, edited by J. Bryant and D. Zillman. Hillsdale N.J.: Erlbaum, pp. 17–41.

Gerbner, G., Gross, L., Signorielli, N., Morgan, M., and Jackson-Beeck, M. 1979. The Demonstration of Power: Violence Profile No. 10. *Journal of Communication* 29:177–196.

Gergen, K. 1985. Social Constructionist Inquiry: Context and Implications. In *The Social Construction of the Person*, edited by K. Gergen and K. Davis. New York: Springer-Verlag, pp. 3–18.

Gilberg, S., Eyal, C., McCombs, M., and Nicholas, D. 1980. The State of the Union Address and the Press Agenda. *Journalism Quarterly* 57:584–588.

Gilmore, W. H. 1980. Arraignment by Television: A New Way to Bring Defendants to the Courtroom. *Judicature* 63:396–401.

Goethe, J. W. 1774. *Die Leiden des jungen Werthers* (The sorrows of young Werther).

Goffman, E. 1959. *The Presentation of Self in Everyday Life*. New York: Doubleday.

Goffman, E. 1961. *Asylums*. New York: Anchor Books.

Goffman, E. 1967. *Interaction Ritual*. New York: Doubleday.

Goldstein, J. 1980. Police Discretion Not to Invoke the Criminal Process: Low-Visibility Decisions in the Administration of Justice. *Yale Law Journal* 69:543–594.

Goldstein, J. 1986. *Aggression and Crimes of Violence*. New York: Oxford University Press.

Goldstein, M. 1973. Exposure to Erotic Stimuli and Sexual Deviance. *Journal of Social Issues* 29:197–219.

Goldstein, M., Kant, H., Judd, L., Rice, C., and Green, R. 1972. Exposure to Pornography and Sexual Behavior in Deviant and Normal Groups. In *Erotica and Antisocial Behavior*. Vol. VII. U.S. Commission on Obscenity and Pornography. Washington, D.C.: U.S. Government Printing Office, pp. 1–90.

Gomme, I. 1986. Fear of Crime Mounting among Canadians: A Multi-Variate Analysis. *Journal of Criminal Justice* 14:249–258.

Gordon, M., and Heath, L. 1981. The News Business, Crime, and Fear. In *Reactions to Crime*, edited by D. Lewis. Thousand Oaks, Calif.: Sage, pp. 227–250.

Gordon, M., and Riger, S. 1989. *The Female Fear*. New York: Free Press.

Gorelick, S. 1989. Join Our War: The Construction of Ideology in a Newspaper Crimefighting Campaign. *Crime and Delinquency* 35:421–436.

Gorn, E. 1992. The Wicked World: The National Police Gazette and Gilded-Age America. *Media Studies Journal* 6:1–16.

Gottfredson, M., and Gottfredson, D. 1980. *Decision Making in Criminal Justice*. New York: Ballinger.

Gottfredson, M., and Hirschi, T. 1990. *A General Theory of Crime*. Stanford, Calif.: Stanford University Press.

Gould, M., and Shaffer, D. 1986. The Impact of Suicide in Television Movies. *New England Journal of Medicine* 315:690–694.

Graber, D. 1979. Evaluating Crime-Fighting Policies. In *Evaluating Alternative Law Enforcement Policies*, edited by R. Baker and F. Meyer. San Francisco: New Lexington Press, pp. 179–200.

Graber, D. 1980. *Crime News and the Public*. New York: Praeger.

Graber, D. 1989. *Mass Media and American Politics*. Washington, D.C.: CQ Press.

Grabosky, P., and Wilson, P. 1989. *Journalism and Justice: How Crime Is Reported*. Sydney: Pluto Press, pp. 121–128.

Graham, H., and Gurr, T., eds. 1979. *Violence in America: Historical and Comparative Perspectives*. Thousand Oaks, Calif.: Sage.

Grant, A. 1987. *The Audio-Visual Taping of Police Interviews with Suspects and Accused Persons by Halton Regional Police Force, Ontario, Canada: An Evaluation*. Ottawa, Ontario: Law Reform Commission of Canada.

Grant, A. 1990. The Videotaping of Police Interrogations in Canada. In *The Media and Criminal Justice Policy*, edited by R. Surette. Springfield, Ill.: Thomas, pp. 265–276.

Grant, J. 1992. Prime Time Crime: Television Portrayals of Law Enforcement. *Journal of Popular Culture* 15:57–68.

Granzberg, G. 1980. The Introduction of Television into a Northern Manitoba Cree Community. In *Television and the Canadian Indian*, edited by G. Granzberg and D. Steinbring. Winnipeg, Manitoba: University of Winnipeg.

Gray, H. 1989. Popular Music as a Social Problem: A Social History of Claims against Popular Music. In *Images of Issues*, 1st ed., edited by J. Best. Hawthorne, N.Y.: Aldine de Gruyter.

Gray, S. 1982. Exposure to Pornography and Aggression toward Women: The Case of the Angry Male. *Social Problems* 29:387–398.

Graybill, D., Strawniak, M., Hunter, T., and O'Leary, M. 1987. Effects of Playing Versus Observing Violent Versus Nonviolent Video Games on Children's Aggression. *Psychology* 24:1–8.

Greek, C., and Thompson, W. 1992. Antipornography Campaigns: Saving the Family in America and England. *International Journal of Politics, Culture and Society* 5:601–616.

Greenberg, B. 1969. The Content and Context of Violence in the Media. In *Violence and the Media*, edited by R. Baker and S. Ball. Washington, D.C.: U.S. Government Printing Office, pp. 423–449.

Greenberg, S. 1987. Why People Take Precautions against Crime: A Review of the Literature on Individual and Collective Responses to Crime. In *Taking Care: Understanding and Encouraging Self-Protective Behavior*, edited by N. Weinstein. New York: Cambridge University Press, pp. 231–253.

Greene, E. 1990. Media Effects on Jurors. *Law and Human Behavior* 14:439–450.

Greene, E., and Loftus, E. 1984. What's New in the News? The Impact of Well-Publicized News Events on Psychological Research and Courtroom Trials. *Basic and Applied Social Psychology* 5:211–221.

Greene, E., and Wade, R. 1988. Of Private Talk and Public Print: General Pre-Trial Publicity and Juror Decision-Making. *Applied Cognitive Psychology* 2:123–135.

Greene, J., and Bynum, T. 1982. TV Crooks: Implications of Latent Role Models for Theories of Delinquency. *Journal of Criminal Justice* 10:177–190.

Greenwood, M. J., Skupsky, D., Tollar, J., Jeske, C., and Veremko, P. 1978. Audio/Video Technology and the Courts. *State Court Journal* 2:26–28.

Grenander, M. 1976. The Heritage of Cain: Crime in American Fiction. *Annals of the American Academy of Political and Social Science* 423:48–55.

Gunter, B. 1987. *Television and the Fear of Crime*. London: Libbey.

Gunter, B. 1994. The Question of Media Violence. In *Media Effects*, edited by J. Bryant and D. Zillman. Hillsdale, N.J.: Erlbaum, pp. 163–211.

Gusfield, J. 1989. Constructing the Ownership of Social Problems: Fun and Profit in the Welfare State. *Social Problems* 36:431–441.

Haas, M. 1988. *TV in the Courts: Evaluation of Experiments*. Memorandum, National Center for State Courts, Williamsburg, Va., February 3.

Hale, D. forthcoming. Keeping Women in their Place: An Analysis of Policewomen in the Movies 1972–1995. *Popular Culture, Crime, and Justice*, edited by F. Bailey and D. Hale. Belmont, Calif.: Wadsworth.

Hall, S., Chritcher, C., Jefferson, T., Clarke, J., and Roberts, B. 1981. The Social Production of News: Mugging in the Media. In *The Manufacture of News*, edited by S. Cohen and J. Young. Thousand Oaks, Calif.: Sage, pp. 335–367.

Hallin, D. 1984. The Media, the War in Vietnam, and Political Support. *Journal of Politics* 46:2–24.

Hamm, M., and Ferrell, J. 1994. Rap, Cops, and Crime: Clarifying the "Cop Killer" Controversy. *ACJS Today* 13:1, 3, 29.

Handy, B. 1995. Our Mutual Houseguest. *Time* October 16, 146:108.

Hanneman, G., and McEwen, W. 1973. Televised Drug Abuse Appeals: A Content Analysis. *Journalism Quarterly* 50:329–333.

Hanratty, M., O'Neal, E., and Sulzer, J. 1972. The Effects of Frustration upon the Imitation of Aggression. *Journal of Personality and Social Psychology* 21:30–34.

Hans, V. 1990. Law and the Media: An Overview and Introduction. *Law and Human Behavior* 14:399–407.

Hans, V., and Dee, L. 1991. Media Coverage of Law. *American Behavioral Scientist* 35:136–149.

Hans, V., and Slater, D. 1983. John Hinckley, Jr., and the Insanity Defense: The Public's Verdict. *Public Opinion Quarterly* 47:202–212.

Hans, V., and Vidmar, N. 1982. Jury Selection. In *The Psychology of the Courtroom*, edited by R. Bray and N. Kerr. New York: Academic Press, pp. 39–82.

Hans, V., and Vidmar, N. 1986. *Judging the Jury*. New York: Plenum.

Hariman, R. 1990. Performing the Laws: Popular Trials and Social Knowledge. In *Popular Trials: Rhetoric, Mass Media, and the Law*, edited by R. Hariman. Tuscaloosa: University of Alabama Press, pp. 17–30.

Harper, T. 1982. When Your Case Hits the Front Page. *American Bar Association Journal* 70:78–82.

Harris, R. 1994. The Impact of Sexually Explicit Media. In *Media Effects*, edited by J. Bryant and D. Zillman. Hillsdale N.J.: Erlbaum, pp. 247–272.

Hartman, M. J. 1978. Second Thoughts on Videotaped Trials. *Judicature* 61:256–257.

Hartsfield, L. 1985. *The American Response to Professional Crime, 1870–1917*. Westport, Conn.: Greenwood Press.

Haskins, J. 1969. The Effects of Violence in the Printed Media. In *Mass Media and Violence*, edited by R. Baker and S. Ball. Washington, D.C.: U.S. Government Printing Office, pp. 493–502.

Haskins, S. 1969. Too Much Crime and Violence in the Press. *Editor and Publisher* 102:12.

Hauge, R. 1965. Crime and the Press. *Scandinavian Studies in Criminology* 1:147–164.

Hawkins, G., and Zimring, F. 1988. *Pornography in a Free Society*. New York: Cambridge University Press.

Hawkins, R., and Pingree, S. 1981. Uniform Messages and Habitual Viewing: Unnecessary Assumptions in Social Reality Effects. *Human Communications Research* 7:291–301.

Hays, W. 1932. President's Report to the Motion Picture Producers and Distributors' Association, Washington, D.C.

Heath, L. 1984. Impact of Newspaper Crime Reports on Fear of Crime: Multimethodological Investigation. *Journal of Personality and Social Psychology* 47:263–276.

Heath, L., and Gilbert, K. 1996. Mass Media and Fear of Crime. *American Behavioral Scientist* 39:379–86.

Heath, L., and Petraitis, J. 1987. Television Viewing and Fear of Crime: Where Is the Mean World? *Basic and Applied Social Psychology* 8:97–123.

Heath, L., Bresolin, N, and Rinaldi, I. 1989. Effects of Media Violence on Children: A Review of the Literature. *Archives of General Psychiatry* 46:376–379.

Heath, L., Gordon, M., and LeBailly, R. 1981. What Newspapers Tell Us (and Don't Tell Us) about Rape. *Journal of Personality and Social Psychology* 47:263–276.

Heinz, A. 1985. The Political Context for the Changing Content of Criminal Law. In *The Politics of Crime and Criminal Justice*, edited by E. Fairchild and V. Webb. Thousand Oaks, Calif.: Sage, pp. 77–95.

Heller, M., and Polsky, S. 1976. *Studies in Violence and Television*. New York: American Broadcasting Company.

Hendrick, G. 1977. When TV Is a School for Criminals. *TV Guide* January 29, pp. 10–14.

Hennigan, K., Heath, L., Wharton, J., Del Rosario, M., Cook, T., and Calder, B. 1982. Impact of the Introduction of Television on Crime in the United States. *Journal of Personality and Social Psychology* 42:461–477.

Hewitt, W. 1990. *Videotaped Trial Records: Evaluation and Guide*. Williamsburg, VA.: National Center for State Courts.

Hewitt, W. 1992. Does Video Court Reporting Have an Effect on Appellate Courts or Appellate Practice? *The Judges' Journal* 31:2–6, 35–36.

Hickey, J. 1976. Terrorism and Television. *TV Guide* July, pp. 8–13.

Higbee, K. 1969. Fifteen Years of Fear Arousal: Research on Threat Appeals, 1953–1968. *Psychological Bulletin* 72:426–444.

Himmelwitt, H. T. 1980. Social Influence and Television. In *Television and Social Behavior: Beyond Violence and Children*, edited by S. Withey and R. Abeles. Hillsdale, N.J.: Erlbaum, pp. 77–95.

Hinds, M. 1993. Teens Lie in Roads Like Film Hero; 1 Dies. *Denver Post* October 19, p. 2A.

Hirsch, P. 1980. The "Scary World" of the Nonviewer and Other Anomalies. *Communications Research* 7:403–456.

Hirsch, P. 1981. On Not Learning from One's Own Mistakes: A Reanalysis of Gerbner et al.'s Findings on Cultivation Analysis, Part II. *Communications Research* 8:3–37.

"Hit Man" Manual Protected by First Amendment. 1996. *The News Media and the Law* 20(4):23.

Hocking, J., Miller, G., and Fontes, N. 1978. Videotape in the Courtroom: Witness Deception. *Trial* 14:52–53.

Hoiberg, B., and Stires, L. 1973. The Effect of Several Types of Pretrial Publicity on the Guilty Attributions of Simulated Jurors. *Journal of Applied Social Psychology* 3:267–275.

Holaday, P., and Stoddard, G. 1933. *Getting Ideas from the Movies*. New York: Macmillan.

Horowitz, I., and Willging, T. 1984. *The Psychology of Law: Integrations and Applications*. New York: Little, Brown.

Hovland, C., Lumsdaine, A., and Sheffield, F. 1949. *Experiments on Mass Communication*. Princeton, N.J.: Princeton University Press.

How Jurors Feel About Videotaped Trials. 1980. *Criminal Justice Newsletter* 11:7–8.

Howitt, D. 1982. *Mass Media and Social Problems*. New York: Pergamon Press.

Howitt, D., and Cumberbatch, G. 1975. *Mass Media Violence and Society*. New York: Wiley.

Huesmann, L. 1982. Television Violence and Aggressive Behavior. In *Television and Behavior*. Vol. 2. *Technical Reviews*, edited by D. Pearl, L. Bouthilet, and J. Lazar. Washington, D.C.: National Institute of Mental Health, pp. 126–137.

Huesmann, R., and Eron, L. 1982. Television Violence and Aggressive Behavior. In *Television and Behavior: Ten Years of Scientific Programs and Implications for the 80s*, edited by D. Pearl, L. Bouthilet, and J. Lazar. Washington D.C.: National Institute of Mental Health.

Huesmann, R., and Eron, L. 1983. Factors Influencing the Effect of Television Violence on Children. In *Learning from Television: Psychological and educational Research*, edited by S. Howe. New York: Academic Press.

Hughes, H. 1940. *News and the Human Interest Story*. Chicago: University of Chicago Press.

Hughes, M. 1980. The Fruits of Cultivation Analysis: A Reexamination of Some Effects of Television Watching. *Public Opinion Quarterly* 44:287–302.

Hughes, S. 1987. The Reporting of Crime in the Press: A Study of Newspaper Reports in 1985. *Cambrian Law Review* 18:35–51.

Humphries, D. 1981. Serious Crime, News Coverage and Ideology: A Content Analysis of Crime Coverage in a Metropolitan Paper. *Crime and Delinquency* 27: 191–205.

Hyman, H., and Sheatsley, P. 1947. Some Reasons Why Information Campaigns Fail. *Public Opinion Quarterly* 11:412–423.

Ibarra, P. R., and Kitsuse, J. J. 1993. Vernacular Constituents of Moral Discourse: An Interactionist Proposal for the Study of Social Problems. In *Reconsidering Social Construction*, edited by J. Holstein and G. Miller. New York: Aldine de Gruyter, pp. 25–58.

Imrich, D., Mullin, C., and Linz, D. 1990. Sexually Violent Media and Criminal Justice Policy. In *The Media and Criminal Justice Policy*, edited by R. Surette. Springfield, Ill.: Thomas, pp. 103–123.

In Re Judicial Conference Guidelines. 1990. *Media Law Reporter* 18:1270–1272.

Inciardi, J. A., and Dee, J. L. 1987. From the Keystone Cops to Miami Vice: Images of Policing in American Popular Culture. *Journal of Popular Culture* 21:84–102.

Inge, T. 1990. *Comics as Culture*. Jackson: University Press of Mississippi.

Intons-Peterson, M., Roskos-Ewoldsen, B., Thomas, L., Shirley, M., and Blut, D. 1989. Will Educational Materials Reduce Negative Effects of Exposure to Sexual Violence? *Journal of Social and Clinical Psychology* 8:256–275.

Irwin, A. R., and Gross, A. 1995. Cognitive Tempo, Violent Video Games, and Aggressive Behavior in Young Boys. *Journal of Family Violence* 10:337–350.

Irwin, J., and Austin, J. 1994. *It's about Time: American's Imprisonment Binge*. Belmont, Calif.: Wadsworth.

Isaacs, N. 1961. The Crime of Crime Reporting. *Crime and Delinquency* 7:312–320.

Israel, H., Simmons W., and Robinson, J. 1972. Demographic Characteristics of Viewers of Television Violence and News Programs. In *Television and Social Behavior: Reports and Papers*. Vol. IV. *Television in Day-to-Day Life: Patterns of Use*. A technical report to the Surgeon General's Scientific Advisory Committee on Television and Social Behavior, edited by E. Rubinstein, G. Comstock, and J. Murray. Washington, D.C.: U.S. Government Printing Office.

Iyengar, S. 1991. *Is Anyone Responsible? How Television Frames Political Issues*. Chicago: University of Chicago Press.

Iyengar, S., and Kinder, D. 1987. *News That Matters: Agenda-Setting and Priming in a Television Age*. Chicago: University of Chicago Press.

Iyengar, S., Peters, M., and Kinder, D. 1982. Experimental Demonstrations of the "Not-So-Minimal" Consequences of Television News Programs. *American Political Science Review* 76:848–858.

Jacobs, H., and Linberry, R. 1982. *Governmental Response to Crime: Crime and Governmental Responses in American Cities*. Washington, D.C.: National Institute of Justice.

Jacobs, J. 1961. *The Death and Life of Great American Cities*. New York: Random House.

Jacobs, T. 1980. The Chilling Effect in Press Cases: Judicial Thumb on the Scales. *Harvard Civil Rights–Civil Liberties Law Review* 15:685–712.

Jaffe, L. 1965. Trial by Newspaper. *New York University Law Review* 40:504–524.

Jameson, F. 1992. *Postmodernism*. Durham, N.C.: Duke University Press.

Janis, I., and Feshbach, S. 1953. Effects of Fear-Arousing Communications. *Journal of Abnormal and Social Psychology* 48:78–92.

Janowitz, M. 1979. Collective Racial Violence: A Contemporary History. In *Violence in America*, edited by H. Graham and T. Gurr. Thousand Oaks, Calif.: Sage, pp. 261–286.

Jarhnig, W., Weaver, D., and Fico, F. 1981. Reporting and Fearing Crime in Three Communities. *Journal of Communication* 31:88–96.

Jeffery, C. R. 1990. Media Technology in Crime Control: History and Implications. In *Media and Criminal Justice Policy*, edited by R. Surette. Springfield, Ill.: Thomas, pp. 289–298.

Jenkins, B. 1975. *International Terrorism: A New Mode of Conflict*. Los Angeles: Crescent.

Jenkins, P. 1992. *Intimate Enemies: Moral Panics in Contemporary Great Britain*. Hawthorne, N.Y.: Aldine de Gruyter

Jenkins, P. 1994. *Using Murder: The Social Construction of Serial Murder*. Hawthorne, N.Y.: Aldine de Gruyter.

Jensen, E., Gerber, L. G., and Babcock, G. 1991. The New War on Drugs: Grassroots Movement or Political Construction? *Journal of Drug Issues* 21:651–667.

Jensen, J. 1993. POW! How Comic Magazines Are Riding High. *Advertising Age* March 8, p. 33.

Jerin, R., and Fields, C. 1995. Murder and Mayhem in *USA Today*: A Quantitative Analysis of the National Reporting of States' News. In *Media, Process, and the Social Construction of Crime*, edited by G. Barak. New York: Garland, pp. 187–202.

Jo, E., and Berkowitz, L. 1994. A Priming Effect Analysis of Media Influences: An Update. *Media Effects Advances in Theory and Research*, edited by J. Bryant and D. Zillman. Hillsdale, N.J.: Erlbaum.

Johnson, C. 1978. Perspectives on Terrorism. In *The Terrorist Reader: A Historical Anthology*, edited by L. Laqueur. Philadelphia: Temple University Press, pp. 267–285.

Johnson, D. 1983. Shooting Down TV's Cop Shows. *TV Guide* April 9, pp. 47–52.

Johnson, M. 1994. *Electronic Media Coverage of Federal Civil Proceedings: An Evaluation of the Pilot Program in Six District Courts and Two Courts of Appeal.* Washington D.C.: Federal Judicial Center.

Johnston, J., Hawkins, D., and Michner, A. 1994. Homicide Reporting in Chicago Dailies. *Journalism Quarterly* 71:860–872.

Jones, E. T. 1976. The Press as Metropolitan Monitor. *Public Opinion Quarterly* 40:239–244.

Jones, S. E. 1987. Judge Versus Attorney Conducted Voir Dire: An Empirical Investigation of Juror Candor. *Law and Human Behavior* 11:131–146.

Joseph, G. 1982. Videotapes as Evidence: Reviewing the Cases. *National Law Journal* 6:1–3.

Joseph, G. 1986. Demonstrative Videotape Evidence. *Trial* 22:60–66.

Jowett, G., and Linton, J. 1980. *Movies as Mass Communication.* Thousand Oaks, Calif.: Sage.

Judges Deny Court Camera Use. 1990. *News Media and the Law* 14:40–42.

Junke, R., Vought, C., Pyszczynski, T., Dane, F., Losure, B., and Wrightsman, L. 1979. Effects of Presentation Mode upon Mock Jurors' Reactions to a Trial. *Personality and Social Psychology Bulletin* 5:36–39.

Jurors' Knowledge of Lie Detector Test Raises Presumption of Partiality. 1984. *Criminal Law Reporter* 35(5), 2082–2084.

Just Like the Movie: Teen Tried to Poison Playmate in Spat Over Film Video. 1991. *Miami Herald* September 1, p. A-1.

Kaminski, E., Fontes, N., and Miller, G. 1978. Videotape in the Courtroom. *Trial* 14:38–42, 64.

Kania, R., and Tanhan, R. 1987. *Rise and Fall of Television Crime.* Paper presented at the annual meeting of the American Society of Criminology, November, Montreal, Canada.

Kaplan, J., and Skolnick, J. 1982. *Criminal Justice.* Mineola, N.Y.: Foundation Press.

Kaplan, S., and Baxter, L. 1982. Antisocial and Prosocial Behavior on Prime-Time TV. *Journalism Quarterly* 59(3):478–482.

Kappeler, V., Blumberg, M., and Potter, G. 1993. *The Mythology of Crime and Criminal Justice.* Prospect Heights, Ill.: Waveland Press.

Katsh, M. 1989. *The Electronic Media and the Transformation of Law.* New York: Oxford University Press.

Katz, E., and Lazarsfeld, P. 1955. *Personal Influence.* New York: Free Press.

Katz, J. 1987. What Makes Crime "News"? In *Media, Culture, and Society*, Thousand Oaks, Calif.: Sage, Chapter 9, pp. 47–75.

Kennedy, D. 1985. Reporters and the Shield Law: A Differing Viewpoint. *Editor and Publisher* 118:44–45.

Kerr, N., Kramer, G., Carroll, J., and Alfini, J. 1991. On the Effectiveness of Voir Dire in Criminal Cases with Prejudicial Pretrial Publicity: An Empirical Study. *American University Law Review* 40:665–667.

Kessler, R., and Stipp, H. 1984. The Impact of Fictional Television Suicide Stories on American Fatalities. *American Journal of Sociology* 90:151–167.

Kessler, R., Downey, G., Milavsky, J., and Stipp, H. 1988. Clustering of Teenage Suicides after Television News Stories about Suicide: A Reconsideration. *American Journal of Psychiatry* 145:1379–1383.

Kirtley, J. 1990. Shield Laws and Reporter's Privilege—A National Assessment. In *The Media and Criminal Justice Policy*, edited by R. Surette. Springfield, Ill.: Thomas, pp. 163–176.

Kirtley, J. 1995. A Leap Not Supported by History: The Continuing Story of Cameras in the Federal Courts. *Government Information Quarterly* 12:367–389.

Kirtley, J. 1996a. Courts Maintain Secrecy of Grand Jury Deliberations. *NEPA Bulletin* January, p. 6.

Kirtley, J. 1996b. Limiting Media Access to Prisoners. *American Journalism Review* March, p. 50.

Kirtley, J. 1996c. Hitting "Hit Man" In the Pocketbook. *American Journalism Review* April, p. 51.

Klain, J. 1989. *International Television and Video Almanac.* New York: Quigley.

Klapper, J. 1960. *The Effects of Mass Communication.* New York: Free Press.

Klein, F., and Jess, P. 1966. Prejudicial Publicity: Its Effects on Law School Mock Juries. *Journalism Quarterly* 43:113–116.

Klein, J., Brown, J., Childers, K., Oliceri, J., Porter, C., and Dykers, C. 1993. Adolescents' Risky Behavior and Mass Media Use. *Pediatrics* 92:24–31.

Knight, S. 1980. *Form and Ideology in Crime Fiction.* Bloomington: Indiana University Press.

Kohn, P., Goodstadt, M., Cook, G., Sheppard, M., and Chan, G. 1982. The Ineffectiveness of Threat Appeals about Drinking and Driving. *Accident Analysis and Prevention* 14:458–466.

Kosky, I. 1975. Videotape in Ohio: Take 2. *Judicature* 59:220–238.

Krafka, C. 1985. *Sexually Explicit, Sexually Violent, and Violent Media: Effects of Multiple Naturalistic Exposures and Debriefing on Female Viewers.* Unpublished Ph.D. dissertation, University of Wisconsin–Madison.

Kramer, G., and Kerr, N. 1989. Laboratory Simulation and Bias in the Study of Juror Behavior: A Methodological Note. *Law and Human Behavior* 13:89–99.

Kramer, G., Kerr, N., and Carroll, J. 1990. Pretrial Publicity, Judicial Remedies, and Jury Bias. *Law and Human Behavior* 14:409–438.

Kraus, S., and Davis, D. 1976. *The Effects of Mass Communication on Political Behavior.* University Park: Pennsylvania State University Press.

Krauss, G., and Bonora, B. 1983. *Jurywork: Systematic Techniques.* 2nd ed. New York: Clark Broadman.

Krutnik, F. *1991. In a Lonely Street: Film Noir, Genre, Masculinity.* New York: Routledge.

Kubey, R., and Csikszentmihalyi, M. 1990. *Television and the Quality of Life: How Viewing Shapes Everyday Experience.* Hillsdale, N.J.: Erlbaum.

Kurtz, H. 1993. *Media Circus.* New York: Random House.

Kutchinsky, B. 1972. Towards an Explanation of the Decrease in Registered Sex Crimes in Copenhagen. In *Erotica and Antisocial Behavior.* Vol. VII. U.S. Commission on Obscenity and Pornography. Washington, D.C.: U.S. Government Printing Office, pp. 263–310.

Kutchinsky, B. 1985. Pornography and Its Effects in Denmark and the United States: A Rejoinder and Beyond. *Comparative Social Research* 8:301–330.

Kutchinsky, B. 1991. Pornography and Rape: Theory and Practice? Evidence from Crime in Four Countries where Pornography Is Easily Available. *Journal of Law and Psychology* 26:47–64.

Lancaster, D. 1984. *Cameras in the Courtroom: A Study of Two Trials.* Research Report No. 14. Bloomington: Center for New Communications, Indiana University.

Lang, D., and Lang, K. 1983. *The Battle for Public Opinion.* New York: Columbia University Press.

Langer, S. 1980. Fear in the Deterrence of Delinquency: A Critical Analysis of the Rahway State Prison Lifers' Program. Ann Arbor, Mich.: University Microfilms International Dissertation, City University of New York.

Langevin, R., Lang, R., Wright, P., Handy, L., Frenzel, R., and Black, E. 1988. Pornography and Sexual Offenders. *Annals of Sex Research* 1:335–362.

Las Vegas, Nevada. 1978. Video Arraignment Demonstration Project. Grant proposal to the Law Enforcement Assistance Administration.

Lasorsa, D., and Wanta, W. 1990. Effects of Personal, Interpersonal and Media Experiences on Issue Saliences. *Journalism Quarterly* 67:804–813.

Lavrakas, P., Rosenbaum, D., and Lurigio, A. 1990. Media Cooperation with Police: The Case of Crime Stoppers. In *Media and Criminal Justice Policy*, edited by R. Surette. Springfield, Ill.: Thomas, pp. 225–242.

Lawyers Aren't Convinced That TV Belongs in Courtrooms. 1979. *American Bar Association Journal* 65:1306–1308.

Lazarsfeld, P., Berelson, B., and Gaudet, H. 1948. *The People's Choice.* New York: Columbia University Press.

Lee, A. 1937. *The Daily Newspaper in America.* New York: Macmillan.

Lefcourt, H., Barnes, K., Parke, R., and Schwartz, F. 1966. Anticipated Social Censure and Aggression-Conflict as Mediators of Response to Aggression Induction. *Journal of Social Psychology* 70:251–263.

Leff, D., Protess, D., and Brooks, S. 1986. Crusading Journalism: Changing Public Attitudes and Policy-Making Agendas. *Public Opinion Quarterly* 50:300–315.

Lefkowitz, H., Eron, L., Walder, R., and Huesmann, L. 1971. Television Violence and Child Aggression: A Follow-Up Study. In *Television and Social Behavior,* Vol. 3, *Television and Adolescent Aggressiveness,* edited by G. Comstock and E. Rubinstein. Washington D.C.: U.S. Government Printing Office.

Leifer, A., and Roberts, D. 1972. Children's Responses to Television Violence. In *Television and Social Behavior.* Vol. 2. *Television and Social Learning,* edited by J. Murray, E. Rubinstein, and G. Comstock. National Institute of Mental Health. Washington, D.C.: U.S. Government Printing Office, pp. 43–180.

Lesser, G. 1974. *Children and Television: Lessons from "Sesame Street."* New York: Vintage Books.

Lesyna, K., and Phillips, D. 1989. Suicide and the Media: Research and Policy Implication. In *Preventive Strategies on Suicide.* New York: World Health Organization Publication.

Letkemann, P. 1973. *Crime as Work.* Englewood Cliffs, N.J.: Prentice Hall.

Leukefeld, C. 1991. The Role of the National Institute on Drug Abuse in Drug Abuse Prevention Research. In *Persuasive Communication and Drug Abuse Prevention,* edited by L. Donohew, H. Sypher, and W. Bukoski. Hillsdale, N.J.: Erlbaum, pp. 21–34.

Levine, J. 1992. *Juries and Politics.* Pacific Grove, Calif.: Brooks/Cole.

Levine, P. 1987. Invasion of Privacy and the News Media. In *The Reporter's Handbook.* Tallahassee: Florida Bar Association.

Levine, P., and Bussian, J. 1987. Through the Long Lens—Legitimate News or Invasion of Privacy. In *The Reporter's Handbook.* Tallahassee: Florida Bar Association.

Lewis, R. 1984. The Media, Violence and Criminal Behavior. In *Justice and the Media*, edited by R. Surette, Springfield, Ill.: Thomas, pp. 51–69.

Lichter, L., and Lichter, S. 1983. *Prime Time Crime*. Washington, D.C.: Media Institute.

Lichter, S. 1988. Media Power: The Influence of Media on Politics and Business. *Florida Policy Review* 4:35–41.

Lichter, S., and Amundson, D. 1994. *A Day of TV Violence 1992 vs. 1994*. Washington D.C.: Center for Media and Public Affairs.

Lieberman, J. K. 1976. Will Courts Meet the Challenge of Technology? *Judicature* 60(2):84–91.

Liebert, R. M., Neale, J., and Davidson, E. 1973. *The Early Window: Effects of Television on Children and Youth*. New York: Pergamon Press.

Lindesmith, A. 1965. *The Addict and the Law*. Bloomington: Indiana University Press.

Linz, D. 1989. Exposure to Sexually Explicit Materials and Attitudes toward Rape: A Comparison of Study Results. *Journal of Sex Research* 26(1):50–84.

Linz, D., Donnerstein, E., and Penrod, S. 1984. The Effects of Long-Term Exposure to Filmed Violence against Women. *Journal of Communication* 34:130–147.

Linz, D., Donnerstein, E., and Penrod, S. 1988. The Effects of Long-Term Exposure to Violent and Sexually Degrading Depictions of Women. *Journal of Personality and Social Psychology* 55:100–110.

Lipetz, M. 1980. Routine and Deviations: The Strength of the Courtroom Work Group in the Misdemeanor Court. *International Journal of Sociology of the Law* 8:47–60.

Lippmann, W. 1922. *Public Opinion*. New York: Macmillan.

Lipsky, M. 1971. Street-Level Bureaucracy and the Analysis of Urban Reform. *Urban Affairs Quarterly* 6(June):391–409.

Liska, A., and Baccaglini, W. 1990. Feeling Safe by Comparison: Crime in the Newspapers. *Social Problems* 37:360–374.

Livingstone, N. 1982. *The War against Terrorism*. Lexington, Mass.: Heath.

Loften, J. 1966. *Justice and the Press*. Boston: Beacon Press.

Long, W. 1995. Video Patrol Takes a Bite out of Crime in Chilean Capital. *Miami Herald* February 5, p. 18A.

Lotz, R. 1979. Public Anxiety about Crime. *Pacific Sociology Review* 22:241–254.

Lotz, R. 1991. *Crime and the American Press*. New York: Prager.

Lowery, S., and DeFleur, M. 1983. *Milestones in Mass Communication Research*. White Plains, N.Y.: Longman.

Lowney, K., and Best, J. 1995. Stalking Strangers and Lovers: Changing Media Typifications of a New Crime Problem. In *Images of Issues Typifying*

Contemporary Social Problems, edited by J. Best. Hawthorne, N.Y.: Aldine de Gruyter, pp. 33–58.

Lowry, D. 1971. Gresham's Law and Network TV News Selection. *Journal of Broadcasting* 15:397–408.

Lynn, K. 1979. Violence in American Literature and Folklore. In *Violence in America: Historical and Comparative Perspectives*, edited by H. Graham and T. Gurr. Thousand Oaks, Calif.: Sage, pp. 133–143.

Lynxwiler, J., and DeCorte, C. 1995. Claims-Making and the Moral Discourse of Hard Core Rap Music. *Perspectives on Social Problems* 7:3–27.

Lyon, D. 1994. *The Surveillance Society*. Minneapolis: University of Minnesota Press.

Macdonald, M. 1995. *Representing Women: Myths of Femininity in the Popular Media*. London: Arnold.

MacKuen, M. 1981. Social Communication and the Mass Policy Agenda. In *More Than News: Media Power in Public Affairs*, edited by M. MacKuen and S. Coombs. Thousand Oaks, Calif.: Sage, pp. 19–146.

MacKuen, M. 1984. Exposure to Information, Belief Integration, and Individual Responsiveness to Agenda Change. *American Political Science Review* 78:372–391.

Madden, W. 1969. Illinois Pioneers Videotaping of Trials. *American Bar Association Journal* 55:457–459.

Maguire, B. 1988. Image vs. Reality: An Analysis of Prime-Time Television Crime and Police Programs. *Crime and Justice* 11(1):165–188.

Maguire, K., and Pastore, A., eds. 1995. *Sourcebook of Criminal Justice Statistics—1994*. Bureau of Justice Statistics and Hindelang Criminal Justice Research Center. Washington D.C.: U.S. Government Printing Office.

Maguire, W. 1980. "Scared Straight!" Discussion. In *Forensic Psychology and Psychiatry*, edited by F. Wright, C. Bahn, and R. Rieber. New York: Academy of Sciences.

Mahan, S., and Lawrence, R. 1996. "Media and Mayhem in Corrections: The Role of the Media in Prison Riots." *Prison Journal* 76(4):420–441.

Major Setback for the News Media. 1983. *Crime Control Digest* 17(13):9.

Making News. 1991. *Consumer Reports* 56:693–694.

Malamuth, N. 1981. Rape Proclivity among Males. *Journal of Social Issues* 37:138–157.

Malamuth, N. 1983. Factors Associated with Rape as Predictors of Laboratory Aggression against Women. *Journal of Personality and Social Psychology* 45:432–442.

Malamuth, N. 1986. Predictors of Naturalistic Sexual Aggression. *Journal of Personality and Social Psychology* 50:953–962.

Malamuth, N., and Briere, J. 1986. Sexual Violence in the Media: Indirect Effects on Aggression against Women. *Journal of Social Issues* 42:75–92.

Malamuth, N., and Ceniti, J. 1986. Repeated Exposure to Violent and Nonviolent Pornography: Likelihood of Raping Ratings and Laboratory Aggression against Women. *Aggressive Behavior* 12:129–137.

Malamuth, N., and Check, J. 1980. Penile Tumescence and Perceptual Responses to Rape as a Function of Victim's Perceived Reactions. *Journal of Applied Social Psychology* 10:528–547.

Malamuth, N., and Check, J. 1981. The Effects of Mass Media Exposure on Acceptance of Violence against Women: A Field Experiment. *Journal of Research in Personality* 15:436–446.

Malamuth, N., and Check, J. 1983. Sexual Arousal to Rape Depictions: Individual Differences. *Journal of Abnormal Psychology* 92:55–67.

Malamuth, N., and Check, J. 1985. The Effects of Aggressive Pornography on Beliefs of Rape Myths: Individual Differences. *Journal of Research in Personality* 19:299–320.

Malamuth, N., and Donnerstein, E., eds. 1984. *Pornography and Sexual Aggression.* New York: Academic Press.

Malamuth, N., and Donnerstein, E. 1982. The Effects of Aggressive Pornographic Mass Media Stimuli. In *Advances in Experimental Social Psychology,* Vol. 15, edited by L. Berkowitz. New York: Academic Press, pp. 104–132.

Malamuth, N., and Spinner, B. 1980. A Longitudinal Content Analysis of Sexual Violence in the Best-Selling Erotic Magazines. *Journal of Sex Research* 16:226–237.

Malamuth, N., Check, J., and Briere, J. 1986. Sexual Arousal in Response to Aggression: Ideological, Aggressive and Sexual Correlates. *Journal of Personality and Social Psychology* 14:399–408.

Malamuth, N., Haber, S., and Feshbach, S. 1980a. Testing Hypotheses Regarding Rape: Exposure to Sexual Violence, Sex Differences, and the "Normality" of Rapists. *Journal of Research in Personality* 14:121–137.

Malamuth, N., Heim, M., and Feshbach, S. 1980b. The Sexual Responsiveness of College Students to Rape Depictions: Inhibitory and Disinhibitory Effects. *Journal of Personality and Social Psychology* 38:399–408.

Mandel, E. 1984. *Delightful Murder: A Social History of the Crime Story.* Minneapolis: University of Minnesota Press.

Mannheim, K. 1952. *Essays on the Sociology of Knowledge.* Edited by P. Kecskemeti. New York: Routledge.

Mannheim, K. 1953. *Essays on the Sociology of Culture.* Edited and translated by E. Mannheim and P. Kecskemeti. New York: Routledge.

Manning, P. forthcoming. Media Loops. In *Popular Culture, Crime, and Justice.* Belmont, Calif.: Wadsworth.

Marcus, P. 1982. The Media in the Courtroom: Attending, Reporting, Televising Criminal Cases. *Indiana Law Journal* (Spring): 235–287.

Marcuse, H. 1972. *One-Dimensional Man.* London: Abacus.

Marighella, C. (n.d.). *Minimanual of the Urban Guerrilla.* Havana: Tricontinental.

Marks, A. 1987. *Television Exposure, Fear of Crime, and Concern about Serious Illness.* Unpublished Ph.D. dissertation, Northwestern University, Evanston, Ill.

Marsh, H. 1991. A Comparative Analysis of Crime Coverage in Newspapers in the United States and Other Countries from 1960 to 1989: A Review of the Literature. *Journal of Criminal Justice* 19:67–80

Marshall, L. 1983. *Juror, Judge and Counsel Voir Dire Perceptions and Behavior in Two Illinois State Courts.* Unpublished Ph.D. dissertation, Boston University, Boston.

Marshall, W. 1988. The Use of Sexually Explicit Stimuli by Rapists, Child Molesters, and Non-offenders. *Journal of Sex Research* 25:267–280.

Martens, F., and Cunningham-Niederer, M. 1985. Media Magic, Mafia Mania. *Federal Probation* 49(2): 60–68.

Martin, D., and Sussman, P. 1993. *Committing Journalism: The Prison Writings of Red Hog.* New York: Norton.

Marx, G. 1985. The Surveillance Society. *Futurist* June, pp. 21–26.

Marzuk, P. M., Tardiff, K., and Hirsch, C. S. 1992. The Epidemiology of Murder-Suicide. *Journal of American Medical Association* 267:3179–3183.

Matelski, M. J. 1991. *Daytime Television Programming.* Boston: Focal Press.

Mathews, J. 1991. LA Sheriff's Deputies Kill 4, but Outrage Is Muted. *Miami Herald* Sunday, October 13, p. 8A.

Mathiesen, T. 1987. The Eagle and the Sun: On Panoptical Systems and Mass Media in Modern Society. *Transcarceration: Essays in the Sociology of Social Control,* edited by J. Lowman, R. Menzies and T. Palys. Brookfield, Vt.: Gower, pp. 59–76.

Mawby, R., and Brown, J. 1984. Newspaper Images of the Victim: A British Study. *Victimology* 9(1):82–94.

Mayer, M. 1987. *Making News.* New York: Doubleday.

Mayhew, P., Clarke, R., Burrows, J., Hough, J., and Winchester, S. 1979. *Crime in Public View.* Home Office Research Study no. 49. London: Her Majesty's Stationery Office.

Mazur, A. 1982. Bomb Threats and the Mass Media: Evidence for a Theory of Suggestion. *American Sociological Review* 47:407–411.

McArthur, C. 1972. *Underworld U.S.A.* New York: Viking Press.

McClosky, H., and Zaller, J. 1984. *The American Ethos: Public Attitudes toward Capitalism and Democracy.* Cambridge, Mass.: Harvard University Press.

McCombs, M., and Shaw, D. 1972. The Agenda-Setting Function of Mass Media. *Public Opinion Quarterly* 36:176–187.

McCombs, M., and Weaver, D. 1973. *Voters' Need for Orientation and Use of Mass Communication*. Paper presented at the annual meeting of the International Communication Association, Montreal.

McConnell, G. 1967. *Private Power and American Democracy*. New York: Knopf.

McCrystal, J. L. 1976. The Case for PRVTTs. *Trial* 12(7):56–57.

McCrystal, J. L. 1978. Videotaped Trials: A Primer. *Judicature* 61(6):250–256.

McGruff Campaign Team (n.d.). National Citizens' Crime Prevention Three-Year Public Education Program, FY 1990–FY 1992. Photocopy, planning document provided by the National Crime Prevention Council, Washington, D.C.

McGuire, W. 1986. The Myth of Massive Media Impact: Savagings and Salvagings. In *Public Communication and Behavior*, edited by G. Comstock. New York: Academic Press, pp. 175–257.

McKenzie-Mohr, M., and Zanna, M. 1990. Treating Women as Sexual Objects: Look to the (Gender Schematic) Male Who Has Viewed Pornography. *Social Psychology Bulletin* 16(2):296–308.

McLeod, J., Becker, L., and Byrnes, J. 1974. Another Look at the Agenda-Setting Function of the Press. *Communication Research* 1:137–144.

McLuhan, M. 1962. *The Gutenberg Galaxy: The Making of Typographical Man*. Toronto: University of Toronto Press.

McLuhan, M. 1964. *Understanding Media: The Extensions of Man*. New York: McGraw-Hill.

McLuhan, M., and Fiore, Q. 1967. *The Medium Is the Message: An Inventory of Effects*. New York: Random House.

McLynn, F. 1989. *Crime and Punishment in Eighteenth-century England*. New York: Routledge.

Mehrabian, A., and Wixen, W. 1986. Preferences for Individual Videogames as a Function of Their Emotional Effects on Players. *Journal of Applied Social Psychology* 16:3–15.

Mehta, M., and Plaza, D. 1994. A Content Analysis of Pornographic Images on the Internet. Queens University and York University. Internet document: http://www.queensu.ca/epu/mehta/porn.htm.

Mendelsohn, H. 1973. Some Reasons Why Information Campaigns Can Succeed. *Public Opinion Quarterly* 37:50–61.

Merton, R. 1946. *Mass Persuasion: The Social Pathology of a War Bond Drive*. Westport, Conn.: Greenwood Press.

Meyer, T. 1972. Effects of Viewing Justified and Unjustified Real Film Violence on Aggressive Behavior. *Journal of Personality and Social Psychology* 23:21–29.

Meyers, M. 1994. News of Battering. *Journal of Communication* 44:47–63.

Meyers, M. 1996. *News Coverage of Violence against Women*. Thousand Oaks, Calif.: Sage.

Meyrowitz, J. 1985a. *No Sense of Place*. New York: Oxford University Press.

Meyrowitz, J. 1985b. Interview by Connie Lauerman, Chicago Tribune Service. *Miami Herald* May 21, p. F1.

Miami Beach Gives Up on Street Anti-Crime Cameras. 1984. *Crime Control Digest* 18(24):2–3.

Miami Beach Police Department. 1983. Micro-Video Project Yearly Report.

Miami Beach Public Information Office. 1982. News release. February.

Milander, J., and Power, T. 1995. Caught on Campus Camera. *Miami Herald* November 5, pp. 1B, 5B.

Milavsky, J., Kessler, R., Stipp, H., and Rubins, W. 1982a. Television and Aggression: Results of a Panel Study. In *Television and Behavior*. Vol. 2. *Technical Reviews*, edited by D. Pearl, L. Bouthilet, and J. Lazar. Washington, D.C.: U.S. Department of Health and Human Services, National Institute of Public Health, pp. 138–157.

Milavsky, J. Kessler, R., Stipp, H., and Rubins, W. 1982b. *Television and Aggression: A Panel Study*. New York: Academic Press.

Milgram, S., and Shotland, R. 1973. *Television and Antisocial Behavior: Field Experiments*. New York: Academic Press.

Miller R., and Holstein J., eds. 1993. *Constructionist Controversies: Issues in Social Problems Theory*. Hawthorne, N.Y.: Aldine de Gruyter.

Miller, G. 1976. The Effects of Videotaped Trial Materials on Juror Response. In *Psychology and the Law*, edited by C. Nemeth and N. Vidmar. Lexington, Mass.: Heath, pp. 185–208.

Miller, G., and Fontes, N. 1979a. Trial by Videotape. *Psychology Today* May, pp. 92, 95–96, 99–100, 112.

Miller, G., and Fontes, N. 1979b. *Videotape on Trial*. Thousand Oaks, Calif.: Sage.

Miller, G., and Siebert, F. 1974. Effects of Videotaped Testimony on Information Processing and Decision-Making in Jury Trials. Progress Report no. 1, February. NSF-RANN Grant #GI 38398, Dept. of Communications. East Lansing: Michigan State University.

Miller, G., and Siebert, F. 1975. Effects of Videotaped Testimony on Information Processing and Decision-Making in Jury Trials. Progress Report no. 2, February. NSF-RANN Grant #GI 38398, Dept. of Communications. East Lansing: Michigan State University.

Minow, N., and Cate, R. 1991. Who Is an Impartial Juror in the Age of Mass Media? *American University Law Review* 40:631–639.

Mischel, W. 1981. *Introduction to Personality*. Austin, Tex.: Holt, Rinehart & Winston.

Molitor, F., and Hirsch, K. 1994. *The Effect of Media Violence on Children's Toleration of Real-Life Aggression: A Replication and Extension of the Drabman and Thomas Experiments*. Paper presented at the International Conference on Violence in the Media, New York, October 3–4.

Molotch, H., and Lester, M. 1981. News as Purposive Behavior: On the Strategic Use of Routine

Events, Accidents and Scandals. In *The Manufacture of News*, edited by S. Cohen and J. Young. Thousand Oaks, Calif.: Sage, pp. 118–137.

Molotch, H., Protess, D., and Gordon, M. 1987. The Media–Policy Connections: Ecologies of News. In *Political Communication Research*, edited by D. L. Paletz. Norwood, N.J.: Ablex, pp. 26–48.

Monteleone, C. D. 1982. Videotape Depositions: Basic Pointers for a Skilled Presentation. *American Bar Association Journal* 68 (July): 863–865.

Mooney, L., and Fewell, C. 1989. Crime in One Long-Lived Comic Strip: An Evaluation of Chester Gould's "Dick Tracy." *American Journal of Economics and Sociology* 48(1):89–100.

Moran, G., and Culter, B. 1991. The Prejudicial Impact of Pretrial Publicity. *Journal of Applied Social Psychology* 21:345–367.

Mos, L. 1980. A Theoretical Perspective on Juvenile Intervention Programs: Discussion. In *Forensic Psychology and Psychiatry*, edited by F. Wright, C. Bahn, and R. Rieber. New York: Academy of Sciences.

Mould, D. 1988. The Pornography–Sexual Crime Debate. *Journal of Sex Research* 25:267–288.

Moynihan, D. 1969. *Maximum Feasible Misunderstanding*. New York: Free Press.

Mullin, C., and Linz, D. 1995. Desensitization and Resensitization to Violence against Women: Effects of Exposure to Sexually Violent Films on Judgements of Domestic Violence. *Journal of Personality and Social Psychology* 69:449–459.

Murdock, G., and Golding, P. 1977. Capitalism, Communication and Class Relations. In *Mass Communication and Society*, edited by J. Curran, M. Gurevitch, and J. Woollacott. London: Edward Arnold, pp. 12–43.

Murray, C. 1994. *Losing Ground*. New York: Basic Books.

Murray, J. 1980. *Television and Youth: 25 Years of Research*. Stanford, Wash.: Boys Town Center for the Study of Youth Development.

Murray, J. 1984. Cross-Cultural TV: Implications for Policy. In *Justice and the Media*, edited by R. Surette. Springfield, Ill.: Thomas, pp. 233–244.

Murray, J., and Clarke, P. 1980. Television and Story Telling: Media Influences on Children's Fantasies. *College and School Innovator* 11:4–7.

Murray, J., Hayes, A., and Smith, J. 1978. Sequential Analysis: Another Approach to Describing the Stream of Behavior in Children's Interactions. *Australian Journal of Psychology* 30:207–215.

Murray, T. 1978. Videotaped Depositions: The Ohio Experience. *Judicature* 61(6):258–261.

Mustonen, A., and Pulkkinen, L. 1993. Aggression in Television Programs in Finland. *Aggressive Behavior* 19:175–183.

National Commission on the Causes and Prevention of Violence (NCCPV). 1969. *Mass Media and Violence*. Vol. 9. Washington, D.C.: U.S. Government Printing Office.

National Institute of Mental Health (NIMH). 1982. *Television and Behavior: Ten Years of Scientific Progress and Implications for the Eighties*. Vol. 1. *Summary Report*. Rockville, Md.: Author.

Nava, M. 1988. Cleveland and the Press: Outrage and Anxiety in the Reporting of Child Sexual Abuse. *Feminist Review* 28:103–121.

Neale, S. 1980. *Genre*. England: British File Institute (distributed by University of Illinois Press, Champaign–Urbana).

Nelson, B. 1984. *Making an Issue of Child Abuse*. Chicago: University of Chicago Press.

Nelson, S. 1989. Crime-Time Television. *Law Enforcement Bulletin* 58(8):1–9.

Nemes, I. 1992. The Relationship between Pornography and Sex Crimes. *Journal of Psychology and Law* 20:450–481.

Nesson, C., and Koblenz, A. 1981. The Image of Justice: *Chandler v. Florida*. *Harvard Civil Rights–Civil Liberties Law Review* 16:405–413.

Nettler, G. 1982. *Killing One Another*. Cincinnati, Ohio: Anderson.

Nevins, F. 1995. Law School Seminar on Popular Fiction and Film. *Murder Is Academic* 3(Nov.):3,5.

New Downtown Video Patrol Program Uses Technology to Reduce Crime. 1996. Press Release from the Downtown Partnership of Baltimore. January 16.

New York City. 1983. Television Arraignment: Feasibility for New York City Criminal Courts. Photocopy, February.

Newman, G. 1990. Popular Culture and Criminal Justice: A Preliminary Analysis. *Journal of Criminal Justice* 18:261–274.

Newman, G. 1993. Batman and Justice: The True Story. *Humanity and Society* 17(3):297–320.

Newman, G. forthcoming. Popular Culture and Violence: Decoding the Violence of Popular Movies. In *Popular Culture, Crime, and Justice*, edited by F. Bailey and D. Hale. Belmont, Calif.: Wadsworth.

Newman, O. 1972. *Defensible Space: Crime Prevention through Urban Design*. New York: Macmillan.

Newman, O. 1975. Community of Interest—Design for Community Control. In *Architecture, Planning and Urban Crime*. Report to NACRO Conference, December 6, 1974, London.

Newman, O. 1976. *Design Guidelines for Creating Defensible Space*. NIJ/LEAA. Washington, D.C.: U.S. Government Printing Office.

Nienstedt, B. 1990. The Policy Effects of a DUI Law and a Publicity Campaign. In *The Media and Criminal Justice Policy*, edited by R. Surette. Springfield, Ill.: Thomas, pp. 193–203.

Nimmo, D., and Combs, J. E. 1983. *Mediated Political Realities*. White Plains, N.Y.: Longman.

Noble, G. 1983. Social Learning from Everyday Television (Children in Front of the Small Screen). In *Learning from Television Psychological and Educational Research*, edited by M. Howe. New York: Academic Press, pp. 101–124.

Noelle-Neumann, E. 1974. The Spiral of Silence. *Journal of Communication* 24:3–51.

Noelle-Neumann, E. 1980. Mass Media and Social Change in Developed Societies. In *Mass Communication Review Yearbook*, Vol. 1, edited by H. Wilhoit and L. de Bock. Thousand Oaks, Calif.: Sage, pp. 657–678.

Noelle-Neumann, E. 1983. The Effect of Media on Media Effects Research. *Journal of Communication* 33:157–165.

Nyberg, A. forthcoming. Comic Books and Juvenile Delinquency: A Historical Perspective. In *Popular Culture, Crime, and Justice*, edited by F. Bailey and D. Hale. Belmont, Calif.: Wadsworth.

O'Keefe, G. 1984. Public Views on Crime: Television Exposure and Media Credibility. In *Communication Yearbook 8*, edited by R. N. Bostrum. Thousand Oaks, Calif.: Sage, pp. 514–537.

O'Keefe, G. 1985a. Taking a Bite Out of Crime: The Impact of a Public Information Campaign. *Communication Research* 12:147–178.

O'Keefe, G. 1985b. Taking a Bite Out of Crime. *Society* 22:56–64.

O'Keefe, G., and Mendelsohn, H. 1984. *Taking a Bite Out of Crime: The Impact of a Mass Media Crime Prevention Campaign.* Washington, D.C.: U.S. Department of Justice, National Institute of Justice.

O'Keefe, G., and Reid, K. 1990. Media Public Information Campaigns and Criminal Justice Policy: Beyond "McGruff." In *Media and Criminal Justice Policy*, edited by R. Surette. Springfield, Ill.: Thomas, pp. 209–224.

O'Keefe, G., and Reid-Nash, K. 1987a. Crime News and Real-World Blues: The Effects of the Media on Social Reality. *Communication Research* 14:147–173.

O'Keefe, G., and Reid-Nash, K. 1987b. *Promoting Crime Prevention Competence Among the Elderly.* Washington, D.C.: U.S. Department of Justice, National Institute of Justice.

O'Keefe, G., Rosenbaum, D., Lavrakas, P., Reid, K., and Botta, R. 1996. *Taking a Bite Out of Crime.* Thousand Oaks, Calif.: Sage.

O'Keefe, T. 1971. The Anti-Smoking Commercials: A Study of Television's Impact on Behavior. *Public Opinion Quarterly* 35:242–248.

O'Neill, J. 1990. Computer to Handle Police Mugs. *Miami Herald* March 3, p. 4B.

Oliver, M. 1994. Portrayals of Crime, Race, and Aggression in "Reality-Based" Police Shows: A Content Analysis. *Journal of Broadcasting & Electronic Media* 38:179–192.

Oliver, M., and Armstrong, G. 1995. Predictors of Viewing and Enjoyment of Reality-Based and Fictional Crime Shows. *Journalism Quarterly* 72:559–570.

Orcutt, J., and Turner, J. 1993. Shocking Numbers and Graphic Accounts: Quantified Images of Drug Problems in the Print Media. *Social Problems* 40:190–206.

Ostroff, M., and Boyd, J. 1987. Television and Suicide. *New England Journal of Medicine* 3(6):876–877.

Ostroff, R., Behrends, R., Lee, K., and Oliphant, J. 1985. Adolescent Suicides Modeled after Television Movie. *American Journal of Psychiatry* 142:989–999.

Ostrow, J. 1993. MTV's "B and B" Ignites Call for Parental Guidance. *Denver Post* October 12, p. E1.

Otto, A., Dexter, H., and Penrod, S. 1991. *Pretrial Publicity and Jury Decision Making: Experimental Studies with Actual Cases.* Unpublished manuscript, University of Minnesota, Minneapolis.

Otto, A., Penrod, S., and Hirt, H. 1991. *The Influence of Pretrial Publicity on Juror Judgments in Civil Cases.* Unpublished manuscript, University of Minnesota, Minneapolis.

Otto, H. A. 1962. Sex and Violence on the American Newsstand. *Journalism Quarterly* 40:19–26.

Owens, D. 1983. Crime Stoppers Generates Valuable Tips. *Miami Herald* February 17, p. 15C.

Packer, H. 1968. *The Limits of the Criminal Sanction.* Stanford, Calif.: Stanford University Press.

Padawer-Singer, A., and Barton, H. 1975. The Impact of Pretrial Publicity on Jurors' Verdicts. In *The Jury System in America: A Critical Overview*, edited by R. Simon. Thousand Oaks, Calif.: Sage, pp. 123–139.

Padawer-Singer, A., Singer, A., and Singer, R. 1974. Voir Dire by Two Lawyers: An Essential Safeguard. *Judicature* 57:386–391.

Paddon, A. 1985. *Television Coverage of Criminal Trials with Cameras and Microphones: A Laboratory Experiment of Audience Effects.* Unpublished Ph.D. dissertation, University of Tennessee, Knoxville.

Padgett, V., and Brislin-Slutz, J. 1987. *Pornography, Erotica and Negative Attitudes Towards Women: The Effects of Repeated Exposure.* Unpublished manuscript, Marshall University, Huntsville, W.V.

Padgett, V., Brislin-Slutz, J., and Neal, J. 1989. Pornography, Erotica, and Attitudes toward Women: The Effects of Repeated Exposure. *Journal of Sex Research* 26:479–491.

Page, B., Shapiro, R., and Dempsey, G. 1987. What Moves Public Opinion? *American Political Science Review* 81:23–43.

Paik, H., and Comstock, G. 1994. The Effects of Television Violence on Antisocial Behavior: A Meta-Analysis. *Communication Research* 21:516–546.

Paisley, W. 1981. Public Communication Campaigns: The American Experience. In *Public Communication Campaigns*, edited by R. Rice and W. Paisley. Thousand Oaks, Calif.: Sage, pp. 15–38.

Palmer, E. 1973. Formative Research in the Production of Television for Children. In *Communications Technology and Social Policy*, edited by G. Gerbner, L. Gross, and R. Melody. New York: Wiley, pp. 229–245.

Palys, T. 1986. Testing the Common Wisdom: The Social Content of Video Pornography. *Canadian Psychology* 27:22–35.

Pandiani, J. 1978. Crime Time TV: If All We Knew Is What We Saw.… *Contemporary Crises* 2:437–458.

Papke, D. 1987. *Framing the Criminal.* Hamden, Conn.: Archon Books.

Parenti, M. 1978. *Power and the Powerless.* New York: St. Martin's Press.

Parish, J., and Pitts, M. 1976. *The Great Gangster Pictures.* Metuchen, N.J.: Scarecrow Press.

Park, R. 1940. News as a Form of Knowledge. *American Journal of Sociology* 45:669–686.

Parke, R. D., Berkowitz, L., Leyens, J., West, S., and Sebastian, R. 1977. Some Effects of Violent and Non-Violent Movies on the Behavior of Juvenile Delinquents. In *Advances in Experimental Social Psychology*, Vol. 10, edited by L. Berkowitz. New York: Academic Press, pp. 135–172.

Pate, J. 1978. *The Great Villains.* New York: Oxford University Press.

Patkin, T. 1994. *The Question of Violence in the Construction of Virtual Environments.* Paper presented at the International Conference on Violence in the Media, St. John's University, Oct. 3 and 4. New York.

Paulin, D. 1988. TV Tips Reap Innocent Suspects. *Miami News* November 29, p. 9A.

Payne, D. 1974. Newspapers and Crime: What Happens During Strike Periods. *Journalism Quarterly* 51:607–612.

Payne, D., and Payne, K. 1970. Newspapers and Crime in Detroit. *Journalism Quarterly* 47:233–238.

Pearl, D. 1984. Violence and Aggression. *Society* 21:17–20.

Pearl, D., Bouthilet, L., and Lazar, J., eds. 1982. *Television and Behavior: Ten Years of Scientific Progress and Implications for the Eighties.* Vols. 1–3. Washington, D.C.: U.S. Government Printing Office, National Institute of Mental Health.

Pease, S., and Love, C. 1984a. *The Prisoner's Perspective of Copycat Crime.* Paper presented at the annual meeting of the American Society of Criminology, November, Cincinnati, Ohio.

Pease, S., and Love, C. 1984b. The Copy-Cat Crime Phenomenon. In *Justice and the Media*, edited by R. Surette. Springfield, Ill.: Thomas, pp. 199–211.

Pember, D. 1984. *Mass Media Law.* 3rd ed. Dubuque, Iowa: W. C. Brown.

Pember, D. 1987. *Mass Media Law.* 4th ed. Dubuque, Iowa: W. C. Brown.

Perez-Pena, R. 1995. "How-To" Film May Have Inspired Subway Attack. *Miami Herald* November 27, p. A-3.

Perse, E., Ferguson, D., and McLeod, D. 1994. Cultivation in the Newer Media Environment. *Communication Research* 21:79–104.

Peterson, P., and Zill, T. 1980. *Television Viewing and Children's Intellectual, Social and Emotional Develop-ment.* Paper presented at the annual meeting of the American Association for Public Opinion Research, May, Washington, D.C.

Peterson, R., and Thurstone, L. 1933. *Motion Pictures and the Social Attitudes of Children.* New York: Macmillan.

Petty, R., and Priester, J. 1994. Mass Media Attitude Change: Implications of the Elaboration Likelihood Model of Persuasion. In *Media Effects Advances in Theory and Research*, edited by J. Bryant and D. Zillman. Hillsdale, N.J.: Erlbaum, pp. 91–122.

Pfau, M., and Parrot, R. 1993. *Persuasion Communication Campaigns.* Boston: Allyn & Bacon.

Pfuhl, E. 1992. Crimestoppers: The Legitimation on Snitching. *Justice Quarterly* 9(3):505–528.

Philadelphia's Popular Police Station. 1979. *Target* 8(2):1. Washington, D.C.: International City Management Association.

Phillips, D. 1974. The Influence of Suggestion on Suicide: Substantive and Theoretical Implications of the Werther Effect. *American Sociological Review* 39:340–354.

Phillips, D. 1977. Motor Vehicle Fatalities Increase Just after Publicized Suicide Stories. *Science* 196:1464–1465.

Phillips, D. 1978. Airplane Accident Fatalities Increase Just after Newspaper Stories about Murder and Suicide. *Science* 201:148–150.

Phillips, D. 1979. Suicide, Motor Vehicle Fatalities, and the Mass Media: Evidence toward a Theory of Suggestion. *American Journal of Sociology* 84:1150–1174.

Phillips, D. 1980. Airplane Accidents, Murder, and the Mass Media: Toward a Theory of Imitation. *Social Forces* 58:1001–1024.

Phillips, D. 1982a. The Behavioral Impact of Violence in the Mass Media: A Review of the Evidence from Laboratory and Non-Laboratory Investigations. *Sociology and Social Research* 66:387–398.

Phillips, D. 1982b. The Impact of Fictional Television Stories on U.S. Adult Fatalities: New Evidence of the Effect of Mass Media on Violence. *American Journal of Sociology* 87:1340–1359.

Phillips, D. 1983. The Impact of Mass Media Violence on Homicide. *American Sociological Research* 48:560–568.

Phillips, D., and Bollen, K. 1985. Same Time Last Year: Selective Data Dredging for Negative Findings. *American Sociological Review* 50:364–371.

Phillips, D., and Carstensen, L. 1986. Clustering of Teenage Suicides after Television News Stories about Suicide. *New England Journal of Medicine* 315:685–689.

Phillips, D., and Carstensen, L. 1988. The Effect of Suicide Stories on Various Demographic Groups, 1968–1985. *Suicide and Life-Threatening Behavior* 18:100–114.

Phillips, D., and Hensley, J. 1984. When Violence Is Rewarded or Punished: The Impact of Mass Media Stories on Homicide. *Journal of Communication* 34(3):101–116.

Phillips, D., and Paight, D. 1987. The Impact of Televised Movies about Suicide. *New England Journal of Medicine* 315:809–811.

Pierce, G., and Bowers, W. 1979. *The Impact of the Bartley-Fox Gun Law on Crime in Massachusetts.* Boston: Center for Applied Social Research, Northeastern University.

Pillsbury, S. 1997. Time, TV, and Criminal Justice: Second Thoughts on the Simpson Trial. *Criminal Law Bulletin* 59(3):3–28.

Platt, D. 1987. The Aftermath of Angie's Overdose: Is Soap (Opera) Damaging to Your Health? *British Medical Journal* 294:954–957.

Poland, J. 1988. *Understanding Terrorism.* Englewood Cliffs, N.J.: Prentice Hall.

Police Adopt Media Guidelines. 1985. *News Media and the Law* 9(3):31–32.

Police Take Shots at Street Crime. 1983. *Security World* 20(9):13, 15.

Porsdam, H. 1994. Law as Soap Opera and Game Show: The Case of the People's Court. *Journal of Popular Culture* 28(1):1–15.

Potter, J. 1996. *Representing Reality: Discourse, Rhetoric, and Social Construction.* Thousand Oaks, Calif.: Sage.

Potter, W. 1986. Perceived Reality and the Cultivation Hypothesis. *Journal of Broadcasting and Electronic Media* 30:159–174.

Powers, R. 1990. Review of *The Police Mystique,* by A. Bouza. *New York Times Review of Books* May 6, p. G8.

Pretrial Publicity—Habeas Corpus. 1984. *Criminal Law Reporter* 35(20):2366.

Price, J., Merrill, E., and Clause, M. 1992. The Depiction of Guns on Prime Time Television. *Journal of School Health* 62(1):15–19.

Prison Ban on Media Interviews Upheld. 1996. *News Media and the Law* 20(4):40.

Pritchard, D. 1985. Race, Homicide and Newspapers. *Journalism Quarterly* 62:500–507.

Pritchard, D. 1986. Homicide and Bargained Justice: The Agenda-Setting Effect of Crime News on Prosecutors. *Public Opinion Quarterly* 50:143–159.

Pritchard, D. 1992. The News Media and Public Policy Agendas. In *Public Opinion, the Press and Public Policy,* edited by D. Kennamer. New York: Praeger.

Pritchard, D., Dilts, J., and Berkowitz, D. 1987. Prosecutors' Use of External Agendas in Prosecuting Pornography Cases. *Journalism Quarterly* 64:392–398.

Privacy Exemption Surmountable. 1985. *News Media and the Law* 9(1):33–35.

Problems Frequent When Seeking Access to Inmates. 1989. *News Media and the Law* 13(4):6–7.

Protess, D., Cook, F. L., Doppelt, J., Ettema, J., Gordon, M., Leff, D., and Miller, P. 1991. *The Journalism of Outrage: Investigative Reporting and Agenda Building in America.* New York: Guilford Press.

Protess, D., Cook, S., Curtin, T., Gordon, M., Leff, D., McCombs, M., and Miller, P. 1987. The Impact of Investigative Reporting on Public Opinion and Policymaking: Targeting Toxic Waste. *Public Opinion Quarterly* 51:166–185.

Protess, D., Leff, D., Brooks, S., and Gordon, M. 1985. Uncovering Rape: The Watchdog Press and the Limits of Agenda Setting. *Public Opinion Quarterly* 49:19–37.

Publicity Didn't Require Venue Changes for Federal Defendants. 1984. *Criminal Law Reporter* 36(8):2140–2141.

Quinney, R. 1970. *The Social Reality of Crime.* New York: Little, Brown.

Quinney, R. 1974. *Critique of Legal Order.* New York: Little, Brown.

Quinsey, V., Rice, M., and Harris, G. 1995. Actuarial Prediction of Sexual Recidivism. *Journal of Interpersonal Violence* 10(1):85–106.

Quinsey, V., Rice, M., Harris, G., and LaLumierl, R. 1993. Assessing Treatment Efficacy in Outcome Studies of Sex Offenders. *Journal of Interpersonal Violence* 8(4):512–524.

Radin, E. 1964. *The Innocents.* Fairfield, N.J.: Morrow.

Radio, TV, Newspapers Rejected in Bid to Use Cameras in Court. 1984. *Criminal Justice Newsletter* 15(20):3–4.

Randall, D., Lee-Simmons, L., and Hagner, P. 1988. Common versus Elite Crime Coverage in Network News. *Social Science Quarterly* 69:910–929.

Random Killings Inspire Increase in People's Fear. 1996. *Orlando Sentinel* June 23, p. A-7

Ray, M., and Wilkie, W. 1970. Fear: The Potential of an Appeal Neglected in Marketing. *Journal of Marketing* 34:54–62.

Raymond, P. 1992. The Impact of a Televised Trial on Individuals' Information and Attitudes. *Judicature* 75(4):204–209.

Real, M. 1989. *Super Media: A Cultural Studies Approach.* Thousand Oaks, Calif.: Sage.

Reinarman, C. 1997. The Social Construction of Drug Scares. In *Constructions of Deviance,* edited by Patricia Adler and Peter Adler. Belmont, Calif.: Wadsworth.

Reinarman, C., and Levine, H. 1989. The Crack Attack: Politics and Media in America's Latest Drug Scare. In *Images of Issues: Typifying Contemporary Social Problems,* edited by J. Best. Hawthorne, N.Y.: Aldine de Gruyter, pp. 115–137.

Reinarman, C., and Levine, H. 1995. The Crack Attack: America's Latest Drug Scare, 1986–1992. In *Images of Issues: Typifying Contemporary Social Problems,* edited by J. Best. Hawthorne, N.Y.: Aldine de Gruyter, pp. 147–186.

Reiner, R. 1985. *The Politics of the Police.* New York: St. Martin's Press.

Rennie, Y. 1978. *The Search for Criminal Man.* San Francisco: New Lexington Press.

Report of the U.S. Task Force on Disorders and Terrorism, National Advisory Committee on Criminal Justice Standards and Goals. 1976. Washington D.C.: U.S. Government Printing Office.

Reppetto, R. 1974. *Residential Crime.* New York: Ballinger.

Riley, D., and Mayhew, P. 1980. *Crime Prevention Publicity: An Assessment.* Study no. 63. London: Her Majesty's Stationery Office.

Riley, S. 1973. Pretrial Publicity: A Field Study. *Journalism Quarterly* 50:17–23.

Roberts, D., and Bachen, C. 1981. Mass Communication Effects. *Annual Review of Psychology* 32:307–356.

Roberts, D., Herold, C., Hornby, M., King, S., Sterne, D., Whiteley, S., and Silverman, T. 1974. *Earth's a Big Blue Marble: A Report on the Impact of a Children's Television Series on Children's Opinions.* Stanford, Calif.: Stanford University Press.

Roberts, J., and Doob, A. 1990. News Media Influences on Public Views on Sentencing. *Law and Human Behavior* 14(5):451–468.

Roberts, J., and Edwards, D. 1989. Contextual Effects in Judgements of Crimes, Criminals and the Purpose of Sentencing. *Journal of Applied Social Psychology* 19(11):902–917.

Roberts, J., and Grossman, M. 1990. Crime Prevention and Public Opinion. *Canadian Journal of Criminology* 32:75–90.

Robinson, J. 1972. Mass Communication and Information Diffusion. In *Current Perspectives in Mass Communication Research,* edited by F. G. Kline and P. J. Tichenor. Thousand Oaks, Calif.: Sage, pp. 71–93.

Robinson, J. 1976. Interpersonal Influence in Election Campaigns: Two Step-Flow Hypotheses. *Public Opinion Quarterly* 40:304–319.

Robinson, M. 1974. The Impact of the Televised Watergate Hearings. *Journal of Communication* 24:17–30.

Robinson, M. 1976. Public Affairs Television and the Growth of Political Malaise. *American Political Science Review* 70:425–445.

Rockwell, J. H. 1983. Videophones and Closed-Circuit Television in Pretrial Proceedings. Memorandum, National Center for State Courts, Research and Information Service, Williamsburg, Va., May 6, Ref. no. RIS 83.056.

Rogers, E. 1973. *Communication Strategies for Family Planning.* New York: Free Press.

Rogers, E., and Dearing, J. 1988. Agenda-Setting Research: Where Has It Been, Where Is It Going? In *Communication Yearbook 11,* edited by J. Anderson. Thousand Oaks, Calif.: Sage, pp. 555–594.

Rogers, E., and Storey, J. 1987. Effects of Mass Communications. In *The Handbook of Social Psychology,* 3rd ed., Vol. 2, edited by G. Lindzey and E. Aronson. New York: Random House, pp. 539–598.

Rollings, H., and Blascovich, J. 1977. The Case of Patricia Hearst: Pretrial Publicity and Opinion. *Journal of Communication* Spring, pp. 58–65.

Rosekrans, M. 1967. Imitation in Children as a Function of Perceived Similarities to a Social Model of Vicarious Reinforcement. *Journal of Personality and Social Psychology* 7:307–315.

Rosekrans, M., and Hartup, W. 1967. Imitative Influences of Consistent and Inconsistent Response Consequences to a Model of Aggressive Behavior in Children. *Journal of Personality and Social Psychology* 7:429–434.

Rosen, R. 1989. Ethical Soap: "L. A. Law" and the Privileging of Character. *University of Miami Law Review* 43:1229–1261.

Rosenbaum, D. 1988. Community Crime Prevention: A Review and Synthesis of the Literature. *Justice Quarterly* 5:323–395.

Rosenbaum, D., and Lurigio, A. 1985. Crime Stoppers: Paying the Price. *Psychology Today* June, pp. 56–61.

Rosenbaum, D., Lurigio, A., and Lavrakas, P. 1986. *Crime Stoppers: A National Evaluation of Program Operations and Effects.* Evanston, Ill.: Center for Urban Affairs and Policy Research, Northwestern University.

Rosenbaum, D., Lurigio, A., and Lavrakas, P. 1989. Enhancing Citizen Participation and Solving Serious Crime: A National Evaluation of Crime Stoppers Programs. *Crime and Delinquency* 35:401–420.

Rosenberg, H. 1990. Talk Shows Retry McMartin Case. Los Angeles Times Service, *Miami Herald* February 3, pp. 1E–2E.

Rosenberg, H. 1995. Nervous in the Naked City. In *The Culture of Crime,* edited by C. LaMay and E. Dennis. New Brunswick, N.J.: Transaction, pp. 103–110.

Rosenblatt, R. 1995. A Nation of Pained Hearts. *Time* Oct. 16, pp. 40–46.

Rosenstock, I. 1960. What Research in Motivation Suggests for Public Health. *American Journal of Public Health* 50:22–33.

Rosenthal, R. 1986. Media Violence, Antisocial Behavior, and the Social Consequences of Small Effects. *Journal of Social Issues* 42:141–154.

Rosenthal, T., and Zimmerman, B. 1978. *Social Learning and Cognition.* New York: Academic Press.

Roshier, B. 1981. The Selection of Crime News in the Press. In *The Manufacture of News,* edited by S. Cohen and J. Young. Thousand Oaks, Calif.: Sage, pp. 40–51.

Rosow, E. 1978. *Born to Lose.* New York: Oxford University Press.

Ross, H. 1989. Lost and Found: The Drunk-Driving Problem in Finland. In *Images of Issues,* edited by J. Best. Hawthorne, N.Y.: Aldine de Gruyter, pp. 177–188.

Ross, H., Campbell, D., and Glass, G. 1970. The British "Breathalyser" Crackdown of 1967. *American Behavioral Scientist* 13:493–509.

Ross, J. forthcoming. The Role of the Media in the Creation of Public Police Violence. *Popular Culture, Crime, and Justice*, edited by F. Bailey and D. Hale. Belmont, Calif.: Wadsworth.

Rothman, D. 1971. *The Discovery of the Asylum*. New York: Little, Brown.

Rottenberg, D. 1976. Do News Reports Bias Juries? *Columbia Journalism Review* May/June, pp. 128–131.

Rubinstein, E., Liebert, R., Neale, J., and Poulos, R. 1974. Assessing Television's Influence on Children's Prosocial Behavior. Stony Brook, N.Y.: Brookdale International Institute.

Rubinstein, J. 1973. *City Police*. New York: Farrar, Straus & Giroux.

Ruel, S. 1994. *Body Bag Journalism: Crime Coverage by the U.S. Media*. Paper presented at the International Conference on Violence in the Media, St. John's University, October 3 and 4, New York.

Rushkoff, D. 1994. Media: It's the Real Thing. *NPQ* Summer, pp. 4–15.

Rushton, J. P. 1976a. Socialization and the Altruistic Behavior of Children. *Psychological Bulletin* 83:893–913.

Rushton, J. P. 1976b. Television and Prosocial Behavior. In *Report of the Royal Commission on Violence in the Communications Industry*. Vol. 4. Ontario: Queen's Printer.

Rushton, J. P. 1980. *Altruism, Socialization, and Society*. Englewood Cliffs, N.J.: Prentice Hall.

Rushton, J. P. 1982a. Imagination, Creativity, and Prosocial Behavior. In *Television and Behavior: Ten Years of Scientific Research and Implications for the Eighties*. Vol. 1. *Summary Report*, edited by D. Pearl, L. Bouthilet, and J. Lazar. Washington, D.C.: National Institute of Mental Health, pp. 45–53.

Rushton, J. P. 1982b. Television and Prosocial Behavior. In *Television and Behavior*. Vol. 2. *Technical Review*, edited by D. Pearl, L. Bouthilet, and J. Lazar. Washington, D.C.: National Institute of Mental Health, pp. 248–257.

Russell, D. 1988. Pornography and Rape: A Causal Model. *Political Psychology* 9:41–73.

Rypinski, I. 1982. Videotaping Depositions. *Hawaii Bar Journal* Winter, pp. 67–76.

Sabom, R. 1993. *Adult Comics: An Introduction*. New York: Routledge.

Sacco, V. 1982. The Effects of Mass Media on Perceptions of Crime. *Pacific Sociological Review* 25:475–493.

Sacco, V. 1995. Media Constructions of Crime. *Annals* 539:141–154.

Sacco, V., and Kennedy, B. 1996. *The Criminal Event: An Introduction to Criminology*. Belmont, Calif.: Wadsworth.

Sacco, V., and Silverman, R. 1981. Selling Crime Prevention: The Evaluation of a Mass Media Campaign. *Canadian Journal of Criminology* 23:191–201.

Sacco, V., and Silverman, R. 1982. Crime Prevention through Mass Media: Prospects and Problems. *Journal of Criminal Justice* 10:257–269.

Salamone, D. 1997. Police Taping Puts Focus on Privacy. *Orlando Sentinel* Feb. 18.

Salas, L. 1984. The Press and the Criminal Justice System: Controversies over Acquisition and Distribution of Information. In *Justice and the Media*, edited by R. Surette. Springfield, Ill.: Thomas, pp. 91–105.

Salcedo, R., Read, H., Evans, J., and Kong, A. 1974. A Successful Information Campaign on Pesticides. *Journalism Quarterly* 51:91–95, 110.

Salvan, S. A. 1975. Videotape for the Legal Community. *Judicature* 59(5):222–229.

Salwin, M. 1986. *Time in Agenda-Setting: The Accumulation of Media Coverage on Audience Issue Salience*. Paper presented at the annual meeting of the International Communication Association, November, Chicago.

Sander, E. 1993. Police Videos. *Miami Herald* October 17, p. 5B.

Sasson, T. 1995. *Crime Talk*. Hawthorne, N.Y.: Aldine de Gruyter.

Saxe, J. 1994. *Violence in Video Games: What Are the Pressures?* Paper presented at the International Conference on Violence in the Media, St. John's University, October 3 and 4, New York.

Schattschneider, D. 1960. *The Semi-Sovereign People*. Hinsdale, Ill.: Dryden Press.

Scheingold, S. 1984. *The Politics of Law and Order*. White Plains, N.Y.: Longman.

Scheler, M. [1926] 1980. *Problems of a Sociology of Knowledge*. Translated by M. Frings; edited by K. Stikkers. Reprint. New York: Routledge.

Schlesinger, P., Tumber, H., and Murdock, G. 1991. The Media Politics of Crime and Criminal Justice. *British Journal of Sociology* 42:397–420.

Schmalleger, F. 1996. *Trial of the Century*. Englewood Cliffs, N.J.: Prentice Hall.

Schmeling, D., and Wotring, C. 1976. Agenda-Setting Effects of Drug Abuse Public Service Ads. *Journalism Quarterly* 53:743–746.

Schmeling, D., and Wotring, C. 1980. Making Anti-Drug-Abuse Advertising Work. *Journal of Advertising Research* 20:33–37.

Schmid, A., and de Graaf, J. 1982. *Violence as Communication*. Thousand Oaks, Calif.: Sage.

Schmidtke, A., and Hafner, H. 1988. The Werther Effect after Television Films: New Evidence for an Old Hypothesis. *Psychiatric Medicine* 18:665–676.

Schneider, J. 1985. Social Problems Theory: The Constructionist View. *Annual Review of Sociology* 11:209–229.

Schram, W., Lyle, J., and Parker, E. 1961. *Television in the Lives of Our Children*. Stanford, Calif.: Stanford University Press.

Schultz, D., and Barnes, B. 1995. *Strategic Advertising Campaigns*. Lincolnwood, Ill.: NTC Business Books.

Schutte, N. S., Malouff, J. M., Post-Gorden, J. C., and Rodasta, A. L. 1988. Effects of Playing Videogames on Children's Aggressive and Other Behaviors. *Journal of Applied Social Psychology* 18:454–460.

Schwartz, J. 1989. Promoting a Good Public Image. *Corrections Today* 51:38–42.

Scott, J. 1985. *Sexual Violence in Playboy Magazine: Longitudinal Analysis.* Paper presented at the meeting of the American Society of Criminology, November, Atlanta.

Scott, J., and Cuvelier, 1987. Sexual Violence in *Playboy Magazine*: A Longitudinal Content Analysis. *Journal of Sex Research* 23:534–539.

Scott, J., and Schwalm, L. 1988a. Pornography and Rape: An Examination of Adult Theater Rapes and Rape Rates by State. In *Controversial Issues in Crime and Justice*, edited by J. Scott and T. Hirschi. Thousand Oaks, Calif.: Sage, pp. 40–53.

Scott, J., and Schwalm, L. 1988b. Rape Rates and the Circulation Rates of Adult Magazines. *Journal of Sex Research* 24:241–250.

Scott, W., and Hart, D. 1979. *Organizational America.* Boston: Houghton Mifflin.

Seaman, W. 1992. Active Audience Theory: Pointless Populism. *Media, Culture and Society* 14:301–11.

Sechrest, D., Liquori, W., and Perry, J. 1990. Using Video Technology in Police Patrol. In *The Media and Criminal Justice Policy*, edited by R. Surette. Springfield, Ill.: Thomas, pp. 255–264.

Secret Court Watch. 1979. *News Media and the Law* 3(4):17–23.

Sennet, R., and Cobb, J. 1973. *The Hidden Inquiries of Class.* New York: Vintage Books.

Shaaber, M. 1929. *Some Forerunners of the Newspaper in England.* Philadelphia: University of Pennsylvania Press.

Shadoian, J. 1977. *Dreams and Dead Ends.* Cambridge, Mass.: MIT Press.

Sharp, A. 1983. Postverdict Interviews with Jurors. *Case and Comment* 88:3–15.

Shaw, D. 1990a. McMartin Verdict: Not Guilty. Where Was Skepticism in the Media? *Los Angeles Times* January 19, pp. A1, A20–A21.

Shaw, D. 1990b. Reporter's Early Exclusives Triggered a Media Frenzy. *Los Angeles Times* January 20, pp. A1, A30–A31.

Shaw, D. 1990c. Media Skepticism Grew as McMartin Case Lingered. *Los Angeles Times*, January 21, pp. A1, A32–A34.

Shaw, D., and McCombs, M. 1977. *The Emergence of American Political Issues: The Agenda-Setting Function of the Press.* St. Paul, Minn.: West Publishing.

Sheley, J. 1985. *America's Crime Problem: An Introduction to Criminology.* Belmont, Calif.: Wadsworth.

Sheley, J., and Ashkins, C. 1981. Crime, Crime News, and Crime Views. *Public Opinion Quarterly* 45:492–506.

Sherizen, S. 1978. Social Creation of Crime News. In *Deviance and Mass Media*, edited by C. Winick. Thousand Oaks, Calif.: Sage, pp. 203–224.

Sherman, B., and Dominick, J. 1986. Violence and Sex in Music Videos: TV and Rock'n'roll. *Journal of Communication* 36:79–93.

Shoemaker, P. 1991. *Gatekeeping.* Thousand Oaks, Calif.: Sage.

Shutkin, J. 1973. Videotape Trials: Legal and Practical Implications. *Columbia Journal of Law and Social Problems* 9:363–393.

Shuttleworth, F., and May, M. 1933. *The Social Conduct and Attitudes of Movie Fans.* New York: Macmillan.

Siebert, F., Wilcox, P., Hough, W., and Bush, T. 1970. *Free Press and Fair Trial.* Athens: University of Georgia Press.

Siegel, A. 1974. The Effects of Media Violence on Social Learning. In *Where Do You Draw the Line? An Exploration into Media Violence, Pornography, and Censorship*, edited by V. B. Cline. Provo, Utah: Brigham Young University Press, pp. 129–146.

Sigal, L. 1973. *Reporters and Officials.* Lexington, Mass.: Heath.

Silvern, S. B., and Williamson, P. A. 1987. The Effects of Video Games Play on Young Children's Aggression, Fantasy, and Prosocial Behavior. *Journal of Applied Developmental Psychology* 8:453–462.

Simon, R. 1966. Murder, Juries, and the Press. *Transaction* May–June, pp. 40–42.

Simon, R. 1977. Does the Court's Decision in *Nebraska Press Association* Fit the Research Evidence on the Impact on Jurors of News Coverage? *Sanford Law Review* 29:515–528.

Simon, R., and Eimermann, T. 1971. The Jury Finds Not Guilty: Another Look at Media Influence on the Jury. *Journalism Quarterly* 48:343.

Simonds, A. P. 1978. *Karl Mannheim's Sociology of Knowledge.* Oxford: Clarendon Press.

Simonett, T. 1966. The Trial as One of the Arts. *American Bar Association Journal* 552:1145–1160.

Skirrow, G. 1986. Hellivision: An Analysis of Videogames. In *High Theory/Low Culture: Analyzing Popular Television and Film*, edited by C. MacCabe. New York: St. Martin's Press, pp. 115–142.

Skogan, W. G. 1984. *The Fear of Crime.* The Hague: Research and Documentation Centre, Ministry of Justice.

Skogan, W. G. 1990. *Disorder and Decline.* Belmont, Calif.: Wadsworth.

Skogan, W. G., and Maxfield, M. 1981. *Coping with Crime.* Thousand Oaks, Calif.: Sage.

Slater, D., and Elliott, W. 1982. Television's Influence on Social Reality. *Quarterly Journal of Speech* 68:69–79.

Slife, B., and Rychiak, J. 1976. Role of Affective Assessment in Modeling Aggressive Behavior. *Journal of Personality and Social Psychology* 43:861–868.

Smith, D. 1976. The Social Content of Pornography. *Journal of Communication* 26:16–24.

Smith, S. 1984. Crime in the News. *British Journal of Criminology* 24:289–295.

Sneed, D. 1985. How to Improve Crime Reporting. *Editor and Publisher* November 9, pp. 39, 56.

Snow, R. 1984. Crime and Justice in Prime-Time News: The John Hinckley, Jr., Case. In *Justice and the Media*, edited by R. Surette. Springfield, Ill.: Thomas, pp. 212–232.

Snyder, R. 1992. Glimpses of Gotham. *Media Studies Journal* 6(1):195–206.

Sohn, A. 1976. Determining Guilt or Innocence of Accused from Pretrial News Stories. *Journalism Quarterly* 53:100–105.

Sommers, E., and Check, J. 1987. An Empirical Investigation of the Role of Pornography in the Verbal and Physical Abuse of Women. *Violence and Victims* 2:189–209.

Soothill, K., and Walby, S. 1991. *Sex Crimes in the News*. New York: Routledge.

Spaniolo, J., and Terilli, S. 1987. The Freedom of Information Act: A Reporters' Map to a Federal Maze. In *The Reporter's Handbook*. Tallahassee: Florida Bar Association.

Sparks, G., and Ogles, R. 1990. The Difference between Fear of Victimization and the Probability of Being Victimized: Implications for Cultivation. *Journal of Broadcasting and Electronic Media* 34(3):351–358.

Spector, M., and Kitsuse, J. 1987. *Constructing Social Problems*. Hawthorne, N.Y.: Aldine de Gruyter.

Sprafkin, J., and Rubinstein, E. 1982. Using Television to Improve the Social Behavior of Institutionalized Children. *Prevention in Human Services* 2:107–114.

Sprafkin, J., Liebert, R., and Poulos, R. 1975. Effects of a Pro-Social Televised Example on Children's Helping. *Journal of Experimental Child Psychology* 20:119–126.

Stack, S. 1987a. Celebrities and Suicide: A Taxonomy and Analysis, 1948–1983. *American Sociological Review* 52:401–412.

Stack, S. 1987b. Publicized Executions and Homicide 1950–1980. *American Sociological Review* 52:532–542.

Stack, W. 1962. Policy and the Pros: An Organizational Analysis of a Metropolitan Newspaper. *Berkeley Journal of Sociology* 17:11–31.

Star, S., and Hughes, H. 1950. Report on an Educational Campaign: The Cincinnati Plan for the United States. *American Journal of Sociology* 55:389–400.

Stark, S. 1987. Perry Mason Meets Sonny Crockett: The History of Lawyers and the Police as Television Heroes. *University of Miami Law Review* 42:229–283.

State Prisons Clamp Down on Prisoner Interviews. 1996. *News Media and the Law* Spring, p. 5.

State Shield Laws: Do They Work? 1982. *News Media and the Law* 6(3):31–33.

Steffens, L. 1931. *The Autobiography of Lincoln Steffens*. Orlando: Harcourt, Brace.

Steigleman, W. 1971. *The Newspaperman and the Law*. Westport, Conn.: Greenwood Press.

Stein, A., and Friedrich, L. 1972. Television Content and Young Children's Behavior. In *Television and Social Behavior*. Vol. 2. *Television and Social Learning*, edited by J. Murray, E. Rubinstein, and G. Comstock. Washington, D.C.: U.S. Government Printing Office, pp. 202–317.

Stein, A., Friedrich, L., and Tahsler, S. 1973. *The Effects of Prosocial Television and Environmental Cues on Children's Task Persistence and Conceptual Tempo*. University Park: Pennsylvania State University Press.

Stempl, G. 1962. Content Patterns of Small Metropolitan Dailies. *Journalism Quarterly* 39:88–90.

Stevens, J., and Garcia, H. 1980. *Communication History*. Thousand Oaks, Calif.: Sage.

Stewart, D., and Mickunas, A. 1974. *Exploring Phenomenology*. Chicago: American Library Association.

Stinchcombe, A., Adams, R., Heimer, C., Schepple, K., Smith, T., and Taylor, G. 1980. *Crime and Punishment: Changing Attitudes in America*. San Francisco: Jossey-Bass.

Stroman, C., and Seltzer, R. 1985. Media Use and Perceptions of Crime. *Journalism Quarterly* 62:340–345.

Sue, S., Smith, R., and Gilbert, R. 1974. Biasing Effects of Pretrial Publicity on Judicial Decisions. *Journal of Criminal Justice* 2:163–171.

Sullivan, H. 1961. *Trial by Newspaper*. Hyannis, Mass.: Patriot Press.

Surette, R., ed. 1984a. *Justice and the Media*. Springfield, Ill.: Thomas.

Surette, R. 1984b. Two Media-Based Crime-Control Programs: Crime Stoppers and Video Street Patrol. In *Justice and the Media*, edited by R. Surette. Springfield, Ill.: Thomas, pp. 275–290.

Surette, R. 1985a. Video Street Patrol: Media Technology and Street Crime. *Journal of Police Science and Administration* 13:78–85.

Surette, R. 1985b. Television Viewing and Support of Punitive Criminal Justice Policy. *Journalism Quarterly* 62:373–377, 450.

Surette, R. 1986. The Mass Media and Criminal Investigations: Crime Stoppers in Dade County, Florida. *Journal of Justice Issues* 1:21–38.

Surette, R. 1988. Video Technology in Criminal Justice: Live Judicial Proceedings and Patrol and Surveillance. In *New Technologies and Criminal Justice*, edited by M. LeBlanc, P. Tremblay, and A. Blumstein. Montreal: Center for Comparative International Criminology, University of Montreal, pp. 407–440.

Surette, R. 1989. Media Trials. *Journal of Criminal Justice* 17:293–308.

Surette, R. 1990a. Law Enforcement Surveillance Projects Employing Media Technology. In *Media and Criminal Justice Policy*, edited by R. Surette. Springfield, Ill.: Thomas, pp. 277–288.

Surette, R. 1990b. Media Trials and Echo Effects. In *Media and Criminal Justice Policy*, edited by R. Surette. Springfield, Ill.: Thomas, pp. 177–192.

Surette, R. 1991. Methodological Problems in Determining Media Effects on Criminal Justice: A Review and Suggestions for the Future. *Criminal Justice Policy Review* 6(4):291–310.

Surette, R. 1992. *Media, Crime, and Criminal Justice: Images and Realities.* Pacific Grove, Calif.: Brooks/Cole.

Surette, R. 1993. *An Empirical Analysis of a Media Echo Effect.* Unpublished manuscript, University of Central Florida, Orlando.

Surette, R. 1994. Media, Violence, Youth, and Society. *The World and I* July, pp. 370–383.

Surette, R. 1995a. Predator Criminals as Media Icons. In *Media, Process, and the Social Construction of Crime: Studies in Newsmaking Criminology*, edited by G. Barak. New York: Garland, pp. 131–158.

Surette, R. 1995b. A Serendipitous Finding of a News Media History Effect. *Justice Quarterly* 12(2):355–364.

Surette, R. 1996. News from Nowhere, Policy to Follow: Media and the Social Construction of "Three Strikes and You're Out." In *Three Strikes and You're Out*, edited by D. Shichor and D. Sechrest. Thousand Oaks, Calif.: Sage, pp. 177–202.

Surette, R. forthcoming. Some Unpopular Thoughts about Popular Culture. In *Popular Culture, Crime, and Justice*, edited by F. Bailey and D. Hale. Belmont, Calif.: Wadsworth.

Surette, R., and Richard, A. 1995. Public Information Officers: A Descriptive Study of Crime News Gatekeepers. *Journal of Criminal Justice* 23:325–336

Surette, R., and Terry, C. 1984. Videotaped Misdemeanor First Appearances: Fairness from the Defendant's Perspective. In *Justice and the Media*, edited by R. Surette. Springfield, Ill.: Thomas, pp. 305–320.

Swanson, C. 1953. What They Read in 130 Daily Newspapers. *Journalism Quarterly* 32:411–421.

Swanson, D. 1988. Feeling the Elephant: Some Observations on Agenda-Setting Research. *Communication Yearbook* 11:603–619.

Tajgman, D. 1981. From *Estes* to *Chandler*: The Distinction between Television and Newspaper Trial Coverage. *Communication/Entertainment Law Journal* 3:503–541.

Tamborini, R., Zillman, D., and Bryant, J. 1984. Fear and Victimization: Exposure to Television and Perceptions of Crime and Fear. In *Communications Yearbook*, edited by R. Bostrum. Thousand Oaks, Calif.: Sage, pp. 492–513.

Tanick, M., and Shields, T. 1985. Courts Wrestle with Venue Problems. *Bench and Bar of Minnesota* 42:15–20.

Tannenbaum, P., and Zillman, D. 1975. Emotional Arousal in the Facilitation of Aggression Through Communication. In *Advances in Experimental Social Psychology*, Vol. 8, edited by L. Berkowitz. New York: Academic Press, pp. 149–192.

Tans, M., and Chaffee, S. 1966. Pretrial Publicity and Juror Prejudice. *Journalism Quarterly* 43:647–654.

Tarde, G. 1912. *Penal Philosophy.* New York: Little, Brown.

Taylor, J. 1995. To Die For. *Nation* 260:440–441.

Terry, W. 1984. Crime and the News: Gatekeeping and Beyond. In *Justice and the Media*, edited by R. Surette. Springfield, Ill.: Thomas, pp. 31–50.

Terry, W., and Surette, R. 1985. Video in the Misdemeanor Court. *Judicature* 69(1):13–19.

Teuchman, G., and Orme, M. 1981. Effects of Aggression and Prosocial Film Material on Altruistic Behavior of Children. *Psychological Reports* June, pp. 699–702.

Thaler, P. 1994. *The Watchful Eye: American Justice in the Age of the Television Trial.* Westport, Conn.: Greenwood Press.

Thomas, W. I. 1908. The Psychology of Yellow Journalism. *American Magazine* March, p. 491.

Thompson, J. 1993. *Fiction, Crime and Empire: Clues to Modernity and Postmodernism.* Urbana: University of Illinois Press.

Thompson, W., Fong, G., and Rosenhan, D. 1981. Inadmissible Evidence and Juror Verdicts. *Journal of Personality and Social Psychology* 40:453–483.

Thrasher, F. 1949. The Comics and Delinquency: Cause or Scapegoat? *Journal of Educational Sociology* 23:195–205.

Tierney, K. 1982. The Battered Women Movement and the Creation of the Wife Beating Problem. *Social Problems* 29(3):207–220.

Toplin, R. 1975. *Unchallenged Violence: An American Ordeal.* Westport, Conn.: Greenwood Press.

Treevan, J., and Hartnagel, P. 1976. The Effect of Television Violence on the Perceptions of Crime by Adolescents. *Journal of Sociology and Sociological Research* 60:337–348.

Treuhaft, D. 1957. Trial by Headline. *Nation* October, pp. 279–282.

Trial by Media. 1984. *U.S. Press* 10(30):4.

Trial Court May Order Trial Proceedings Closed to Public If It Follows Certain Procedural Safeguards. 1985. *Criminal Law Bulletin* 21(2):180.

Tuchman, G. 1973. Making News by Doing Work. *American Journal of Sociology* 79:110–131.

Tuchman, G. 1978. *Making News: A Study in the Construction of Reality.* New York: Free Press.

Tucker, K. 1993. Reno and Butthead. Do Movies and Television Have an Image Problem? *Entertainment Weekly* No. 195, November 5:44–47.

Tumber, H. 1993. Selling Scandal: Business and the Media. *Media, Culture, and Society* 15:345–361.

Tunnell, K. 1992. Film at Eleven: Recent Developments in the Commodification of Crime. *Sociological Spectrum* 12:292–313.

Tunnell, K. 1995. Silence on the Left: Reflections on Critical Criminology and Criminologists. *Social Justice* 22:89–101.

Tunnell, K. forthcoming. Reflections on Crime, Criminals, and Control in Newsmagazine Television Programs. *Popular Culture, Crime, and Justice*, edited by F. Bailey and D. Hale. Belmont, Calif.: Wadsworth.

Turnbo, C. 1994. News at Eleven. *Federal Prisons Journal* 3(3):47–50.

Turner, C., and Fern, M. 1978. Effects of White Noise and Memory Cues on Verbal Aggression. Papers resented at meetings of the International Society for Research on Aggression.

Tuska, J. 1987. *The Detective in Hollywood.* New York: Doubleday.

Tyler, T. 1980. Impact of Directly and Indirectly Experienced Events: The Origin of Crime-Related Judgments and Behavior. *Journal of Personality and Social Psychology* 39:13–28.

Tyler, T. 1984. Assessing the Risk of Crime Victimization: The Integration of Personal Victimization Experience and Socially Transmitted Information. *Journal of Social Issues* 40:27–38.

Tyler, T., and Cook, F. 1984. The Mass Media and Judgments of Risk: Distinguishing Impact on Personal and Societal Level Judgments. *Journal of Personality and Social Psychology* 47:693–708.

Tyler, T., and Lavrakas, P. 1985. Cognitions Leading to Personal and Political Behaviors: The Case of Crime. In *Mass Media and Political Thought: An Information Processing Approach*, edited by S. Hraus and R. M. Perloff. Thousand Oaks, Calif.: Sage, pp. 141–156.

U.S. Commission on Obscenity and Pornography. 1972. *Erotica and Anti-Social Behavior.* Vol. 7. Washington, D.C.: U.S. Government Printing Office.

U.S. Department of Justice. 1986. *Final Report of the Attorney General's Commission on Pornography.* Vols. 1–2. Washington, D.C.: U.S. Government Printing Office.

U.S. Department of Justice. *Sourcebook of Criminal Justice Statistics—1994.* Washington, D.C.: U.S. Government Printing Office, pp. 160–161, 220–227.

U.S. Senate Judiciary Committee on Juvenile Delinquency. 1969. *Interim Report on Judiciary Investigation of Juvenile Delinquency in the U.S.* Reprint. Westport, Conn.: Greenwood Press.

U.S. Surgeon General. 1987. Report of the Surgeon General's Workshop on Pornography and Public Health. *American Psychologist* 42:944–945.

Valentine, P. (1997) "Baltimore Police Begin Patrolling Streets by Video Camera. *Washington Post,* June 20, p. B2.

Van Alstyne, S. 1977. The Hazards to the Press of Claiming a Preferred Position. *Hastings Law Journal* 28:761–781.

Van Dijk, J. 1978. The Extent of Public Information and the Nature of Public Attitudes toward Crime. In *Public Opinion on Crime and Criminal Justice.* Vol. XVII. *Collected Studies in Criminological Research,* edited by A. Coenen and J. van Dijk. Strasbourg Cedex, France: Council of Europe, pp. 7–42.

Van Dyke, J. 1977. *Jury Selection Procedures.* New York: Ballinger.

Van Noonen, L. 1994. *Feminist Media Studies.* Thousand Oaks, Calif.: Sage.

Video Transmission to Counter Hijacking. 1986. *Security World* 23(7):18.

Vidmar, N., and Judson, J. 1981. The Use of Social Science in a Change of Venue Application. *Canadian Bar Review* 59:76–102.

Violent Movie Didn't Cause Youth's Death. 1989. *News Media and the Law* 13(4):33–34.

Voumvakis, S., and Ericson, R. 1984. *News Accounts of Attacks on Women.* Toronto: Centre of Criminology, University of Toronto.

Wakshlag, J., Bart, L., Dudley, J., Groth, G., McCutcheon, J., and Rolla, C. 1983. Viewer Apprehension about Victimization and Crime Drama Programs. *Communication Research* 10:195–217.

Wakshlag, J., Vial, V., and Tamborini, R. 1983. Selecting Crime Drama and Apprehension about Crime. *Human Communication Research* 10:227–242.

Walker, S. 1983. *The Police in America.* New York: McGraw-Hill.

Walker, S. 1985. *Sense and Nonsense about Crime.* Pacific Grove, Calif.: Brooks/Cole.

Walsh, J. 1995. Special Report: The Simpson Verdict. *Time* 146:62–64.

Warr, M. 1980. The Accuracy of Public Beliefs about Crime. *Social Forces* 59:456–470.

Warr, M. 1991. America's Perceptions of Crime and Punishment. In *Criminology: A Contemporary Handbook*, edited by J. F. Sheley. Belmont, Calif.: Wadsworth.

Warren, S., and Brandeis, L. 1890. The Right to Privacy. *Harvard Law Review* 4:193–199.

Watt, J., and Krull, R. 1978. Examination of Three Models of Television Viewing and Aggression. *Human Communication Research* 3:99–112.

Weaver, D. 1980. Audience Need for Orientation and Media Effects. *Communications Research* 7:361–376.

Weaver, J. 1987. *Effects of Portrayals of Female Sexuality and Violence against Women on Perceptions of Women.* Unpublished Ph.D. dissertation, University of Indiana, Bloomington.

Websdale, N., and Alvarez, A. forthcoming. Forensic Journalism as Patriarchal Ideology: The Newspaper Construction of Homicide-Suicide. In *Popular Culture, Crime, and Justice*, edited by

F. Bailey and D. Hale. Belmont, Calif.: Wadsworth.

Weimann, G. 1983. The Theater of Terror: Effects of Press Coverage. *Journal of Communication* 33(1):38–45.

Weimann, G. 1993. The Newsworthiness of International Terrorism. *Communication Research* 12(3):333–355.

Weimann, G., and Winn, C. 1994. *The Theater of Terror: Mass Media and International Terrorism.* White Plains, N.Y.: Longman.

Weinstein, N. 1987. Cross-Hazard Consistencies: Conclusions about Self-Protective Behavior. In *Taking Care: Understanding and Encouraging Self-Protective Behavior,* edited by N. Weinstein. New York: Cambridge University Press, pp. 325–336.

Weis, J. 1977. Electronics Expand Courtrooms' Walls. *American Bar Association Journal* 63:1713–1716.

Weis, K., and Borges, S. 1973. Victimology and Rape: The Case of the Legitimate Victim. *Issues in Criminology* 8:71–115.

Weiss, M. J. 1982. Trial by Tape. *American Film* June, pp. 61–64.

Wertham, R. 1954. *Seduction of the Innocent.* New York: Rinehart.

West, S., Hepworth, J., McCall, M., and Reich, J. 1989. An Evaluation of Arizona's July 1982 Drunk Driving Law: Effects on the City of Phoenix. *Journal of Applied Social Psychology* 19(14):1212–1237.

Westin, A. 1982. *Newswatch: How TV Decides the News.* New York: Simon & Schuster.

Wheatley, J. 1971. Marketing and the Use of Fear or Anxiety-Arousing Appeals. *Journal of Marketing* 35:62–64.

Whitaker, M. 1995. Whites v. Blacks. *Newsweek* October 16, 126:28–34.

White, D. M. 1950. The Gatekeepers: A Case Study in the Selection of News. *Journalism Quarterly* 27:383–390.

White, T., Regan, K., Waller, J., and Wholey, J. 1975. *Police Burglary Prevention Programs.* Washington, D.C.: U.S. Department of Justice, Law Enforcement Assistance Administration.

Whitlark, J. 1988. *Illuminated Fantasy: From Blake's Visions to Recent Graphic Fiction.* Rutherford, N.J.: Fairleigh Dickinson University Press.

Whitney, C., Wartell, E., LaSorsa, D., Danielson, W., Olivarez, A., Lopez, R., and Klijn, M. 1997. Television Violence in "Reality" Programming: University of Texas, Austin Study. In *National Television Violence Study.* Vol. 1. Thousand Oaks, Calif.: Sage, pp. 269–304.

Wilbanks, W. 1984. *Murder in Miami: An Analysis of Homicide Patterns and Trends in Dade County (Miami) Florida. 1917–1983.* New York: University Press of America.

Wilcox, W. 1970. The Press, the Jury, and the Behavioral Sciences. In *Free Press and Fair Trial: Some Dimensions of the Problem,* edited by C. R.

Bush. Athens: University of Georgia Press, pp. 49–105.

Willard, D., and Rowlanel, J. 1983. *The Politics of TV Violence.* Thousand Oaks, Calif.: Sage.

Williams, J. 1994. Comics: A Tool of Subversion? *Journal of Criminal Justice and Popular Culture* 2(6):129–147.

Williams, J., Lawton, C., Ellis, S., Walsh, S., and Reed, J. 1987. Copycat Suicide Attempts. *Lancet* 2:102–103.

Williams, P., and Dickinson, J. 1993. Fear of Crime: Read All about It? *British Journal of Criminology* 33:33–56.

Williams, T. ed. 1986. *The Impact of Television: A Natural Experiment in Three Communities.* New York: Academic Press.

Wills, G. 1977. Measuring the Impact of Erotica. *Psychology Today* November, pp. 30–34.

Wilmer, L. [1859] 1970. *Our Press Gang.* New York: Lloyd.

Wilson, B., Kunkel, D., Linz, D., Potter, J., Donnerstein, E., Smith, S. Blumenthal, E., and Gray, R. 1997. Violence in Television Programming Overall: University of California, Santa Barbara Study. In *National Television Violence Study.* Vol. 1. Thousand Oaks, Calif.: Sage, pp. 3–267.

Wilson, G., and O'Leary, K. 1980. *Principles of Behavior Theory.* Englewood Cliffs, N.J.: Prentice Hall.

Wilson, J. Q. 1975. *Thinking about Crime.* New York: Basic Books.

Wilson, J. Q., and Herrnstein, R. 1985. *Crime and Human Behavior.* New York: Simon & Schuster.

Winkel, M., Novak, D. M., and Hopson, H. 1987. Personality Factors, Subject Gender, and the Effects of Aggressive Video Games on Aggression in Adolescents. *Journal of Research in Personality* 21:211–223.

Winks, R., ed. 1988. *Detective Fiction.* Woodstock: Foul Play Press.

Wise, D. 1986. Bar Report Recommends Curbs on Pretrial Comments to Media. *New York Law Journal* 196:1, 3.

Wisehart, M. K. [1922] 1968. Newspapers and Criminal Justice. In *Criminal Justice in Cleveland,* edited by R. Pound and F. Frankfurter. Montclair, N.J.: Patterson Smith.

Witek, J. 1989. *Comic Books as History.* Jackson: University Press of Mississippi.

Wober, J. 1978. Televised Violence and Paranoid Perception: The View from Great Britain. *Public Opinion Quarterly* 42:315–321.

Wood, W., Wong, F., and Chachere, G. 1991. Category Accessibility: Some Theoretical and Empirical Issues Concerning the Processing of Information. In *Social Cognition,* Vol. 1, edited by E. Higgins, C. Herman, and M. Zanna. Hillsdale, N.J.: Erlbaum, pp. 161–197.

Wooldridge, F. 1981. Micro Video Patrol. Grant application, Community Development Block Grant Program (HUD), August, Miami Beach.

Worchel, S., Hardy, T., and Hurley, R. 1976. The Effects of Commercial Interruption of Violent and Nonviolent Films on Viewers' Subsequent Aggression. *Journal of Experimental Psychology* 12:220–232.

Wurtzel, A., and Lometti, G. 1984a. Researching Television Violence. *Society* 21:22–30.

Wurtzel, A., and Lometti, G. 1984b. Smoking Out the Critics. *Society* 21:36–40.

Yagade, A., and Dozier, D. 1990. The Media Agenda-Setting Effect of Concrete versus Abstract Issues. *Journalism Quarterly* Spring, pp. 3–11.

Yankelovich, D., Skelly, S., and White, A. 1978. The Public Image of Courts: Highlights of a National Survey of the General Public, Judges, Lawyers, and Community Leaders. In *State Courts: A Blueprint for the Future, Proceedings of the Second National Conference on the Judiciary*, edited by T. J. Fetter. Williamsburg, Va.: National Center for State Courts, pp. 5–69.

Zaner, L. 1989. The Screen Test: Has Hollywood Hurt Corrections' Image? *Corrections Today* 51:64–66, 94, 95, 98.

Zeisel, H., and Diamond, S. 1978. The Effect of Peremptory Challenges on Jury and Verdict: An Experiment in a Federal District Court. *Stanford Law Review* 30:491–531.

Zillman, D. 1971. Excitation Transfer in Communication-Mediated Aggressive Behavior. *Journal of Experimental Social Psychology* 7:419–434.

Zillman, D., and Bryant, J. 1982. Pornography, Sexual Callousness, and the Trivialization of Rape. *Journal of Communication* 32:10–21.

Zillman, D., and Wakshlag, J. 1985. Fear of Victimization and the Appeal of Crime Drama. In *Selective Exposure to Communication*, edited by D. Zillman and J. Bryant. Hillsdale, N.J.: Erlbaum, pp. 141–156.

Zillman, D., Johnson, R., and Hanraham, J. 1973. Pacifying Effect of Happy Ending of Communication Involving Aggression. *Psychological Reports* 32:967–970.

Zucker, H. 1978. The Variable Nature of News Media Influence. In *Communication Yearbook*, Vol. 2, edited by B. Ruben. New Brunswick, N.J.: Transaction Books, pp. 225–240.

Case Cites

Broddie v. *ABC*, 881 F2d 1318 [11th Cir. 1989].

Chandler v. *Florida*, 101 S. Ct. 802 [1981].

Craig v. *Maryland*, 89 U.S. 478 [1990] [Md. Ct. App. 1989].

Estes v. *Texas*, 381 U.S. 532 [1965].

Florida v. *Globe Communications Corp.*, No. 91–011008 nm A02. Fla. Cir. Ct., Palm Beach County. Information May 9, 1991.

Gannett Co. v. *DePasquale*, 443 U.S. 368 [1979]

Illinois v. *Allen*, 90 S. Ct. 1057 [1990].

In re Press-Enterprise v. *Riverside Superior Court*, Sup. Ct. 106 S. Ct. 2735 [1984]).

In re Farber, 394 A.2d 330 [1978].

In re Knight Pub. Co., 743 F.2d 231 [4th Cir. 1984].

Jankovics v. *United States*, 22 F.3d 1091 [2d Cir. 1994].

Miami Herald v. *Tornillo*, 418 U.S. 241 [1974].

Murphy v. *Florida*, 421 U.S. 794 [1975].

Mutual Film Corporation v. *Industrial Commission of Ohio*, 236 U.S. 230 [1915].

Nebraska Press Association v. *Stuart*, 427 U.S. 539 [1976].

New York v. *Class*, U.S. 106 S. Ct. 960 [1986].

Nixon v. *Warner Communications*, 435 U.S. 591 [1978].

Patton v. *Yount*, 104 S. Ct. 2885 [1984].

Pell v. *Procunier*, 94 S. Ct. 2800 [1974].

Penn. v. *Munk*, 110 S. Ct. 2714 [1990].

People v. *Taylor*, Ill. Sup. Ct., No. 58258 [1984].

Post-Newsweek Stations v. *United States*, 461 U.S. 931 [1983].

Press-Enterprise v. *Riverside Superior Court* (Sup. Ct. 106 S. Ct. 2735 [1984]).

Rice v. *Paladin Enterprises, Inc.* No. AW 95–3811, 24 Med.L. Rptr 2185 (D Md 1996).

Richmond Newspapers v. *Virginia*, 448 U.S. 555 [1980].

Rideau v. *Louisiana*, 373 U.S. 723 [1963].

Saxbe v. *Washington Post*, 94 S. Ct. 2811 [1974].

Sheppard v. *Maxwell*, 384 U.S. 333 [1966].

Sidebottom v. *Schiro*, 927 F. Supp. 1221 [May 1996].

State v. *Kirkland*, Mont. Sup. Ct., 11/21/79.

State v. *Hauptmann*, 115 N.J.L 412 [1935] cert. denied, 296 U.S. 649 [1935].

United States v. *Briley*, 726 F.2d 1301 [8th Cir. 1984].

United States v. *Burke*, 700 F.2d [1983] cert. denied, 104 S. Ct. 72 [1983].

United States v. *Burr*, 25 F. Cas. 49, 49 [C.C.D. Va. 1807] [No. 14692g].

United States v. *Culter*, 6 F. 3d 67 [2nd Cir. 1993].

United States v. *Debango*, 780 F.2d 81 [D.C. Cir. 1986].

United States v. *Gurney*, 558 F.2d 1202 [5th Cir. 1977], cert. denied sub nom.

United States v. *Hastings*, 695 F.2d 1278 [11th Cir. 1983], cert. denied sub nom.

United States v. *Zamora*, 784 F.2d 1025 [10th Cir. 1986].

Index